"In his almost minute-by-minute account of the most famous infantry charge in history, Phillip Thomas Tucker provides a thoughtful and challenging new look at the great assault at Gettysburg, from planning to aftermath. Not afraid to lay blame where he thinks it belongs, Tucker is fresh and bold in his analysis and use of sources. Even though any reader knows in advance the outcome, still *Pickett's Charge* maintains suspense to the sound of the last gun."

—William C. Davis, author, *Crucible of Command: Ulysses S. Grant and Robert E. Lee—The War They Fought, The Peace They Forged*

"Replaces 150-plus years of uninterrogated mythology with meticulously researched history to give us a new and long-overdue understanding of what tradition dismisses as Robert E. Lee's most tragic error in pursuit of a 'Lost Cause.'"

—Alan Axelrod, author, *The 20 Most Significant Events of the Civil War*

"A thought-provoking and eye-opening study of this pivotal moment in American history."

—Louis P. Masur, Rutgers University professor of history author, *The Civil War: A Concise History*

"You are certainly emerging as one of the most prolific Civil War historians."

—James McPherson, acclaimed Civil War historian, professor emeritus, Princeton University, to Phillip Thomas Tucker

Alexander Hamilton's Revolution

Alexander Hamilton's Revolution

His Vital Role as Washington's Chief of Staff

PHILLIP THOMAS TUCKER, PhD

Skyhorse Publishing

Skyhorse Publishing books may be purchased in bulk at special discounts for sales promotion, corporate gifts, fund-raising, or educational purposes. Special editions can also be created to specifications. For details, contact the Special Sales Department, Skyhorse Publishing, 307 West 36th Street, 11th Floor, New York, NY 10018 or info@skyhorsepublishing.com.

Skyhorse® and Skyhorse Publishing® are registered trademarks of Skyhorse Publishing, Inc.®, a Delaware corporation.

Visit our website at www.skyhorsepublishing.com.

10 9 8 7 6 5 4 3 2

Library of Congress Cataloging-in-Publication Data is available on file.

Cover design by Rain Saukas
Cover art from *Alexander Hamilton (1757–1804) in the Uniform of the New York Artillery* by Alonzo Chappell, 1856

Print ISBN: 978-1-5107-1659-9
Ebook ISBN: 978-1-5107-1660-5

Printed in the United States

To America's distinguished chiefs of staff and Captain Louis McLane Hamilton, the grandson of Alexander Hamilton. The youngest captain in the United States Army and a proud member of the 7th Cavalry, Captain Hamilton, as promising in the early years after the Civil War as his grandfather had been at the beginning of the American Revolution, was killed during a charge by one of the first hostile shots fired during Lieutenant Colonel George Armstrong Custer's surprise attack on the Southern Cheyenne village on the Washita River on a snowy November 27, 1868.

Contents

Prologue

Despite being only twenty-six years old and still considered by elitists inside and outside the Continental Army as only a lowly immigrant and newcomer from the West Indies when situated just outside the British and Hessian defenses of Yorktown, Virginia, Lieutenant Colonel Alexander Hamilton had gained one of the most important combat missions of the American Revolution in October 1781. However, Hamilton was a combat veteran and not concerned about the risks or dangers of the battlefield; this was exactly the kind of a vital assignment that he had long coveted. Of Scottish heritage on his father's side and with handsome Scottish looks that were almost boyish—much to the delight of the ladies—Hamilton was every inch of a grizzled fighter, a distinctive quality of a Celtic heritage and his undying belief in the cause of liberty.

Not long after the red-streaked sunset of October 14, 1781, descended over the autumn-hued landscape of the Virginia Tidewater, Hamilton prepared to lead a desperate assault on one of the most formidable British defensive bastions along Yorktown's siege lines, Redoubt Number Ten. If his relatively small force of Continental light troops could overwhelm the imposing earthen redoubt, and if the French allies could capture adjacent Redoubt Number Nine on this chilly autumn night, then Lord Charles Cornwallis, who had been handed the mission to conquer the South, would be forced to surrender his entire garrison.

As he fully realized, General George Washington had chosen precisely the right officer to lead this crucial attack on Redoubt Number Ten, which anchored Cornwallis' left flank along with Redoubt Number Nine. Washington knew this highly capable native West Indian extremely well, ever since he had joined his staff at Morristown, New Jersey, on March 1, 1777. Therefore, Washington possessed complete confidence in what the newly married Continental officer could accomplish against any odds. No one in the Continental Army was quite like the irrepressible and brilliant Lieutenant Colonel Hamilton, and Washington had early realized as much.

As a tactically flexible leader on the battlefield, Hamilton had long ago far exceeded the highest of expectations as Washington's invaluable right-hand man at his headquarters for most of the war. Most importantly, there was nothing insignificant about young Hamilton's many outsized accomplishments on and off the battlefield, especially as Washington's trusted chief of staff in the modern sense from March 1777 to early 1781. Hamilton's tenure was not only the longest (nearly four years) of any member of Washington's staff, but also by far the most important and crucial from beginning to end.

In a desperate dash across open ground in the autumn blackness, Hamilton led the charge on imposing Redoubt Number Ten, while sending a Continental battalion—under the command of his best friend, Lieutenant Colonel John Laurens—swinging around to gain the bastion's rear: a clever pincer movement guaranteed to catch the enemy by surprise. Once again and as so often in the past, this gifted young man in a blue Continental officer's uniform had proven that he could succeed in almost any goal that he sought to attain.

Hamilton's remarkable tactical success in capturing this strategic redoubt, in conjunction with the capture of the adjacent redoubt by the French, sealed the fate of Yorktown and the British-Hessian-Loyalist army. Lord Charles Cornwallis had no choice but to surrender his entire army: a turning point not only in American history, but also in world history. As he did so often in the past, Alexander Hamilton had played a vital role in Washington's (and the French allies') decisive victory at Yorktown, guaranteeing a bright beginning and promising future for an infant people's republic, the United States of America.

Introduction

In America's capital city filled with impressive monuments to America's Founding Fathers, military heroes, and political leaders, no official memorial or monument has ever been erected to Alexander Hamilton in Washington, DC. Instead, a lone bronze statue of Hamilton sits on the south patio of the US Treasury Building. This notable omission in the nation's capital is a classic irony, because no Founding Father played a larger role in the creation of America as we know it today than this remarkable man from the faraway West Indies. Even more, no Founding Father of America overcame greater adversity and more setbacks early in life than Alexander Hamilton, who became a master at doing the impossible, regardless of the odds. This irrepressible young man elevated himself to lofty heights because he possessed an uncanny ability to dream big and almost miraculously overcome the seemingly insurmountable obstacles stemming from family tragedies, cruel twists of fate, and hard luck that were no fault of his own.

Despite his unpromising beginnings on the tropical islands of Nevis, where he had been born, and St. Croix, as the only Founding Father not born and raised on American soil, Hamilton succeeded by way of his own impressive array of abilities (a true self-made man) as one of the most extraordinary men not only of the Revolutionary War Era, but also of American history. Quite simply and although long overshadowed by the other Founding Fathers who possessed higher social standing and achieved far less (especially on the battlefield) during the war years, Hamilton was one of the best and brightest of his generation. No Founding Father was more naturally gifted or accomplished than Hamilton both on and off the battlefield, other than perhaps General George Washington himself.

Nevertheless, Hamilton became the most paradoxical, and hence least-understood, most controversial, and unappreciated, of all Founding Fathers. In fact, no Founding Father has been more unfairly maligned by untruths and unappreciated for less justifiable reasons than Hamilton, including during the war years, when he was the only Founding Father besides Washington to fight on the battlefield and compile a distinguished military record. And no

Founding Father has been more thoroughly distorted by more misconceptions than Hamilton, in part because of his perceived foreignness and dysfunctional upbringing. But ironically, his past in this once-remote tropical paradise saddled the young man with the demons that motivated and relentlessly drove him to excel and to do what seemed absolutely impossible for a lowly immigrant to achieve on American soil, year after year.

Today, Hamilton's fame as a Founding Father has continued to rest almost entirely on his key political and economic contributions after the American Revolution to lay a central foundation upon which America's superpower status has long rested. Indeed, he played a leading role with President George Washington in forging the new nation and his legacy lives with us today. Before today's popular Broadway play *Hamilton*, which has raised the level of overall awareness about the fiercely driven West Indian, Americans have long mostly known about Hamilton from his fatal duel on July 11, 1804, with Vice President Aaron Burr. What generations of Americans have known least and have little appreciated about Hamilton—in the past and even today—have been his many distinguished military contributions, both on and off the battlefield, especially in regard to his long-overlooked chief-of-staff role and the all-important French Alliance.

And, of course, Hamilton's image has become readily familiar to generations of Americans since 1928 from his handsome, chiseled face on the ten-dollar bill: a distinguished portrait of the mature Hamilton, the established politician, wealthy attorney, and married man of post–Revolutionary War America. Perpetuating the traditional image of Hamilton in the popular memory, he is depicted in aristocratic civilian attire in this famous portrait, rather than in the military uniform of a lieutenant colonel in the Continental Army. This enduring popular image has also helped to effectively obscure his all-important wartime role as the dashing young officer, who was the most gifted and dynamic leader of Washington's staff.

In both war and peace, the central foundation of the modern American nation was laid and created by the most brilliant leadership team in American history, Washington and Hamilton. But this post–Revolutionary War leadership team of two idealistic nationalists would not have forged or excelled for years had not this vital working relationship been first cemented by an inordinate level of trust and mutual respect created by the challenges of the difficult war years, from early 1777 to 1781—a relationship forged in adversity and unprecedented challenges not readily understood, even today.

Fortunately for Washington and America, Hamilton was an innovative intellectual and deep-thinking genius, who excelled in multiple fields of endeavor upon which the life of the infant United States often hung by a thread during the war years.

Ironically, however, Hamilton's beginning could not have been more unpromising, unlike the other Founding Fathers. He endured a broken family (a rogue father and a wayward mother), illegitimate and then orphan status, humble origins, and a host of tragedies before he migrated to America just before the Revolutionary War. These setbacks only fueled Hamilton's desire to succeed almost at any cost. Paradoxically, a perceived "foreignness" of the erudite Hamilton by provincial Americans—including those (even some other Founding Fathers of the aristocracy) who were jealous and suspicious of his many gifts—tarnished his historical image. However, Hamilton was actually more fiercely nationalistic than those America-born leaders who unfairly criticized him and had never risked their lives on the battlefield. Although the high-ranking elitist politicians, especially in Congress, who detested him because this commoner boldly took his better-educated and highly respected elders to task for their many failures that endangered the life of the army and the revolution, Hamilton did whatever he could for America's benefit as a diehard nationalist at the expense of his own image and reputation. Ironically, his elitist distracters later condemned him for his lack of support for the common man, when he was the most common man among the Founding Fathers.

Most importantly, he evolved into America's first chief of staff, in the modern sense, for General Washington at his headquarters by the spring of 1777. This was a historic development and a distinguished first in the annals of American military history: the birth of the chief of staff, the second most important position after the army's commander, in the modern sense. Despite holding only a lieutenant colonel's rank, and being the youngest staff officer of the general's military "family," Hamilton nevertheless played multiple invaluable roles that have been generally unappreciated to this day.

It has been long assumed by generations of American historians that Washington managed the Continental Army largely on his own without a chief of staff, which is one of the great myths of the American Revolution and one that has stubbornly persisted to this day, partly because of the longtime hero worship of the "Father of our Country." But in truth and far more than has been realized by most American historians, Washington benefitted immeasurably from Hamilton's influence, whose contributions made Washington a much better and more capable general in the end.

Fortunately for Washington's management of the Continental Army and dealing with almost insurmountable problems, the general had early possessed a distinct genius (perhaps his most overlooked talent) for recognizing superior ability and talent, especially in regard to young Hamilton's seemingly boundless potential and promise. As the commander-in-chief's favorite aide-de-camp and top staff officer—a meticulous workaholic blessed with sound judgments and brilliant insights—for nearly four years, Hamilton contributed significantly to the war effort because he was an original, brilliant, and bold thinker who constantly challenged convention for the overall good of America and the army. Significantly, the famed General Staff of the German military establishment of the World Wars had long cultivated the boldest and most unorthodox (nonconformists and mavericks) individuals from among its most promising students to be original thinkers because they were the ones who eventually excelled in the art of war by thinking outside the dominance of the entrenched, traditional thinking of opposition leadership—a forgotten key to success. Washington was most fortunate because Washington fit all of these requirements of an ideal General Staff officer of the modern period.

Not one of the thirty-two men who served on his personal staff known as the "family"—and even general officers of the Continental Army—was more vital to Washington year after year than Hamilton. He was literally the commander-in-chief's chosen one and golden boy, who could accomplish almost any task or mission required by "His Excellency," despite the odds or obstacles. From beginning to end, therefore, Hamilton was Washington's indispensable right-hand man with a can-do attitude and perfectionist mentality that early transformed him into the primary driving force of Washington's headquarters staff, the nerve center of the Continental Army and America's overall resistance effort.

Consequently, Hamilton became inseparable from Washington while serving in his invaluable role as the first chief of staff in the modern sense. Historians have long incorrectly portrayed how Washington operated in little more than a vacuum in his major decision-making at headquarters year after year. In one of the great paradoxes of Revolutionary War historiography, generations of historians have simply assumed and deliberately emphasized that Washington made notable achievements that should actually be credited to Hamilton. Fortunately for America, the talents of each man—Washington and Hamilton—almost perfectly compensated for and complemented what the other lacked to create an unbeatable whole: the most dynamic and successful leadership team of the American Revolution and then of post-war America in regard to the highest office in the land, when Washington served as the nation's first president.

In part because Hamilton had only recently arrived as a lowly immigrant from the West Indies thanks to influential backers, there long remained an enduring suspicion (especially among his military and political enemies of the upper-class elite, including other Founding Fathers) that he was unworthy of the name *American*. After the war, he was constantly attacked in the press by Jeffersonian opponents (whose political leader from Monticello never fought on a battlefield or made significant wartime contributions like Hamilton) for being un-American, as if he had never played such a vital role by Washington's side for so long and during some of the crucial campaigns of the American Revolution. But, in fact, after Washington, no Founding Father contributed more to America's ultimate victory on the battlefield and overall success as a nation than the much-maligned Hamilton. Therefore, one of the great conundrums and contradictions of American history was how Hamilton's long list of impressive wartime accomplishments could have become so unappreciated by the nation that he so often risked his life to save, and helped to create both on and off the battlefield for years. For one, history has not been kind to Hamilton. Aristocratic Founding Fathers like John Adams and Jefferson held Hamilton in contempt because of his immigrant status. For such reasons, the Jefferson Memorial stands in impressive fashion from the tidal basin in Washington, DC, while no comparable memorial to Hamilton can be seen to this day.

Hamilton's remarkable success story—literally a case of rags to glory—was the very personification of the American dream to people around the world today: taking advantage of existing opportunities and rising higher on one's own abilities and hard work, overcoming the odds regardless of background, religion, or social status, not to mention the fact that in a nation that was built through successive tides of immigrants looking for a coveted piece of the American dream, Hamilton was one of the original immigrants. Possessing an uncanny ability to rise above adversity and hardship that were too great for most people to overcome, Hamilton's meteoric rise from Caribbean obscurity and dysfunctional family background to the leading player on Washington's staff and a revered war hero was a true Horatio Alger story.

After he became disillusioned with America's failing war effort and lack of unity, this cerebral young man was focused on solving infant America's seemingly insolvable military, economic, and political problems while serving on Washington's staff during the war. Nevertheless, he still remained an outsider and maverick—actually assets—in fundamental ways, especially as an innovative problem solver which set him apart from a mostly conservative officer corps, consisting mostly of traditional America-born men of a higher class and social standing. These orthodox types were the least likely individuals to develop original ideas that provided solutions to new and complex problems. Partly because of such reasons and his outstanding success in multiple fields of endeavor, Hamilton made a good many wartime enemies, including influential members of Congress, and, he remained at odds with powerful politicians of the Virginia Dynasty, especially Thomas Jefferson, and other Anti-Federalists, after the war.

As Washington fully recognized, Hamilton was very different from his peers who were far more provincial and less gifted. Hamilton's overall outlook of life reflected his sharply dissimilar and broader background, which embodied more wide-ranging experiences, including on an international level in the Caribbean. Therefore, Hamilton was a free-thinking and open-minded newcomer to America without the burden of regional biases or prejudices that damaged America's war effort from the beginning. This "Hamilton difference" provided keen insights, original thinking, and accurate assessments that served him so well in advising Washington, especially during high-level dealings with upper-class French military leaders.

Hamilton's well-grounded and sophisticated progressive opinions were cosmopolitan beyond his years and well beyond the narrow regional views of many revolutionary leaders, especially during the American Revolution. This was especially true in regard to slavery, specifically the young man's hatred of slavery. As he emphasized in an appeal to the Continental Congress in 1779, Hamilton believed in black equality to whites, which was a view extremely rare in his day and unmatched by any Founding Father, especially slave owners—a significant difference among the Founding Fathers that has been long overlooked. He utterly rejected the prevalent concept of black inferiority with a self-assured ease, and boldly appealed to Congress to allow slaves to fight for their freedom and that of America. In time, Hamilton became a principal leader of the New York Manumission Society. For a wide variety of reasons and especially in regard to his lowly immigrant background, Hamilton's life was very much a paradox: The ultimate outsider who became the ultimate insider and visionary nationalist who stood at the very center of some of the most dramatic moments in America's story from Washington's headquarters to his presidency of the world's newest republic.

Today, Hamilton has become known primarily because of his disproportionate and significant contributions in the drafting of the United States Constitution, and his service as America's first Secretary of the Treasury. He also founded the national bank, established a solid base for future industrial growth, and played a leading role in the adoption of stronger government institutions. His innovations were intended to make the new republic financially stable and functional, thus ensuring a bright future, while helping to preserve the fragile union of diverse states: the laying of the very foundation for the modern American nation. These contributions were especially significant and timely because the upstart United States of America was fully expected by many people, especially European leaders, to fail miserably and to be shortly relegated to the dust bin of history.

However, the breadth of these well-known postwar achievements has obscured Hamilton's astonishing career as one of the most remarkable officers of the Continental Army, when he served by Washington's side for nearly four years. As fate would have it and in Washington's giant shadow, he was largely unseen behind the scenes at Washington's headquarters, especially in regard to decision-making and coordinating intelligence activities. This was no accident. The stoic Hamilton actually allowed the limelight to shine on Washington, because he was the symbol of self-sacrificing patriotism and the overall resistance effort that had to be promoted at all times.

As only a lieutenant colonel in his twenties and a relative newcomer to America's shores who had spent most of his life in the West Indies, Hamilton's wartime responsibilities, as early delegated to him by his appreciative commanding general who knew that the young man could always get the job done, were truly sweeping for the fulfillment of a chief of staff's responsibilities. Washington's trust in this young man of such exceptional promise, which shortly grew to a heavy dependence that continued unabated for most of the war and even during his presidency after the war, was demonstrated in the most important fields of endeavor: strategy, politics, intelligence, planning, logistics, training, and diplomacy with the Continental Congress, politicians, generals, and the French allies. Hamilton's diplomatic skill and fluency in French paid considerable dividends in regard to America's proud and sensitive primary partner, which was absolutely necessary for easy communications and better understanding between culturally dissimilar allies (former enemies in the previous war) that were essential to eventually achieving decisive victory in the end.

Equally significant for America's successful war effort, Hamilton played an invaluable role in protecting Washington's leadership position and reputation when the rising tide of criticism, including that coming from ambitious fellow generals and members of Continental Congress against the Virginian with losing ways, and when more successful rivals sought to replace him by Machiavellian means. Year after year, therefore, Lieutenant Colonel Hamilton served as Washington's ever-vigilant guardian angel, helping to ensure that he securely remained the army's commander and symbol of America's resistance effort until the war's end.

In multiple roles of extreme importance, Hamilton repeatedly rose to the fore when the battlefield situation was especially crucial, from the battle of Trenton as a New York artillery commander, to the battle of Monmouth Court House as Washington chief of staff, and all the way to the battle of Yorktown as the tactically astute commander of light infantry in the crucial attack. Incredibly and like very few others, Hamilton excelled in every branch of the service, except cavalry, and only because he never had an opportunity to do so.

While women of all ages loved Hamilton, he made enemies of men very easily, and often without significant cause, thanks to his brilliance and success that generated considerable jealousy. Partly because of his many enemies of influence, high-ranking generals and politicians, (especially Jefferson after the war), who grossly distorted the historical record to diminish his many significant contributions and political and economic legacies, Hamilton has become America's most controversial Founding Father for reasons mostly unjustified. On the other hand, he could count on the loyal friendship of many of America's leading men, especially Washington, who fully understood his true value to himself and America, and never lost his faith in Hamilton.

His determined and dogged perseverance, born of his earlier life struggle for existence in the Caribbean, was another key to Hamilton's amazing wartime and postwar successes that continuously astounded Washington and other Founding Fathers. In the West Indies as well as in America, Hamilton fought to overcome a series of formidable obstacles and social prejudices set firmly in place to block his rise because of the arbitrary dictates of class, wealth, and social background. This was one fundamental reason why he so enthusiastically embraced America's egalitarian spirit and struggle for liberty that boldly defied the unfair social foundations of the aristocratic elite and the traditional ruling class.

As fully demonstrated at the battles of Trenton (late 1776) and Princeton (early 1777) and other hard-fought contests when he earned distinction while commanding a New York state battery with tactical skill, Hamilton was early recognized as a gifted young officer by senior leaders, including Washington. Hamilton's sterling reputation and seemingly endless promise opened the door to Washington's invitation—one of his best decisions and far more than he realized at the time—to join in his staff on March 1, 1777. For ample good reason, he was nicknamed Washington's and the Continental Army's "Little Lion." Hamilton's sobriquet of Little Lion did not stem from either his youth or slender form, but from his eagerness to win battlefield distinction, and an almost suicidal courage that repeatedly defied death in crisis situations. Some observers even believed that the young man possessed a death wish.

During this era, the term "little" referred to humble origins. The dashing Hamilton, who wore a resplendent uniform with meticulous care as if educated at a European military academy, actually stood above average height of the time at five foot and seven inches in a lithe, well-proportioned form. But Hamilton's lively personality, intelligence, leadership abilities, and other natural gifts were truly outsized. As mentioned, this scholarly intellectual was also a man of action. During the battle of Monmouth Court House, New Jersey, on June 28, 1778, Hamilton, with saber in hand and dashing back and forth on horseback, played a key role. Here, he rallied shaken troops and even led a counterattack to help save the day, after having shouted "let us all die here rather than retreat" in the face a spirited British counterattack. This is but one example of Hamilton's fighting spirit in a key battlefield situation.

Besides achieving ultimate victory and creating a strong nation for survival in a dangerous world, Lieutenant Colonel Hamilton, imbued with the republican spirit of the Age of the Enlightenment ideologies, most of all wanted America to truly live-up to its lofty ideals. To him, this meant that America should end slavery to remain true to its most basic founding principles. Ahead of his time and at the risk of his career and good standing in serving as Washington's chief of staff, he boldly advocated for the use of black soldiers to fight for their own and America's freedom in the South. He was a leading advocate of this audacious proposal to Congress risking his reputation, especially among the highest-ranking Southern politicians and military men in America.

In addition, Hamilton also early befriended when Washington initially remained cool to still another opportunistic foreign officer (especially when he had been endorsed by rival General Horatio Gates) seeking higher rank and served as a liaison officer early on to Prussian Baron Freidrich Wilhelm von Steuben. Von Steuben later led the way in transforming the Continental Army into a well-drilled military organization to match their professional and superior opponent. Hamilton early recognized the Prussian's true value, while helping to make the German's acclimation into the Continental Army a relatively smooth one.

For the first time in any single volume, the primary emphasis of this book will be to reveal how a young immigrant from the West Indies made so many all-important contributions as the commander's principal aide-de-camp and closest confidant during most of the war years, the invaluable chief of staff role: the often overlooked story of the dynamic leadership team of Washington and Hamilton during the war's most critical periods at headquarters and on the battlefield. What has been most often forgotten was the fact that this was a truly symbiotic relationship between these two men, separated by social standing and in age by more than two decades and dissimilar life experiences, a close rapport which played a vital role not only in America's ultimate success in the end, but also the nation's long life in the future.

Therefore, this book will present the long overlooked and generally unappreciated story of the detailed inter-workings of America's most important leadership team and most vital partnership during the America Revolution's most crucial years. Quite simply and what has been almost entirely forgotten was the fact that after General Washington, Hamilton filled the most important position in America's military from March 1777 to early 1781.

Indeed, this ultra-nationalist team of Washington and Hamilton played a leading role in not only winning the war, but also in charting the new nation's future course well into the twenty-first century. The symbiotic Washington–Hamilton relationship was America's most important and crucial partnership in early American history, and the chief of staff role was the vital glue that kept this dynamic relationship together in both war and peace.

Generations of military and academic historians have long wondered about what was the most important link that so closely united these two Founding Fathers and bonded them tightly together for so long, especially when their relationship was an impersonal, work-based one. Consequently, this book has been written to answer this enduring mystery—Hamilton's all-important role as Washington's chief of staff, comparable to that of the equally brilliant Louis Alexandre Berthier for Napoleon. Significantly, just as Berthier was the most important chief of staff of the Napoleonic Wars and was one of the forgotten secrets of Napoleon's string of amazing successes across Europe, so too did Hamilton serve as the invaluable chief of staff who made Washington a much better general.

In the end, Hamilton's many invaluable and diverse contributions for such an extended period might well have saved not only the commander-in-chief position of George Washington, but also played a larger role in separating winner from loser in the American Revolution. Although obscured by Washington's giant shadow that has long diminished the importance of his unparalleled and unprecedented role as chief of staff in the modern sense, Hamilton's wartime years have presented a striking paradox, because no one accomplished more during the war years and gained less credit for what he achieved for such an extended period at such a high level. For good reason when he gave his farewell address and submitted his resignation as commander-in-chief to Congress at Annapolis, Maryland, on December 23, 1783, Washington especially thanked his trusty aides-de-camp, and no one was more deserving of his most sincere thanks than Hamilton, because his larger-than-life role from beginning to end.

In one of the great ironies of Revolutionary War historiography, the most important position in the Continental Army (Washington's indispensable right-hand man for most of the war), after commander-in-chief of course, has been long minimized by historians in one of the most glaring omissions in the historical record. Generations of American historians have long focused exclusively on the accomplishments that Washington achieved, as if these successes were made entirely on his own—as if his gifted chief of staff named Alexander Hamilton never existed. Therefore, one of the most important roles of any military officer in the annals of American history has been long overlooked for reasons based more on jealousy, pettiness, and heated postwar politics than the facts.

Phillip Thomas Tucker, PhD
Washington, DC
August 15, 2016

Chapter I

A Natural Rebel with Much to Prove

Alexander Hamilton, a brilliant young immigrant from the Caribbean, made his dreams come true in America in spectacular fashion and in relatively short time. America, like Hamilton, overcame the odds to reach its full potential, but only after a great deal of heartache and struggle, winning its independence after eight years of bitter conflict. When he first stepped on the shores of America in the summer of 1773 not long before the American Revolution, few young men seemed so unlikely to reach such soaring heights as Hamilton.

For such reasons, Hamilton embraced the totality of the American dream and a heady new nationalism like a holy shroud, and quickly distanced himself from his dark West Indian past. Despite his future successes, the emotional pain of that dark past of a troubled life never left him. With a chip on his shoulder from the snubs and humiliations of his past because of his low social standing, the young man made for a natural revolutionary who fit neatly into the mainstream of angry Americans determined to shake off the bondage of the mother country.

Hamilton's unpleasant early life in the Caribbean was no fault of his own. Hamilton's father, James—a Scottish aristocrat and aspiring merchant with little business savvy—deserted the family and was not seen again. James Hamilton was the fourth of eleven children from the family estate at Ayrshire, southwest Scotland. However, a branch of the Hamilton family had been centered in the township of Hambleton, England. Handsome and personable, Hamilton's father was a Scottish nobleman and proud of it, but at the same time was a ne'er-do-well, whose Caribbean business ventures too often went awry. He never married Hamilton's mother, the considerably younger Rachel Faucette-Lavien, and their informal relationship represented the relatively loose morality of West Indian Creole society. She was a feisty woman of French Huguenot descent. Strong-willed and a force to be reckoned with, Rachel hailed from a respected family who owned a small sugar cane plantation on the Caribbean island of Nevis. Having the greatest influence on Alexander's life than anyone else, she was a remarkable woman of moral courage and intelligence, and ahead of her time in many fundamental ways.

Before James Hamilton's arrival, Rachel Faucette's first husband had resulted in an ill-fated and disastrous relationship for the spirited young woman. When she was only sixteen, Rachel had been swept off her feet and married a Dane, Johann (John) Michael Lavien, more than ten years her senior, in 1745. Rachel eventually realized her grave mistake. Around 1750, after about a half decade of marriage, she struck out on her own way rather than endure a loveless, perhaps even abusive, relationship. Rachel simply left, after her husband had used up her inheritance that had once been a "snug fortune." Rachel ended her relationship much like her mother Mary did before her, who had gained a legal separation from her husband.

A fancy dresser with an outsized ego, Lavien (Lavine in Alexander Hamilton's spelling) was a German-Jewish merchant from Copenhagen, Denmark. Like most ambitious transplants from the cities of western Europe, he had aspired to seek his fortune in the West Indies and become a sugar and cotton planter and small slave-owner on the Danish island of St. Croix. Lavien also hoped that Rachel would return to him, but her independent spirit and ways dictated otherwise, which resulted in a personal vendetta from an embittered husband.

After having been an apprentice with a leading Glasgow businessman and textile merchant in the growing linen industry, James Hamilton had been working for a St. Christopher (better known as St. Kitts) mercantile firm that had extensive ties to Glasgow, including sugar refineries. James first met Rachel in the Leeward Island of St. Kitts. She had briefly moved from St. Croix with son Peter Lavien, her only legitimate child, born in 1746, to rejoin her mother, who was living with a large landowning planter on the island of Nevis. However, Rachel returned to St. Croix, where she supported herself by renting out her three slaves (Flora, Esther, and Rebecca inherited from her grandmother), and by a small sewing business. Under pressure from debtors and her vindictive husband who had her imprisoned at the main fort in Christianstead (the capital of St. Croix) for adultery, the persecuted Rachel fled to the English island of St. Kitts in 1750, abandoning all that she had known, including her son Peter: a drastic step that now made a legal separation from her estranged husband impossible and would doom any future children (James Hamilton, Jr., and Alexander Hamilton) as illegitimate.

Destiny seemed to have ordained a fateful meeting on St. Kitts between Rachel and James Hamilton in the early 1750s. Because divorce was such a rare and expensive undertaking at this time, and remarriage was now not possible for Rachel in legal terms under convoluted Danish law on St. Croix, Alexander's mother (although legally still married to Lavien) lived an unconventional life-style with James Hamilton. Under the circumstances, it was impossible for Rachel to legitimize their relationship and common law marriage in legal terms. She lived with James for perhaps as many as fifteen years, a period in which he was unable to acquire riches in the Caribbean. Born around 1718 and raised in his landed family's Kerelaw Castle, which overlooked the port town of Stevenston, Scotland, James had grown up with the finer things in life. Like most West Indies planters, James had planned to retire in his native homeland after he made his riches in the Caribbean.

The two were polar opposites. Rachel's dominant traits were not only prac-ticality and commonsense but also intelligence, while James was more of a dreamer that ensured some "indolence." However, James Hamilton was blessed with a pleasing personality and charming ways. Fortunately for him, Alexander Hamilton benefitted from this union by gaining the most admirable qualities of each parent. Even by Caribbean standards, this common-law marriage was scandalous, but less so if on the mainland, when Alexander Hamilton—the couple's second son after James, Jr.—was born in Charlestown, the capital of Nevis in the British Caribbean, on Saturday, January 11, 1755. Lacking the work ethic necessary to succeed but burdened with a sense of entitlement of a proud Scottish nobleman, James, Sr. dealt the hard-luck Rachel another severe blow. After having failed as a husband like in his business ventures, he deserted the family in 1766. After having brought his common-law wife and two sons from Nevis to St. Croix's busiest port, Christiansted, Hamilton disappeared for good. Alexander never saw his father again.[1]

After nearly a decade of having fled St. Croix, Lavien filed for divorce in 1759 in order to protect his one legitimate heir, Peter Lavien, while ensur-ing that Alexander and James were declared bastard and "whore children," who could never legally inherit any of his property. With the 1759 decision of the judge sitting on the Danish divorce court, Lavien was allowed to remarry, unlike Rachel. Rachel had been disgraced by her husband's wrath, including what might well have been trumped-up charges of adultery that caused her to be jailed in Christiansted for a short period.

As sad fate would have it, Alexander Hamilton paid a high psychological and emotional price for all of these unfortunate developments, and the unconventional nature of his mother's relationship with his father, and his illegitimate status. This was especially the case in the port of Christiansted, where his mother had suffered her greatest setbacks and humiliations, weighing heavily on a woman valiantly struggling against the odds. As a result, Alexander's first education came in the school of hard knocks.

Although from a broken family herself and not raised by her father, Rachel had found the long-term relationship with the affable Scotsman, relatively secure. Alexander certainly benefitted from this early stability of a nuclear family. Despite being destined to experience hard times in the Caribbean, Alexander never lived in a lower class dwelling. Before relocating to St. Croix with James Hamilton in the spring of 1765, Rachel had lived with him in a stone waterfront home located on the foreshore of Gallows Bay in the port of Charlestown on Nevis' southwestern side near the Customs House. Situated on the main street that ran parallel to the bay and near Anglican Churches, Rachel had inherited this property from her father. The large, two-story house stood on a flat, sandy plot of land located not far from the luminous blue-green wide bay.[2]

Because of the family's dysfunctional past, young Alexander suffered from the inevitable social backlash while growing up on St. Croix, especially after his father's departure. He was forced to fight for his reputation, name, and honor in Christiansted's streets, learning firsthand about the harshness and unfairness of the outside world, hard lessons that he never lost and wounds that never disappeared. Rather remarkably, however, he never held any resentment or bore a grudge toward his "charming scamp of a father," for abandoning the family. In social terms, the Celtic background of the family of Alexander's Scottish father was distinguished and respectable, which was so vitally important in class-conscious eighteenth century society and especially to a young man without a stable family life. The distinguished heritage became a source of pride for Alexander in his dark moments.

Despite the hardships brought about by his father's hasty departure when he was ten, and his mother's upcoming death from yellow fever on February 18, 1768, when he was only thirteen, Alexander developed a tough-mindedness, hardened exterior, and resiliency that served as an emotional and psychological buffer for protection, qualities that served him well in meeting life's stern challenges in the future. Cruel twists of fate and adversity shaped a young Hamilton out of necessity into a responsible individual mature well beyond his years. With a passion and ample justification because he had suffered in this class-based environment, the ever-egalitarian Hamilton long denounced the rigid artificiality of class distinctions and aristocracy on both sides of the Atlantic. He sincerely believed that non-aristocratic "blood is as good as that of those who plume themselves upon their ancestry."[3]

The place of Alexander's birth, Nevis, lay in the Queen's Leewards, consisting of five tropical islands situated amid turquoise waters. Only thirty-five square miles in size, Nevis was positioned near its oddly shaped sister island of St. Kitts (first known as St. Christopher and about twice Nevis' size), from where James Hamilton hailed. These two islands rose up from the same mountain range that had been thrust upward from the ocean's floor millions of years ago.

Alexander Hamilton's life at the port of Charlestown, Nevis, till age ten, and then later Christiansted, St. Croix, to age seventeen, was filled with the sights and sounds of the busy wharf and dock: noisy fishermen and sailors from around the world; the sight of large numbers of black slaves; stately royal palms and orange trees loaded with ripe fruit; flocks of low-flying brown pelicans flying low over blue waters in search of unwary fish; lucrative island commerce from nations around the world; and African slaves gathering at the town's marketplace every Sunday to sell their produce. Towering above Charleston, Nevis was distinguished by snow-covered Mount Nevis, which dominated the island's center. Standing at 3,200 feet above sea level and often obscured in clouds, this imposing mountain towered over a green carpet of sugar cane plantations that covered the fertile lowlands. Christopher Columbus had allegedly christened this picturesque island *Nuestra Señora de las Nieves* (Our Lady of the Snows) because of the extinct volcano's frigid peak. Bustling Charlestown was the island's largest and busiest port.[4]

In an environment that was the antithesis of the traditional backgrounds and native environments (mostly small farms or larger Southern estates near the east coast) of the other Founding Fathers, the beauty of Nevis and St. Croix contrasted sharply with the harsh realities of life—including slavery's horrors—on these tropical islands. He had seen men, women, and children sold on the auction block. The horrors and agonies of slavery left a deep impression upon young Hamilton, who became a hater of slavery and a diehard abolitionist. In fact, Alexander's early experiences that confirmed the humanity of slaves—which had been denied by so many whites—allowed him to stand high above most of his fellow Founding Fathers in moral terms.

Rachel became the owner of five full-grown female slaves after her mother's death, which had allowed her to inherit two additional slaves who were likewise hired out. She assigned a young slave boy named Ajax to Alexander as a body servant. Charlestown prospered as the island's primary slave market, part of the lucrative international mercantile system. Besides the endless source of cheap labor performed by the unfortunate Africans in the broad fields, the rich volcanic island soil, warm weather, and bright sunshine all fueled the island's primary cash crop of sugar cane. Nevis was covered by flowing cane fields that stretched as far as the eye could see. The sprawling planter estates were dotted with rounded stone windmills that provided the wind energy, along with slave labor, that crushed the green stalks into cane juice.[5]

The basic core of Hamilton's personality, including his hated of slavery, was formed in his personal struggles and humiliations on St. Croix. The world of the Danish West Indies shaped and molded the man destined to become one of America's most unforgettable Founding Fathers, although that significant influence has been long minimized by generations of historians. Ironically, St. Kitts would send much-needed supplies to General George Washington's Army during the first two years of the American Revolution, which might have been a source of pride to Hamilton, while serving his country.

Distinguished by a sound business sense, financial smarts, strong will, and work ethic, Rachel was tough and resourceful out of necessity. The independent-minded Rachel was autonomous to a degree not usually seen in a woman at this time. She defied a patriarchal society's lowly expectations, especially when on her own. After James Hamilton abandoned the family and was seen no more, the irrepressible Rachel was primarily responsible for providing for herself and two sons, Alexander and James, Jr., by her own resourcefulness and brainpower to create a decent life for the hard-luck family on St. Croix. A bright woman who had mastered the art of survival on her own, Rachel was a skilled businesswoman who continued to defy convention. Her entrepreneurial sense and never-say-die spirit were passed down to her precocious son, who was destined to put these admirable qualities to good use on American soil.

A hard worker, Rachel successfully operated a small store from her rented two-story house (the upstairs was the residence and downstairs was the business) at No. 34 Company Street in Christiansted. Rachel's wealthy brother-in-law, James Lytton, paid the rent and donated the Spartan furnishings. He might also have contributed the silver utensils and porcelain water basins and plates owned by Rachel. Conducting a profitable business to support her family unlike the fumbling James at a time when women seldom operated an independent business enterprise, she sold a variety of goods imported from the American colonies through the import-export mercantile firm of David Beekman and Nicholas Cruger of New York City. These imports, especially salt pork and flour, were sold by Rachel to plantation owners, who exclusively grew crops of sugar cane to utilize all available acreage. In addition, Rachel's good looks and stylish dress at age thirty-six did nothing to hurt business among admiring male customers.

Most importantly, Alexander learned at an early age how to effectively manage and operate the store, gaining an understanding of financial matters and becoming an expert at accounting. Hamilton also learned the advantages of promptly paying debts while working by his mother's side and gaining a well-honed knowledge for business. Meanwhile, his enterprising mother also gained income from the five slaves, whom she continued to rent out. Despite its small size, Alexander's Caribbean world was cosmopolitan and lively, thriving at the crossroads of imperial destinies and mercantile ambitions of the major European powers. Sailing ships from around the world docked at the Caribbean's major ports, including those in St. Croix. Christiansted was the thriving commercial center, situated on St. Croix's north central side, while Frederiksted was located on the island's west side. Named in honor of Danish kings, these bustling towns were laid out and built in traditional Danish-style, with whitewashed homes and buildings gleaming in the Caribbean sunshine.

Hamilton saw little romance on the tropical islands of either Nevis or St. Croix, only the harsh realities of what was often a short life in the hell of the tropics, especially from the ravages of disease. Because of the stain on the family name and the geographic-social constraints for future advancement, Hamilton's ambitions were early frustrated. Therefore, he soon found a satisfying refuge in books, including thirty-four volumes owned by his mother. These books were almost certainly bought or donated by her well-to-do brother-in-law, James Lytton, who had married her sister Ann. This small library, which almost certainly included the Holy Bible, was a rare luxury for a relatively young woman of only modest means, speaking well of Rachel's intellectual abilities and foresight in regard to her sons. Hamilton viewed St. Croix's eighty-four square miles and three hundred eighty sugar plantations as little more than a prison that confined his growing ambitions and dreams.[6]

Processing bills of lading, bookkeeping, accounting, and tabulating funds as a teenage apprentice at the mercantile firm of Beekman and Cruger (eventually to become Kortright and Cruger which continued to be based in the great mercantile center of New York) was a dead-end occupation for Hamilton's lofty aspirations. His mother had secured this entry position for Alexander since he was eleven, when his education in business continued unabated after having worked at his mother's store: a wise decision that ensured the young man a livelihood and mentor, Nicholas Cruger. Rachel had done all that she could to place her precious son in a professional position, and she succeeded admirably in her mission.

Rachel died on February 19, 1768, of a yellow fever epidemic at age thirty-eight, thanks in part to an excessive bleeding procedure prescribed by her physician. The same epidemic nearly took Alexander's life, and he was fortunate to have survived. Thankfully, to provide Alexander with some consolation, social humiliation did not follow Rachel in death because of her past social indiscretions. She was buried at nearly St. John's Anglican Church, and the religious-minded young man envisioned her good soul ascending to heaven, where it belonged, contrary to the harsh opinions of most self-righteous people in Christiansted.

Then, as if not enough tragedy had marred Alexander's life, Rachel's still vindictive Danish husband Lavien suddenly returned and laid claim to his wife's meager estate because she had not left a will. With evil intent in his personal war that never ended against Rachel and her memory, he deprived Alexander and his brother, now orphans and on their own, of their inheritance, which included Rachel's five adult female slaves. Alexander and James continued to suffer only because they were illegitimate. Again, the relentless Lavien was determined that everything was to go to his legitimate son of Rachel, Peter. The court agreed, and all of Rachel's estate went to Peter. The two young men were then placed under the legal guardianship of Peter Lytton, a cousin in his early thirties. However, during the summer of 1769, a troubled Peter Lytton committed suicide, leaving his estate to his black paramour, Ledja, and their mulatto children. Then, less than a month later, wealthy brother-in-law James Lytton also died: still another stunning setback for the forlorn Alexander and James, Jr., whose fortunes continued to spiral downward at a rapid rate. Displaying the strength of character long demonstrated by his mother, as if he

were compensating for his wayward father's shortcomings, Hamilton chan-
neled the family setbacks and humiliations to his maximum advantage. He
developed an uncanny ability to turn negatives into positives, with reversals
only strengthening his will to succeed in life. Hamilton was consumed with his
great dream, to escape the Caribbean at the first opportunity, because he hated
"the groveling and [lowly] condition of a clerk," as he lamented in a letter dated
November 11, 1769, at age fourteen.[7]

Alexander finally benefitted from a decent break in life. While older brother
James Hamilton, Jr., became an apprentice to a carpenter, Alexander was taken
in by the family of wealthy merchant Thomas Stevens on King Street, after
his mother's death. Alexander also gained a best friend in the merchant's son,
Edward "Ned" (also "Neddy" as Hamilton penned in letters, including the one
on November 11, 1769) Stevens, who was near his own age. The two young
Creoles were much alike, even sharing a hatred of slavery. But this promising
son of one of Christiansted's leading merchants left for America to complete
his education. In November 1769, while languishing as a teenage apprentice
to Beekman and Cruger, where he had been working before Peter Lytton's
death, Hamilton worked long hours at the company's headquarters near the
busy wharf. Alexander's desire to escape from St. Croix was so strong that he
wrote his best friend, Ned Stevens, who was studying at King's College (now
Columbia University) in New York City, that he had "to confess my weakness,"
which was a soaring ambition.[8] Significantly, in regard to his future ascent in
life, the many "harrowing experiences of his youth did not embitter Hamilton
against the world [but] instilled in him an inflexible resolution to conquer it"
rather than be conquered.[9]

Year after year, Hamilton engaged in thankless employment for Nicholas
Cruger, a New York City merchant of Dutch heritage, at King Street's lower
in downtown Christiansted. Here, at the company's store and large warehouse
near the wide harbor and the wharf, Hamilton demonstrated his considerable talents and superior abilities over an extended period. Nicholas Cruger,
Alexander's boss, was the son of a leading mercantile and political family of
New York City, which had elected two Cruger mayors. Nicholas was a junior
partner of St. Croix's most lucrative exporter of sugar and molasses to England's
thirteen colonies. Hamilton now had connections to New York City, where he
was eventually bound, while putting his French to good use, because of the
firm's business links to the French West Indies, especially St. Domingue (the
future Haiti).

Blessed with a strong work ethic and stamina for long hours of labor, Hamilton's knowledge of finance and commerce became more refined. In 1769 when Hamilton was fourteen, and after having worked as a clerk for around three years, David Beekman departed the firm. He was replaced by New Yorker Cornelius Kortright. However, Hamilton's lowly status did not change at Kortright and Cruger.

But then an opportunity unexpectedly developed. Hamilton's promise increased in Cruger's eyes when he excelled by taking charge and making smart decisions, after excelling at extra responsibilities far beyond a clerk's duties. This golden opportunity to demonstrate the full extent of his abilities came by accident. Despite only being sixteen, Hamilton suddenly benefitted from rising from a lowly clerk's position in October 1771 to become a very effective manager during Cruger's temporary absence. With his trademark boundless energy and savvy in money matters, Hamilton had even improved the business by making tough decisions, including having to fire the company's attorney and ship captain who had drained the company's profits. Cruger imported the same commodities, including fine "Philadelphia flour" that Rachel had sold at her provisioning store, whose goods supplied the sugar planters. But after effectively managing the firm's St. Croix business operations like a veteran manager many years his senior, Hamilton returned to his former clerk position when a recovered Cruger reappeared to take over.

Since he was mostly self-taught, Hamilton continued to read and write as he grew older, nursing a desire to become a distinguished man of letters, perhaps as a ticket out of the detested tropics and bleak island exile. He became more ambitious when a newspaper was established in Christiansted in 1770, which fueled his literary efforts. In early April 1771, he wrote a romantic poem, which was published in St. Croix's primary English newspaper. Displaying no bitter feelings about the family's abandonment, Alexander also wrote a riveting letter to his wayward father, who was living somewhere in the southern Caribbean, about a tropical hurricane's devastation of St. Croix.

Hamilton's hurricane letter was republished in the *Royal Danish American Gazette* on October 3, 1772. At age seventeen, Hamilton drew widespread attention for his masterful prose and colorful vocabulary distinguished by a precocious blend of passion, religion, and wit that seemingly could only have been written by an older (cynical and worldly) and more experienced writer. As demonstrated in the past, he proved himself adept as thoroughly with poems treating sexual topics as he was with religious themes. The sermon-like hurricane letter reminded readers of the supreme folly of man, who was deserving of such divine retribution for earthly sins. Hamilton's words had a dramatic impact on the upper-class elite of St. Croix, even garnering the governor's attention. With his promise and intelligence so bright, a group of benevolent local backers, almost certainly organized by Reverend Hugh Knox and no doubt including men like his employer Nicholas Cruger and his guardian Thomas Stevens, decided to send Hamilton to America to further his education by studying medicine. Doctors were always needed on the disease-ridden tropical island, where yellow fever had taken so many lives, including Hamilton's own mother. Hence, young men from the islands, like Hamilton's good friend "Neddie" Stevens now a student at King's College, studied medicine in America.[10]

Reverend Knox's personal and spiritual influence in assisting Hamilton to fulfill his dreams can hardly be overestimated. Arriving on St. Croix in early 1772, the enlightened Scottish Presbyterian minister who had been educated in divinity at the College of New Jersey (later Princeton University), became not only Hamilton's mentor but also his savior. As the pastor of the Scottish Presbyterian Church in Christiansted, Knox's influence resulted in Hamilton's spiritual turn to religious poetry, and then to more lofty writing pursuits. From Knox, born among the Irish Presbyterians of Ulster Province, north Ireland, and his extensive library, Hamilton gained not only a greater spiritual faith, but also an early education in Enlightenment ideologies and philosophies. Desiring for this gifted young man to succeed in life beyond a lowly clerk trapped on a remote island, the handsome Knox played the key role in paving the way for Hamilton to go to America to fulfill his lofty ambitions. After he secured Knox's letters of introduction to friends in America and learned of the availability of donated funds in America for continuing his education, the opportunities in America beckoned to the young Hamilton as never before.

On a day that he never forgot, Alexander Hamilton walked out along the same lengthy Christiansted wharf from which he and his family had arrived from Nevis in the spring of 1765 less than a decade before. When he finally sailed away from tiny St. Croix and the Caribbean forever in summer 1773 with few possessions, he had no desire to ever return to the place of so much personal suffering and pain. Hamilton left behind almost too many pained memories to count and no regrets.

Most of all, the young West Indian wanted nothing more than a new place and identity to start anew, because he was determined to make a name for himself. At only age eighteen, he was now highly motivated to prove wrong and show up all the haughty upper-class individuals who looked down upon him and his mother with such arrogance and disdain by gaining more distinction than all of them put together. Small wonder that this dreamy young man had early turned to reading, studying history, and writing as a comforting buffer against harsh realities of life in the Caribbean. He was smart, confident, and self-reliant, which boded well for whatever he embarked upon in America.

Phoenix Rising

After embarking upon a three-week journey from St. Croix and experiencing a close call when the ship had caught fire on the open sea, eighteen-year-old Alexander Hamilton landed on the mainland of British America in the summer of 1773. He arrived at the port of Boston, Massachusetts, with high hopes for a brighter future. Hamilton never saw the Caribbean again. He was fiercely motivated to excel in this new environment, despite being a perfect stranger to America and without a friend in this new world. Without family or social connections, he would have to excel on his own in a strange land that he had never seen before. But he had a soaring ambition and keen intelligence that were destined to serve him well in the days ahead. The humiliations of St. Croix failed to diminish his sense of optimism and hope for a brighter future. In fact, the family reversals and social embarrassments in the Caribbean had only fueled his desire to succeed at any cost. As fate would have it, he had entered a world as turbulent as his own past, because of stirrings of a people's revolution were in the air.

Unlike anything seen on St. Croix, Hamilton found that America was a brewing cauldron of revolutionary sentiments fueled by heady Age of Enlightenment idealogy. He immediately journeyed south from Boston to New York City to pick up his allowance from his St. Croix backers for his education at the headquarters of Kortright and Company. Here, his friend Ned Stevens (the only person that he knew in America) studied at King's College, and this was where Cruger's associates lived. However, making an excellent initial impression with his smart dress, erect carriage, and winning personality, Hamilton easily cultivated new friends and associates. Hamilton met a radical merchant named Alexander McDougall, one of the leading Sons of Liberty, in New York City. On July 6, 1774, McDougall was destined to give a rousing speech that galvanized patriot support and greatly impressed

Hamilton. Already an anti-establishment man with a long list of personal grievances against the ruling elite and upper class that he detested on St. Croix, Hamilton soaked up the fiery revolutionary sentiment of America and its heady egalitarian promise. Without the rise of this brewing conflict and his arrival in America occurring at exactly the right time, Hamilton would very likely have remained an obscure unknown individual lost to the pages of history.

Hamilton finally began to study at Elizabethtown (today's Elizabeth), New Jersey, located just southwest of New York City on Newark Bay. The town was founded in 1664 and named after Queen Elizabeth I. Reverend Hugh Knox, his benevolent St. Croix mentor and chief supporter who had early recognized the young man's potential, had given him introductory letters that allowed his entry into the Elizabethtown Academy. He did not have any relations in American nor hard currency except for the letters of credit secured from the Kortright and Company in New York City. Hamilton only had great expectations and winning ways in abundance to propel himself upward and onward. Here, just northwest of the northern edge of Staten Island and just west of the Hudson River, Hamilton thrived in his preparatory studies before gaining entry to college. More importantly, he excelled in the vibrant social world of Elizabethtown, where he made invaluable connections and lifelong friends of the social, political, and professional elite, including many attorneys: William Livingston, Elias Boudinot, William Alexander (Lord Stirling, who was of noble Scottish blood like Hamilton), and John Jay. Significantly, all of these men were destined to play leading roles in the struggle for liberty.

After six months of study at the academy (a prep school) thanks to Knox's letter of introduction, Hamilton's plan to attend school at the College of New Jersey (now Princeton University), a center of Presbyterian revolutionary sentiment, failed. Hamilton's excessive academic ambitions required an accelerated course of study, which he boldly proposed to the school's head, Scotland-born John Witherspoon. Hamilton's proposal was rejected by letter from the board of trustees. Not deterred by the setback, Hamilton then applied to New York City's King's College (today's Columbia University), where friend Ned Stevens studied, partly because he had new sponsors, such as William Alexander, who served on the college's governing board. In addition, Hamilton was sufficiently urbane to thoroughly enjoy the bustling life of New York City, the throbbing economic center of America, compared to the dreary New Jersey backwoods of remote Princeton. To Hamilton's delight, despite the fact that this educational institution was Anglican and Loyalist, King's College accepted his plan to embark upon an accelerated course of study. He had finally fulfilled his desire to proceed on the fast track by the fall of 1773. More importantly, Hamilton's rejection at Princeton thrust him into the heart of the swelling tide of revolution and among leading New York City patriots.

Only age eighteen, Hamilton had also targeted New York City because this was where the Cruger family had long conducted business. Hamilton possessed personal contacts through Kortright and Company, whose representative in St. Croix was Kortright and Cruger, which managed his educational allowance. In lower Manhattan, he boarded with an Irish immigrant tailor named Hercules Mulligan, and his wife Elizabeth. A handsome Irishman with blue eyes, Mulligan hailed from Coleraine, County Antrim, Ulster Province, north Ireland. The son of an accountant, he had migrated to America with his Scotch-Irish family at age six. Educated at King's College and an Episcopalian born on the Emerald Isle in 1740, Mulligan was an influential leader of New York City's Sons of Liberty and an active member of the New York Committee of Correspondence. Mulligan's brother was a junior partner in the firm of Kortright and Company, while his father operated an accounting business, where he had once worked as a clerk: an experience shared by Hamilton in St. Croix. Hamilton and Mulligan were both gregarious and became fast friends.

Even more multi-cultural than the Caribbean, New York City was swept with a flood of new Enlightenment ideas about the meaning of freedom. Without hesitation, Hamilton had sided with the Americans in their quarrel against England, embracing a new patriotism and a nascent nationalism. Hamilton also continued to receive enlightened Presbyterian lessons (first learned from Reverend Knox in St. Croix) that emphasized the sacredness of republicanism and egalitarianism. Thanks to his dual educations from the New York Sons of Liberty and the egalitarian teachings of Presbyterianism, Hamilton quickly evolved into a champion of America's destiny with a passion. Across America, a heightened sense of morality and religious faith, especially Presbyterianism, lay at the heart of the rise of republicanism.

Strengthened by Knox's spiritual and liberal teachings before he had departed St. Croix, Hamilton's Presbyterianism and his father's faith from Scotland of the Great Awakening fused with the righteousness of revolutionary defiance toward Great Britain's threats and dominance. The timely fusion was a natural fit for Hamilton, as he became a diehard revolutionary and nationalist. After all, he already had a considerable chip on his shoulder in regard to exploitive, arbitrary aristocratic authority and the abusive class structure on both sides of the Atlantic. Proving that he was very much his mother's son, he naturally took to opposing the autocratic abuses of the ruling elite and wealthy planters, who had long arrogantly flaunted their high social standing to young men of a lower class like Hamilton.

After experiencing a freer life in an invigorating new land that was larger and more dynamic than he had imagined, Hamilton's patriotism soared higher in the excitement of the times. His growing sense of nationalism had been fueled by meeting with the leading revolutionaries of New York City like McDougall. Born in Scotland, McDougall gave his most patriotic speech at the New York City Common, known as "The Fields," near King's College in July 1774, denouncing the harsh trade sanctions imposed by the British government on Boston, after the Boston Tea Party. But he was outdone by a slight, unknown teenager, who was a college student and an unknown to the people of New York City. Evidently without preparation, Hamilton took the stage and delivered a masterful speech on America's behalf—which advocated a strong pro-Boston Tea Party stance and a commercial boycott of British goods—that left the crowd spellbound by its oratorical brilliance.

Quite by accident, the leaders of the Sons of Liberty had suddenly found a gifted spokesman. In another case of excellent timing, Hamilton needed New York City—America's second largest city after Philadelphia—as much as New York's relatively small group of zealous revolutionary leaders, needed a gifted writer, captivating street speaker, and deep thinker in the escalating propaganda war for the hearts and minds of citizens. After all, America's largest commercial center was largely a Tory city. New York's powerful provincial legislature consisted of faithful Loyalists with extensive political, economic, and personal connections to England. If not outright active Tories, many New Yorkers remained neutral, desiring only to stay out of the encroaching conflict. By contrast, the band of enthusiastic New York City revolutionaries, including their bright shining star named Hamilton, represented "the most daring spirits and the loftiest minds of the colony."[11]

After New York City had grown into America's major metropolis, Theodore Roosevelt, in 1906, concluded without exaggeration how "the purest and ablest New Yorkers were to be found in the ranks of the revolutionists. . . . The young men of ardent, generous temper, such as Alexander Hamilton, John Jay and

Gouverneur Morris" played key roles in leading the way to revolution for New York's patriots.[12]

Rising Up Against England's Might

Like so many others of his day who fought for America, Hamilton had no prior military or political experience, but these class-based limitations did absolutely nothing to dim the young man's ardor or confidence. Nevertheless, and as he had prophetically predicted to "Neddie" Stevens in regard to an armed conflict as a younger man (at age fourteen) in St. Croix in November 1769, Hamilton saw the encroaching war as an opportunity to earn distinction and win the respect from his peers to ensure his advance in a revolutionary society dedicated to equality.[13]

Of all the Founding Fathers, Hamilton was a man without a past (as he preferred under the circumstances) when he first arrived in New York City. America's struggle offered the best chance of his life to literally reinvent himself into an entirely new man. Thanks to his own natural inclinations combined with the heady influence of New York City's Sons of Liberty, Hamilton envisioned a people's republic where anyone could rise on merit rather than social standing and wealth as on his detested St. Croix. Indeed, of "all the Founding Fathers, Hamilton was especially suited to fight for a new society where men could live together free of ancient customs and outworn prejudices" that had made his life difficult in St. Croix.[14]

Because he hailed from a faraway speck of a tropical island that was considered foreign to most Americans, especially because it was located in the Danish West Indies, Hamilton wanted to prove that he was a true American and republican. After his early July 1774 "Fields" speech that displayed his oratory skills that had mesmerized the crowd, Hamilton demonstrated his patriotic worthiness by advocating for American rights and an enthusiastic support for the First Continental Congress, and America's liberty with brilliant writing that flowed so effortlessly from his hand. Clearly, even as this early date, Hamilton was demonstrating that he was a formidable dual threat—by way of pen and oratory—in the propaganda war to defy British dominance.

Hamilton gained greater public notice as a hard-hitting pamphleteer (under the appropriate name of "A Friend of America") in an influential and timely piece of thirty-five pages published entitled "A Full Vindication of the Measure of Congress," in December 1774. With analytical clarity, attorney-like precision, and a masterful style, Hamilton made the case that "Americans are entitled to freedom," and systematically eviscerated the anti-Congress arguments of the gifted Loyalist writer and Anglican rector Samuel Seabury of Westchester, New York. In "A Westchester Farmer," the Yale and Oxford man had wielded highly effective propaganda that dealt a severe blow to the patriot cause.

At this time, when a masterful rebuttal was needed to bolster patriot sentiment, especially in New York City, Hamilton was still a member of the student literary society at King's College on the northern edge of New York City. A systematic dismantling of a brilliant writer who was a privileged, pompous Anglican clergyman and just the kind of authority figure that an outlier and natural rebel like Hamilton loved to mock and reduce in size, utilizing cleverly worded insults that packed powerful punches.

After Seabury answered his pamphlet, Hamilton then reentered the pamphlet war by releasing an even more hard-hitting attack in eighty pages, published on February 23, 1775, *The Farmer Refuted*. He especially emphasized his two greatest intellectual strengths, economics and politics, which revealed the immense depth of his knowledge and even prophetic insights that relatively few Americans had embraced at this time. Ever the optimistic visionary, Hamilton emphasized America's future greatness and special destiny, if only the colonists would unite in their resistance against a common foe. Hamilton's writings in his two masterful "Farmer" essays were broadly appealing and presaged central arguments later included in the Declaration of Independence, that many people believed that John Jay, a leading revolutionary and New York delegate of the First Continental Congress, was the author.

Hamilton early coveted the privilege of battling for the liberties of a freedom-loving people, joining the Sons of Liberty in February 1775 not long after his twentieth birthday. Thanks to his hard-hitting style on behalf of America in speech and pamphlet, he became "the darling" and "boy wonder" of the most diehard revolutionaries, especially the Sons of Liberty, in New York City. While still only a student in college, Hamilton had evolved into a respected patriot leader entirely in his own right.

Like Hamilton on his father's side, Alexander McDougall was of Scottish descent, which represented another example of the importance of the extensive Celtic and Presbyterian contributions to America's struggle for liberty. After all, the Scottish peoples' own dream of independence had been crushed by English military might, and in many respects the fight in America was very much a continuation of an ancient war between Celtic people and Anglo-Saxons. For centuries, the English had become masters in the brutal art of smashing desperate liberation bids and budding nationalism among the Celtic people in Wales, Ireland, and Scotland: bloody lessons not lost to the immigrant sons of these conquered Celtic regions now living on American soil. Born on the island of Islay, Scotland, McDougall would form the First New York Regiment, and lose his beloved soldier son in America's disastrous Canadian Campaign during the winter of 1775–1776.

Hamilton's passion for independence early caused him to take the initiative in other ways besides masterful writing and fiery speechmaking. Hamilton enlisted in a volunteer infantry company of Manhattan men and boys known as "the Corsicans" under Captain Edward Fleming, a British Army veteran, with the news of the first clashes at Lexington and Concord, Massachusetts, in April 1775. He then gained invaluable knowledge about artillery from an experienced gunner, who almost certainly had served in the British Army like Fleming.

The ever-opportunistic Hamilton saw greater future possibilities for himself in service with the artillery arm than in the infantry. After learning about the proper useage of artillery from one of "the Corsicans," therefore, he then helped to organize a volunteer artillery company, known as the "Heart of Oaks," from a group of students in his literary society at King's College in late 1775. Along with school mates Nicholas Fish and Robert Troup, former members of "the Corsicans," and although still too young to shave, Hamilton wore a fancy and tight-fitting green uniform coat with a stylish brown leather cap distinguished by the words, "Liberty or Death." He carried a flintlock pistol and a powder horn with his name carved in it. He also etched symbols on the powder horn that represented the true path to future success from his readings of Sir Francis Bacon. Hamilton's hand-carved designs emphasized his motto of always looking forward to a brighter future, including the visualization of goals. He, therefore, carved a unicorn, which symbolized personal aspirations, with the design of a five-petal flower from the Hamilton family coat of arms on the hindquarters. After studying military manuals, meanwhile, he drilled his fifty student-gunners of the Heart of Oaks volunteer company on the grassy, open grounds of the churchyard of nearby St. Paul's Church each morning before class at King's College.

Then, May 10, 1775, Hamilton bravely intervened to quell an angry mob to save King's College president Dr. Myles Cooper, who had been accused of Loyalist activities. Employing his masterful oratory before Cooper's locked door, Hamilton bought time for the panicked president to escape in the nick of time. Clearly, even as a leading Sons of Liberty revolutionary in New York City, Hamilton had not lost his compassion or humanity for a Loyalist. Meanwhile, he continued his effective writing on behalf of the patriotic cause, including condemning the Quebec Act, because it extended the boundary of French Catholic Canada south and all the way to the Ohio River to infringe on America's ambitions, especially colonies like Virginia, to extend farther west. Hamilton's forceful arguments were printed in two essays published in the *New-York Gazetteer*, New York City. Not long thereafter, the native West Indian continued to demonstrate his skill with the pen with articles in the *New York Journal*. He produced a stunning total of fourteen essays in as many weeks under the pseudonym of "Monitor." As usual, Hamilton emphasized how it was a conspiracy of corrupt and evil men of Parliament in London who were conniving to economically and politically enslave the American people.

Revealing that he was also a man of action, Hamilton was then part of a daring night raid that captured a large number of British cannon at the Grand Battery, located just south of rectangular-shaped Fort George at the southern tip of lower Manhattan Island, on the warm night of August 23, 1775. At the imposing artillery bastion—which contained two dozen large caliber cannon that faced New York harbor and had long protected the city from attack by water—Hamilton and more than a dozen King's College volunteers played a role in rescuing the guns. With the sixty-four-gun British warship *Asia* close and seemingly about to send forth a shore party to take possession of the cannon, Hamilton and his comrades hauled off twenty-one of the precious guns. He risked his life in helping to evacuate cannon from the battery while under cannon-fire from the warship and musketry from soldiers manning a British patrol boat. On his own and ignoring the danger, Hamilton then returned to the battery and then coolly retrieved his musket, misplaced by his friend Hercules Mulligan, that had been left behind.[15]

He resumed his studies at King's College, but the drilling and training continued unabated on the grounds of St. Paul's Church throughout the fall of 1775. When he left King's College in January 1776 after around two years of study, Hamilton was determined to go his own way, despite not having formally graduated. Wartime requirements beckoned Hamilton, and he left his studies behind without regrets, because he knew that this people's revolutionary provided unprecedented opportunities for a gifted young man on the rise.

Long seen as a haven of Loyalists, King's College was transformed into a hospital by the patriots. Ironically, the same classrooms where Hamilton had sat as a student were turned into prison cells for rebels, after the British captured New York City later in 1776.

At this time, the stern requirements of the revolutionary struggle called, and Hamilton's days as one of America's most effective pamphleteers and a Corsican and Hearts of Oak militiaman were over. Hamilton wanted to see action even to the point of rejecting lofty positions that guaranteed social connections and advancement. "I am going into the army," he wrote on February 18, 1776, and Hamilton's life would never be the same. Clearly, the young man was not a soulless mercenary type in this regard. When he was offered a prestigious position on the staff of his old friend Brigadier General William Alexander (Lord Stirling) through his friend Elias Boudinot, Hamilton declined. This was a surprising decision for any young officer except Hamilton, who was a true outlier in this regard. He utterly detested the concept of taking a subordinate role, although a staff officer's position could provide a path to upward mobility on the coattails of a successful general.

Hamilton was determined to fulfill his ambition for active field command rather than staff duty. In consequence, he turned his sights on becoming a captain as a battery commander, after New York City friend Alexander McDougall, former ship captain and Sons of Liberty leader, recommended him as the commander (captain) of the New York artillery unit in February 1776. This artillery unit was to be raised by the New York Provincial Assembly to protect the city. Hamilton, consumed by revolutionary zeal and patriotic sentiment, was eager for action to prove his worth to one and all.

However, he lacked the necessary experience, and officers' commissions only seemed to be awarded to well-known members of New York City's social and political elite, and not to recent immigrants from a small Caribbean island or a young man fresh out of King's College. This new artillery unit was the only battery that represented New York City, providing high visibility and widespread recognition for stirring accomplishments, if demonstrated on the battlefield. Even though he was an idealist in regard to America's struggle, the young man from the West Indies had no illusions about the cost of fighting for freedom, and wrote on February 18, 1776, with his usual flair: "perhaps ere long [I] may be destined to seal with my blood the sentiments defended by my pen. Be it so, if heaven decree it. I was born to die and my reason and conscience tell me it is impossible to die in a better or more important cause."[16] Revealing that intellectual reasoning applied to scrutinizing his own motivations even in the midst of a sacred struggle for liberty, Hamilton excused his burning ambition to excel on the battlefield as just a common feature of human nature that was largely beyond his control: "The desire for reward is one of the strongest incentives for human conduct," he wrote.[17]

An enigma and perhaps the most complex Founding Father, Hamilton was a rare blend of a man of action and scholarly intellectual. He was "one of the first Americans of the War of Independence to unlimber a cannon" in the name of America.[18] However, despite the majority having no military experience themselves, the well-dressed aristocrats of the New York Provincial Assembly had to be convinced that this recent immigrant and a smooth-faced college student could command the respect of his older American-born volunteers to gain distinction on the battlefield for the city and assembly. Influential patrons continued to speak up in his behalf to support this young man unknown to Americans only a few months before. These included John Jay, of Huguenot descent, and Colonel Alexander McDougall, who was the son of a "Scots milkman." But even this support was not enough to win Hamilton the coveted position; he would have to do it himself. As so often in the past, Hamilton then applied his can do aptitude for overcoming obstacles. He studied long and hard for the examination required to secure the coveted position. Improving upon what he had already learned as a college student outside of the classroom on the training ground of King's College, Hamilton shortly became an expert in artillery, the army's most technical arm, at a time when few Americans knew anything about it.

Hamilton's graceful manners and dignified style revealed a confident natural leader of men, including those who were much older, and a proper gentleman that were viewed as so important in colonial and colonial society: requirements for the right kind of leadership in the eyes of New Yorker leaders, who also placed faith in McDougall's and Jay's vote of confidence. His diverse range of abilities also impressed the patriotic members of the New York Provincial Assembly. At age twenty-one, Hamilton won the appointment to command the New York "Provincial Company of Artillery" with the rank of captain on March 14, 1776. Hamilton became one of the youngest captains in America's militia. Most importantly, he proved that he adhered to his own words that had been read by large numbers of Americans in a recent pamphlet: "the law of nature which gives every man a right to his personal liberty, and therefore confer no obligation to obedience."[19]

Exhibiting a dashing style and a meticulous eye for detail that in part made him a good commander, Hamilton wore a splendid blue uniform coat newly made at a New York City tailor shop. Hamilton had always been a sharp dresser when he could afford to be, and he now continued his distinct style as a proud New York artillery officer. His captain's fine uniform was very likely made at Hercules Mulligan's tailor shop on Water Street in lower Manhattan, located near the wharves along the East River. Hamilton became a model officer, who would never lord over his men like most military leaders of the day. Assisted by Mulligan in scouring lower Manhattan, Hamilton had recruited a good many Irish and Scots to serve in his battery, including illiterate immigrants, and an occasional Dutchman with roots in the former New Amsterdam Colony. Hamilton's artillery unit, the New York Provincial Company of Artillery, soon contained sixty-eight gunners, whom he trained intensely to become some of the best artillerymen in the service. These artillerymen wore blue coats with white shoulder belts of leather and brass buttons to reflect the "smart" appearance that Hamilton required of himself.

Hamilton was described by a Pennsylvania officer as "under middle size, thin in person, but remarkably erect and dignified in his deportment. His hair was turned back from his forehead, powdered and collected in a club behind. His complexion was exceedingly fair, and varying from this only by the almost feminine rosiness of his cheeks . . . as to figure and colour, an uncommonly handsome face [and] when in conversation it easily assumed an attractive smile."[20]

The young officer was determined to prove himself, after having mastered the artilleryman's art and win distinction on the battlefield. He had dressed and equipped his cannoneers, now some of the best-uniformed soldiers, who wore buckskin pants, in America, by using the remaining college funds provided by his St. Croix sponsors. Hamilton developed into a highly respected commander: Hard-working, conscientious, and always concerned for his men's welfare to ensure their loyalty and full support.[21] His well-honed business experience from his St. Croix days paid invaluable dividends in organizing and supplying his New York battery.[22]

Week after week, Hamilton trained and prepared his young New York artillerymen to oppose the finest British regulars in defending New York City. But he still found time to study the books to continue his education, while transforming his men into a very good artillery unit distinguished by its "appearance and the regularity of their movements." He proved to be an ideal and popular commander, who early gained the respect of his gunners. Hamilton realized that it was only a matter of time before Great Britain launched a mighty expedition with the mission of crushing the rebellion. Ironically, as revealed in his late 1774 writings, when he was more naïve but still amazingly prophetic, Hamilton had been convinced that only "the grossest infatuation of madness itself [could cause the English monarchy to] enforce her despotic claims by fire and sword." Then, in his *The Farmer Refuted* in early 1775 and with the keen insight for which he was becoming known, Hamilton "may have been the first in print to maintain that Britain could not win the war" in the end.[23]

Dramatic Meeting at Bayard's Hill

On the orders of General William Alexander (Lord Stirling), Hamilton and his New Yorkers fortified some of New York's highest ground on the north side of the city on Bayard's Hill, hoping to stop British warships from sailing north up the Hudson. Young Captain Hamilton first met General George Washington there in lower Manhattan in mid-April. The austere Virginian and member of the Virginia elite with extensive French and Indian War experience inspected the newly built defensive bastion on Bayard's Hill known as Fort Bunker Hill, bristling with a dozen cannon, which overlooked the city and the wide Hudson that led north to Albany, New York. Like Lord Stirling and New Englander General Nathanael Greene who had offered him a staff position that was also rejected, Hamilton made a highly favorable impression on the commander-in-chief. Looking and acting anything but like a recent immigrant from the West Indies as carefully cultivated, Hamilton garnered Washington's compliments for him and his New York gunners for their "masterly manner of executing the work."[24]

However, at this point in the conflict, Hamilton's real war was now not on a battlefield against the British but rather against the mismanagement of authorities, who denied his gunners vital supplies. Knowing the importance of keeping up the spirits of his New York artillerymen, Hamilton fought for a fair share of supplies, including rations, and pay for his gunners: equal to that of Continental artillerymen. In an impassioned letter on May 26, 1776, to the provincial congress of New York in seeking equal treatment for his artillerymen, Hamilton made a righteous appeal to justice in his usual diplomatic style: "I am not personally interested in having an augmentation [of pay] because my own pay will remain the same that it now is; but I make this application on behalf of the company, as I am fully convinced such a disadvantageous distinction will have a very pernicious effect on the minds and behavior of the men. They do the same duty with the other companies and think themselves entitled to the same pay."[25]

Hamilton's First Combat as Artillery Commander

On his own initiative or perhaps under direct orders, Captain Alexander Hamilton laid plans to launch a daring night raid with the arrival of warmer and less rainy weather just after mid-June, after the spring rains had stopped. Envisioning a surprise attack, he targeted the British defensive position around the lighthouse at the northern end of Sandy Hook, New Jersey, south of New York Harbor and just southeast of Staten Island. Situated at the entrance of New York harbor, Sandy Hook, a thin peninsula that thrust north from the New Jersey mainland, was a strategic position. Hamilton struck in the darkness in an assault in which he carefully coordinated the fire of his New York artillery pieces and infantry attackers. Conducting his first offensive strike, the young captain mixed musketry with artillery fire of approximately one hundred men, taking advantage of the darkness and the element of surprise. But the enemy's defensive position was too strong to be overcome. Hamilton revealed his trademark hard-hitting style: "I continued the attack for two hours with [his New York] fieldpieces and small arms, being all that time between two smart fires from the shipping [British warships just outside Sandy Hook] and the [defensive position around] the lighthouse, but could make no impression on the walls" of the British defensive position. This sharp clash at Sandy Hook has become one of the forgotten fights of the American Revolution.

Meanwhile, Washington was placed in a no-win situation by the rising chorus of demanding politicians of the Continental Congress and the impossible mission of defending New York City. Because Manhattan Island was surrounded by a network of waterways, Washington was unable to develop an adequate tactical solution for defending the city. Nothing could counter the powerful Royal Navy, which guaranteed that America's largest city would fall, after England had dispatched the largest fleet and expeditionary force ever set forth, under General William Howe. On June 28, and not long after he returned from his Sandy Hook raid, Hamilton watched the execution of Irishman Sergeant Thomas Hickey in lower Manhattan, near the Bowery, for his role in a plot to murder General Washington in a city swarming with Loyalists. Hamilton fully approved the execution that he hoped would cow "those miscreants," the large Tory population of New York City.

In early July, General William Howe finally made his first tactical move, disembarking thousands of British and Hessian troops onto Staten Island from warships of his brother Lord Richard Howe's fleet. Hamilton and his gunners saw their first action on July 12, barely a week after the signing of the Declaration of Independence in Philadelphia. The spirits of Hamilton and his men were high, after Washington announced the issuing of the declaration to his troops assembled on the New York City Common, where the native West Indian had made his impassioned speech two years before. Still smarting from having recently lost his purse containing his officer's pay, (which happened on July 6, perhaps from too much drinking from America's first Fourth of July celebration), Hamilton might have been in a bad mood. If so, he was presented with an opportunity to finally unleash his wrath on the enemy.

Two British warships, the *Rose* and the *Phoenix* of the powerful fleet of Admiral Richard Howe, the brother of General William Howe, caused panic on Manhattan Island by sailing up the Hudson to probe the strength of the American defenses, including Fort Bunker Hill. Nothing could stop the two warships that demonstrated the tactical superiority and skill of the British Navy: an ill-omen for American forces in regard to attempting to defend a city surrounded by waterways. From this high point on Manhattan Island, Hamilton gave the command to fire. His men opened up with their guns at the British vessels. King George III's sailors returned fire upon Hamilton's earthen fort atop the commanding heights. Because of inferior artillery in terms of caliber, Hamilton's resistance proved largely ineffective, allowing the two warships to continue sailing up the broad Hudson. Several New York artillerymen were injured when the barrel of one Hamilton's guns exploded, most likely because the barrel was defective because of age or inferior quality. Contrary to the opinions of some historians, Hamilton was not at fault for what was nothing more than an accident.

With an elaborate defensive network protecting New York City that Washington attempted to hold in the hope of inflicting another defeat like at Bunker Hill (Breed's Hill just outside Boston)—if General Howe was foolish enough to order frontal assaults as on that bloody day last June—the British wisely refused the bait of launching infantry attacks. Unfortunately, feeling that he had to face the British Army's might—now swollen to forty-two thousand men to outnumber Washington's Army—partly because this upcoming confrontation was a "point of honor" and under political pressure from the Continental Congress to defend New York City, Washington was already in serious trouble long before the first shot in the showdown for New York City was fired in anger. He had dispersed his troops over a wide area to defend Manhattan and Brooklyn, which Hamilton correctly believed was indefensible. In fact, this precocious young man sensed the fast-approaching disaster, because Washington had divided his army, which was now separated across a sizeable body of water, the Upper Bay just below the East River.

Finally, Howe struck when he felt the opportunity was right. The Royal Navy sailed from Staten Island and landed thousands of troops on the southern end of Long Island at Gravesend Bay. After coming ashore via new, innovative landing crafts on the warm morning of August 22, Howe's troops then skillfully maneuvered inland. Around seventeen thousand British and Hessian soldiers marched seven miles to the northeast to outflank American defensive positions, and eased themselves into an ideal position to strike Washington's rear south of Brooklyn Heights, to catch the badly outnumbered homespun rebels by surprise. Lord William Howe's professional troops struck a powerful blow that sent the American forces reeling on August 27 during the battle of Long Island.

Meanwhile, maintaining his longtime defensive position on Manhattan Island to the northwest, Hamilton and his New York gunners from atop Bayard's Hill, the highest point in the city, listened to the battle roaring on Long Island. Washington was driven to new levels of frustration by the rout. The embarrassing defeat—a new low for the novice Continental Army and the largest battle to date—showed that the amateurs in rebellion (this was Washington's first experience in commanding an army in a sizeable battle) were no match for well-trained troops led by experienced, professional leaders.[26]

After the survivors of the disastrous battle of Long Island were transported west in flat-bottomed boats by Colonel John Glover's New England mariners across the mist-covered East River on the night of August 29 to Manhattan Island's safety during the narrow escape, Washington still attempted to hold the strategic island, which only guaranteed the same inevitable bleak results, because of the Royal Navy's vast superiority. However, the sound arguments of his top lieutenant, General Nathanael Greene, had convinced the commander-in-chief otherwise. Washington wisely decided to abandon New York City before it was too late, because the British Navy could land large numbers of troops north of Washington at anytime to trap his army on Manhattan Island. At a commanders' conference on September 12, it was decided that the army of ill-trained troops, who were no match for redcoat regulars, should retreat north up the Hudson to the easily defendable high ground of Harlem Heights.

Two young officers who would win distinction in the years ahead played key roles in protecting Washington's withdrawal ("I was among the last of our army that left the city" bragged Hamilton for good reason) northward up Manhattan Island. After sailing up the East River, Howe's forces landed at Kip's Bay, around nine miles southeast of Harlem Heights, on a Sunday that Washington never forgot. What happened at Kip's Bay was an alarming reminder of what could also happen on the island's west side along the Hudson, because of the Royal Navy's strength and capabilities: the British could land large numbers of troops at will north of Washington's Army to cut-off escape from Manhattan Island. Here, at this natural indentation located on the island's east side above New York City, a heavy cannonade of nearly eighty guns from Admiral Howe's warships and the unnerving sight of thousands of British-Hessian troops rowing toward shore in barges caused a rout of the raw New England soldiers on September 15, 1776. Without losing a single soldier, Howe succeeded in negating the American riflemen in defensive positions—the old Bunker Hill formula for success—with a massive artillery bombardment.

But two highly capable young officers had restored a measure of honor to the Continental Army during the dismal withdrawal. As a strange fate would have it, the destinies of Hamilton and Aaron Burr were already intertwined on the American stage by the time of the retreat to Harlem Heights. Despite now wearing Continental officer uniforms of blue, one of these promising men was destined to take the other's life in a little more than a quarter century. Hamilton's New York battery had been now reduced in firepower, after having been forced to leave their heavy guns behind, at Fort Bayard, after Washington had issued orders for New York City's evacuation. Therefore, Hamilton now commanded only three light guns of his reduced New York battery.[27]

A historian before he became the nation's twenty-sixth president in September 1901, Theodore Roosevelt emphasized the value of the Hamilton-Burr connection in protecting Washington's vulnerable rear during his withdrawal north from New York City. Washington's "divisions, on their retreat, were guided by a brilliant young officer, Aaron Burr, then an aide-de-camp to [General Israel Putnam, while the army's] rear was protected by Alexander Hamilton and his company of New York artillerymen, who in one or two slight skirmishes beat off the advance guard of the pursuers."[28]

During the cheerless withdrawal north to Harlem Heights, and assisted by Burr's knowledge of the road leading north, Hamilton repeatedly rose to the challenge of protecting the army's rear, demonstrating leadership abilities noticed by his superiors, including Washington. As planned, Washington took good defensive position on the commanding ground of Harlem Heights just over a dozen miles north of New York City. He naturally hoped that Howe would commit the folly of assaulting the fortifications situated atop dominant terrain. Fulfilling his rearguard role for the army, young Captain Hamilton was one of the last Americans to reach the safety of the new defense line. Forced to drag their guns because artillery horses had been lost, he and his New York gunners arrived after dark on another warm September night with their two New York cannon, after one of his guns broke down and had to be left behind, along with the artillery unit's baggage. Only because the British pursuit lacked vigor, Hamilton was fortunate not to have been captured.

Here at the rocky plateau known as Harlem Heights, including bluffs ascending to a height of around sixty feet, was a panoramic view of the southern end of Manhattan Island, where Hamilton selected a good position in Washington's newly constructed defensive line and carefully placed his two light guns for the best fields of fire. Even the survivors of the Kip's Bay disaster were emboldened by Washington's high ground defensive position brimming with artillery, including Hamilton's New York guns. Washington again viewed Hamilton's organization skill and military bearing at his new defensive position that had been bolstered by light earthworks to protect his two cannon. Washington was impressed by what he saw.

But Howe had learned his Bunker Hill lesson well on June 1775, and never forgot his frightfully high losses. He refused to take the bait of attacking the formidable Harlem Heights, although fighting did erupt on September 16. Once again, the Royal Navy landed large numbers of Howe's troops north of Washington's stationary position to negate the high ground advantage. The out-maneuvered revolutionaries were once again forced to withdraw north from Harlem Heights toward Manhattan Island's upper tip, when the leaves of October had already turned to their autumnal hues of red and gold, especially the maples, to reveal a natural beauty that seemed to mock America's sinking military fortunes and the creeping darkness that surrounded the increasingly vulnerable life of an infant republic.

Rising to the Challenge at White Plains

After being forced to depart from his excellent defensive position along Harlem Heights, Washington retreated farther north to White Plains, New York. Here, he fortified another good high ground position, presenting Howe with still another formidable defensive array. But Chatterton's Hill, part of a ridge looming at around one hundred eighty feet in height at this point on the vulnerable American right and overlooking the Hudson River just to the west of Washington's main defensive position, was a vulnerable point of this weak defensive line. Washington had massed most of his troops on the high ground to the east, forcing Howe to look elsewhere to strike.

Therefore, correctly ascertaining a good tactical opportunity west of the Bronx River on October 28, Howe ordered the capture of the vulnerable Chatterton's Hill. Positioned on the high ground overlooking the Bronx River, Hamilton had a bird's eye view of the surrounding countryside. He became alarmed by the dire threat posed by the advance of Howe's troops in fording the Bronx River, that flowed between Chatterton's Hill (to the west) and Washington's main line (to the east), and then Howe's surge up the hill in a bid to turn Washington's right flank. Responding quickly to the day's most serious threat to the defenders of Chatterton's Hill, who numbered only about a thousand, Hamilton immediately ordered two of his light guns dragged into an excellent firing position on a rocky ledge of the hill that overlooked the river. From this elevated vantage point, Hamilton opened fire on the German Hessians, crack mercenary troops led by highly capable professional officers, in the river valley below, who were attempting to cross the river by wading and ascending the commanding elevation.

Just as the Hessians seemed about to overrun Chatterton's Hill, out-flank Washington's Army, and win the day, Hamilton's timely and accurate fire proved effective in turning the tide. With well-aimed fire, combined with an eruption of musketry from the Delaware and Maryland Continentals who protected the flanks of his New York cannon, Hamilton stopped the determined Hessian attempt to turn Washington's weak right flank. With only two guns, Hamilton's leadership decisions and quick actions saved the day. Despite this,

Howe's resurgent troops eventually captured the hill, forcing Hamilton to retire to save his two guns. However, the resistance effort fueled by Hamilton's guns helped to convince Howe to conclude his offensive effort on October 28. Young Captain Hamilton basked in his sparkling success which for once allowed Washington to inflict more losses than he suffered, in an inversion of the usual formula of the disastrous New York Campaign. At only age twenty-one, Hamilton reveled in an impressive battlefield performance.

After so many American reversals around New York City, the euphoria stemming from the signing of the Declaration of Independence had evaporated among patriots by the fall of 1776. New York City had been lost and Washington had been defeated in a series of battles during the nightmarish New York Campaign. Washington could not hold Manhattan due to the powerful Royal Navy, thousands of well-trained British and Hessian troops, and General Howe's tactical skill. Before withdrawing to the mainland, Washington left large numbers of troops at the five-pointed star-shaped earthen walls of Fort Washington. Located on the high ground known as "Mount Washington" that dominated Manhattan Island's northern end and overlooked the Hudson River, the ill-fated Fort Washington represented the Americans' last fatal grip on Manhattan.

Nested on the commanding high ground located between Harlem Creek to the east and the Hudson, this massive fort in Upper Manhattan had been named after the commander-in-chief. Fort Washington stood across the wide Hudson from Fort Lee, New Jersey, just slightly to the southwest. But its inevitable dismal fate was only a matter of time, proving the folly of Washington's strategic plan of fortified posts. Fort Washington's fall and the capture of more than two thousand of the army's best Continental troops on November 15, 1776, represented still another bitter defeat and a stunning blow to the reeling homespun revolutionaries. Then, after Fort Lee's fall on November 20, Washington had no alternative but to withdraw southwest through New Jersey, as desertions skyrocketed during this exceptionally dark period for America's fortunes.[29]

Winning Glory along the Raritan River

Reinforced by another ten thousand troops for his invasion of New Jersey after Fort Lee's capture, a supremely confident Howe then turned his sights on vulnerable Philadelphia, America's capital. General Howe followed Washington's reeling army deeper through the lowlands of New Jersey, pushing southwest across a landscape bathed in bright autumn colors of perhaps during what could have been the last autumn for the independent republic, if the British and Hessians continued their winning ways. Washington implored General Charles Lee, who commanded a separate portion of the Continental Army, to watch over the New York Highlands, to join him. The Virginian now envisioned making a united stand on the Raritan River, one of New Jersey's major rivers, near New Brunswick in north central New Jersey and southwest of New York City. But the cunning Lee, who had ambitions of replacing Washington as commander-in-chief, refused to march south to Washington's assistance. Washington and his ever-dwindling band of soldiers were now on their own to make the best out of a very bad situation that continued to get worse, while retiring to avoid certain destruction from what appeared to be an unbeatable opponent.[30]

During the long withdrawal toward Philadelphia to the southwest, Hamilton led his New York artillery past the Elizabethtown Academy, New Jersey, where he had once studied with visions of a bright future on America soil without the horrors of war. During this period of gloom, he was described by an officer as "small, slender, and with a delicate frame." But these undistinguished outward appearances of this serious-minded and intense young man were deceiving, a characteristic that Washington had already learned, and would soon see again.

After crossing the Raritan River on the "New Bridge" and reaching New Brunswick, nestled on the river's south bank, Washington gained the protection of a river between him and his pursuers. But because of massive desertions, he lacked the necessary strength to make a defensive stand. Consequently, Washington planned to continue his retreat toward eastern Pennsylvania and Philadelphia. The wooden bridge spanning the Raritan River had been erected in early 1776 to replace the ferry, providing Washington with an easy means of crossing the river with his ragtag army. After the motley collection of the remaining troops crossed over the wide Raritan that was tidal at this point, they hurriedly removed the large wooden planks to prevent Howe's troops from crossing. Therefore, only a nearby ford now offered Howe a good crossing point. Consequently, this key location needed to be defended to buy precious time.

In a timely defensive stand on the south bank of the Raritan to protect Washington's withdrawal south toward Trenton, New Jersey, on November

29, Hamilton's leadership abilities and skills as an artillery commander were once again demonstrated. Fortunately for Washington and his retreating men, Hamilton had transformed his artillery command into "a model of discipline" by this time. Here, along the high riverbank, Hamilton's two blazing six-pounders kept the encroaching British and Hessians at bay hour after hour. Animated by the hot action and his heavy responsibility to hold fast in the army's rear, the energetic captain in his neat-fitting blue uniform was everywhere at once, shouting instructions and instilling confidence among his New York gunners, who hoped to hold Howe's legions at arm's length.

The twenty-one-year-old artillery officer bought precious time, helping to save Washington's depleted army as it limped slowly toward eastern Pennsylvania and an unknown fate. Imploring his New York artillerymen to fire faster and more accurately from their protected ledge of high ground along the Raritan, Hamilton experienced one of his finest days. He encouraged his New York cannoneers to maintain a blistering fire, resulting in a lengthy duel with a row of British artillery.

With Hamilton commanding his New York guns with skill, Colonel Henry Knox's faith in his young battery commander was well-rewarded. He had placed his trust in what Hamilton could accomplish against the odds in a true crisis situation. Meanwhile, to the southwest, Captain Hamilton's barking guns were beautiful music to Washington's ears, providing him with a sense of relief that his vulnerable rear was now well-protected during the long withdrawal to Princeton, New Jersey. Most importantly for an extended period, with his accurate covering fire, Hamilton had succeeded in keeping an aggressive enemy at arm's length, while Washington led his weary survivors south toward Princeton. All of this was accomplished at great risk to himself and his New York gunners. With the enemy drawing closer, Hamilton ordered his men to switch from cannonballs to canister to dissuade Howe's finest light troops from crossing the at the ford: a wise decision that bought more precious time for Washington's army to farther slip to safety.

After a job well done, Captain Hamilton became the talk of a thankful army, because his defiant last stand ensured that the Continental Army would escape to live and fight another day. Having seen Hamilton's spirited defense of the Raritan ford in a critical situation, Washington sent one of his aides back to the front for the express purpose of learning the name of the officer who commanded the guns at the ford, because Colonel Knox had ordered the timely placement of Hamilton's guns after Washington departed. Wishing that he had a good many more fighting men of Hamilton's caliber after Knox had sung the young man's praises, Washington was "charmed by the brilliant courage and admirable skill" of the young artillerist, who always performed at his best in the greatest crisis situation. Not having seen the action at the Raritan ford, Washington later informed Congress in an early December letter about the sudden appearance of "several parties on the heights opposite Brunswick and were advancing in a large body towards the crossing place [and] we had a smart cannonade," in which the trusty Hamilton had played the leading role.[31]

Captain Hamilton's impressive battlefield accomplishments seemed to contradict a placid façade, boyish handsomeness, and slight physique which gave little hint of the hard-fighting qualities and fiery nature of the "Little Lion" that lay just beneath the calm surface. Hamilton was described by an older and much larger soldier, who could hardly believe his eyes, as "a mere stripling [who wore in jaunty fashion] a cocked hat pulled down over his eyes," while leading his artillerymen with skill and boldness.[32]

Equally shocked by the sight of the boyish Hamilton and his powder-grimed gunners when they reached Princeton after their spirited defiance along the Raritan, another one of Washington's men marveled at the finely uniformed commander who so often skillfully led the New York battery, which "was a model of discipline; at their head was a boy, and I wondered at his youth, but what was my surprise when he was pointed out to me as that Hamilton of whom we had already heard so much."[33]

With a look that was guaranteed to win the hearts of the ladies, Hamilton was fine-boned, slender with an erect military bearing, and of only medium height. With reddish-brown hair and an "almost pretty face," and one that was "never to be forgotten," wrote one woman, Hamilton's appearance gave little clue of the depth of the boldness of this young officer, who would fight to the last artillery round and last man if necessary. He performed so well and audaciously, but not recklessly, on the battlefield that onlookers, military and civilian, were amazed by his growing list of martial exploits that gained the admiration of the army's senior leaders, including Washington. Captain Hamilton was indeed Washington's feisty "Little Lion," whose roar was familiar to a large number of British and Hessian troops.

But Captain Hamilton's military gifts were manifested in other ways. Two years before his defiant stand along the Raritan, Hamilton had already outlined that strategy that would eventually result in the defeat of the British

Army. As an undergraduate student at King's College and barely out of his teenage years, he had written with prophetic vision and wise insight in making a bold claim that England could not win this war: "The circumstances of our country put it in our power to evade a pitched battle [because] it will be better policy to harass and exhaust the [British] soldiery by frequent skirmishes and incursions than to take the open field with them, by which means they would have the full benefit of their superior regularity and skills. Americans are better qualified for that kind of fighting which is most adapted to this country than regular troops."[34]

Surprise Attack at Trenton

Meanwhile, Washington's gloomy retreat though New Jersey continued unabated during America's darkest hour to date. Washington finally took a tenuous defensive position on the Delaware River's west bank on the Pennsylvania side, after crossing the brownish river just ahead of the pursuit of Lord Charles Cornwallis, Howe's capable top subordinate. But with time running out for the enlistments of so many Continentals at year's end, Washington's situation was becoming even more critical. Knowing that a victory was desperately needed to lift the patriots' flagging spirits after so many recent reversals, Washington decided to launch a daring strike on the early morning of December 26: the kind of wise guerrilla-like strategy that Hamilton had advocated in his masterful *The Farmer Refuted*, written while a King's College student even before he had ever seen a battle.

Washington was presented with a golden tactical opportunity, after Howe decided that the campaign of 1776 was over, before delivering a knock-out blow. He therefore established winter quarters and an over-extended line of defensive posts that stretched across New Jersey and all the way back to New York City. A lover of high living, the aristocratic Howe returned to New York City to enjoy urban delights, including his mistress. Washington took full advantage of the suddenly more favorable situation. He outlined his audacious battle plan at a commanders' conference to his top lieutenants and other officers, including Captain Hamilton. Hamilton had been recently stricken with a "long and severe fit" of illness, in his own words. Unable to perform any duty, he had been bedridden "in the back room" of Colonel Knox's headquarters at the John Chapman House, located on the north side of Jericho Mountain in Bucks County, Pennsylvania.

Despite the risks involved in such an audacious strike that called for a risky river crossing and a lengthy march of nine miles south to Trenton amid the dead of winter, the young man had literally willed himself out of the sickbed in order to get back on his feet just for the opportunity to lead his New York artillerymen (now reduced to fewer than thirty followers) in the upcoming operation. At this time, his splendid performance during the long New Jersey retreat, especially in the defense of the Raritan ford, was still the talk of the army.[35]

In a critical situation, Washington was now going for broke because he had no choice. It was now literally a case of do or die for the patriot cause. He planned to transport his remaining Continentals to the east side of the Delaware River in order to launch a surprise attack on the sizeable Hessian garrison of Trenton by sunrise of December 26. Quite simply, this was Washington's last opportunity to reverse the fast-declining fortunes of a dying revolution. A desperate Washington hoped to vanquish the seasoned and well-trained professional Hessian soldiers, which had proved impossible in the past. Fortunately, Washington could count on some very good men, including Captain Hamilton, for undertaking his supreme challenge. The stoic soldiers who now remained by Washington's side were now the very backbone of the resistance effort and quite literally America's best and brightest like Hamilton, after the mass desertions and casualties.

In the fast-fading daylight of a bleak Christmas Day, Washington's ragtag revolutionaries assembled in silence on the Delaware's west bank. Here, they prepared to cross the ice-clogged river at McConkey's Ferry about nine miles above Trenton. Not long after the sun dropped in a frozen sky that brought the first harsh offerings from a winter storm that had suddenly descended over the Delaware River Valley, the first of Washington's soldiers began to cross the swift Delaware in Durham boats. These sturdy wooden boats were manned mostly by Colonel John Glover's mariners from the Massachusetts seacoast, especially the fishing port of Marblehead that overlooked a beautiful bay. After Washington's ill-clad infantrymen had been rowed across the Delaware's swirling waters following much effort by Glover's hardy men during the tempestuous night, the first of Colonel Henry Knox's eighteen guns were pushed and pulled onto the wide bottoms of the ferry boats for the perilous crossing not long after midnight.

Wearing a makeshift cape fashioned from an old blanket for slight protection against the icy rain, snow, and biting cold of late December, Captain Hamilton made sure that his six-pounder guns and battery horses were aboard the ferry boat. Hamilton's guns were transported safely across the angry Delaware without incident during the nerve-racking crossing, when the Durham boat was rocked by chunks of ice slamming into its side. Hamilton must have wondered about the strange course of his life that had brought him to this crossing on one of the coldest of nights of the year and so far from the tropical warmth of his native Caribbean. During his St. Croix exile, he had prophetically dreamed about winning glory and distinction, writing in his November 11, 1769, letter to his good friend Edward Stevens, "I wish there was a war": a great dream of youth that had come true, but one that perhaps Captain Hamilton now regretted, given the circumstances.

While a mixture of snow, rain, and sleet poured down across a landscape already shrouded in a fresh blanket of snow, Hamilton attempted to stay warm as best that he could amid the howling December winds. He fondly recalled the warm ocean breezes and blue turquoise waters glittering in the Caribbean sunshine during the grueling ordeal. The young man often showed his love for his New York cannon, even "patting [the barrel of one], as if it were a favorite horse or a pet plaything," wrote one amused older officer.[36] Hoping to exceed his Raritan River exploits, Hamilton was encouraged by the resolve of his stoic men and his commander's adherence to guerrilla-like tactics that he had long advocated. Bolstering his confidence for a successful outcome at Trenton, Hamilton believed that Washington's remaining Continental soldiers, tough and seasoned regular troops, were "ready, every devil one of them" for the great challenge that lay ahead.[37]

After eight hours of high anxiety on a nightmarish night, Washington finally transported all 2,400 of his best men (mostly Continentals) and artillery pieces across the Delaware under Knox's supervision while sleet and snow poured down. Once safe on the small plot of flat ground on the river's eastern bank, Hamilton quickly mustered his New York gunners, who were now wet and cold. Then, he went to work getting his guns and half-frozen men for the advance east up high ground from the river to eventually gain the road that led the nine miles south over the white expanse to Trenton's northern edge.

Finally, Washington gave the word for his hopeful troops to move out in the blackness. Hamilton led his New York artillerymen up the timbered hill shrouded in snow. After pushing east up the ascending terrain, now white with freshly fallen snow, to gain the high ground above the Delaware, the soldiers of the lengthy column continued east before turning south down the Scotch Road that led to Trenton. The first major natural obstacle encountered by Washington's troops on the march south was the heavily wooded environs of Jacob's Creek. Here, the unfamiliar terrain descended sharply into the narrow creek valley, a deep gorge cut by the now-raging watercourse, amid the silent woodlands. With much effort and as gently as possible, Hamilton and his gunners eased their cumbersome artillery pieces down the steep slope leading to the creek, after Washington's column of infantrymen had churned up the ground, making it more slippery for weary soldiers and horses.

With Hamilton working beside his men and shouting orders, the New York artillery pieces were hauled across the creek's freezing waters, after much effort. Hamilton's gunners, including their captain, who was not mounted like Washington at the head of his troops, got their feet wet while crossing the swollen stream. After gaining the high ground on the creek's south side, the lengthy column moved out once again, heading south during a trek toward Trenton. At the small community of Birmingham, New Jersey, Washington divided his column into two divisions to strike Trenton from two directions.

General John Sullivan, a hard-fighting Presbyterian of Scottish heritage like Hamilton, commanded the First Division. Commanding his division of mostly New Englanders with skill, General Sullivan, who had been taken prisoner at the battle of Long Island but was exchanged shortly before the battle of Trenton, was ordered by Washington to march southwest to gain the snow-covered River Road that paralleled the Delaware and then entered Trenton's southwestern edge. Meanwhile, Washington and Hamilton remained at the head of General Nathanael Greene's Second Division. Part of the brigade commanded by his old friend Lord Stirling (William Alexander), Hamilton's New York battery was placed in front of Greene's column. Hamilton's guns were in an advanced position in the column to occupy the strategic high ground at the town's northern edge to command Trenton nested in the river valley below to the south, once the vanguard of Greene's column reached its objective. Once in position, the two arms of Washington's pincer movement were then to close tightly around the three regiments of Colonel Johann Gottlieb Rall's Hessian brigade in the river valley. But besides the disproportionate amount of artillery, the key to Washington's masterful battle plan was to strike as closely to sunrise as possible, although his delicate timetable had been ruined by the time-consuming river crossing and the raging storm that had slowed the march south.

After trekking nine miles and finally reaching the strategic high ground at Trenton's northern edge, Washington and Hamilton rejoiced that all three

Hessian regiments had been caught by surprise. Knowing that the key to the battle's outcome now depended upon placing all of Colonel Knox's artillery, including Hamilton's New York State battery, in a row along the commanding high ground that overlooked Trenton, Washington and Knox ordered the guns into their elevated positions atop the freshly fallen snow. At the head of Greene's column, Hamilton shouted to his gunners to hurriedly unlimber their cannon on the windswept heights.

Finally, after getting the field pieces through the snow, the New Yorkers placed their guns in their assigned positions at the head of Queen Street, just east of King Street. These two parallel main streets ran through Trenton, from north to south, and down the slope to the Delaware. Once his field pieces were aligned on the heights and his cannoneers took careful aim at their targets below in the town situated on the banks of the Delaware, Hamilton gave the order to fire. The young artillery officer from King's College described how, "one of the first groups [of Hessians] was cut down by" the fire from his New York guns.[38]

As he had fought during the defensive stand against the odds along the Raritan River, Captain Hamilton also excelled in the stiff challenges of urban combat. Contrary to myth, the Hessians were not drunk for a late night celebration. Instead, they were ready to fight back with great spirit. Therefore, the showdown at Trenton was one of the hardest-fought battles of the American Revolution. To inflict additional damage on the Knyphausen Regiment (Colonel Rall's rightmost, or easternmost, command) that had hurriedly aligned along Queen Street, Hamilton aggressively employed his guns like "flying artillery." Demonstrating tactical skill and flexibility, he ordered some guns pushed south down the snowy street, easing closer to the splendidly uniformed members of the Knyphausen Regiment to provide greater assistance to Washington's charging infantrymen battling in the snow-covered streets, their first experience in urban warfare. Then, exploiting the opportunity to the fullest, the tactically astute captain played a key role in the Hessians' encirclement. Such aggressive tactics made the surrender of Rall's fusilier and grenadier brigade inevitable. The brave Colonel Rall had fallen from his horse, mortally wounded by riflemen in the bitter street fighting, while leading a daring counterattack west and back into the heart of Trenton.[39]

Sealing the fate of the Hessian brigade, Captain Hamilton had no idea at this time that his effective artillery fire was made possible by a precious reserve of black powder (many infantrymen's muskets were wet and unable to fire in the snowstorm) that had been smuggled to America from the same tropical islands where he had been raised. Clearly, the many ironies of Hamilton's life were played out in a variety of ways at Trenton, where America's struggle for liberty was revitalized by Washington's remarkable victory. But that promising life had almost come to an abrupt end at Trenton, where he had "narrowly escaped [Hessian] cannonballs, which whizzed by his ears" on this day of destiny.[40]

Washington Strikes Again: Princeton

Emboldened by his elimination of an entire seemingly invincible Hessian brigade (along with its dynamic Colonel Rall who had never previously known defeat on American soil) at Trenton and to continue to fan the flames of a rekindled resistance effort to restore faith in the revolution's prospects, Washington decided to again cross the Delaware on December 30. With his fighting blood up after his Trenton success, he planned to strike again at the college town of Princeton, garrisoned by the British, to make a mockery of the British claim that New Jersey had been subjugated and that the war was all but over. Picking off isolated New Jersey garrisons offered the tantalizing possibility of forcing the British to withdraw all the way back to New York City.

However, Lord Charles Cornwallis, bent on revenge after the sharp setback at Trenton that had caught him by surprise, reinforced Princeton on January 1, 1777. Cornwallis believed that he now had Washington trapped on the river's east side at Trenton, which he reached the following day. Washington made a defensive stand on high ground above Assunpink Creek on the south of Trenton, repelling Cornwallis' attack by massive artillery fire, including from Hamilton's guns. After having left Princeton too lightly defended following what has been called the Second Battle of Trenton (also known as the Battle of Assunpink Creek), Cornwallis never expected that Washington would then dare to launch a strike in his rear, however.

Displaying tactical audacity after leaving campfires burning and sentinels in place to fool Cornwallis who remained on the Assunpink and confident that his opponent would be easily destroyed with the sunrise, Washington then stole a march on Howe's most capable top lieutenant by pushing north in the night to deliver an audacious attack. Under cover of darkness, he skillfully sidestepped Cornwallis' advanced force by easing quietly to the right, marching a dozen miles upon Princeton. To maintain silence while stealthy passing by Cornwallis' troops, the wheels of Hamilton's New York guns were wrapped in rags and blankets. Washington's nighttime maneuver was masterful, and reminiscent of his daring strike on Trenton. Just outside Princeton on the morning of January 3, the advance of Washington's troops, under Scotland-born General Hugh Mercer, then ran into a seasoned brigade of redcoats on the march to link with Cornwallis. Appreciating the irony, Hamilton entered the fray at Princeton, where he had first attempted to enroll as a student at the prestigious college not long after his arrival in America.

Exploiting the tactical advantage gained by Washington's troops in hurling the British rearward like at Trenton, Hamilton and New York gunners of a "model" artillery command went into action with high spirits. But they shortly faced a formidable challenge at Nassau Hall, which was the College of New Jersey's and the town's largest building. Located just south of the Post Road, this sturdy structure was now filled with hundreds of British soldiers, who found timely refuge there. They had been hurled rearward by General Sullivan's attackers, but the Britons were now determined to hold firm. To reduce the defensive bastion after setting up his guns in the yard of the college and at close range, Hamilton opened up with his six-pounders on the rear of Nassau Hall, which no doubt brought some personal satisfaction to the young man who never forgot a slight from his so-called social superiors.

Almost as if to eliminate that embarrassing setback from his memory, with Princeton rejecting him only a few years before, Hamilton's guns continued to unleash a hot fire at Nassau Hall, where British soldiers returned musketry from windows, from which panes of glass had been knocked out. Solid iron projectiles from Hamilton's two field pieces tore through the walls and bounced off rear walls around the defenders. A cannonball from one of Hamilton's guns that relentlessly pounded the main building scored a direct hit, tearing through the wall of the prayer hall (chapel) of the stately building and hitting the large portrait of King George I. Allegedly, the iron projectile symbolically struck the monarch's head, tearing it from the large painting that had been long revered like a sacred relic. Later, Washington learned of Hamilton's direct hit, perhaps from the captain himself.[41]

More importantly, the accurate fire directed by Hamilton at Nassau Hall had a decisive effect in breaking the defenders' spirit and will to resist, forcing hundreds of British soldiers to surrender. A white flag waved from one of the windows. Then, in one American sergeant's words, "a haughty crabbed set of men" in red uniforms surrendered, to Hamilton's delight, because of what his guns had achieved.[42]

Again catching British leadership, especially Cornwallis, by surprise, Washington won the day at Princeton. Captain Hamilton enjoyed the sweet taste of victory, basking in the two remarkable successes that had turned the tide of the revolution, thanks to Washington's adherence to unorthodox tactics that he had long advocated. Washington was hearing more about this dynamic young artillery officer, who had risen magnificently to every challenge. Hamilton later concluded with glee that Washington's bold "enterprises of Trenton and Princeton [represented] the dawning of [a] bright day which afterwards broke forth with such resplendent luster."[43]

With Cornwallis in pursuit, Washington retreated to the west, after burning bridges to slow the redcoats bent on revenge. He then led his army into winter quarters at Morristown, New Jersey, where Hamilton once again took to a sick bed out of urgent necessity after the winter campaign's rigors. Providing some consolation to him during his illness, he basked in his recent accomplishments. At the battles of Trenton and Princeton, Captain Hamilton continued to demonstrate courage, leadership ability, and tactical skill that caught the notice of the Continental Army's officer corps. During the Trenton-Princeton Campaign that reversed the revolution's course when it seemed all but impossible to do so, Hamilton's feats and dynamic leadership style continued to be the talk of the army. Contrary to myth, he had first become known to Washington for intelligence and exceptional promise through Colonel Joseph Reed, Washington's adjutant general, during a prisoner (for officers) exchange mission in which he played a role in September 1776. However, because of his youth and recent immigrant background, Hamilton had still needed an influential patron to sing his praises as a highly capable officer and a proper gentleman.

Colonel Henry Knox, Washington's young chief of artillery from Boston who had most closely seen Hamilton's potential and promise at the Raritan, Trenton, and Princeton, was that man. The scholarly Knox, a self-educated man with a can-do attitude and innovative mind, closely identified with Hamilton, including with the young man's difficult past in the West Indies. Much like Alexander's family's abandonment by hard-luck James Hamilton, Knox's own father had left his family, suddenly sailing off to the West Indies to leave his responsibilities behind. Knox and Hamilton, therefore, had been forced to work at young ages to provide for their families, gaining worldly experience, maturing out of necessity, and learning the meaning of responsibility. Not surprisingly, Knox had taken an early interest in the bright artillery officer under his command, because they were very much kindred spirits and self-made men of outstanding promise. For good reason, in a letter to Washington at a later date, Hamilton described how, "General Knox has the confidence of the army and is a man of sense."[44]

Recognizing talent and ability, General Nathanael Greene, Washington's top lieutenant, had also praised the young Hamilton to the commander-in-chief, especially after seeing him in action at Trenton and Princeton.

This steady flow of favorable accounts praising Hamilton's abilities and talents had been passed on to the commander-in-chief for some time. At his always-busy headquarters, Washington needed such a dynamic young man with a lively intellect and outstanding abilities (seemingly boundless) on his personal staff. Washington had also seen for himself what Hamilton could accomplish during the recent campaign. He understood that Hamilton, brilliant and assiduous, was a very special officer of unlimited promise. Consequently, only three weeks after his surprising victory at snowy Princeton, while settled into winter quarters in a protective valley at Morristown (and with a staff vacancy open after George Baylor's departure to cavalry service), Washington inquired about "the suitability" of young Hamilton as an aide-de-camp to serve on his small staff, where the demands were disproportionately large and challenges endless.

In a formal setting that reflected proper protocol, Washington then met with Hamilton, after he had been invited to a dinner at headquarters. Like everyone else, the commander-in-chief was greatly impressed by the young man with refined manners, gentlemanly behavior, and boundless charm. Washington realized that this was exactly the kind of gifted officer who he needed on his personal staff. After all, Hamilton was nothing short of a "boy genius," which had been recognized by the Continental Army's top leaders. Indeed, and even more than Washington now realized, because "of all the founding fathers, Hamilton best understood the full breath of the Revolution—from war to politics to organization" at every level.

Consequently, Hamilton shortly received a coveted personal invitation (Washington's note of January 20, 1777) to become a member of the general's personal staff at his headquarters and to join the elite group of young staff officers of his "family." However, this was not an easy decision for the young man. He still lusted most of all for independent command, in part because he knew that "the regiments of artillery were multiplied [and] I had good reason to expect that the command of one of them would have fallen to me. . . ."[45]

And, if Hamilton gained command of a regiment, then he envisioned eventually winning command of a brigade and a corresponding brigadier general's rank. After having previously refused to take aide-de-camp positions for two generals, Hamilton gave Washington his answer only after deliberation that took some time (nearly six weeks that included the period when ill), because he was not looking forward to a desk job that would deprive him of battlefield opportunities. Joining Washington's staff ensured an advance from the rank of captain to lieutenant colonel: a significant increase in rank for a mere youth of twenty-two and recent immigrant lacking social standing and wealth in America. This was the kind of fast track advancement that Hamilton relished, although he had been a frustrated clerk working at a desk in a dead-end position in St. Croix only four years before.

However, he correctly sensed Washington's best qualities, and instinctively knew that he could rise higher, if the Virginian succeeded in winning this war for America's heart and soul. Despite his serious initial reservations, Hamilton finally made up his mind. As Hamilton emphasized in his own words from a letter and directly contrary to innermost inclinations, he was bound by a deep sense of patriotism and admiration toward Washington "to *accept his invitation to enter into his family.*"[46]

In his general orders of March 1, 1777, Washington officially announced that Hamilton "is appointed Aide-De-Camp to the Commander in Chief, and is to be respected and obeyed as such."[47] No longer a captain of a New York battery (state service) and after he turned over his command to a faithful lieutenant, Hamilton's star was on the rise, after becoming the nineteenth man who had been appointed to Washington's staff since July 5, 1775. Serving with Washington at his headquarters was considered to be the highest honor and a great opportunity. But this would only remain true as long as Washington was successful on the battlefield or just avoided decisive defeat. The young man's career was about to soar to unprecedented heights, far beyond what anyone (including Washington and Hamilton) could imagine, especially at a time when many Americans, including those in high places, doubted Washington's leadership and tactical abilities. With his New York battery now depleted by disease, losses, enlistment expirations, and desertions, Hamilton was fortunate to have been presented this golden opportunity to accept such a prestigious position. Clearly, this lofty position on Washington's staff represented an example of Hamilton doing what he had to do to get ahead, especially in regard to proving his worth and value to the leader of America's revolutionary resistance effort. Fortunately, for Hamilton, this peoples' revolution and its egalitarian nature allowed talented men to rise up on their own ability, despite the lack of social standing or wealth. Hamilton was at the right place, right time, and now with the right person in charge to make a name for himself. He was now in a position to excel as never before. But Hamilton could not imagine that by linking his fortunes with Washington, he was about to begin "one of the most important and creative associations in American history."[48]

Chapter II

George Washington's Chief of Staff

After departing a relatively obscure position of a New York battery commander, Hamilton's life changed forever when Washington appointed him an aide-de-camp. Washington had established winter quarters at Morristown in January 1777, which had allowed Hamilton easier acclimation into Washington's staff than if during a period of active campaigning. This "very clever little village" of Morristown was located on a level plateau at the foot of one of the chains of three low, heavily forested ridges of the Watchung Mountains, also known as the Blue Hills, in central New Jersey.

General Washington had chosen a strategic location in the sprawling lowlands of eastern New Jersey that was sufficiently close to New York City to monitor British movements, especially in regard to the launching of offensive operations. Morristown was situated near the main road that connected America's two largest and most important cities, Philadelphia and New York City. At this strategic point almost directly west of New York City, Washington also could keep an eye on British garrisons at Brunswick and Amboy to the south, and if the enemy suddenly descended upon Philadelphia to the southwest. Washington had first ridden through Morristown in May 1773 on his way to New York City, probably never imagining that he would command an army at this place only a few years later.

Although he did not fully realize this fact at the time, Hamilton was not about to embark upon an ordinary or routine assignment as another staff officer in Washington's "family." He shortly became not only Washington's primary aide, but also a key focal point for the army's management and overall functioning.[1] Setting the stage for this development and opportunity had been no accident or due to luck and fate. In fact, he had known from the beginning of his military service that he had to perform on and off the battlefield in an exceptional manner to catch the eye of his superiors. Therefore, by setting himself apart by way of his battlefield successes and aggressive leadership style, he had in no small part orchestrated his own rise to gain the opportunity to join Washington's staff, because he could not rely on social standing, wealth, and family connections like so many others. He had won over influential patrons, especially Colonel Knox, and his past efforts had now paid dividends.

With the days growing longer and with new buds of fresh spring growth appearing, Hamilton was ready for a new challenge, despite a recent bout with reoccurring illness. With his trademark youthful confidence of being able to excel as a respected member of Washington's staff, Hamilton mounted his favorite horse to proceed to Washington's Morristown headquarters to open a new chapter in his unpredictable military service. Deep in thought after having left behind his New York artillery comrades forever, he rode slowly over the hilly ground at the foot of this chain of heavily forested mountains, to Washington's headquarters for his first day of duty. No record has been left of the goodbyes between Hamilton and his New York artillery-men, but they were certainly heartfelt.

Surrounded by timbered hills that provided protection against the harsh winds of winter, Morristown consisted of less than a hundred houses centered beside a village green, much like a town in old England. One forgotten reason that explained Washington's choice of Morristown for the army's winter quarters was its largely Presbyterian population. The quaint village had been settled by English Presbyterians around 1715. During a conflict that was as much of a civil war as a revolution, this religious demographic made it more likely that the residents would not spy for the British. Washington's headquarters had been established in Jacob Arnold's three-story tavern, on the northwest side of the village green and located directly across from the Morris County Courthouse.

General Washington had readily accepted Arnold's offer to use his spacious tavern, which was one of the town's two most popular establishments. He had chosen a second floor room for his headquarters office, which overlooked the eight-acre village green and presented a pleasant view for some reflection, if so inclinced, when not overloaded with work. The large-sized fireplaces on the tavern's first floor allowed the heat to rise to the second floor, where Washington's bedroom, near his office, was located. Situated just before the town's Baptist Church, the tavern was painted white, and built on a solid stone foundation for protection against the rain and melting snow. Arnold's Tavern provided the adequate space needed for Washington to conduct the hectic pace of army business and management throughout the winter and early spring (from January to May 1777). Assigned to various duties from sunup to sundown, Washington's hardworking staff officers were also billeted in the large tavern, as was customary, to be near the commander-in-chief at all times.[2]

On Saturday, March 1, and with spring in the air, Hamilton galloped up to Arnold's Tavern to embark upon his new assignment. Looking younger than his years and possessing a distinctive Scottish physical appearance with blue eyes and reddish-brown hair, he then walked up the three steps to the wide porch of the building, entered the tavern, and then formally introduced himself to General Washington and accepted his new position without fanfare. The general greeted him heartily. Giving no hint of his troubled past in the Caribbean, the eager young man in a resplendent new lieutenant colonel's uniform of dark blue was shortly given an assignment at the busy headquarters known for the heavy workload that could wear out even the most energetic men.

The commander-in-chief first assigned Hamilton as military secretary, a position created by Congress and delegated to Washington when the Continental Army was formed. Although not realized at the time, it was a strange, but most fortuitous, destiny that had brought Washington and Hamilton together to create a perfect match. But this fortunate synthesis was no accident on the commander-in-chief's end, because it had been planned and carefully orchestrated by the far-sighted Washington, who knew that he could benefit immeasurably from the "boy genius." First and foremost, he fully appreciated an urgent need to reorganize his staff and make it more professional—ironically, one that needed to be fundamentally more "British" than American.

Most of all, Washington realized that he needed a highly capable individual to head his staff to make it more efficient, where previously there was no such leader of Washington's staff. In time, this also meant delegating some authority, allowing his most talented staff officer to take over some of his heavy workload. The overburdened Virginian had long lacked such an officer to organize and coordinate the endless tasks that had to be completed for the effective management of a popular people's army that was still evolving and maturing. In his own words, Washington needed an intelligent and energetic officer who "can think for me as well as execute orders." Hamilton's arrival was a giant step in fulfilling this all-important objective. Quite simply, an army only operated smoothly and efficiently if its commander and staff worked together harmoniously as a team, and this requirement now called for a talented leader of the staff.

As Washington's primary military secretary and a tireless workaholic, Hamilton shortly outperformed the two most experienced members of Washington's military "family," Tench Tilghman and John Fitzgerald, who were both more than ten years older than him. These men had been severely overworked for some time, and badly needed assistance and even some guidance in regard to coordinating their activities. They were delighted by Hamilton's arrival and take-charge personality to relieve their heavy workload and organize their efforts more smoothly to fit Washington's requirements and meet his lofty expectations.[3]

Blessed with his father's charm and his mother's sharp business sense, Hamilton made an exceptional first impression to one and all at headquarters. Besides beginning good working relationships with his fellow staff officers, he also quickly struck up lasting friendships that came easily to the gregarious officer with a quick smile and joke, while maintaining an easygoing presence even in highpressure and tense situations at headquarters. Hamilton got along very well with the lighthearted Irish-born Colonel Fitzgerald. As skilled in business as in the aristocratic society of his hometown of Alexandria, the versatile Son of Erin was described by Martha Dangerfield Bland, age twenty-five, during her visit to Washington's Morristown headquarters, as "an agreeable, broad-shouldered Irishman."[4] Around age thirty-four, the handsome and well-mannered Fitzgerald, who once had been the "favorite of the Scotch and English maidens of Alexandria," was now married to Jane Digges, a fellow Catholic who had captured his heart and vice-versa.[5]

The wife of Virginian Colonel Theodorick Bland described Tench Tilghman as "a modest, worthy man who from his attachment to the General voluntarily lives in his family and acts in any capacity that is uppermost without fee or reward."[6] But like everyone else, she was most impressed with the attractive and dashing Hamilton, who drew women like moths to a flame. Martha wrote how he was a "sensible, genteel, polite, young fellow, a West Indian."[7] Hamilton's distinctive Caribbean Creole qualities, including his slight island accent (perhaps tinged with some Danish linguistic influences) and polished ways that were more European than American, were duly noted by this refined lady of the upper class.

Hamilton's arrival at Washington's headquarters just before the spring of 1777 could not have been more timely for the exhausted staff and for

Washington. The hardworking commander, who always demanded a great deal of his "family" members like himself, was short of staff. At this time, he had only three staff officers on duty at Morristown: the aforementioned Tilghman (an enthusiastic volunteer aide-de-camp from a wealthy Philadelphia merchant family), and Fitzgerald (the enterprising merchant from Alexandria, Virginia), as well as the relatively inexperienced George Johnston, Jr. Johnston was the brother-in-law of Robert Hanson Harrison, who also was an invaluable member (military secretary) on Washington's staff since his January 20, 1777, appointment. Johnston had served as aide-de-camp with the necessary zeal, but unfortunately he lacked experience that reduced his efficiency. Martha Dangerfield Bland noted that Johnston, a member of the Virginia upper class elite and a prewar associate of Washington, was "exceedingly witty at everyone's expense," but without causing resentment among his good-natured targets. He was destined to die of disease in October 1777: the only disease death of any "family" member during the history of Washington's staff.

Known for his "astute mind," Tilghman's pleasing and unpretentious personality made him a universal favorite, especially to Hamilton. Two aides-de-camp, William Grayson (serving in this capacity since August 1776) was the well-educated son of a Scottish immigrant, and Lieutenant Colonel Samuel "Sam" Blachley Webb, the Connecticut-born stepson of Yale graduate and diplomat Silas Deane and who also had been appointed to Washington's staff in 1776, had departed "the family" to take command of respective regiments during the first week of January. Tilghman, Webb, who was a bit too "fond of . . . gaiety," in Washington's words, and Grayson had served Washington as aides-de-camp during the disastrous New York Campaign, when America's fortunes plummeted to new lows.

Meanwhile, Colonel Robert Hanson Harrison, Washington's principal lawyer from Alexandria, Virginia, and a companion fox chaser who had ridden across Mount Vernon's lands before the war, was now sick, leaving a large void at the role of military secretary. Ironically, Webb's transfer to a command position in the field probably saved his life. Known as Washington's "unlucky aide," Webb already had suffered three wounds. Colonel George Baylor, a Caroline County, Virginia, planter, was also now absent from Washington's headquarters, after having entered cavalry service. He had served on the staff since August 15, 1775. The Virginian had played a distinguished role at Trenton, while serving at Washington's side when the army's often-beaten commander had scored his first victory. As a cruel fate would have it, Baylor was destined to die of lingering war wounds in 1784. Virginian John Walker had been appointed to Washington's staff in February 1777, but he was about to depart on a mission to the Continental Congress, then located in Baltimore, Maryland, in early March. Therefore, because of the staff's depletion, the workload at headquarters was now exceptionally heavy, and the hours were long (working late at night and then up early in the morning). Even the robust Washington suffered from exhaustion, affecting his health and attitude during the dreary winter days. Most of all, the staff lacked coordination of effort and efficiency to Washington's disadvantage.[8]

Hamilton, consequently, was early busy with a number of assignments. On March 3, he embarked upon addressing a host of complex prisoner exchange concerns, especially the legal status of captives. After all, the Americans were rebels in revolt against a legitimate government of a world power. These complex communications and negotiations became one of Hamilton's many specialties, thanks to his lawyer-like grasp of details and legalese.

Washington already knew that Hamilton possessed excellent prisoner exchange negotiation skills because in September 1776 he had helped to complete the formal exchange of around four hundred American prisoners, including the irrepressible Captain Daniel Morgan. These men had been taken during General Richard Montgomery's ill-fated bid to capture Quebec and make Canada the fourteenth colony. They had patriotically refused to drink tea even in captivity in Quebec, before signing paroles in August. Aboard five ships, the American prisoners finally reached New York City on September 11, setting the stage for an official exchange on American soil at Elizabethtown Point, New Jersey, near where Hamilton had attended school before King's College. In time, therefore, Washington "put Hamilton in charge of coordinating all prisoner exchanges," after he had proved to be the right man for this demanding job. After much effort and skillful diplomacy, Hamilton, blessed with a meticulous mind and natural problem solver, eventually succeeded in negotiating an effective prisoner exchange policy in a most delicate situation that was more about politics than manpower issues.[9]

Washington required a gifted writer with broad intelligence and skillset to work closely with the commander-in-chief. But this talented writer also needed to be a natural politician with the ability to be extremely careful and concise, but yet firm, in his correspondence to Washington's many subordinates in the field. Most importantly, an inordinate degree of delicate diplomacy was also needed in sensitive communications and personal dealings with the prerogative-minded Continental Congress and sensitive civil authorities (governors) of thirteen fractious states torn by political rivalries, jealousies, and pettiness. Filling these crucial voids of a "ready Pen-m[a]n" in Washington's words, with typical aplomb and finesse, Hamilton was a master of communicating at the highest level with skill and care (orally or in writing) in the most delicate military and political matters upon which an army's existence and nation's life depended.[10]

To maintain good relations with civil authorities, subordinate commanders, and politicians in an ever-sensitive environment that called for the utmost delicacy and tact, Washington had long sought a single individual who could express exactly and concisely what the commander wanted by mere suggestion and hint: all-important, highly detailed communications written in the most artful manner possible, requiring an inordinate degree of diplomacy, yet sufficiently forceful to get the necessary results to fulfill Washington's wishes. It was a delicate balancing act, and Hamilton was the man who made Washington's highest expectations and wishes come true by his diplomatic wording that was presented in concise form in a neat secretarial script.

Consequently, Hamilton's influence established a highly effective working process at headquarters that became the standard routine: Washington opened by discussing a specific topic with Hamilton, who then wrote a draft of the general's thoughts, ideas, and specific requirements for the prompt execution of orders. Hamilton perfected the ability to seemingly read Washington's mind, and place his desires on papers in record time. He was even to take the general's most scattered and sketchiest ideas into a proper form to get the necessary results. As in all things, Hamilton was highly productive, churning out whatever Washington felt, desired, and wanted to convey in the most polished manner possible. The principals then reviewed and corrected the draft for a final copy (created by his military secretary) to be signed by Washington upon final approval. All in all, this was no easy task except for Hamilton, requiring literary polish, political savvy, and diplomatic skill, all of which he possessed in abundance. As Washington's chief military secretary after taking over for Harrison, Hamilton early filled this crucial void like no other member of Washington's staff. Washington had earlier lamented how "Mr. Baylor, contrary to my expectation, is not in the slightest degree a penman, though spirited and willing."[11]

Fortunately for Washington, Hamilton was the very antithesis of Baylor and other staff officers, which made him the best possible man for even the most demanding job at headquarters. Indeed, Washington now possessed a young officer who many believed was the most gifted and best "penman" in America. In communicating with the leading political and military revolutionaries across America, especially in Congress at Philadelphia, Washington had long sorely needed a more experienced and highly educated man (a true intellectual with practical experience) than himself (still very much a provincial Virginia planter) to put his words into their most polished and sophisticated form. After all, the precise choice of words in concise form to address the most complex military and political situations was absolutely essential for maintaining the all-important good relations with the politically focused (versus military-focused) congressmen, civil officials, and a vast array of military leaders with inflated egos, regional prejudices, and often almost infantile sensitivities. Most importantly, such self-important congressmen financed and supplied the Continental Army for its survival, and needed to be carefully cultivated with extreme tact and politeness. Thanks in part to his experiences in St. Croix, where he had long dealt with smart merchants and businessmen from around the world, Hamilton possessed not only a natural and well-honed talent but also genius for fulfilling this vital role with almost effortless ease, because he was so analytically gifted.[12]

Despite Hamilton's position as military secretary at the very center of Washington's headquarters, earning a salary double than that of an aide-de-camp, it was not exactly what he most desired. Hamilton lusted for action and not a military career sitting behind a desk at headquarters far from the front lines. Therefore, Hamilton had willingly "subordinate[d] his desire for a combat command to the recognition that he was doing essential service and would still be at the general's side whenever battle offered."[13]

Before Hamilton's arrival, no staff member of Washington's "family" had been able to replace the invaluable services of Lieutenant Colonel Joseph Reed, until Hamilton made the commander-in-chief forget all about him. Raised in Trenton, Reed was a savvy former lawyer whose disloyalty (doubting Washington's military ability and expressed favor of another commander-in-chief as a replacement) to Washington had proved his undoing. Bright and capable, Reed had become Washington's top staff officer not long after the Virginian took command of the army. Washington's dependence upon Reed had grown so great that when his top staff officer was absent, the commander-in-chief pleaded with Reed in a January 23, 1776, letter: "Real necessity compels me to ask you, whether I may entertain any hopes of our returning to my Family?"[14]

Then, revealing his dependence on his brightest staff officer, an almost desperate Washington continued to explain to Reed how "if you can make it convenient, and will hint the matter to Colo. [Robert Hanson] Harrison [a Marylander who officially served as Washington's military secretary since 1776], I dare venture to say that Congress will make it agreeable to you in every shape they can—My business [at headquarters] Increases very fast, and my distresses for want of you, along with it—Mr. Harrison is the only Gentleman of my Family that can afford me the least assistance in writing," which was absolutely crucial to the commander-in-chief.[15]

But Hamilton not only effectively replaced but also far surpassed what Reed had to offer and accomplished for Washington before the former attorney's abrupt departure in May 1776.

Hamilton shortly became not only Washington's top staff officer, but also his most trusted "family" member. All in all, this was a rather remarkable development because of Hamilton's young age and recent immigrant status, when most other staff officers were older and had secured their coveted positions on Washington's staff largely because family, social, and political connections. He was not only the first, but also the only West Indian to serve on Washington's staff, bringing to a provincial staff a distinctive international flavor, broader outlook, French language skills, and a more open overall mindset.

Washington had visited the West Indies in his first and last trip from the American mainland, and even developed a certain affinity for West Indian Creoles like Hamilton. (Ironically, Hamilton was later condemned by his political enemies for being a "Creole," who did not have America's true interests at heart.) Washington had flirted with historical obscurity when he almost died of smallpox at age nineteen in November 1751, during his visit to Barbados in the British Caribbean. Likewise, another ambitious teenager (Hamilton) also had seemed relegated to an equally dark obscurity had he not escaped from the Caribbean only recently.

After accompanying his ailing half brother Lawrence (Mount Vernon's original owner) in a futile bid to improve the older man's health in Barbados, Washington had been stricken by a nearly fatal case of the disease, but this now proved a blessing in disguise. Consequently, Washington had gained an early immunity to smallpox that served him well while commanding the army, when the ravages of disease took far more American lives than the enemy. Because Lieutenant Colonel Hamilton shared in this advantage of immunity to smallpox with Washington, this factor was another reason why the two men served together as such a highly durable and long-lasting team from early 1777 to nearly the war's end.[16]

Although already heavily burdened, Hamilton received another new assignment at Washington's headquarters on March 12. Washington became alarmed when a number of Morristown civilians were suddenly stricken with smallpox among his soldiers quartered in town. He knew that his command encamped nearby in winter quarters was now vulnerable to this deadly contagion that might cause havoc among America's primary army. Washington had learned his lesson in the summer of 1776 in commanding at New York City, when at least 20 percent of his troops could not fight because of sickness, including smallpox.

Washington, consequently, made the decision to begin the smallpox inoculation process to safeguard the army, before the disease spread. Written by Hamilton and signed by the Virginian, Washington's March 12, 1777, orders initiated the army's smallpox inoculation program. Some inoculations had initially been introduced as early as January 1777, because some soldiers, including Robert Hanson Harrison from Alexandria, Virginia, had already become sick.[17] Clearly, Washington was as proactive in regard to the growing serious threat of an epidemic, refusing to take an unnecessary risk that demonstrated his wisdom. He early informed Harrison, who served capably in the "family" from November 1775 to March 1781 (longer than anyone): "I shudder at the consequences of this disorder if some vigorous steps are not taken to stop the spreading of it."[18]

Washington's prompt actions unleashed his private war against smallpox and "sav[ed] the lives of tens of thousands of soldiers and civilians [which] was as important a factor in winning a victory as important as in any battle."[19] Despite being immune to smallpox, Washington nearly lost his life during this period at Morristown. Because of an extreme, if not obsessive, devotion to duty that guaranteed long hours and overexertion, Washington had worn himself down. He also had become especially vulnerable after a winter snow storm struck the army's winter encampment on February 24. Thanks to the ever-growing workload and with too few available aides-de-camp, Washington had been severely overburdened over an extended period. Laboring with Hamilton at his desk late every night in this typical "micro-manager" style, Washington's hectic pace of work at his Morristown headquarters had steadily eroded his strength to severely affect his health by the time that Hamilton arrived.

Supervising the heavy snow removal from the winter encampment as if still managing daily operations on his Mount Vernon plantation that had given him far more experience in supervising enslaved laborers than soldiers, Washington was exposed to the elements. In attempting to do everything at once in the midst of winter, Washington caught a nasty cold and a severe sore throat. The forty-five-year-old general was soon bedridden after his condition rapidly worsened. Ironically, periodic bleeding (the day's accepted medical practice) by a well-meaning army physician only made the commander-in-chief weaker and more vulnerable to the grim reaper.

During this crucial period in March 1777 when Washington lingered near death, Hamilton was often by the general's side to assist and seek instructions. The army needed to continue functioning without its inspirational driving force. Hamilton, therefore, not only took on increased responsibilities, but also began to take charge at headquarters, a situation resembling his experience when Nicholas Cruger became sick and teenaged clerk Hamilton had stepped in to operate the Kortright and Cruger Company at St. Croix with skill for nearly six months. When Washington felt that it was necessary to inform General Nathanael Greene that this highly capable Rhode Islander would be his successor if his death came which now appeared likely, Hamilton was shocked. Washington's new military secretary heard the unofficial passing of the torch for temporary command of the Continental Army, until the Continental Congress made an official appointment. Hamilton, "Tilghman, Harrison, and Johnston [sic] all believed the general might die and urged Greene to prepare himself to lead the army [and] the young aides even discussed the problems of holding Washington's funeral in the snow."[20]

The same heavy workload that had played a role in eroding Washington's health also affected Hamilton in physical terms. Still not fully recovered himself from a recent sickness before joining the staff to embark upon an even heavier workload, Hamilton was at considerable risk. Ironically, however, the intense workload seemed to act like a tonic on Hamilton, but only initially. With Washington bedridden, Hamilton and a handful of aides-de-camp labored overtime and far into the night, picking up the slack as much as possible. With Hamilton leading the way by example, the other "family" members shouldered the heavy workload in Washington's absence to fill the sizeable void.

Severely overtaxed and physically worn down, Hamilton briefly fell sick again, before his first two weeks of service on Washington's staff had passed. In a March 10, 1777, letter to report Washington's declining physical condition to his old friend and supporter General Alexander McDougall, the New York City merchant and Sons of Liberty leader, Hamilton warned his Celtic friend how Washington "has been very much indisposed for three or four days past, insomuch that his attention to business is pronounced by the doctor [Pennsylvania-born John Cochran, the promising son of Irish immigrant parents] to be very improper; and we have made a point of keeping all from him which was not indispensably necessary [and therefore] I detained your express a day in hopes of a convenient opportunity to communicate your letter to him; but though he has grown considerably better than he was, I find he is so much pestered with matters, which cannot be avoided, that I am obliged to refrain from troubling him on the occasion; especially as I conceive the only answer he would give, may be given by myself."[21]

To keep the seriousness of Washington's illness a secret from the army and especially the enemy, Hamilton emerged as the principal leader of not only the "family," but also the principal mastermind of the "elaborate cover-up." Hamilton issued a stream of directives in Washington's name, after the stricken general whispered his orders for the army's daily operations to him. Caring for their revered chief, Hamilton and his young cohorts of the "family" quietly maintained the appearance of absolute normality at headquarters as if Washington's life was not in serious danger, while seamlessly continuing the business of the army's daily operations. In this way, the ever-energetic Hamilton "took charge of Washington's staff with characteristic, electrifying speed."[22]

Fortunately, Martha Washington reached the Morristown headquarters from Mount Vernon on March 15. Washington had wisely convinced Martha to receive an inoculation against smallpox in May 1776 to safeguard her for her future visits to his headquarters. Martha's loving care, gentle hand, and home tonics (successful in formerly treating her husband back home) began to restore Washington's health and spirits. Indeed, Washington had a very close "brush with death," far more than anyone realized outside of the close-knit military "family." Like a phoenix rising, Washington was soon back on his feet. Within two weeks of his arrival at Washington's headquarters, Hamilton had nearly witnessed the death of the man who symbolized America's resistance effort and the revolution itself.[23] Like his other near-death experiences on and off the battlefield, Washington's close brush with death in the winter gloom of

Morristown gave him another reason to believe that he was now under "the miraculous care of Providence."[24]

Thanks to the stealthy efforts of Hamilton and other staff officers, Washington's near-premature demise was never leaked out so as not to additionally weaken the already fragile collective mindset of the resistance effort, which was as much a civil war as a revolution. The intimate details of Washington's activities became closely guarded secrets kept from the public, and especially the ever-gossipy newspapers in Philadelphia and British headquarters in New York City, only thirty miles distant. In this way, Washington's image as the father of the army and linchpin of revolutionary resistance remained firmly intact. Washington's revered image as the symbol of the revolution was a necessary ingredient to support the morale of a homespun, ragtag revolutionary army. As demonstrated during this period, Washington's little military "family" was just that: an insular and secure world that was secretive (because of omnipresent security concerns, especially in regard to protecting the commander-in-chief and his reputation), which was paramount for America's overall well-being, including the image projected to nations aboard.[25]

Significantly, Washington learned a valuable lesson while he had been bedridden. His staff officers, especially Hamilton, had effectively managed the army's daily functioning for an extended period. In the future, therefore, Washington wisely decided that he would no longer tirelessly work himself to utter exhaustion and risk a dangerous relapse. He had learned exactly of the true value of his staff, especially Hamilton who had taken charge and led the way. Washington now realized the wisdom of delegating far more authority and responsibility to this highly capable right hand man of his "family." Washington's late March 1777 decision was significant, but not entirely an easy one, at least initially, for the micro-managing Virginian.

Out of necessity, Washington put aside his ego (after all, he was addressed as "His Excellency" by one and all, including Hamilton) and ubiquitous plantation owner leadership style by looking a stark reality in the face, allowing him to astutely recognize his own shortcomings and limitations as a mature man in his mid-forties. A very good judge of character, but even a better judge of another person's capabilities and potential, Washington early recognized the outstanding talents of gifted individuals, such as Generals Greene and Knox. More sophisticated and cosmopolitan than the commander-in-chief, Hamilton filled in the gap for some of Washington's shortcomings: a realization that resulted in the creation of a dynamic team with two very different halves, which made a most impressive whole by neatly complimenting each other.

Therefore, Hamilton right at the outset proved nothing less than a godsend to Washington. Although Washington was twenty-three years older than Hamilton, the two men were worldly and both cynics as a result of the hard knocks and cruel twists of fate life had taught them. Hamilton's early crash course in adversity and personal disappointments in the Caribbean had accelerated this process, explaining his maturity and wisdom beyond his years that was actually closer to the world-weariness of a middle-aged man like Washington.

General Washington now fully realized this was a conflict (a war of attrition) that was longer than anyone had originally imagined, involving challenges anticipated by few at the war's beginning. He needed not only a principal staff officer but also a trusty right-hand man to expertly coordinate activities among staff members and to serve as an effective buffer between Washington and his generals and the politicians. Quite simply, what Washington most of all needed was a chief of staff, in the modern sense, to meet the many complex challenges of an unprecedented nature, and far beyond the responsibilities of a traditional staff officer as in the past. Most importantly, Washington needed a man of Hamilton's rare and seemingly endless abilities to work behind the scenes to solve problems, mediate disagreements, and confront issues, including those before they come to the commanding general's attention. All in all, Hamilton's role was to make Washington's job as commander-in-chief easier by making the overall functioning of headquarters more efficient in a professional sense.

Indeed, Hamilton was exactly the right man at exactly the right place for the dramatically expanded role of extreme increased importance. Although not fully appreciated or recognized by historians to this day, Hamilton was to be America's first chief of staff in Continental Army's history, and his appointment an important first step in the overall evolution of war-making in the modern era. Washington's new awareness about the urgent need of easing his heavy burden of responsibility and delegating authority coincided perfectly with Hamilton's abilities. As officially only "Washington's favorite aide-de-camp" but with an ever-growing amount of duties well beyond even the staff's adjutant general's position, Hamilton was shortly given a host of widening responsibilities and roles not yet seen by any military aide in the evolution of modern warfare.[26]

Although unrecognized by American and European historians who have assumed that Washington did virtually everything on his own, Hamilton was truly America's father of the modern chief of staff on the operational and war-fighting level in the evolution of modern war-making as we know it today. But the perception that Washington made decisions by himself in a vacuum has become one of the most enduring myths of the American Revolution. Even Alexander the Great inherited an experienced general staff from the Macedonian Army built by his father King Philip, before his conquest of the vast Persian Empire. Hamilton's vital role as chief of staff, including as military advisor, in the modern sense was downplayed by the young man to maintain Washington's lofty image as the leader of the revolutionary struggle. Although the title of chief of staff did not officially exist, Washington basically said as much when he, never one to bestow lavish praise, described Hamilton as his "principal and most confidential aide."[27]

Washington made this key decision not only because he needed a chief of staff in terms of overall responsiblities but also because he believed in all that Hamilton had to offer on the operational level: a solid vote of confidence that almost seemed like a leap of faith at first glance from a much older man and America's foremost revolutionary leader, who as an international figure was now admired around the world. In consequence, what was created at Morristown was a union and team that "were unbeatable" for the seemingly endless stern challenges that lay ahead.[28] In Hamilton, Washington had been most fortunate to have found "a man with all of those qualities that this post required: determination, organization, communication skills, and loyalty."[29]

Washington had early explained what he needed from staff members, but now this key requirement had been dramatically increased to embody new responsibilities, and it was destined to grow in the years ahead: "It is absolutely necessary for me to have persons that can think for me as well as execute orders."[30] Future staff officer to Washington, Timothy Pickering revealed Hamilton's success in this significant effort, because the young man "had to *think* as well as to *write*" for the commander-in-chief to be the most effective. Washington had also early emphasized how "Aid de Camps [*sic*] are persons in whom entire confidence must be placed [and] It requires men of Abilities to execute the duties with propriety and dispatch, where there is such a multiplicity of business as much attend the Commander in Chief of such an Army as ours. . . ."[31]

Hamilton fulfilled all of these much-needed requirements and like no other officer to date. By way of his own decision, Washington had forged one of the most dynamic and best leadership teams in American history. Washington had already learned a lesson in regard to the mistake of making staff appointments too hastily, not only in regard to New Jersey attorney Reed, but also to young Aaron Burr. Burr had been first accepted as a "gentleman volunteer" by General Benedict Arnold in the late summer of 1775. Without having accomplished much of anything and despite the fact that Burr was still only a teenager, Ireland-born General Richard Montgomery then made him an aide-de-camp just before leading the ill-fated invasion of Canada that ended in the failed attack on Quebec on the last day of December 1775. This had been a casual appointment that was the antithesis of Washington's far more judicious and careful appointment of Hamilton to his staff and then his delegation of greater responsibilities to the young man, after he demonstrated his outstanding abilities at headquarters.[32]

Unlike Burr, who had only served briefly on Washington's staff in June 1776, what Washington got in Hamilton was even far more than he could fully comprehend at this time. With his penetrating mind and masterful skill in interpersonal relationships, especially in a working environment, Hamilton was not only a prodigy but also very much of a genius. In fact, "so quick was Hamilton's comprehension that a word often sufficed to make Washington's wishes clear [and] his skill in arranging, analyzing, and presenting arguments and his knowledge of the technical side of the military art made him invaluable at headquarters. Distrustful of his own literary powers, Washington fell easily to the habit of turning his correspondence over to [Lieutenant] Colonel Hamilton." Therefore, Robert Troup, who was a King's College friend, summarized how the "pen of our army was held by Hamilton" and more than anyone else.[33]

Despite the increased workload at headquarters, Hamilton had not forgotten either his own friends or former comrades of his old New York battery. John "Jack" Laurance was one such friend from New York City, where he had migrated in 1767. The England-born Laurance, a lawyer, now loved America as much as his fellow immigrant Hamilton, because it was a place where dreams and ambitions could come true. Addressed to "My dear Jack," Lieutenant Colonel Hamilton sought to help not only an old friend but also his former battery from New York at the same time. He wrote: "Agreeable to your request, I inquired of Gen. [Henry] Knox, concerning a vacancy of a Captain's birth in his [Artillery] Corps [and] I was in hopes you might be prevailed with to accept a company in the Artillery. He was much pleased with the idea [and] desired me to make you a tender of the remains of my old [New York artillery] company, which will be a considerable help to you [and] I shall be very happy if you determine to enter in a Corps so respectable in itself."[34]

To be fair, the other members of Washington's staff were impressive in their own right, even if they did not shine as bright at headquarters. Amazed by the overall quality of this most remarkable group of young men whom she first saw at Washington's Morristown headquarters in April 1777, Martha Dangerfield Bland explained how Hamilton, Tilghman, Johnston, Fitzgerald, and Harrison "are the General's family, all polite, sociable gentleman, who make the day pass with a great deal of satisfaction to the visitors" to headquarters.[35]

But what Bland could not ascertain was that Hamilton had emerged as the staff's leader by this time. The Marquis de Lafayette, the young French noble who volunteered to fight for America even before the all-important French Alliance of 1778, and won an appointment to major general from Congress at age twenty (without a father—like Hamilton—after he had been killed by the English in 1759), perhaps said it best. Lafayette explained the wisdom of Washington's choice of Hamilton to head his staff to make it far more efficient and professional: "There are few men to be found of his age who have a more general knowledge than he possesses, and none whose soul is more firmly engaged to the cause, or who exceeds him in probity and sterling virtue."[36]

Hamilton's broad range of knowledge and keen instincts about the complexities of politics (both inside and outside the army), insightful judgment about people's character (virtues and vices, strengths and weaknesses), natural diplomatic sense, organizational and diplomatic skills, and artful tact all combined to neatly fulfill Washington's demanding requirements in multiple fields of endeavor: a fact early noted by a good many of America's leaders, civilian (especially the Continental Congress) and military (from generals to staff officers) in regard to young Lieutenant Colonel Hamilton.

While Washington and Hamilton remained polite and formal with Congress to maintain good relations and the proper military–civilian divide as dictated by a republican government's core values, both men were diehard nationalists, who saw America's future destiny with clarity. They early saw the need for stronger government to provide the army with the necessary means to wage a more successful war. However, Hamilton was not without criticism in his private correspondence, which in time strongly condemned the incompetence of Congress for ample good reason, while searching for novel solutions to the problems that were sabotaging America's best resistance efforts.

Most of all, Washington's wisdom was demonstrated in his choice in the versatile and talented leader of his military "family," but he also based his decision on the views of others, including Generals Greene, McDougall, Knox, Alexander (Lord Stirling), and others. Besides his superior intellect combined with a practicality and common sense, Hamilton's sound judgment and nonprovincial views demonstrated a mental flexibility that American political and military leaders ascertained long before he joined Washington's staff.

A Precocious Wisdom

With sage insight, Hamilton had early warned of the self-destructive actions of the country's most radical revolutionaries. He had been appalled by the inherent dangers when New Englanders (the so-called Connecticut Light Horse) from Connecticut crossed the state border to create unrest in New York City, including destroying the office of Hamilton's pamphlet printer James Rivington, during the third week of November 1775. This highly combustible situation threatened to create an even wider divide between New Yorkers and New Englanders to sabotage the fragile unity of Americans. Like Washington, Hamilton had early focused on what was best for the overall national good, and always selflessly labored on that behalf. Therefore, despite a recent arrival from the West Indies, this gifted prodigy had seen the danger of disunity from the folly of sectional prejudices, and sought an immediate solution.

Although only an aspiring student at King's College and still too young to even vote or hold office in New York, Hamilton took timely action. With his keen outsider views, untainted by prevalent regional prejudices, he penned a long letter to his older (by more than a decade) and established friend John Jay, a brilliant lawyer and New York delegate of the Continental Congress, emphasizing what was necessary to restore unity among patriots at a crucial early period. Hamilton was deftly acting as a sage political adviser for Jay in regard to the complex nuances of the combustible brew of human nature and politics based on his extensive "reading and my own experience."[37] As he informed Jay in his letter, Hamilton had feared that this volatile situation would lead to a deep "division and quarreling among ourselves [and] many ill consequences will be prevented if your body [Continental Congress] gently interposes a check for the future [and] believe me sir it is a matter of consequence and deserves serious attention" by Congress.[38]

Hamilton's late November 1775 initiative to a respected congressional delegate had been entirely correct. Hamilton had provided wise council on an important nature to more-established older men (Jay and other members of Congress), while at the same time advising an inexperienced Congress about the best way to proceed in the perplexing game of revolution to avoid its many pitfalls.[39] Then, when New York Loyalists cleverly called for new assembly elections to circumvent the grassroots support for the Continental Congress, Hamilton once again skillfully maneuvered and countered with a hard-hitting response. He went on the political offensive like a pugnacious pit bull on behalf of America's interests. In a December 31, 1775, letter, he had advised Jay about the measures that were necessary "to keep the attention of the people united" behind Congress, because Hamilton realized that "the whigs [patriots] I doubt not constitute a large majority of the people."[40] Ascertaining opportunities from the rising difficulties by using the elections to the patriots' benefit, Hamilton had even diplomatically hinted for Jay to depart Congress in Philadelphia and journey to New York City in order to provide more effective leadership and rally support among the city's patriots. As Hamilton had then penned with a gentle touch exactly when needed: "If you approve the hint, I should wish for your presence here."[41]

Then, when New York called for elections on January 2, 1776, Hamilton had increased pressure on Jay to depart Congress and lead the way for New York City's patriots, who were in the minority. On January 4, 1776, and with his usual deep insights about psychology, propaganda, and politics, he wrote in no uncertain terms although still masked by a friendly persuasion wrapped in the polite language used among proper aristocratic gentleman of the day: "The Tories seem to give out that there will be no opposition, but I suspect this as an artifice to throw the people off their guard [and] I should be glad to see you here with all convenient dispatch; though perhaps your presence may not be absolutely necessary, yet I like to hazard anything, or to neglect any step which may have the least tendency to insure success."[42]

An Empowered Chief of Staff in the Modern Sense

Even while serving on Washington's staff, Hamilton also sagely advised America's inexperienced leaders and government—not only in the New York legislature but also the Continental Congress and the Confederation Congress that eventually hammered out the Articles of Confederation (America's earliest constitution)—about the day's most pressing concerns, serving in effect as America's "junior statesmen" in the process. For an extended period, with his knowledge and intellect growing by leaps and bounds while he continued to develop expertise in multiple fields, Hamilton provided a flow of wise council to many American leaders, while building a political base of supporters and admirers, "not only on how the war should be managed but also on the directions the new nation should take."[43] Within two months of joining Washington's staff, Hamilton wrote to New Jersey's Governor William Livingston on April 29, advising how to quell the rising tide of Tory sentiment in the strategic Garden State.[44]

Meanwhile, Washington's recent incapacitation from illness at Morristown and thoughts about improving the overall quality of the functioning of his headquarters staff also made him realize that he needed to enlarge his staff. Quite simply, a larger group of staff officers was needed not only for the overall smoother functioning of headquarters, but also now to support the symbiotic team of Washington and Hamilton and the young man's enlarged responsibilities. Washington's staff had been only recently bolstered by two new additions. Lieutenant Colonel Richard Kidder Meade hailed from Nansemond County in the Virginia Tidewater area near the Atlantic. Meade's grandfather had been North Carolina's governor, and he brought a greater measure of social prestige and status to Washington's staff. A bachelor at age thirty, he joined the staff in March 1777. Meade and John Walker, who joined the staff in February 1777, were the latest additions to the military "family."[45]

Like Washington, Meade was a Virginian and a fine horseman in the cavalier tradition. A former captain of the Second Virginia Continental Regiment, Meade's superior equestrian skill ordained that he often served as a "riding aide" (like Baylor had been before his departure) as a dispatch rider, messenger, and reconnaissance officer, which he performed along with his other official staff duties.[46] Possessing a fine education from the prestigious Harrow School in northwest London, Meade primarily delivered Hamilton's directives (written for Washington) far and wide until he left the "family" in 1780 to get married. Quite simply, "Alexander Hamilton did the 'head work' for Washington while" Meade 'did the riding.'" Meade admired Hamilton because "few men [were more] estimable, fewer amiable" than the native West Indian.[47]

As the undisputed leader of Washington's military "family," Hamilton excelled in an entirely different environment and atmosphere from his battery commander days with his beloved New Yorkers. Social by nature and blessed with winning ways that made him popular, he thrived not only in the professional but also in the familial setting of headquarters because of the close interaction, good humor, and camaraderie among fellow staff officers. Washington's close-knit "family" members became exceptionally devoted to each other. They worked closely together from sunup to sundown and often spent the night in the same room, because they had to be near Washington's presence night and day since the commander-in-chief requests might come at anytime, day or night. More than any other staff member, Hamilton found not only a "family," but also a new home as a highly respected member of not only the military but also the upper class—more of a collegiate setting than a traditional military headquarters but very businesslike—in the bosom of Washington's staff. In fact, Hamilton basked in this environment of "familial warmth" that he had made even warmer with the sunshine of his personality. Hamilton's dark and rootless past had vanished for all practical purposes with his miraculous regeneration into a new person with a new role, Lieutenant Colonel Hamilton.

Of course, Hamilton was naturally flattered that Washington had so early recognized his talents and delegated more authority to him. His confidence soared accordingly. With versatile abilities and expertise in multiple fields in abundance, Hamilton's only perceived flaw (if it could be considered such) was over-eagerness, if not a subtle aggressiveness just below the surface, to demonstrate his worth. But in fact, Hamilton had only to be himself around not only Washington but also other staff members, who fully appreciated all that he offered to "the family" that worked hard at managing the Continental Army. He had finally found a place where he would be judged on his merits and abilities rather than his monetary worth (scant indeed) and highly questionable social background. Even Hamilton's elevation to chief of staff failed to cause internal problems within the staff since he had suddenly appeared at headquarters on March 1, because they recognized Hamilton's abilities without argument or debate: a situation that ensured a level of harmony not often seen on other general's staffs, where egos so often rose to the fore.

Consequently, the "family" was not marred by clashes of personalities or ego-driven rivalries. With Hamilton's pleasing and diplomatic personality ("a bright gleam of sunshine," emphasized General Greene) casting a glow, the cooperative working relationships at headquarters increased the staff's productivity and efficiency, while the overall work setting improved dramatically. Washington, as penned in a wartime letter, placed a high premium on his young "Gentlemen of the Family," who "are with me," through the good times and the bad.[48] (As revealed in a letter, Hamilton used this popular terminology for members of Washington's staff, "Gentleman of the family."[49])

From the beginning, Hamilton thrived in this familial, collegial environment, which he not only relished but also fully appreciated: a situation that literally brought the best out of him, negating his own well-founded cynicism. He embraced the warm feelings radiated by staff members and returned the sentiment of literally brothers in arms. After all, at this time and despite his worldliness and outgoing affect on those around him, Hamilton was very much of a loner at heart, because of the demons that still haunted him from his dark Caribbean past. As Hamilton explained his personal code in a letter to his best friend John Laurens in April 1779, (Lauren served beside him on Washington's staff by the late summer of 1777 and was someone who also had been born out of wedlock in South Carolina): "You know the opinion I entertain of mankind, and how much it is my desire to preserve myself free from particular attachments [deep personal friendships and love relationships with women], and to keep my happiness independent on the caprice of others."[50]

Hamilton concealed a deeply held caution about establishing close human relations with a giddy and almost frivolous exterior in social situations. After all, he had lost every person who he had every loved: his father, mother, and first cousin Peter Lytton who had committed suicide. Therefore, as a world-wise and die-hard cynic who knew only too well about the dark side of human nature, he was deeply wary of risking deep emotional attachments, male or female, even though he made friends easily and was "girl crazy" toward upper class women, possessing an active and healthy libido, perhaps more so than any other Founding Father. John Laurens was the greatest exception to the rule for Hamilton in regard to open affection during this early period. The depth of this friendship (even more than brothers) eventually began to change the hard-edged young man with the passing of time, overcoming his caution about genuine closeness to another person and making him more receptive to a complete surrender to a permanent love, if he met the right woman which eventually happened. But this world-weary young man would be extremely circumspect and careful in his final choice of a wife, preferring to remain a playboy on the make and playing the field.[51]

By excelling as a respected leader of Washington's staff in an all-important position, Hamilton had beaten the odds by way of his own merits rather than wealth, family name, or because of a privileged social background, which were the traditional avenues of achieving such a dramatic rise in status. Like other generals according to the custom of the day, Washington had been long committed to selecting capable men from the best families with fine educations and gentlemen (he needed educated and trustworthy "confidential" men from respected families, including those with important political influence like Laurens) to serve on his staff. Educated in London and from an aristocratic Virginia planter class family, Lieutenant Colonel Richard Kidder Meade was one such example. Young Aaron Burr, a Princeton man, also fit these specialized requirements that were socially based. Consequently, membership to Washington's prestigious military "family" was very much about class, economics, family background, and education. However, Hamilton was the notable exception to the rule, further emphasizing that his rise was little short of remarkable, if not miraculous, because he was largely a self-made man unlike the others. As proud members of the America's newest generation of a landed aristocracy on the rise, these men were true bluebloods of an infant republic and they basked in this distinction—all except Hamilton.

Washington's aides-de-camp, or his "Confidential Officers" in the general's words, when Hamilton entered Washington's "family" in early 1777 consisted of individuals of considerable merit and promise: before his recent departure, John Baylor, who had been one of the staff's best horsemen and who had carried the silk regimental battle-flags of the Hessians captured at Trenton to Congress, then in Baltimore where it had relocated after fleeing from threatened Philadelphia; mature Robert Hanson Harrison, the former lawyer, whom Hamilton and other young aides called the "ancient [military] secretary" before he took over the job; the rambunctious Tench Tilghman who was duty-minded but also had a keen eye for the ladies like Hamilton who possessed a distinct talent for seduction; the personable Caleb Gibbs who was destined to command Washington's personal body guard known as Washington's Life Guard; John Walker, and George Johnston, who joined this unique military "family" of the austere Virginian in mid-January 1777. Hamilton rose swiftly above them all on his own abilities and achievements rather than social and economic standing and connections: a remarkable development by any measure.

Especially sensitive about his unfortunate family background because of his illegitimacy, Hamilton genuinely believed that he was part of an aristocracy that went back to his father's native Scotland. In Hamilton's mind, this ancient Celtic lineage was even more distinguished and certainly of longer duration than those of Washington's esteemed "family" members, most of whose families had been in America for several generations. Since Scotland was now part of Great Britain after this imperialist nation's conquest of still another Celtic people whose dream of independence had been crushed by British might, Hamilton was proud of his legitimate connections to his father's Scottish family that boasted of the best blood of this ancient Celtic land. In this sense, he even felt superior to the so-called colonial elite who had been in America only a relatively short time compared to the Hamilton family of Kerelaw Castle, Stevenston, Scotland, where his father had been raised.

For an easy acclimation into the "family," Hamilton also knew exactly how to act, dress, and talk just like a proper gentleman without any hint of a less-distinguished West Indies past that was unknown to Washington and other staff officers. In this way, he was to gain universal acceptance and especially able to dazzle the ladies of the upper class, and move easily in what normally would be a forbidden social order for him. Instead of being perceived as a pretentious upstart who had no business serving not only as a member but also as the leader of Washington's staff, Hamilton rose higher with a smooth, natural ease without causing discord or even the usual jealousy for an over-achieving newcomer. By his own abilities, Hamilton had opened the door to the possibility of an exclusive membership into America's aristocracy. He grew so close to Washington that the general referred to Hamilton with pride as "my boy": the ultimate compliment from the most respected man in America.

But unlike other aides-de-camp who basked in the overall headquarters experience, the young man from St. Croix was not entirely enamored of life at Washington's headquarters, but not because of the heavy workload or any personality clashes. He was simply not temperamentally suited for the job. Despite his success at headquarters, Hamilton still remained an ambitious man of action (a veteran artillery officer with a distinguished combat record) and a diehard romantic imbued with the Age of Enlightenment's loftiest ideals, which fueled his desire to aspire higher, especially on the field of strife at the head of an independent command. Therefore, Hamilton's ambition of winning battlefield distinction was now a dream deferred. But this was not a simple case of a mindless or unrealistic longing for glory like that of an infatuated youth. As previously demonstrated on the battlefield, Hamilton knew that he was a very good soldier and a capable leader of men. In this regard, Hamilton was not vain as much as he was precisely in tune to his own leadership abilities and full potential. Because of his situation of having no family or fortune, Hamilton had long seen military glory as his sole avenue to earn greater recognition: a strategy that had already worked to his benefit, and resulted in his position on Washington's staff.

The antithesis of a traditional "glorified clerk" of a commander's staff at headquarters, Hamilton possessed a host of refined interpersonal, diplomatic, and political skills that had been finely honed from the combined experience of working in Christiansted combined with his extensive readings in classical history and politics. Hamilton also was very much of a classical scholar and a natural philosopher who fully utilized the most invaluable lessons of the past to apply them to the current situation. Therefore, in making decisions and bestowing sage advice at Washington's headquarters, he often offered the appropriate timeless lessons (military and political) from his readings of classical history. As if still studying at King's College, Hamilton borrowed books whenever possible. He studied into the night to continue his thorough education on practically all subjects, while other aides slept at headquarters.

A longtime personal inclination that in part revealed the legacies of a troubled past, Hamilton especially detested any hint of subservience, however. In this sense, Hamilton was not entirely suited for closely structured and narrowly defined military life that often sapped personal initiative and set deeply entrenched restrictions of a traditional nature, because of his independent ways partly inherited from his headstrong parents. Even as a young student and recent immigrant who remained an outlier, he had boldly attempted to gain permission to embark upon an independent course of study at Princeton, hoping to be allowed to go his own way.

However, Hamilton never allowed this powerful disinclination—a special sore spot with him—to clash with Washington's autocratic ways until one brief moment in mid-February day in 1781, in a classic case of sacrificing personal desires and ambitions for America's overall good because he knew that fully supporting Washington was the best way that he could assist the American cause. Therefore, from the beginning, he had enthusiastically engaged in all assignments and responsibilities while winning Washington's ever-lasting admiration and respect in the process. Blessed with the ability to compartmentalize, Hamilton fit neatly into not only Washington's family, but also his leadership role as head of the staff. After his quick elevation to the nerve center of the highest level action at Washington's headquarters, Hamilton possessed the rare ability to submerge his own personal feelings and psychological needs to faithfully serve Washington for the greater good and excel in the process, as if he was fulfilling his fondest personal ambition. A true nationalist who was devoted to America and its promising future thanks in large part to the immigrant experience, he saw this struggle as a righteous one which he embraced with his heart and soul.

As mentioned, Hamilton's dysfunctional family background and his many unrewarding years of working as a lowly clerk on St. Croix had shaped him into a far different kind of person than the privileged bluebloods of Washington's "family." He learned how to survive in a harsh world, and this required flexibility and skills in adjusting to new circumstances. Part of his former job at Kortright and Cruger called for skillfully maneuvering the tricky ground of dealing with wealthy merchants and wily sea captains from around the world, bestowing upon him a wide range of experiences. Hamilton was not entirely satisfied even being Washington's chief of staff. As Hamilton later confessed in a wartime letter: "I always disliked the office of an Aide de Camp as having in it a kind of personal dependence [and therefore] I refused to serve in this capacity with two Major General's [Lord Stirling—General William Alexander—and General Nathanael Greene] at an early period of the war. Infected however with the enthusiasm of the times [March 1777], an idea of the Generals character induced me to *accept his invitation* to enter into his family."[52]

Despite this deep-seated resentment of subservience that was masked by his polished style, pleasing personality, and work ethic that knew few limitations, Hamilton headed this hardworking military "family" without the hint of any dissatisfaction on his part. Most importantly, Hamilton brought a fresh breath of new life, a quick mind, and a rejuvenating sense of vitality to Washington's worn and overworked staff—invaluable qualities that energized and inspired staff members during the long hours of work that often went late into the night. In some cases, he and other aides composed, wrote, and copied more than a hundred letters per day. Fortunately for Washington, Hamilton was not only a dynamic type-A personality, but also a tireless workaholic with an uncanny ability to solve even the most difficult problems.

Partly because of his difficult past, Hamilton was also wise and savvy well beyond his years. Consequently, in his dealing with America's top military and civilian leaders, Hamilton was not at any intellectual or psychological disadvantage whatsoever because of his family background, youth, recent immigrant status, or West Indian birth. The headquarters environment provided Hamilton with an open avenue for social acceptance and ascendency that was unattainable in civilian life. With a gentleman's flair and flawless manners of the upper class elite, he tactfully led the "charmed circle" of Washington's "family" with his outstanding abilities and winning ways during the long hours of work, and then allowed his sparkling personality to shine after hours in a more relaxed setting of socialization, including dinners and dances.[53]

For good reason, Washington relied heavily upon what Hamilton had to offer as a right-hand man at headquarters. The commander-in-chief and Hamilton accomplished more together as a dynamic team with each passing week. Although Hamilton was only twenty-two, Washington had "rapidly expanded Hamilton's duties, putting him in charge of all headquarters operations in order to give himself more time for other work."[54] Washington and Hamilton often "pored over maps [and] discussed upcoming battles" with Hamilton playing a role in formulating strategy almost like a senior general in a dynamic relationship that endured long after the war.[55]

Like John Jay, who benefitted from Hamilton's political advice about the proper course that Congress should take to improve America's fortunes, Washington shortly learned that he could immeasurably benefit from his chief of staff's well-thought-out advice on multiple levels of complexity. In one of his most amazing delegations of authority in America's entire war effort and almost immediately, Washington freely "gave Hamilton surprising powers and responsibilities, permitting him to interview deserters, meet spies, communicate with generals, chair meetings of officers, and talk to local ministers and merchants on his behalf [and] he also allowed him to write public proclamations and newspaper columns signed with Washington's name [and of course] the general had no objections to the frequent [sound] political and economic advice that the talkative Hamilton offered to congressmen, governors, state legislators, and anyone else who would listen. He saw a young version of himself in Hamilton, but a more brilliant self."[56] Hamilton was a true "intellectual, but, unlike many men of great learning, he was also a well-organized and hard-working administrator who streamlined the chain of command and served as the buffer between the commander-in-chief and the entire army [and most importantly] Washington had a brilliant and innovative thinker, and also someone who got things done": the best of both worlds for Washington's maximum benefit and to his delight.[57] With unsurpassed skill, Hamilton from the outset served as Washington's "chief agent" in the most complex matters of diplomacy and intelligence gathering, and "special agent to [Washington's] field commanders" of the Continental Army.[58]

As mentioned, John Laurens became Hamilton's best friend and closest confidant during the war years, and it was a durable relationship of great strength. Like other Age of Enlightenment romantics and idealists, the two young men were kindred spirits. They shared a deep Hellenistic-like affection (not unlike Alexander the Great and Hephaestion, but without the physical love between them) that they expressed to each other in very personal and often emotional letters over an extended period. Like Hamilton, Laurens was another one of Washington's "Little Lions," who possessed a fiery republican spirit and roared his loudest on the battlefield, where their daring and courage were revealed.[59]

The breadth of Hamilton's abilities were so widely realized that leading New York politicians like Gouverneur Morris—of French Huguenot descent like Hamilton (his mother's side)—repeatedly sought his advice and ideas, especially because he was an adopted New Yorker himself. These opportunistic New Yorkers early solicited for Hamilton to serve as "the state's confidential military liaison" and a direct communications link to the army's headquarters not long after he joined Washington's staff. As if Hamilton's heavy daily work-load was not enough, he was presented with a special request from the three-man Committee of Correspondence, which included his friend John Jay, of the New York Convention. Hamilton was asked to serve as their chief correspondent to inform them about the army's condition and the war's overall progress.

Of course, these highly placed New Yorkers were hoping to gain deep insight into the inner workings of Washington's headquarters, in order to increase their influence and promote their own self-interests and agendas. However, the request complimented Hamilton because it came from a body of distinguished political leaders and from older members of America's ruling class. These respected legislative committee members—New York's leading revolutionary politicians—correctly saw Hamilton as a young man with great expectations. Hamilton was sufficiently politically savvy to know that this offer presented an excellent opportunity by allowing him direct access and greater influence among New York's leading politicians and revolutionary leaders. Naturally, given his ambitions, he took full advantage of the opening by writing the Committee's twice-weekly reports, despite his hectic headquarters schedule that left little spare time.

Eager to take advantage of every opportunity, Lieutenant Colonel Hamilton readily accepted this additional workload and commitment to the Committee. "With chearfulness [*sic*], I embrace the proposal of correspondence with your convention, through you; and shall from time to time as far as my leisure will permit, and my duty warrant, communicate [in order] to convey a true idea of what is going on in the military line," penned Hamilton in his March 20 acceptance letter. With heightened interpersonal and diplomatic skills rarely seen of someone his age and humble background, Hamilton showed prudence in his new responsibilities. Significant ethically, he refused to cross boundaries and go beyond proper protocol even for his own advantage. Mindful of customary military procedures of a strict nature and in no uncertain terms, he made these New York committee members fully aware that what he wrote to them was only the "private sentiments" of a Continental officer, which were not "an echo" of the personal opinions of "the General."[60]

Hamilton was now in an advantageous position of greater empowerment with his growing political connections. He personally was invested with the power of "deciding what the state's politicians [of New York] should be told of Continental military affairs."[61] Only two days later, Hamilton advised his New York friends of what he had gleaned from the latest intelligence combined with his own personal insights: "The British army continues to decrease by the daily loss of prisoners and deserters . . . which is a striking symptom that the situation of affairs with the enemy is not so favorable as it might be [and] It is my opinion the enemy will make no grand movement [on the capital of Philadelphia because of their desire to capture cities, especially the capital] before the beginning of May [1777]; and perhaps not then" at all.[62]

Hamilton also freely voiced his many ideas to Washington on any issue that the commander-in-chief solicited and in more detail and with greater expertise than even what the Virginian expected: General Greene had learned as much the first time that he had invited Hamilton, overflowing with good ideas, to dinner in the spring of 1775. As their working and personal relationship grew through daily close contact, Washington became more candid around Hamilton, gradually letting down a stiff formal façade of a traditional Virginia Tidewater aristocrat to a degree. The recent immigrant from the West Indies viewed the commander-in-chief as synonymous with America's struggle for life against the world's superpower and imperial giant: an all-important symbol and image that needed to be supported by Hamilton as much as possible for the revolution's very survival.

Meanwhile, Washington's appreciation for Hamilton continued to steadily grow with each passing day in part because he had learned his lesson from bitter experience concerning the pain of disloyalty surrounding someone on his own personal staff, Joseph Reed. Well educated at London's Middle Temple, Reed was brilliant but not as brilliant as Hamilton. Worst of all, this 1776 betrayal by a proper gentleman of the upper class had shocked the Virginian to the core. After the loss of Forts Washington and Lee in the fall of 1776, Adjutant General Reed (like many other Americans) had lost all faith in Washington's generalship. Reed wrote letters that had even encouraged General Charles Lee to believe that he was Washington's best replacement: the ultimate betrayal.

One historian concluded how the clandestine activities of Reed, whom Washington had trusted completely, were overt "acts of treason." After declaring that Washington was not capable of achieving victory, Reed had implored Lee: "I think yourself and some others should go to Congress and form the plan of the new army."[63] After Washington discovered Reed's betrayed friendship and trust, the adjutant general shortly resigned. Whereas Reed was Washington's most disloyal staff officer, Hamilton was Washington's most loyal.[64]

Esteemed Family Members

As mentioned, Lieutenant Colonel John Fitzgerald was a key member of Washington's staff born in County Wicklow, Leinister Province, located just south of Dublin, among the rolling hills, known as the "Garden of Ireland" because of its natural beauty. Fitzgerald had migrated to America in 1769 to make a fresh start in life. This enterprising immigrant had then made his American dream come true. Of the Catholic faith, Fitzgerald had been a leading merchant of the port of Alexandria, Virginia, which was located on the Potomac's west bank just north of Mount Vernon. Starting in 1774 with a fellow Irishman named Valentine Peers, Fitzgerald successfully engaged in the lucrative linen trade with Ireland.

A man of action and a fine officer like Hamilton, Fitzgerald had first served as a captain of the 3rd Virginia Continental Regiment before earning a major's rank. He joined Washington's "family" in the fall of 1776. Blessed with a gregarious personality and a good sense of humor, Fitzgerald possessed political ambitions and would become Alexandria's mayor after the American Revolution. This merry Irishman and Hamilton were soon fast friends, exchanging witticisms and jokes. Most symbolically, the fact that two of Washington's best aides were born beyond America's shores has been generally unappreciated by historians, who have long presented an overly homogenous portrait of Washington's "family" like the Continental Army in general.[65]

Hamilton also grew close to Robert Hanson Harrison, who had been appointed to Washington's staff in early November 1775. Because his infantry command had been formed in Alexandria only three days after Christmas 1775, Lieutenant Colonel Harrison had also served in the 3rd Virginia Continental Regiment like Fitzgerald, before becoming Washington's aide-de-camp and then military secretary. As mentioned, Washington knew Harrison well before the war. The southern Marylander had been born in Charles County, across the Potomac (east side) from Virginia and southeast of Alexandria, but had moved west to Fairfax County, Virginia. An experienced lawyer when the revolution erupted, Harrison had served as Washington's attorney from his office in Alexandria, where Fitzgerald's mercantile business thrived. A faithful Episcopalian, Harrison had often visited Mount Vernon on both personal visits and business calls. Respected in Alexandria like Fitzgerald, Harrison was an early leading revolutionary in rallying support to the patriot cause, having served on Alexandria's Committee of Correspondence.

Therefore, the bonds of friendship and business ties between Washington and Harrison were strong. Like Hamilton, Harrison had not been spared the tragedies of life. His wife had died before the war, and he was the now the single father of two daughters, Sarah and Dorothy. As an older man, Harrison's health was not nearly as robust as Hamilton's and younger staff officers. To fight for his country's freedom, nevertheless, Harrison had left his daughters with his parents at the Charles County, Maryland, family home located at or near Walnut Landing, on the Potomac River. Harrison's family had been living in southern Maryland for more than a century.

During the autumn of 1776, Harrison became one of Washington's first aides-de-camp and one of his favorites. He had first joined his old friend from Mount Vernon at the army's Cambridge, Massachusetts, encampment located just outside Boston. Here, Harrison served as one of the general's two aides along with Reed. In 1776, Harrison was officially appointed as Washington's military secretary, garnering the rank of lieutenant colonel. Because of their age difference of a decade and with obvious relish that revealed how he enjoyed to poke good-natured fun at those whom he liked, Hamilton called Harrison, born in 1745, the "Old Secretary." Harrison was actually only in his early thirties. (Hamilton's nickname for Harrison was no show of disrespect. Martha

Washington often openly referred to her husband around his staff at headquarters as "her 'Old Man' as she calls him.") Harrison served on Washington's staff until March 1781, when he then returned to his southern Maryland home to care for his two daughters.[66]

Revealing his less serious side, Hamilton freely teased and joked with Harrison not only about his ample eccentric qualities, but also about his case of hemorrhoids due to long hours of being seated and writing at a desk: a forgotten personal price paid by a hard-working staff officer at headquarters. Hamilton utilized his poetic and humorous side to his supreme delight when he wrote about Harrison with a sarcastic flair: "His sedentary exploits are sung in strains of laborious dulness [and] The many breeches he has worn out during the war are enumerated—nor are the depredations which long sitting have made on his ___ unsung."[67]

Harrison's admiration for Hamilton and what Hamilton could accomplish as Washington's most dynamic and gifted staff officer never wavered. He bestowed the sobriquet of "Little Lion" upon Hamilton for the young man's boldness in society, especially with pretty women he charmed with such effortless ease, among senior leaders at the conference table, and on the battlefield.[68]

Good Times at Headquarters

With everyone on the headquarters staff in their twenties except Harrison and Johnson, Washington's "family" was a lively, high-spirited bunch, especially after all work was completed. As delegated by Washington, Hamilton served as the principal driving force among Washington's staff during both work and off-work hours. As a reward for the day's exertions, Washington's staff often engaged in organized social activities, especially extended dinners, when not busy with other duties during active campaigning. Washington declined to play the host, and it was Hamilton who presided over these social events, especially the dinners. At first, Washington rotated this role among aides, but shortly Hamilton became the permanent host.

In keeping with Washington's longtime practice at Mount Vernon, the main dinner of the day was held in mid-afternoon. These dinners were almost always attended by other generals, whose own regimental or brigade headquarters were located nearby, as well as the officer of the day. However, political leaders, including Congressmen and state government officials, and an occasional businessman, also attended the main meal of the day in a formal setting. Female friends, wives, and relatives were also often included in the formal dinner arrangements, swelling the number of participants to as many as twenty people.

These social gatherings reached their zenith during winter, brightening the otherwise dreary existence at winter quarters, when less work was required after active campaigning ceased. Especially during the coldest season, therefore, dinners at Washington's headquarters drew everyone closer together, forging deeper bonds and keeping spirits high under adverse conditions. According to the day's custom, dinners were followed by a round of toasts and drinking that often continued late into the night.

But it was the talkative Hamilton, with his winning smile, easy laughter, sharp sense of humor and well-known wit, who most excelled in these social situations, especially when pretty ladies were present. Allowing his charm and sunny personality to dominate the proceedings, he opened conversations, told the appropriate stories with tact and humor, and made everyone feel comfortable. Consequently, he "presided at the headquarters dinner table and kept the conversation lively" night after night.[69]

One impressed Pennsylvania officer described how the erudite Hamilton masterfully "presided at the General's table [and] he acquitted himself with an ease, propriety and vivacity that gave me the most favorable impression of his talents and accomplishments."[70]At these customary social settings at headquarters, Hamilton combined witty conversations with the tradition of leading rounds of toasts and singing popular ballads and drinking songs in "his rich singing voice."[71]

The young man's seamless blending of hard work and leisure times in a formal social setting, where his polished manners and intelligence shined brightly to impress participants, was a winning combination that impressed admirers. The ladies were especially charmed by Hamilton and his pleasing personality. Despite the young man's sociability and love of merriment, the wife of a cavalry officer described him as "sensible"—the model Continental officer on Washington's staff. As he revealed in a wartime letter, Hamilton lived by the "maxim of [his] life [which was] to enjoy the present good with the highest relish & to soften the present evil by a hope of future good."[72]

During work hours and especially in the more lighthearted hours after required duties were completed, Hamilton relied on his cutting-edge satire, sharp wit, and "rapier-swift jokes" that enlivened daily life at headquarters to lighten the heavy workload. On one memorable occasion, Hamilton voiced his opinion against a plan to kidnap Sir Henry Clinton, who was the top commander at New York City. An armchair general, he was not known for his aggressiveness or military skill. Hamilton, consequently, explained to Washington with a wry smile how keeping Clinton in command of England's war effort was actually to America's advantage. Indeed, General Clinton's strategic blundering and hubris eventually paved the way to the surrender of an entire British-Hessian-Tory army at Yorktown, Virginia, in October 1781, when Hamilton's military skills and reputation reached a zenith. Therefore, Hamilton had been entirely correct when he wisely advised Washington long before how the kidnapping of General Clinton from his stately Broadway residence "would be to our misfortune, since the British government could not find another commander so incompetent to send in his place."[73]

During daily interaction with the staff in a calculated bid to keep spirits up, Hamilton allowed his exuberant sense of humor to lighten the load of bureaucratic red tape and long hours of toil. Without exaggeration, New York's Governor George Clinton complimented Hamilton by writing how he was "O'ver-run with wit." His well-honed humor that dominated headquarters and formal dinners often appeared occasionally in official army correspondence. In one letter to Brigadier General "Mad" Anthony Wayne (nicknamed for his combativeness, not lack of sanity) who was one of Washington's finest top lieutenants and a real fighting general of ability, Hamilton recommended that one zealous religious man, Doctor W. Mendy, should be appointed chaplain in the general's command, because he "will fight," and possessed no failings "except that he does not drink and will not insist on your going to Heaven whether you want to or not."[74]

A distinguished French general of the nobility and Age of Enlightenment intellectual, the Marquis De Chastellux, described his initial impressions of Hamilton during a memorable visit to Washington's headquarters, when he first met Washington, who "conducted me to his house, where I found the company [family] still at table, although the dinner had been long over. He presented me to [his] Generals . . . and his *family*, then composed of Colonels Hamilton and Tilgman [*sic*], his secretaries and aids-de-camp . . . and other officers attached to the general, form what he called his family."[75]

Lengthy Work Hours

But, of course, hard work and long hours dominated Washington's headquarters far more than frivolity. Daily life at headquarters was usually Spartan to an extreme degree, especially during active campaigning. A young Marylander who had been raised in the tobacco country of St. Michael's river country and who had been a wealthy Philadelphia merchant before the war, Lieutenant Colonel Tench Tilghman became one of Hamilton's closest friends despite their age difference of more than ten years. In August 1776 at age thirty-two, he had been appointed to Washington's "family." Blessed with a lively, fun-loving personality, Tilghman had served in a Philadelphia company of the Flying Camp in August 1776, before working closely beside Hamilton who became a respected mentor and good friend. Hamilton discovered a kindred spirit in the Marylander. In an August 15, 1776, letter to his father, Tilghman described the businesslike diligence that was required by Washington of his staff members, including even while headquartered briefly in New York City: "my acquaintance is confined to two or three young Gentlemen of the Generals Family, and to the last you cannot conceive what a constant Scene of Business we are engaged in."[76]

Only three days later in another letter to his father, who owned a tobacco plantation in County Talbot, near the town of Easton, Maryland, Tilghman admitted with grim resolution of Washington's demanding requirements from sunup to sundown, especially for young men in the prime of life, writing: "I take your Caution to me in Regard to my Health very kindly, but I assure you, you need be under no Apprehension of my losing it on the Score of Excess in living, that Vice is banished from this Army and the Generals Family in particular. We never sup, but go early to bed and are early up."[77]

Washington held Tilghman in high esteem. Washington wrote in a wartime letter how Tilghman "joined my family, and has been in every action in which the main army was concerned. He has been a zealous servant . . . [and] his modesty and love of concord placed the date of his expected commission at the first of April 1777, because he would not take rank of Hamilton and [Richard Kidder] Meade, who were declared aids in order (which he did not choose to be), before that period, although he had joined my family and done all the duties of one from the first of September preceding."[78]

The hectic level of non-stop activity at Washington's headquarters was fully revealed in the letters of another member of the general's "family," John Laurens. He joined Washington's staff on September 6, 1777, as a volunteer aide-de-camp. A true Southern blueblood born in Charleston, South Carolina, Laurens had received an excellent overseas education, including in Geneva, Switzerland, because of his wealthy father's emphasis on his eldest son obtaining the very best schooling. In a March 25, 1778, letter to his father Henry Laurens, who was then the president of the Continental Congress (the second, after John Hancock of Boston) since November 1, 1777, and had an eerie foreboding that his too often reckless—or too courageous—son would die in battle far from home, John wrote: "I have long anxiously desired to see you, but the unabated flow of business in the general's family restrained me from asking leave" from headquarters.[79]

In another letter that revealed how little time he possessed to write even a short note, while laboring on Washington's staff with so many assigned duties, John even apologized to his father on this occasion, "I was going to speak privately on several public matters, but the horses are order'd, and what I write must be dispatched hastily."[80] And on October 14, 1777, John Laurens' letter to Henry emphasized the heavy workload at Washington's headquarters and the scarcity of free time, including even to sit down and write to his family: "Between copying and composing [letters, orders, and messages for Washington] I have inked a great deal of paper, and it begins to be time for me to join in the concert of my snoring companions [of Washington's family], who are extended before the fire in the style which we practiced in the interior [western frontier] parts of So. Carolina."[81] As revealed in Laurens' letter, one of these snoring members of Washington's family was Hamilton, because the aides usually sleep in a single room, unless he was up late studying or reading as was often his habit.

Since March 1, 1777, Hamilton thrived in this busy environment and in his daily assignments that literally had no end. First among these duties were extensive writing chores that were the normal part in the daily operations of Washington's headquarters. In the beginning, Hamilton worked long hours in writing out Washington's orders, instructions, and directives that revealed the hand of a master composer of eloquent verse and prose. Consequently, Hamilton often labored overtime, succeeding in each new assignment in the writing of too many letters to count. All the while, Hamilton continued to prove to Washington that he was one of America's most gifted writers.[82]

The spectrum of Hamilton's writing gifts already had even played a key role in helping to early educate a generation of colonists that it was in America's best interests to break away permanently from the British Empire. And as he had demonstrated repeatedly in the past, including in bestowing wise advice to leading Congressional members, Hamilton was one of the most politically astute and savvy members of Washington's Army. Consequently, besides communicating with Washington's subordinates in various commands, Hamilton proved invaluable in Washington's ultrasensitive dealings with Congress, state governors, and committees across America in his dual military-civilian role. On one occasion and seemingly to contradict his own aristocratic manners and speech, Hamilton's egalitarian side (the real person hidden by a polished and carefully cultivated aristocratic facade) was fully evident when he expressed concern that if a separate senate in New York was elected by only propertied voters, then such a government institution might then "degenerate into a body purely aristocratical"[83]

The Fiery Young Nationalist

Significantly, Lieutenant Colonel Hamilton was far more than just another Continental Army officer on the rise. Washington now possessed the best writer in the Continental Army, and one who benefitted far more from the young man's talents than has been generally recognized by many historians. Even as a precocious teenager, Hamilton's political talents and instincts had earned him a name not only in the Caribbean but also in America. Hamilton's writing skills had served as his ticket out of dead-end St. Croix, which he was destined to never see again after he sailed away in 1773, as he preferred. His literary talents that resulted in two published works in the island's largest English newspaper and had so thoroughly impressed the ruling elite with his talents, helped Hamilton to reach America's shores. Quite simply, the young man successfully wrote his way out not only out of the Caribbean forever, but out of the obscurity of dreary St. Croix. Then, once reinvigorated by the endless possibilities of America, Hamilton owed his dramatic rise to an unmatched literary skill and mastery of the English language, which Washington now utilized to the fullest at headquarters. Even before Thomas Jefferson wrote of "the pursuit of happiness" in the Declaration of Independence, Hamilton had already penned that identical phrase to additionally inspire the American people with revolutionary zeal. It is not known, but almost certainly Washington had read the early works by the young immigrant, that partly explained why Hamilton may have been invited to join Washington's headquarters in the first place.

With New York divided in sentiment and as mentioned, a masterful Loyalist writer who was an Anglican rector, under the pseudonym of "A Westchester [County, New York] Farmer," had launched a hard-hitting propaganda campaign in October 1774. This upper class Loyalist propagandist proved effective in convincing many Americans to remain loyal and disregard the alleged siren's song of the Continental Congress. Published in local newspapers, this convincing Tory voice had to be immediately refuted to keep large numbers of people securely in the patriot camp. Hamilton had been exactly the right man for the job, while still only a young student at King's College.

Launched only a month later on December 15, 1774, to limit the extensive damage caused by the Loyalist's pen, Hamilton's subsequent "A Full Vindication of the Measures of the Congress" was a most forceful reply to the "Westchester Farmer." Indeed, what Hamilton wrote was far more brilliant than the Loyalist's arguments that he systematically dismantled with his usual blend of common sense, wit, and brilliance. In his revolutionary pamphlet published by James Rivington, New York City, under the pseudonym of a "Friend to America" and advertised as the "Westchester Farmer's" biting "Wit ridiculed" of which he was a master, Hamilton launched an analytical assault with brilliantly composed arguments that appealed to and educated a new generation of Americans. With a forceful style all his own, to prove that he was the ultimate nationalist not long after he first stepped on America's shores, Hamilton thoroughly denounced the Loyalists, because they "are enemies to the natural rights of mankind is manifest; because they wish to see one part of their species enslaved by another. . . . They endeavor to persuade us, that the absolute sovereignty of parliament does not imply our absolute slavery; that is it a Christian duty to submit to be plundered of all we have, merely because some of our fellow-subjects are wicked enough to require it of us, that slavery, so far from being a great evil, is a great blessing."[84]

With pinpoint logic and artful eloquence, Hamilton emphasized to Americans to awake, because of the great threat that they now faced: "There is less reason now than ever to expect deliverance . . . from the hand of oppression. The system of slavery, fabricated against America, . . . is the offspring of mature deliberation [and] This being the case, we can have no resource but in a restriction of our trade, or in a resistance *vi & armis*. It is impossible to conceive of any other alternative."[85]

Then, Hamilton thoroughly discredited the Loyalist writer by informing the American people, "I can venture to assure you, the true writer of the pieces signed by A. W. Farmer, is not in reality a Farmer. He is some ministerial emissary, that has assumed the name to deceive you . . . to cheat you out of your liberty and property, to serve their own purposes. You would be disgrace to your ancestors. . . ."[86]

Like a veteran Parliamentarian in London or an experienced Philadelphia lawyer articulating a brilliant argument in an American courtroom, Hamilton saved the best argument for last. He warned of the dire consequences of the folly of not faithfully following the Continental Congress and giving it full support: "I caution you, again and again, to beware of the men who advise you to forsake the plain path, marked out for you by the Congress. They only mean to deceive and betray you. . . . If you join with the rest of America in the same common measure, you will be sure to preserve your liberties inviolate; but if you separate from them, and seek for redress alone, and unseconded, you will certainly fall a prey to your enemies, and repent your folly as long as you live."[87]

After his devastating literary attack on the previously successful Loyalist writer to win more supporters to America's cause not only in New York City but also across the land, Hamilton had then continued to make a distinguished name for himself among the patriots across America. As mentioned, he next wrote his "Remarks on the Quebec Bill" in a two-part assault on the Quebec Act on June 15 and June 22, 1775. Hoping to alert Americans of the dangers, Hamilton warned Americans of the evil British plot to subvert American liberties, denouncing "this act as an atrocious infraction on the rights of Englishmen."[88]

Clearly, all of these notable examples clearly proved that Washington had gained arguably the most brilliant young writer in America: the most valuable asset that a commander-in-chief could possibly possess in an unprecedented people's revolution against a monarch, that was also a civil war with Americans badly divided in loyalties. Therefore, unlike any member of Washington's staff, the politically and diplomatically minded Hamilton intimately "understood how the various governors, state officials, and Congressional delegates viewed the war" on every level, and knew how they should be dealt with in writing and in person.[89] Hamilton also continued to advise America's top political leaders not only upon how to most effectively conduct the war, but also what was needed for the creation and preservation of a truly efficient republican government.[90]

Most importantly and armed with seemingly endless insights of considerable merit, Hamilton also served as the commander-in-chief's invaluable point man on the most complex military and civilian affairs. After having replaced Harrison (and Tilghman to a lesser degree) as the most intimate staff member to Washington and in carrying the burden of the military secretarial responsibilities, politically related functions, and vital chief-of-staff duties, Hamilton had become a force to be reckoned with. He provided invaluable expertise as Washington's most trusted adviser well into early 1781, which was the year of decision because of victory at Yorktown. Washington hinted as much by writing how Hamilton was the primary and "most confidential aide" on his staff. One recent book correctly emphasized in its subtitle the importance of the Washington and Hamilton relationship that lasted for twenty-two years to shape the American nation like no other partnership: quite literally, the "Alliance that Forged America."[91] Consequently, like best friends and kindred spirits due to their undying faith in America and its promise, the "two were constantly together, whether in the office, at dinner, or riding with exuberance . . . through the countryside in the late afternoon" for recreation.[92]

The closeness of their relationship even developed a sort of conversational shorthand, because they saw eye-to-eye on so many things, especially in regard to the army and nationalism. Washington needed only to say a few words at a personal meeting with Hamilton, who seemed to possess prophetic and clairvoyant-like views about military strategy (even the war's ultimate outcome). Hamilton was able to then instantly address concerns and develop solutions with laser-like precision, and to begin writing lengthy letters that reflected Washington's way-of-thinking and requirements about the most complex matters: Most importantly, a situation that reaped good results and high dividends because of the polished yet forceful manner in which they were written. Hamilton presented the commander's thoughts in the most concise and graceful form for the proper execution of precise orders that were easily understood and acted upon without confusion, a contribution absolutely necessary for an efficient chain of command and a smooth functioning of a military machine imbued with too much democratic tendencies.

For instance, Hamilton was early tasked with writing a forceful, but tactful, letter in order not to alienate one of America's best fighting generals in order to get the best results, which required extreme care and delicacy. In keeping with Washington's strategic goals, Hamilton's objective was to discourage the overly ambitious General Benedict Arnold, known for his boldness and aggressiveness often to the point of recklessness, from attacking Newport, Rhode Island. Washington approved Hamilton's diplomatic letter to the mercurial Arnold, who was a true fighting general and one of America's best leaders but also perhaps the most sensitive senior officer in the Continental Army: "Unless your strength and circumstances be such that you can reasonably promise a *moral certainty* of succeeding [then] relinquish the [offensive] undertaking and confine yourself, in the main, to a defensive operation."[93]

As Washington's brilliant chief of staff who seemed to have all the answers, Hamilton's workload was excessive. However, the overall quality of his work never suffered, and even more responsibilities mounted over time. With a masterful style and in concise sentences that got to the point to emphasize the Virginian's wishes, he not only wrote Washington's correspondence in the general's name and composed his speeches, but also penned orders (diplomatic and polite wording but still sufficiently firm to get quick results) to generals, Congressmen, and other civilian leaders. Of course, what Hamilton wrote for Washington with such skill was approved by him, before the precisely written missive was dispatched by a mounted courier on his way to a subordinate or the Continental Congress at Philadelphia.[94]

To assist his chief of staff with his ever-increasing number of assignments, Washington had assigned Lieutenant Colonel Tench Tilghman as the recent immigrant's personal assistant. Hamilton and Tilghman were much alike in regard to tastes and inclinations. They were even eventually attracted to the same vivacious woman, whom the "Little Lion" married before the war's end. Just as Hamilton was Washington's right-hand man, so Tilghman became Hamilton's right-hand man: another perfect match that made the work at headquarters flow more smoothly. For more than four years, Tilghman served as Hamilton's "faithful assistant" to make his job easier, allowing the native West Indian to focus on more important matters that had been delegated to him by Washington. After watching Hamilton perform at his best and echoing the views of other staff members, Tilghman had nothing but lavish praise for the younger man from what he considered a foreign land. If the war had lasted longer, Tilghman admitted that he would have gladly served another five years beside and under Hamilton, which he considered a great honor.[95]

One American described the creation of a most dynamic and formidable team: "General Washington, versed as all great men are in the discovery of talents, and in the employment of them, made [Hamilton] at once his aid-de-camp and secretary, a post of eminent as important in the American army. From that time his correspondence with the French, which language he speaks and writes perfectly well, the details of every kind, political and military, entrusted to him developed those talents, the general had known how to discover, and put in activity; whilst the young soldier, by a prudence and secrecy still more beyond his age than his information, justified the confidence with which he was honoured."[96]

Paying another tribute, Robert Troup, an ex-college roommate from King's College who had served with Hamilton in the volunteer student company, summarized the importance of his friend's masterful prose that garnered results: "The pen of our army was held by Hamilton; and for dignity of manner, pith of matter, and elegance of style, General Washington's letters are unrivaled in military annals."[97]

Hamilton's unique blend of wise judgment, military instincts, and political astuteness ensured that he served as "Washington's most trusted advisor on matters both military and political [and] Washington wouldn't go into battle or even communicate with government officials about the needs of his army without first consulting Hamilton, and Hamilton usually replied with acumen far beyond his age and experience."[98]

But Hamilton was not an insufferable and arrogant know-it-all, who grated on nerves by boasting about his gifts and carelessly flaunted them in the face of others. He, of course, possessed a host of shortcomings like everyone else, but he knew to hide his deficiencies: a talent learned from his difficult and hard-luck days in the Caribbean, where wearing a mask was often necessary for survival.

But Hamilton possessed at least one limitation. To keep up with one of America's finest horsemen because Washington was physically fit and one of the finest riders in the Virginia Tidewater, Hamilton needed to improve in riding skills merely to ride by the side of Washington, especially on the battlefield. One of Washington's "family" who was frustrated in attempting to keep pace with the commander-in-chief's equestrian skills, that had been refined by longtime love of fox hunting across the fields and meadows of Fairfax County, Virginia, John Laurens requested of his wealthy father, who owned a large South Carolina plantation: "I am exceedingly in want of a vigorous steed that can gallop and leap well, not younger than four, but I would rather have him of six or seven years of age."[99]

Washington's military "family" was bound closely together not only by a lofty sense of duty and honor, but also the gentleman's code of conduct. As mentioned, the close-knit world of Washington's staff existed as an independent entity and distinct subculture in the secrecy of headquarters, operating apart from the rest of the army. More than he initially realized, Hamilton was fortunate in this regard, because he was relatively sheltered from the vicious backstabbing of army politics. This was an all-important consideration, because of the extent of Hamilton's talents and successes were sure to garner a great deal of jealousy and envy among high-ranking officers of less ability. In the insular world of Washington's headquarters, the opinionated, smart Hamilton, who boldly and freely spoke his mind, benefitted from a protective shield that sheltered him from older and less talented officers who were unable to rise as fast as this brilliant young man, who was still viewed by them as nothing more than an upstart foreigner. In this sense, Hamilton's military career benefitted from Washington's good graces that provided protection.

As this time, the typical Continental officer considered himself a proper gentleman who was superior, especially in moral terms, to non-gentlemen (lower ranks of society) in civilian and military society: Ironically, not unlike how the British viewed colonials in America. And only a proper gentleman of higher education and moral standing was considered best suited to lead men of a lower class on the battlefield. In a striking paradox, this class distinction dominated the thinking of the officer corps of both sides.[100]

Washington, from the upper echelon of planter class society, was bound by this strict moral code of a proper gentleman, including even in regard to having first taken command of the nascent American Army at Cambridge, Massachusetts, in the summer of 1775. As he had penned to Martha at Mount Vernon, "it was utterly out of my power to refuse this appointment without exposing my character to such censures, as would have reflected dishonour upon myself, and given pain to my friends [and] must have lessened me considerably in my own esteem."[101] Like Hamilton, Lieutenant Colonel John Laurens, born in Charleston, South Carolina, was awed by Washington and what he meant to America in symbolic, psychological, and moral terms, writing: "If ever there was a man in the world whose moderation and Patriotism fitted him for the command of a Republican Army" of homespun, idealistic revolutionaries.[102]

As a recent immigrant to America, Hamilton also possessed the rare advantage of remaining neutral and without the usual views tainted by emotion or petty provincialism in the sectional tensions that divided Washington's Army, the same regional and cultural fissure between North and South that was destined to lead to America's national nightmare from 1861–1865. Significantly, because Hamilton was not an overly proud son of any state and was not beset by local or regional prejudices, his overall perspectives in sensitive matters were never distorted by the pervasive narrow-focused sectional animosities that existed between North and South. This rare objectiveness from the young man also greatly benefitted Washington, who possessed a good many strong regional prejudices. And Hamilton was smart enough not to take sides in this ever-widening sectional divide that carried strong passions and ancient prejudices (not even Washington, a lifelong Virginia planter, was immune) of an irrational nature, because the staff was composed of men from North and South.

Benefitting from the rare luxury of a cool and calculated dispassion in regard to regional differences as in almost all matters, Hamilton had long deplored the seemingly endless regional prejudices and local rivalries (far stronger than the nascent American nationalism) that posed a grave danger to the unity of America's resistance effort and nascent nationalism. A disgusted Hamilton had lamented the folly of the destructive sectional rivalries in a November 26, 1775, letter to his friend and fellow Presbyterian John Jay, New York delegate to the Continental Congress: "Antipathies and prejudices have long subsisted between this province [New York] and New England [and] To this may be attributed a principal part of the disaffection now prevalent among us."[103]

Agreeing with Hamilton, an observant New England physician in the Continental Army, James Thacher, noted in his journal in September 1776 about "another evil of a very serious complexion [has developed]. Since the troops from the Southern states have been incorporated and associated in military duty with those from New England, a strong prejudice has assumed its unhappy influence, and drawn a line of distinction between them. Many of the officers from the South are gentlemen of education, and unaccustomed to that equality [classless without concerns from gentleman's upper-class ways] which prevails in New England [and the two groups] differing in manners and prejudices" led to deep animosity. Therefore, as Thacher recorded in his journal: "Hence we too frequently hear the burlesque epithet of *Yankee* [New Englanders] from one party [Southerners], and that of *Buck-skin* [Virginians], by way of retort, from the other," or New Englanders.[104]

Fortunately for Washington and happily for Hamilton, who hated these silly regional prejudices and "ancient animosities," in his own words, that threatened to sabotage the fragile national unity and the overall war effort, he was not a "Yankee" or a "Buckskin." Being a West Indian with a broad range of experiences with people from around the world now served Hamilton (and Washington in consequence) extremely well. Therefore, free of limitations imposed by sectional prejudices, provincialism, and a narrow-minded regionalism, Hamilton's open-mindedness allowed him to work smoothly not only with all members of Washington's staff, but also with military and civilian leaders regardless of their origins, class backgrounds, or where they resided.[105] Almost symbolically now that his boss was a Virginian who had fought on the western frontier during the French and Indian War, Hamilton's first uniform as the New York battery commander had been "buckskin breeches," like so many Virginians, especially the western Virginia riflemen of Washington's Army, with an accompanying blue military coat. But there was nothing traditionally Southern in Hamilton as Washington clearly noted by his manner, distinctive style, and talk that revealed his West Indies and more worldly background: perhaps another factor in his choice of Hamilton to serve on his staff.[106]

Along with his precocious worldliness and intelligence from a truly labyrinthine mind that impressed one and all, Hamilton's charm, refined manners, and sense of humor were factors that also cemented the divergent elements of Washington's staff for greater overly harmony, especially in high-stress and crucial situations. Most importantly, Hamilton's personal and professional qualities made Washington's staff more efficient and, most importantly, more professional. Thanks in no small part to all that he had to offer to Washington's staff as a dynamic leader in his own right, Hamilton created and led an efficient working body of highly capable men in the most challenging circumstances, especially during active campaigning and crisis situations.

Indeed, Hamilton's personality and high spirits also had a positive effect on Washington and the staff in general, making headquarters an overall better workplace under a commander who was extremely demanding and sometimes short tempered. For such reasons, not only Washington but also other staff members took a permanent shine on the native West Indian, and their admiration and respect for him never wavered. Indeed, most of all, "it was Hamilton, though, spouting his political views, telling stories, lampooning British politicians, and diving into every subject from literary criticism and haughty Philadelphia merchants [and he was] the charismatic figure at these parties, always encouraged by Washington. He, like the others, took great enjoyment in the stories and humor of Hamilton."[107]

Chapter III

Washington's Dependable Right-Hand Man

No single role embraced by Hamilton was either more important or timely than serving as Washington's chief of staff, in the modern sense, although that title did not officially exist in the American army of the 1770s. While this is now one of the most crucial positions in the United States military establishment, in Hamilton's day it was the first such position in the annals of the Continental Army. He set the bar high. Hamilton and his contributions transformed Washington's staff into a truly professional organization, making it more efficient, stable, and productive to meet the demands of a lengthy war of attrition. Because Washington had been forced to rely upon friends, prominent families, and political connections for choosing staff officers, he had long lacked a take-charge officer like Hamilton who was so unlike other staff members: An outsider with broad views that were more nationalistic than regional and whose position was not based on lofty social and political standing. Paradoxically, this outsider from what was considered a foreign land evolved into the ultimate insider of Washington's military "family" of promising officers. For his entire life, Hamilton had been looking for such an opportunity, because his role as Washington's chief of staff provided perhaps the best example of how not only the Continental Army but also this little military "family" was a true meritocracy: the environment in which he could truly excel on his own ideas and abilties.

As mentioned, one of the greatest misconceptions about the American Revolution—America's most mythical chapter—is that Washington operated alone in an isolated vacuum to orchestrate his army's complex operations and campaigns from his headquarters. In this sense, Washington's mythical and romantic image has cast a giant shadow, which has long obscured the importance of Hamilton's vital role and his vital contributions as Washington's right-hand man whose influence and role was far greater than long assumed. Clearly, Hamilton's rise had been as dramatic as it had been meteoric for a relatively little-known man who was not only the youngest member of Washington's staff, but also the most recent arrival to America's shores.

Natural in the creation of a nation's birth, the excessive glorification of Washington and his achievements in the annals of American history has long portrayed him as having practically won the revolutionary entirely on his own. Even one of America's leading Revolutionary War historians whose work has been masterful over the years, Thomas Fleming, has been guilty of perpetuating this popular myth. He concluded incorrectly in his 1963 book *Beat the Last Drum, The Siege of Yorktown 1781* how Washington "was always his own chief of staff."[1] But to be fair, Fleming is not to blame, because this misconception and popular assumption has existed since the American Revolution.

Because of his lofty "father of the country" status, this longtime assumption that Washington had no chief of staff has been routinely and widely accepted by generations of American historians. While this situation was more the case near the war's beginning when Washington first took command of the army at Cambridge, it ended not long after Hamilton's arrival at his Morristown headquarters on March 1, 1777. But what should be acknowledged is that Washington's genius was fully recognizing Hamilton's genius and to early delegate so many key responsibilities to the young man. During most of the revolutionary struggle, no one worked longer or made more significant contributions at the army's vibrant nerve center than Washington's most trusted confidant. As mentioned, Hamilton's specialty was the ability to excel at the most sensitive and delicate missions that required the highest level of well-honed diplomatic, interpersonal, and political skills that he possessed in abundance.

Above all, the breadth of Hamilton's skills were put to good use by Washington in solving some of his greatest problems, especially in crisis situations. Working behind the scenes in Washington's shadow, Hamilton made disproportionate contributions from beginning to end. Having the uncanny ability to literally "possess the Soul of the General" which was necessary to decipher exactly what was most required by him and then pass it along to others, Hamilton was essentially Washington's alter ego while holding "one of the highest offices in the land" as Washington's chief of staff.[2]

The Incomparable Berthier of the Continental Army

By way of historical comparison, a brilliant chief of staff was also one of the secrets of Napoleon Bonaparte's astonishing successes on battlefields across

Europe. Like Washington, Napoleon possessed the genius for surrounding himself with the best talent and most brilliant minds. Napoleon's campaigns unleashed massive armies that flowed smoothly with unprecedented precision and coordination over vast areas of Europe, especially in catching armies of opposing monarchs by surprise, thanks in part to the forgotten contributions of an expert staff, especially his invaluable chief of staff. The Napoleonic staff at all levels (army, division, and corps) was very large compared to American army staffs, which by contrast continued to remain small well into the nineteenth century, including on both sides during the Civil War. While the Napoleonic model for strategy and tactics was warmly embraced by American officers, especially during the Civil War, for generations, such was not the case in regard to the staff or the chief of staff role. All in all, this was an unfortunate development that long guaranteed that the American military was less professional and effective than its European counterparts across the continent.

No one (after Napoleon) was more responsible for Napoleon's remarkable string of successes year after year than the incomparable performance of his brilliant chief of staff who was without a peer in the nineteenth century, Louis Alexandre Berthier. He first served in his important role in the Army of Italy during Napoleon's Italian Campaign, where the young native Corsican, long-haired and slim in his early days, first made a name for himself as a gifted independent commander with brilliant tactical and strategic insight. Like Hamilton beginning in March 1777, Berthier, a former engineer of immense ability and son of an architect, made sure that Napoleon's staff functioned smoothly during the French emperor's most famous campaigns.[3]

Although Alexander the Great had benefitted by a general staff in his conquest of the Persian Empire in ancient times in marching his army beyond the limits of the known world and all the way to India, the modern roots of the General Staff and a Chief of Staff went back to the Prussian Army, when a group of chosen officers provided direct service to the King, the commander-in-chief. Then, in a development in regard to Washington that took place in the Continental Army after Hamilton's arrival on the first day of March 1777, it "was natural that [the Prussian monarch] should need such a staff, and should come to rely on the Chief of his General Staff as his principal operational assistant."[4]

However, Napoleon had been long recognized as the first commander to utilize a chief of staff on the modern sense, but this has been a misleading conclusion and simply not the case. In truth, it was Washington and not Napoleon who should rightly have this distinction. Leading the way and performing much like the incomparable Berthier, Hamilton served as the principal "driving force of the staff" and headquarters during most of Washington's tenure (nearly four years) as commander-in-chief.[5] In bestowing Hamilton with broad responsibilities and duties of extreme importance, Washington never regretted one of his best decisions of the war.[6] From beginning to end, Hamilton gave wise strategic council not only to Washington, but also to his top lieutenants, including General Nathanael Greene.[7] Therefore, whenever he faced a new dilemma and seemingly insurmountable problem (like the case of Berthier and Napoleon, who summonsed his chief of staff seventeen times one hectic night in 1809) the most commonly heard words year after year at Washington's headquarters were "Call Colonel Hamilton!"[8]

Because so many other Continental officers fawned upon him in the never-ending game of self-serving politics and personal advancement, Washington fully appreciated that Hamilton spoke with honesty and candor about anything and everything (except about his dark family past), making him an ideal trustworthy military and political advisor to a still novice general who was still learning on the job and often failed to receive the truth from subordinates who seemingly always sought to curry favor. Washington knew that he could always get the straight story and unvarnished truth from Hamilton, who freely spoke his mind and from the heart. As the Virginian realized, this was an amazing young man who could be trusted and depended upon without question. It was also a characteristic that would earn the young lieutenant colonel many enemies, because he was Washington's favorite which was the most coveted of positions. General Washington early realized that Hamilton, despite his ambition that he held in check to serve as the chief of staff, was not one who sought to win favor by saying what he thought the commander-in-chief wanted to hear like so many others.

Despite his increasing success as chief of staff that almost seemed impossible for someone in his early twenties to achieve, Hamilton still desired to win distinction by his own achievements on the field of strife. This passion continued to consume him, but his strong will kept it in check. Hamilton, therefore, remained focused solely on his daunting tasks at headquarters. Although he was outspoken on almost every subject, Hamilton was no flatterer—except toward attractive women—even when often surrounded by some of America's most revered men, who expected a respectful silence from one so young. . When he saw failings of policies or individuals at the highest levels, Hamilton freely spoke his mind, offering solutions to the most vexing governmental, military, and economic problems of a sensitive nature. This was a rare quality that had earlier seen the self-assured teenager even correctly criticizing his superior's questionable judgment and business decisions when he had successfully managed the firm's St. Croix business operations in Cruger's absence.[9]

Keen Strategic Insights

Besides possessing prophetic military insights and understanding tactical aspects of waging war, Hamilton also developed a keen strategic mind that was first revealed when he had boldly predicted that England could never win this war even before the conflict began at Lexington and Concord, Massachusetts. From gathering intelligence about his opponent, Hamilton's astute strategic sense and insights about General William Howe's intentions were revealed in his March 10, 1777, letter to General Alexander McDougall, the New York City radical and leader of the Sons of Liberty who had early fueled Hamilton's revolutionary zeal before the war, only days after he joined Washington's staff at Morristown: "It is greatly to be lamented that the present state of things does not admit of having the requisite number of troops at every post; on the contrary the most important, are deficient . . . but those posts must suffer which, from their situation ought only to be of a secondary attention. We have, I think, the most decisive evidence that the enemy's operations will be directed on this quarter; to this end they are drawing all their forces into the Jerseys, and as soon as the weather will permit 'tis expected they will move towards Philadelphia. Not being very numerous 'tis unlikely they should attempt such an object, without collecting their whole force; and for that reason 'tis not much to be appreciated they should make any stroke of the kind you mention."[10] As Hamilton's prophetic letter revealed, it is hard to imagine that such a keen strategic analysis was written by a mere youth, who was new to Washington's headquarters.

Because he advised Washington on some of the day's most complex and pressing matters, Hamilton also continued to pay close attention to political developments. Hamilton remained in the loop of politics at the highest levels during the winter and spring of 1777. From the Morristown encampment on May 19, 1777, he penned one penetrating letter to Gouverneur Morris, a respected delegate to New York's constitutional convention, in regard to the new state constitution of New York: "That there is a want of vigor in the executive, I believe will be found true. . . . On the whole . . . I think your Government far the best that we have yet seen, and capable of giving long and substantial happiness to the people."[11]

But Hamilton's insights were as astute in military as in political matters, especially on the eve of the new campaign. Waiting for the enemy's next move to initiate the 1777 spring campaign, Hamilton busily wrote a series of letters containing Washington's directives to his top lieutenants. On June 4, 1777, Hamilton wrote to Major General Benjamin Lincoln, at Middlebrook, New Jersey, to be ready for movement when ordered: "As the enemy appear from different Quarters to be in motion it is necessary that the army be in readiness to march [and] it is therefore ordered that the tents be immediately struck—the baggage and camp equipage loaded . . . and all the men [should be] ready to march at a moment's warning."[12]

During the early summer of 1777, Hamilton offered other strategic insights to Morris. Knowing that the army's survival was the primary strategic goal in a war of attrition against a superior opponent, he advised how the "liberties of America are an infinite stake. . . . We should not play a desperate game for it, or put it upon the issue of a single cast of the die. The loss of one general engagement may effectively ruin us, and it would certainly be folly to hazard it."[13]

A diehard nationalist who fully understood the potential of this new people's republic and America's promise, Hamilton's belief in the struggle for liberty never wavered, even when his spirits sank because of the loss of the revolutionary faith among many Americans, especially with so many Loyalists providing opposition. Hamilton reminded one general with the same ease with which he communicated with state governors, in order to emphasize what he considered to be the proper patriotic duty. America's revolutionaries struggled mightily against the odds because "our all is at stake [because] It is not a common contest we are engaged in."[14]

By July 1777, Hamilton finally found some time for long-neglected personal correspondence, including a letter to his old spiritual mentor from his St. Croix days, Reverend Hugh Knox. On July 1, he even described his entry into Washington's "family" with a sense of satisfaction to the good reverend who had been a key player in organizing the support behind Hamilton's journey to America and start of a new life, writing: "I found General Washington at Morris Town, and have been with him ever since."[15]

Hamilton also described the overall strategic situation to Reverend Knox. He revealed a solid understanding of the value of asymmetrical (guerrilla) warfare that mirrored his astute strategic and tactical insights first expressed as a King's College student: "There have been a number of trifling skirmishes [but] they served to harrass [*sic*], and waste away the enemy, and teach our men to look them in the face with confidence."[16] Hamilton's July 1, 1777, letter indicated that he had gained recent intelligence about his opponent just before the campaign's beginning. By this time, Washington and Hamilton embarked upon measures to prepare the army at Morristown for a movement to meet Howe's next maneuver. But even more revealing, Hamilton presented his insightful strategic view that was the secret to success: "Our own army is continually growing stronger in men and discipline. . . . We can maintain our present number . . . while the enemy must dwindle away; and at the end of the summer [of 1777] the disparity between us will be infinitely great, and facilitate any exertions that may be made to settle the business with them. . . . Our business then is to avoid a General engagement and waste the enemy away by constantly goading their sides, in a desultory way."[17]

A Professional Intelligence Network

Benefitting Washington in additional ways, Hamilton's abilities spilled over into other important areas, especially intelligence work, which long has been the most forgotten side of the American Revolution, because of its secrecy and the lack of primary documentation. With Hamilton now available at headquarters, Washington now had the right time and person to focus on creating an intelligence service. Washington had made his initial efforts to establish a spy network in February 1777 only a short time before the bright-eyed native West Indian arrived at headquarters.

Hamilton's arrival was most timely, because his personal New York City connections were invaluable in recruiting covert agents in the city, which now served as the center of British power in America. Of course, Hamilton knew the city and inhabitants far better than Washington, who specifically requested that Hamilton utilize the most capable and patriotic New Yorkers for covert activities. Therefore, he went to work in setting up a wide-reaching intelligence organization to get the edge on his more experienced opponent in the information war. Tapping into his New York City network, Hamilton began to recruit civilians, such as his old friend Hercules Mulligan and his brother, as well as the Culper Ring of covert agents, who provided a flow of information to Hamilton. Such intelligence allowed Hamilton early on to ascertain that the British were planning a mighty offensive effort in the spring targeting Philadelphia, America's capital.

Blessed with an analytic mind ideally suited for espionage, Hamilton developed acute detective-like instincts and skills that were tailor-made for the intelligence field, where he excelled. While Washington was not his own chief of staff as long assumed by traditional historians, he was more of his own chief of intelligence with Hamilton second-in-charge. But in time, Hamilton began to take over more of the burden during the ongoing intelligence war that was as crucial as battlefield showdowns. Relying upon his intelligence-gathering skills that had been first learned as a young officer in the French and Indian War, an experienced Washington had evolved into a master at the complicated covert game. Once again, Washington and Hamilton made an ideal team in working closely together. Hamilton often dealt with the most intimate details of spy operations, including even deciphering reports and letters from spies that were written in invisible ink. Despite his youth, Lieutenant Colonel Hamilton had no illusions about either the importance of or the serious nature of covert activities. Hamilton had received the British Captain John Montresor who was carrying a flag of truce and information about the lethality of this covert game. He first brought the news that Washington's spy Nathan Hale had been hanged in New York City before a crowd of gawking onlookers, including Montresor, who reported Hale's heroism in the face of death to Hamilton, on September 22, 1776.

With Washington managing a vast intelligence network with Hamilton, one historian concluded: "Washington particularly liked having his fearless young cavalrymen as intelligence officers [that] included Captain [Allen] McLane, Benjamin Tallmadge [the promising Long Island-born son of clergymen on both sides of the family, a Yale classmate of Nathan Hale, and former Continental light dragoon officer, who was destined to be appointed the head of Washington's intelligence network outside of headquarters in the summer of 1778], and Henry Lee. His aides Robert Hanson Harrison, John Laurens, and Alexander Hamilton, also became adept in the work."[18]

But as so often is the case in regard to the native West Indian's hidden contributions, this historian's words devalued Hamilton as Washington's top intelligence officer: resulting in part from the lack of information about these secret activities and Hamilton's desire not to take credit for his own achievements, including in the secretive intelligence field, while in part to maintain Washington's lofty symbolic image that was necessary for a successful resistance effort. In truth, Hamilton "handled much of the general's intelligence work," and far more than has been generally recognized by historians: another forgotten success story by the chief of staff. Ironically, one of the intelligence reports—dated March 10, 1777—read by Hamilton at headquarters, had been sent from another young, ambitious officer, Aaron Burr. Hamilton had almost certainly first met Burr in the summer of 1773, when he arrived fresh from St. Croix.[19]

Other intelligence reports destined to reach headquarters in the days ahead were forthcoming from Hamilton's old friend, the Irishman Hercules Mulligan, who operated as a subagent of the Culper Ring. He possessed a perfect cover as Hamilton fully realized, having married Elizabeth Sanders, the daughter of a British admiral. In his mid-thirties, Mulligan was energetic, resourceful, and intelligent: an ideal secret agent. Mulligan gathered intelligence while operating his popular tailor shop at 23 Queen Street (now 218 Pearl Street), which catered to the elite. Here, Loyalists and British officers freely spoke their minds, bragging about their upcoming military exploits, and revealing military secrets. Mulligan's brother Hugh, Jr., likewise gathered intelligence that was read by Hamilton with great interest.

But Hamilton's old friend Hercules from their Sons of Liberty days provided the lion's share of the intelligence that was delivered to Hamilton in person by his trusty slave Cato. Most importantly, because of Hamilton's past association with the Mulligan boys, their intelligence was guaranteed to be authentic, which came as a great comfort to Washington, because so few people in New York City could be trusted.[20]

Continuing to perform as a well-honed, dynamic team, Washington and Hamilton concocted a clever scheme to not only catch a British spy, but also to present a false impression (misinformation) to mask the army's paltry numbers at the Morristown winter encampment. All of this was calculated to fool the wily General Sir William Howe, the overall commander of British forces in North America. A wealthy philanthropist, attorney, and New York merchant who had relocated to Morristown to escape Loyalist persecution, Elias Boudinot had also served with Hamilton in the prisoner exchange negotiations. Destined to become the future president of the Continental Congress and an invaluable connection, he was Hamilton's friend and associate from a time of greater innocence, before the war.

Washington and Hamilton relied upon Boudinot "to coordinate intelligence activities" to a degree. He was a Presbyterian whose parents had migrated to America from the West Indies, and one of the first members of the American Bible Society. Like Hamilton, Boudinot believed that God had blessed America's cause. While spending a year in New Jersey, as a college student at the Elizabethtown Academy, and thanks to Reverend Hugh Knox's and Nicholas Cruger's efforts, Hamilton had stayed in the Boudinot home, known as the "Great House," distinguished by its elegance and mansard roof.

After departing for King's College and deeply affected by the death of Boudinot's pretty daughter Maria, who he had long fawned over in a familial setting, Hamilton could only express his deep feelings in writing. He had written a heartfelt poem on September 4, 1774. Still philosophical even when overwhelmed by his own emotions, he gently implored the grieving family to "weep Maria's fate no more; She's safe from all the storms of life." Washington's "Little Lion," whose heart was especially big toward children no doubt because of how he had suffered as a child, had a sentimental side that was masked by a dashing ladies' man façade.

At one point, Hamilton learned that a spy was reporting to Howe's headquarters about Washington's plans, which was a most disturbing intelligence leak obviously from an inside source. Therefore, at the Morristown encampment located just north of the Watchung Mountains, Washington wrote out a twelve-page bogus report, at Hamilton's urging, that detailed the army's strength by regiment. Most importantly, this report exaggerated the Continental Army's strength at Morristown from the actual number of around three thousand to an inflated total of twelve thousand troops. Then, with the spy present, Hamilton suddenly departed the room with the phony excuse of needing to search for additional papers. He of course conveniently left Washington's report sitting on his desk. Naturally, in Hamilton's absence, the spy closely scanned the "top secret" document. Therefore, the manpower figure—four times higher than the army's actual number—was later reported by the spy to Howe, who was completely taken in by the clever ruse.[21]

Additionally whenever Washington was absent from headquarters, Hamilton filled in to perform capably as the army's chief intelligence officer. Hamilton not only deciphered secret agent dispatches to learn of the most recent intelligence, but also acted upon them in a timely manner, especially in critical situations. In July 1780, while Washington was away from headquarters and after receiving new intelligence from covert asset Abraham Woodhull in New York City, Hamilton was alarmed by what he read from the latest report. Therefore, on the afternoon of July 21, he made the independent decision to immediately warn the commander, General Jean Baptiste Donatien de Vigneur, Comte de Rochambeau, of the French expeditionary force, that he had "just received advice . . . that the enemy are making an embarkation with which they menace the French fleet and army [because] fifty transports are said to have gone up the [Long Island] Sound to take in troops and proceed directly to Rhode Island."[22]

To gather and evaluate intelligence, Hamilton also personally interrogated New Jersey Loyalists who had been rounded up and brought to the Morristown headquarters. Relying upon his good judgment and laser-like ability to ascertain the truth, he determined "who were innocent or guilty of trivial offenses from those whose crimes were of a capital or heinous nature."[23]

Overall, Hamilton advocated less harsh measures than Washington, after separating fact from fiction (rumor in his case) like an experienced sleuth, adhering to the axiom that all suspects were innocent until proven guilty. Because of Hamilton's morally based penchant for fairness—seldom seen from angry patriotic Americans toward Loyalists in this increasingly bitter civil war, the board of inquiry bestowed true justice. The most serious offenders were sent to Governor William Livingston of New Jersey for punishment, while the board released (to Hamilton's satisfaction because he had deemed that they posed no threat) Loyalists who posed no threat. Reasoning like a fair-minded lawyer in advising against harsh measures because the confiscation of Tory property "is not recognizable by martial law," Hamilton's morality and sense of fair play, stemming in part from having been dealt with so unfairly by Danish law and his mother's vindictive first husband, were based upon his egalitarian conviction that the top priority should be "the least encroachment either upon the rights of citizen or of the magistrate."[24]

Meanwhile, the spring campaign of 1777 lingered on the horizon, offering new hopes to win America's independence on the battlefield. In what little spare time that was stolen away from his headquarters duties and like most healthy young men who wanted to demonstrate their manhood, the warmer weather fueled Hamilton's romantic side. Throughout the long winter in Morristown, Hamilton had enchanted Martha Washington and her circle of ladies—seemingly any female, almost regardless of age, who happened to come into his orbit. He enjoyed tea with ladies in Morristown, and very likely a good deal more with any attractive, young woman who allowed herself to be seduced with his sweet words and charm. Having seen the ardent Hamilton long in heated pursuit of female prey at headquarters' social events, Mrs. Washington considered Hamilton a love-minded tomcat, seemingly always on the prowl for ladies at night.[25]

With the refined charm of a true Creole from the West Indies, the swashbuckling ladies' man finally focused the main thrust of his romantic attentions on a single target not long after taking his new position at Washington's headquarters. A significant leap in social status enhanced the possibilities of a successful conquest of the heart of an old friend, the aristocratic daughter of New Jersey's first governor, William Livingston. While a student at the Elizabethtown Academy, Hamilton had first become enchanted with the seventeen-year-old lady and her Presbyterian upper class world, when he visited her father's home in Elizabethtown. But now, six years later, Hamilton possessed considerably more experience and knowledge about the ways of upper class American women of the aristocracy instead of the more common Caribbean girls of his past.

At Morristown, Hamilton openly flirted with Catherine "Kitty" Livingston, now age twenty-three, with his usual aggressive style softened by wit, humor, and well-chosen words. After she later asked Hamilton in a letter to send her information about the military and political situation, he had the audacity (in the typical Hamilton style of no-holds-barred) to pry open the door to what he hoped would be a romantic relationship with the attractive daughter of one of America's wealthiest men. In an April 11, 1777, letter that revealed his very forward intentions of a bedroom nature that he hoped might lead to marriage, Hamilton also displayed the rare blend of his refined sense of humor and well-honed seductive skills. He simultaneously boasted and teasingly warned "Lady Kitty" how, "you know, I am renowned for gallantry" with the ladies. Boldly offering to become the lover of a wealthy governor's daughter if she only agreed to embrace his ample charms while simultaneously answering her military-related questions, he emphasized how he "shall always be able to entertain you. . . . After knowing exactly your taste, and whether you are of a romantic, or discreet temper, as to love affairs, I will endeavor to regulate myself by it. . . . But amidst my amorous transports, let me not forget, that I am also to perform the part of a politician and intelligencer. . . . Of this, I am pretty confident, that the ensuing campaign will effectually put to death all their hopes; and establish the success of our cause beyond a doubt. You and I, as well as our neighbors, are deeply interested to pray for victory, and its necessary attendant peace."[26]

When Kitty replied to his April 11 letter, Hamilton passed it around to the other aides like a romantic trophy. This callousness (considered more so in the morally strict American religious-based culture rather than the much looser Caribbean value system of the tropics) also suggested that she might have had some mutual interest to Hamilton's rather indiscrete proposal. After all, a letter from a pretty governor's daughter, who had all the things coveted by a young man hoping to move fast up the social ladder and as high as possible, was something that was eagerly devoured by staff officers. As in the case of the ravishing "Kitty" Livingston, Hamilton's success with attractive women became as well known as his aggressiveness on the battlefield.

As he bragged his credo to Ms. Livingston in his response to her which displayed a bold facade of confidence, if not arrogance, that masked deep-seated insecurity from his dysfunctional past—and the complete antithesis of the privileged life of Kitty—"ALL FOR LOVE is my motto." Hamilton's written words revealed his playboy tendencies, which seemed to contradict his intellectualism and high-minded philosophical nature of this Renaissance man: "Phlegmatists may say I take too great a license at first setting out, and witlings may sneer and wonder how a man the least acquainted with the world should show so great facility in his confidences—to a lady."[27]

While Hamilton was writing his letter to pretty Kitty Livingston and dreaming about a romance that never evolved to his satisfaction, thriving instead in his fertile imagination, he also was eager to strike a blow at his adopted nation's invaders, who were dealing harshly with patriots, both soldiers and civilians, in the occupied areas. As he penned in an early summer 1777 letter that was decidedly moralistic and philosophical: "it is painful to leave a part of the inhabitants a prey to enemy depredations; and it is wounding to the feelings of a soldier, to see an enemy parading before him and daring him to fight which he is obliged to decline. But a part must be sacrificed to the whole, and passion must give way to reason."[28]

Hamilton and Washington's "family" received assistance near the end of June 1777, when Colonel Timothy Pickering arrived at headquarters, after accepting the adjutant general position on Washington's staff. Pickering was an aspiring Harvard College graduate from the cod fishing port of Salem, Massachusetts, located just north of Boston. Representing the fifth generation of his family in New England, he was also the son of a Congregational deacon who was a fiery abolitionist. Like Hamilton, Pickering was initially reluctant to join Washington's staff. He had greater familial responsibilities than Hamilton, including a wife, Becky White-Pickering, and son, John, at home. Unlike Hamilton who was the ultimate nationalist, Pickering had been initially lukewarm to the idea of America's independence. But now all of those doubts had vanished, and Pickering, in his early thirties and nearly ten years older than Hamilton, became another respected member of the "family."[29]

A Doomed Philadelphia

Hamilton had served in Washington's little military "family" for less than six months before the first serious threat to America's capital of Philadelphia emerged. As the top intelligence officer at headquarters after Washington, Hamilton sought to ascertain Howe's true strategic intentions from the flow of recent intelligence reports by the secret network of New York City spies, as well as British deserters from the New York City garrison. As early as March 10, 1777, and with seemingly prophetic insight, Hamilton already knew about Howe's next strategic move: "We have, I think, the most decisive evidence that the enemy's operations will be directed on this quarter [and Howe] will move towards Philadelphia."[30]

In an insightful letter to the New York Committee of Correspondence, he correctly advised how the British had targeted Philadelphia for capture, because of their "well-grounded rule in war to strike first at the capital towns and cities."[31] Therefore Hamilton repeatedly cautioned Washington to keep the army near Philadelphia to protect it instead of taking the tempting bait of clever British feints, or even more serious threats posed by Howe. Such British tactics were calculated to draw Washington away from America's capital and into the unfavorable tactical situation of a large-scale conventional battle on open ground, where the ill-trained and less-capable Continental Army could be destroyed.[32]

Hamilton was so confident about the wisdom of his strategic insights that he correctly informed the members of the New York Committee of Correspondence—who were alarmed by rumors that the British planned to advance up the Hudson to capture Albany—that Howe had Philadelphia in his sights and not Albany. On Saturday April 5, 1777, Hamilton presented his sound strategic-political reasoning based upon his own analysis and from what he had gathered from the intelligence that flowed into headquarters: "As to your apprehensions of an attempt up the North [Hudson] River I imagine you may discard any uneasiness on that score, though it will be at all times adviseable to be on the watch. . . . Philadelphia is an object calculated to strike and attract their attention. It has all along been the main source of supplies towards the war and the getting it into their possession would deprive us of a wheel we could very badly spare in the great political and military machine."[33] The aristocratic Lord Howe, who had led British troops in America during the French and Indian War and had an affinity for Americans in general, could not have said it better himself.

In a May 7, 1777, letter from Washington's Morristown headquarters, Hamilton took quill pen in hand to explain to the New York Committee of Correspondence how the British "will no doubt embark for some expedition by water . . . either . . . to Philadelphia or up the North [Hudson] River. . . . The testimony of every person, that comes from them, confirms this fact, that their horses are in such miserable condition as to render them incapable of any material operations by land [in a march up the Hudson for Albany and] I know not how it will be possible for them to penetrate any distance [north deeper into New York] in the Country."[34]

Tactical Maneuvers in New Jersey

Based in part on what Hamilton had ascertained from intelligence and his sound advice to ignore British feints up the Hudson, and march south to oppose Howe's main intention to advance on Philadelphia in overwhelming numbers, Washington moved the army south around twenty miles from Morristown to strong, elevated positions North of Middlebrook, in east-central New Jersey, on May 28, after crossing the Passaic River. Here, Washington established his army in a good defensive position, and ordered the digging of light defenses. From the fortified ridge of one of the chains of the Watchung Mountains south of Morristown, he could keep a closer watch on his opponent and perhaps even contest Howe's long-anticipated advance southwest toward Philadelphia, if a good tactical opportunity was suddenly presented. Situated only seven miles from the British outpost of Brunswick, New Jersey, Washington waited on tactical developments in an excellent defensive position.[35]

During the third week of June, Howe evacuated Brunswick. He then withdrew around a dozen miles slightly northeast to Perth Amboy, New Jersey, on Raritan Bay which the Raritan River entered. Based on accurate intelligence combined with his own strategic insights, Hamilton had already predicted and revealed Howe's next bold movement in his May 7 letter to the New York

Committee of Correspondence: "We have reason to suspect the enemy will soon evacuate Brunswick and push for Amboy."[36]

Sensing a possible tactical opportunity when Howe finally departed Brunswick as expected by Hamilton, Washington ordered his troops to advance into the sprawling farmlands of central New Jersey's plains east of the three Watchung Mountain chains. The experienced Howe, with a far larger army, planned to lay a tactical trap. Howe maneuvered on May 26 in the hope of cutting Washington off from the high ground of Middlebrook. However, as Hamilton advised, Washington withdrew west from the New Jersey lowlands rather than risk almost inevitable defeat if he had attempted to stand up against a seasoned general and thousands of well-trained professionals in an open field fight.

But Washington's hasty retreat back to the good defensive ground of Middlebrook caused the politically minded Hamilton more than usual concern. With his astute political sense, Hamilton knew that Washington had left himself open to political attack from the naysayers, including from Congress, by his withdrawal even before a vastly superior opponent. Therefore, in an attempt to nip the inevitable criticism in the bud and acting almost like Washington's guardian angel in protecting the commander-in-chief's reputation, Hamilton went to work in the art of damage control with his customary zeal. He wrote Robert R. Livingston, a respected New York politician of the Committee and graduate of King's College, to justify the strategic wisdom of Washington's retrograde movement on May 28. Hamilton praised the Virginian's tactical decision of not risking the army's life against a superior opponent, while placing the strategic situation in the proper historical and political perspective: "I know the comments that some people will make on our Fabian conduct. It will be imputed either to cowardice or to weakness: But the more discerning, I trust, will not find it difficult to conceive that it proceeds from the truest policy. . . . The liberties of America are an infinite stake. We should not play a desperate game for it or put it upon the issue of a single cast of the die. The loss of one general engagement may effectively ruin us, and it would certainly be folly to hazard it, unless our resources for keeping up an army were at an end, and some decisive blow was absolutely necessary; or unless our strength was so great as to give certainty of success. Neither is the case . . . Their affairs will be growing worse—our's better;—so that delay will ruin them. It will serve to perplex and fret them, and precipitate them into measures, that we can turn to good account. Our business then is to avoid a General engagement and waste the enemy away [and] in a desultory teazing [*sic*] way."[37]

With additional active campaigning in the spring 1777 campaign about to open, Washington and Hamilton busily made preparations for detailed troop movements, after securing as many new recruits as possible. On May 30, 1777, worried that Howe might attempt crossing the Delaware, Hamilton wrote to Captain Francis Grice, Assistant Deputy Quartermaster, to emphasize the timely importance of making "use of wagons" for "transporting the twelve boats you mention. The General expects it will be done with all possible dispatch, as it is absolutely necessary we should have all the boats we can collect at and about Coryel's ferry [twenty-five miles north of Trenton on the Delaware], in case we should want to make use of them. The General expected, that by this time, all the boats were removed from Trenton to Coryel's" Ferry, because they "may be serviceable to the Enemy, should they make a sudden push that way" to Trenton.[38]

On July 1, 1777, in a letter to Reverend Hugh Knox, Hamilton described the most recent military developments centered around the possession of Philadelphia, the primary bone of contention during the 1777 Campaign because of the political, military, and psychological importance of the capital: "On the 20th of June, the Campaign may be said to have opened by a general movement of the British army, to put into execution a project they had been preparing for all winter—the possessing themselves of Philadelphia. But they have been disappointed in this expectation. Our army was situated in a strong position on the heights of Middlebrook. . . . They manoeuvered [*sic*] a while . . . but finding they could not bring us to battle [and] that the country people [militia] were gathering with great spirit to reinforce us, . . . they were compelled to decamp [and then] return to their old" position.[39]

Howe's setback in unsuccessfully attempting to force Washington to engage in an open field fight in the New Jersey lowlands left Hamilton in a confident mood, anticipating positive developments for America's military fortunes. Compared to the losses and fiascos of 1776, Washington was now a much better general, thanks in part to more thorough intelligence analyzed and coordinated by Hamilton, and to his sage advice on seemingly all matters. Presenting his broad strategic analysis, Hamilton had earlier concluded his letter to Reverend Knox by emphasizing how he was "unable to form any conclusion satisfactory to my own judgment [but] I think they will hardly be mad enough to plunge again into that nest of Hornets, the Eastern States."[40]

Hamilton possessed ample good reason to gloat about Howe's thwarted New Jersey ambitions in his letter, because Washington had made the correct tactical moves. After a brief encounter known as the battle of Short Hills on the Scotch Plains on June 26, Howe had finally realized that no opportunity existed to destroy an increasingly wary Washington. The Virginian possessed the advantage of retiring to his strong position in the Watchung Mountains at Middlebrook, whenever threatened. An appropriate historical analogy revealed Hamilton's extensive knowledge of ancient Roman history and tactics. Roman leader Quintus Fabius Maximus had smartly withdrawn before the brilliant generalship of Hannibal and his North African army of multi-ethnic warriors, including blacks, in 217 BC to avoid a general engagement that might prove disastrous. As Hamilton emphasized in regard to a policy that he had believed was the true secret to success even when a student at King's College, Washington's decision to withdraw was tactically correct, earning him a reputation as "our American Fabius." A frustrated Howe retired all the way to the safety of Staten Island, after having failed to strike a decisive blow upon Washington's elusive army that was no longer easy prey.

"Gentleman Johnny" Burgoyne's Descent Toward Albany

Meanwhile, new strategic developments were taking shape far to the north near the Canadian border. Built in 1755 by the French with the most advanced European engineering skills of the day, the star-shaped bastion of Fort Ticonderoga, located in northern New York above Albany, was captured by British forces in early July 1777. British and Hessian forces, under Lieutenant General "Gentleman Johnny" Burgoyne, had placed cannon atop the hills surrounding the largest fortress in all North America, forcing the garrison's capitulation.

Having proudly worn a scarlet uniform since age fifteen, Burgoyne had also served as an indolent playboy member of Parliament. He even enjoyed connections to the upper class elite and King George III. Now it seemed like Albany—the vital supply base of America's northern army under General Philip Schuyler (Hamilton's future father-in-law who had no means of saving Fort Ticonderoga, but unfairly suffered severe criticism as if the fort's loss was all his fault)—might be threatened from the north by Burgoyne, who continued to advance south, and simultaneously by Howe, who could march north to meet this offensive from Canada. Even if Howe failed to advance north up the Hudson River, Fort Ticonderoga's fall opened up a strategic avenue for Burgoyne to push south all the way to New York City to isolate New England from the other states.

Therefore, Washington, Hamilton, and his headquarters staff needed to acquire additional intelligence to ascertain what exactly these new British movements meant to the overall strategic picture, while contemplating their next move to counter the most serious threat. The situation was crucial, because if Washington's main army was not immediately threatened by Howe, then the commander-in-chief could reinforce General Schuyler in the north against Burgoyne, who possessed an open land corridor south down the Hudson.

After Howe withdrew to Staten Island, Washington moved his headquarters to Smiths Clove in Orange County, New York. Washington worried that Burgoyne might link up with Howe to form a formidable concentration of military might that could deliver a knock-out blow to the Continental Army. From Smiths Clove, Hamilton wrote to Gouverneur Morris on July 22, 1777, about the latest strategic developments. Once again revealing his keen insight, Hamilton was prophetic in predicting that Burgoyne would meet with disaster if he advanced too far south parallel to the Hudson and deeper into New York's depths on his own and without adequate support: "I am doubtful whether Burgoigne [sic] will attempt to penetrate far, and whether he will not content himself with harassing our back [western frontier] settlements by parties assisted by the savages. . . . The doubt rises from some appearances that indicate a Southern movement of General Howes army, which, if it should really happen, will certainly be a barrier against any further impressions of Burgoigne [sic]; for it cannot be supposed he would be rash enough to plunge into the bosom of the Country, without an expectation of being met by General Howe. . . . I confess however that the appearances I allude to do not carry a full evidence in my mind; because . . . I cannot conceive upon what principle of common sense or military propriety Howe can be running away from Burgoigne [sic] to the Southward."[41]

Only two days before Hamilton wrote this prophetic letter to Morris, who served as a member of the New York Committee of Correspondence, General Howe ordered thousands of troops aboard a vast flotilla of more than two hundred eighty ships that filled New York harbor. Without Washington, Hamilton, or the "family" knowing what was happening in the next phase of the 1777 campaign, Howe's mighty armada sailed from Sandy Hook Bay that led out to the Atlantic on July 23.[42]

Ironically, the confusion at Washington's headquarters about Howe's next tactical move was less than the confusion at British headquarters. London's March 1777 strategic plan called for Howe to march north to meet Burgoyne, who was pushing south down the Hudson, after he captured Fort Ticonderoga: an excellent strategy calculated to sever the infant United States in two and deliver a death stroke the revolution with the timely unity of two strong forces. However, not adhering to London's ambitious strategic plan for the summer campaign in which Burgoyne played the leading role, Howe focused instead on capturing Philadelphia. Therefore and unknown to him, Burgoyne was now on his own in marching south along the Hudson toward Albany in "happy ignorance" of the systematic unraveling of London's strategic plan that seemed to promise decisive victory. Once again, Hamilton was prophetic and his strategic insight was right on target. He seriously doubted that Howe would make the smart strategic decision of moving north to link with Burgoyne instead of targeting Philadelphia, since the often feuding British military leaders "generally acted like fools."[43]

With Burgoyne's Army pushing south through northern New York without meeting opposition but moving at a leisurely pace, Hamilton began to grow increasingly worried about the overall strategic situation because of the lack of resistance, however. From the "Head Quarters Camp Near German Town," Pennsylvania, and about ten miles north of Philadelphia, on August 7, 1777, Hamilton wrote to Robert R. Livingston, a King's College graduate (Class of 1765) and former member of the Continental Congress: "I am with you exceedingly anxious for the Safety of your State" of New York.[44]

What now troubled Hamilton was the ease with which General Burgoyne's forces advanced steadily south through upstate New York with impunity. The people of New York had not rallied to meet the ever-growing threat. He feared that "the loss of [New York] would be a more affecting blow to America than any that could be struck by Mr. Howe to the southward." Hamilton expressed his growing concern because of "the panic in the army (I am afraid pretty high up) and the want of zeal in the Eastern States are the only alarming Considerations, for tho' Burgoine [*sic*] should be weak in numbers I suppose him, if the army Tumble at his name, & those who Command it ready to fly from the most defencible [*sic*] Ground at the Terror of small Scouting Parties of Indians, and, if to Crown the Whole the Eastern States go to Sleep & leave New York dismembered & Exhausted, as it is, to play the whole Game against a Skilful [*sic*] & Enterprising Antagonist; I say if that is to be the Case, we can look for nothing but Misfortune upon Misfortune, & Conquest without a blow."[45]

Lieutenant Colonel Hamilton's early warnings about Howe's ambitious designs on capturing America's capital were verified on August 22, when the British fleet of more than two hundred fifty ships was finally reported in the Chesapeake Bay and sailing north toward Philadelphia and not up the Hudson to assist Burgoyne. General Howe knew that by approaching Philadelphia from the south, he would force Washington to move out of a good defensive position and into the open, where he could be vanquished.

Meanwhile, Washington's Army had remained stationary during this period because Howe's intentions were not entirely clear. America's extensive intelligence network, including Hamilton's best efforts, faltered on this occasion, because the immense fleet and thousands of troops had simply disappeared from view and could not be tracked. After intelligence reports had reached headquarters that Howe's troops had boarded ships in New York harbor in early July, Washington could only wait on the next development. It had been generally assumed that Howe would proceed up the Hudson to link with Burgoyne.

With the new intelligence in August which confirmed that Philadelphia was Howe's true target, Washington and Hamilton now realized the elusive answer to the riddle. In consequence, Washington led his army from the Germantown area around thirty-five miles southwest to Wilmington, Delaware, to ease into a good position to protect Philadelphia on the south. Explaining why he had not entered Delaware Bay, Howe had decided not to risk running past the strong American forts positioned on the narrow Delaware River, which entered the head of Delaware Bay, below Philadelphia, and possibly losing ships from defensive obstacles sunk in the shallow waters. Instead, he had wisely chosen to advance overland on the America's capital, after leaving Chesapeake Bay, which paralleled Delaware Bay to the east. Consequently, Howe's Army of around eighteen thousand men poured ashore at Head of Elk Landing, in Maryland's northeastern corner and located at Chesapeake Bay's head, for the march on Philadelphia only around thirty-five miles to the northeast.

On September 1 from the commercial port of Wilmington, northeast of the Head of Elk Landing and located at the upper end of Delaware Bay, where Washington had established the army's encampment after having marched through the dusty streets of Philadelphia to a cheering populace, Hamilton wrote another letter to Governor Morris, who had long benefitted from his sage political and military advice. After having acquired intelligence about Howe's Army, Hamilton was perplexed by the lack of more vigorous movement (which he had long worried about) by Howe toward Philadelphia, although his army was encamped on Pennsylvania soil within easy striking distance of America's capital.

Perplexed by Howe's lack of aggressiveness, Hamilton expressed how Howe "still lies there in a state of inactivity; in a great measure I believe from the want of horses, to transport his baggage and stores. It seems he sailed [from Staten Island] with only about three weeks provendor and was six at sea. This has occasioned the death of a great number of his horses, and has made skeletons of the rest. He will be obliged to collect a supply from the neighboring country before he can move [on Philadelphia and] The enemy will have Philadelphia, if they dare make a bold push for it, unless we fight them a pretty general action."[46]

Hamilton's aggressive instincts had once again risen to the fore at a time when a more cautious Washington, hoping to avoid a showdown, still embraced his Fabian policy in the hope of wearing down the invaders and depriving them of supplies. But Hamilton, whose insights and instincts indicated that a good tactical opportunity existed, sensed that Howe might well be vulnerable at this time, after having ventured inland across unfamiliar country. He therefore believed that Howe could be caught by surprise and defeated by a sudden attack, because his army was in overall poor condition.

As Hamilton stressed in no uncertain terms in the same Monday September 1 letter to Morris, and revealed a bold tactical viewpoint that he had almost certainly mentioned earlier to Washington: "I opine we ought to do it [strike the stationary Howe], and that we shall beat them soundly if we do. The [Pennsylvania] Militia seem pretty generally stirring [to resist Howe]. Our army is in high health & spirits. We shall I hope have twice the enemy's numbers. I would not only fight them, but I would attack them; for I hold it an established maxim, that there is three to one in favour of the party attacking."[47]

In overall tactical terms, Lieutenant Colonel Hamilton was essentially correct in appreciating the possibility of benefitting from another Trenton-like strike to catch Howe—who was smug and complacent—because he would be caught by surprise, after his amphibious landing and long voyage by ship. While serving as Washington's chief of staff, Hamilton had his own mind (clearly, a most aggressive one) and a very keen strategic one—not only prophetic but also almost clairvoyant in regard to Burgoyne's and Howe's monumental strategic efforts in 1777 at that: A fact fully appreciated by Washington, who continued to benefit from what this young officer had to relate to him with clarity and confidence.

Confirmed by solid intelligence that had been corroborated, Hamilton's strategic and tactical sense continued to be right on-target to an amazing degree. Relying on experience and his readings of military history, he envisioned the unleashing of a surprise attack that might reap dramatic results because it was always best to strike a blow against an amphibious invader as close to the time of landing as possible before he gained additional strength, if Washington saw proper merit in such a possibility. An overconfident Howe was indeed vulnerable, while positioned in unfamiliar territory, far from his supply base of New York City, and encamped in an unfortified position without due caution. As mentioned, Hamilton correctly predicted that Burgoyne—whose "vanity [would evolve] into rashness," in his words—would meet with disaster, if he penetrated too far south from his logistical base (Canada) on his own, into the wilderness depths of upstate New York. In a classic case of divide and conquer, Hamilton fully realized that defeating or forcing Howe to retire would leave Burgoyne more vulnerable, ensuring that the two forces never linked to deliver a fatal blow.[48]

Most of all, Hamilton knew that twin blows delivered upon Burgoyne and Howe to thwart their uncoordinated ambitious designs might turn the tide of the revolutionary struggle. Besides his sound tactical and strategic insights, the foundation of Hamilton's natural aggressiveness lay in part in other often overlooked factors, including his strong religious faith and a sense of righteousness about America's cause. Hamilton waged war like a holy warrior and Crusader of old. In a wartime letter to Hamilton, Reverend Knox emphasized that America's fight was a "glorious struggle," and the native West Indian wholeheartedly agreed. For Hamilton and Knox and so many others, Presbyterianism was a key factor which additionally fueled the revolutionary faith that America was the Promised Land and a New Israel, which had been chosen by God for the benefit of a new people, the Americans.

Especially as a recent immigrant who had been remade by the American experience in only a remarkably short time, Hamilton was the very embodiment of not only the new warrior, but also the new man in America in a truly New World transformation. Appropriately in the land of so many immigrants, mostly from western Europe, that was larger than anything he had ever seen before which were two key factors that made America so unique, Hamilton had been reinvigorated by the American experience. With a righteous zeal of a true son of the Age of Enlightenment in defense of what was considered a Promised Land, Hamilton waged war against an opponent who represented the worst Old World abuses. Hamilton embraced the enlightened concepts of American exceptionalism like a holy shroud, because he knew that was indeed the case, after his dark childhood experiences in the West Indies.

When so small that he had to be "placed standing by her side upon a table," he had early learned about the Old Testament's moral laws of the ancient Hebrews from an elder Jewish female scholar on Nevis. At that time, he had even learned to recite the Decalogue in Hebrew. Hamilton believed that the blessings of liberty were a gift from God: the American people's true higher authority and certainly not the only too human autocrat King George III, as he had repeatedly emphasized in his prewar political writings to influence the colonists. Hamilton saw America as a blessed land with limitless possibilities and destined for future greatness, if the homespun revolutionaries under Washington could prevail in this war to save the golden and righteous vision of "a City upon a Hill," in the memorable 1630 words of Massachusetts governor John Winthrop.[49]

The same age as Hamilton, John Laurens, the idealistic South Carolinian who hailed from a wealthy upper class family that owned hundreds of slaves, served as a volunteer member of Washington's staff and made significant contributions. He was almost a mirror-image of Hamilton, not only with a youthful handsomeness and a lively personality, but also a similar hot temperament, dashing qualities, and hatred of slavery. They were bound together by an all-consuming passion in behalf of America's cause that they viewed as sacred. The two young men became the closest of friends, risking their lives side-by-side on the battlefield. Less of a master of his emotions than Hamilton, Laurens had first applied for an official position on Washington's staff on August 4, 1777. However, despite having only three staff officers serving in his military "family," Washington had inexplicably refused Laurens's request to join him.

Nevertheless, Washington needed the talented Laurens, whose sense of dedication, energy, and enthusiasm was boundless like Hamilton's. He was the well-educated son of South Carolina congressman, merchant, large planter, and the future president (the fifth in November 1777) of the Continental Congress, Henry Laurens. John was of French Huguenot heritage (like Hamilton's mother) like so many other patriots in not only South Carolina, where the lower Santee River country had early served as a Huguenot haven. Washington had then formally asked the young Southerner, in his early twenties, of so much promise to "become a Member of my Family."[50]

Therefore, Laurens first joined and served in Washington's staff as a volunteer aide-de-camp. He informed his father by letter how he desired either a "glorious Death, or the Triumph of the Cause" of America. Such words correctly made his father concerned about his son's attitude that guaranteed a daredevil recklessness on the battlefield. Laurens gained his official appointment to aide-de-camp on October 6, 1777.[51]

Brandywine Creek Defeat September 11

As the final showdown to confront the advance of Howe's Army loomed, the fighting spirit in Washington's Army was high in the spring and summer of 1777. The recent march of Washington's men through Philadelphia had been a festive event that heightened the army's morale and confidence: among the careful considerations that had convinced Hamilton that Howe could be attacked with success, before he neared Philadelphia. More than ten thousand Continental soldiers, wearing recently washed uniforms and sprigs of green in hats, had marched with disciplined step and pride through their nation's capital, while the crowds cheered wildly. Washington, Hamilton, and the common soldiers in the ranks also now fought under a new flag. The Second Continental Congress had recently passed the Flag Resolution on June 14, 1777, to create the truly first national flag, the earliest "Stars and Stripes."[52]

On September 10, Washington positioned his army in a lengthy north-south defensive line along the east bank of Brandywine Creek, located less than thirty miles southwest of Philadelphia and flowing into the Delaware at Wilmington to the southeast, before Howe's steady advance north toward the capital from the Head of Elk southwest of Wilmington and Philadelphia. Forced upon Washington who had no choice but to now attempt to defend the approach to Philadelphia for pressing strategic, political, and psychological reasons, the showdown between the two armies of about equal size was now inevitable. As usual, Washington hoped that Howe would rashly unleash frontal assaults as at Bunker Hill, but this rosy scenario lingered only as a fantasy.

Washington's defensive line on the Philadelphia side (east) of Brandywine Creek was over-extended for six miles in a north–south line along the creek's east bank to guard against a crossing by Howe's troops. Because of mounting political pressures from Congress and the populace to save the capital, Howe had correctly calculated that Washington would be forced to fight in the open in order to protect Philadelphia, providing him the long-awaited opportunity to destroy the Continental Army. The consummate professional, Howe correctly reasoned that Washington would not allow him to march north unopposed into the young nation's capital without a determined fight to appease Congress and the people of a new republic. Therefore, Washington had established his aforementioned defensive position.

When Washington mistakenly believed that Howe, because of highly effective tactical feint at the American center with a full third of his army, would attempt to cross Brandywine Creek at Chadd's Ford, he left himself vulnerable on his right flank on the north to a stealthy British flank movement to the northwest. Howe boldly divided his army, concluding that Washington was awaiting the frontal assaults that he would never unleash. Consequently, as if reading the Virginian's tactical mind, Howe knew that Washington would remain stationary, forfeiting the initiative and allowing him to maneuver at will. Consequently, on the afternoon of September 11, Howe led the largest part of his army on a march north up the creek's west bank. Attacking from the north, Earl Charles Cornwallis easily turned Washington's weak right flank, which seemed to dangle in mid-air. After a nearly fifteen-mile forced march north, and then crossing two little-known fords (Washington was unfamiliar with the region and the ford's locations), north of the lengthy lines of most American troops at Chadd's Ford, to the south, Cornwallis' flank movement around Washington's right was a brilliant tactical stroke, attempting to repeat his one-sided Long Island success.

With his right flank turned and after General John Sullivan, a hard-fighting Scotch-Irish general, had been victimized by Cornwallis' flank maneuver like at Long Island in late August 1776, an alarmed Washington, Hamilton, Laurens, and other staff members departed headquarters in a hurry and mounted up. With an escort of dragoons, they galloped to the crisis point to the north on the double. Leading the way, Washington's muscular charger easily leaped over one rail fence after another, and Hamilton and other staff officers followed suit in the wild ride. In this fast-paced crisis situation at the north, Washington and Hamilton did all that he could to rally the troops. Hamilton even reverted back to his old familiar role of a New York artillery captain to orchestrate the positioning of guns in a desperate effort to stem the tide. Hamilton then mounted his war horse, and rode down the line to inspire the shaky troops with raised saber, while shouting words of encouragement.

But all of the best efforts of Washington, Hamilton, Laurens, and the Marquis de Lafayette were to no avail. When Lafayette, only age twenty, was shot in the leg and fell from his horse, Hamilton rushed to his Gallic friend's aid. With the British advancing in overwhelming numbers in this collapsing sector north of Chadd's Ford, Hamilton pulled his young French friend, who had long enjoyed the native West Indian's fluency in French, to safety. Meanwhile, in keeping with his reputation, Laurens' recklessness and courage were displayed in full, and "it was not his fault that he was not killed or wounded," wrote an amazed Lafayette.

Clearly, as if a replay of the humiliating defeats around New York City in 1776, Washington became a victim of Howe's tactical masterpiece and abundant professional experience. With thousands of redcoats about to gain his rear behind his right to the north combined with renewed offensive pressure at Chadd's Ford on his center, Washington had no choice but to order his out-flanked army to retreat, which shortly became a rout. In the encroaching darkness of September 11 (one of the most humiliating days in the history of the Continental Army), Washington and Hamilton and other stunned staff members rode north toward Philadelphia amid the chaos of a routed army.

Although having been tactically befuddled by Howe's adroit maneuvering that caught him by surprise, and suffering about double the losses of the British as a consequence, Washington still remained in a defiant position between Howe and Philadelphia to safeguard the capital, after retiring to the northeast. Washington had been beaten, but his army remained intact to face the next challenge that was sure to come. Most importantly, Howe had been unable to deliver a knockout blow on the resilient Americans, despite the many tactical errors typical of amateurs in rebellion.[53]

For sound political and strategic reasons, an undaunted Washington was still determined to defend the new nation's capital. But his army was in overall bad shape after the humiliating Brandywine defeat and high losses. Not discouraged, Hamilton was still eager for any opportunity that might emerge to strike a blow and drive Howe away from Philadelphia. Most of all, he wanted to redeem America's tarnished honor and the army's reputation after the sharp setback. Meanwhile, Washington was forced to guard a lengthy stretch of the south bank of the Schuylkill River, the last natural barrier protecting the republic's capital, to keep Howe from crossing the river.

However, Washington was suddenly stunned to receive an urgent cavalry report at headquarters that redcoats were pushing toward Swede's Ford, where shallow waters and a rocky bottom made for an easy crossing of large numbers of troops, a half dozen miles northwest of Philadelphia. In the dark, Washington now needed precise intelligence about Howe's movements for any realistic chance of successfully defending America's capital. Was this a feint or the beginning of a full-scale assault?

As usual, Washington knew that he could depend upon Hamilton for providing him with an accurate and reliable report of the most recent tactical developments, when the existence of America's capital was at stake. Therefore, Washington ordered Lieutenant Colonel Hamilton, Captain Henry "Light-Horse Harry" Lee, and eight Virginia cavalrymen to immediately embark upon a risky mission to gather intelligence. Hamilton was also ordered to destroy the flour mills at Daverser's Ferry along the Schuylkill to deny provisions to Howe's Army. A resourceful and aggressive cavalryman of outstanding ability, Lee (the dashing father of General Robert Edward Lee, who was destined to engage in his own revolutionary struggle on behalf of still another republic and eighty-six years later targeted Philadelphia for capture at the zenith of the 1863 Gettysburg Campaign) was the right man—along with Hamilton—for this crucial mission upon which so much now depended.[54]

Hamilton's Narrow Escape

As the highest-ranking officer of the scouting party, Lieutenant Colonel Hamilton led his contingent of mounted men to the Schuylkill. Here, on September 18, Hamilton scouted along the tree-lined river bank before returning to Daverser's Ferry to destroy the flour mills. Hamilton had discovered that the "enemy are on the road to Sweedes [Swede's] ford, the main body about four miles from it." Then, while he and his men were torching the flour mills at Daverse's Ferry, Hamilton was caught by surprise by the sudden appearance of the British Army's advance. However, thinking ahead as usual, he had been sufficiently prudent to have tied up a flatboat on the riverbank just in case a hasty departure was needed. With the British dragoons drawing close, Hamilton and four comrades raced for the riverbank and jumped into the flatboat. They then cast off as quickly as possible, but the Britons were too close, and hurriedly gained the shoreline.[55] In Hamilton's words: "They sent a party this evening to Davesers ferry, which fired upon me and some others in crossing it, killed one man, wounded another, and disabled my horse."[56]

This was another close call for Hamilton, and even more precarious than he mentioned in his typical modesty. The British advance party consisted of elite cavalrymen, who knew how to efficiently kill and capture rebels, especially when they were isolated too far before the main army. Despite the fact that the fast-thinking Lee had drawn attention by riding away with his men in a different direction to bait the British dragoons into pursuit, Hamilton and several comrades found themselves in serious trouble. The river's current prevented a quick escape, leaving Hamilton and his men little more than sitting ducks to the line of dragoons along the riverbank. Consequently, Hamilton was only able to escape the volleys by diving from the flatboat and going underwater. As mentioned, one of Hamilton's oarsmen was killed and another fell wounded, while his horse was hit by close-range volleys fired from cavalry carbines that swept the flat-bottomed boat. Hamilton, a good swimmer, stayed underwater for so long that his comrades believed that he had drowned.

Hamilton, who had learned to swim when he had played in the Caribbean's waters as a youth, then swam across the wide Schuylkill under this hot fire, escaping to the Philadelphia side of the river. As Hamilton later penned on the evening of September 18: "They came on so suddenly that one [flat]boat was left adrift on the other side, which will of course fall into their hands and by the help of that they will get possession of another, which was abandoned by those who had the direction of it and left afloat, in spite of every thing that I could do to the contrary."[57]

Alarmed about the impending grim fate of members of Congress (hanging of rebel political leaders if captured) with enemy troops edging so close to Philadelphia, and without Washington able to stop the British from crossing the Schuylkill at Swede's Ford, Hamilton knew that he had to act fast. He was still wet and in an agitated state when he penned a hasty note to John Hancock, the president of the Continental Congress. With his political priorities foremost and fearing the worst, Hamilton knew that America could not afford to have Congressmen captured, tried, and executed like so many Irish rebels for centuries. From an express rider dispatched by Hamilton in a hurry to Philadelphia, Hancock received the lieutenant colonel's September 18 dispatch just after midnight on September 19. Hamilton's urgent warning stunned the wealthy merchant from Boston: "If Congress have not left Philadelphia, they ought to do it immediately without fail."[58]

Hamilton's warning was based on his existing knowledge of the strategic situation and revealed what he or any prudent leader would have done if commanding a highly efficient British Army to fully exploit the advantageous tactical advantage: "These two [captured] boats will convey fifty men across [the river] at a time so that in a few hours they may throw over a large party, perhaps sufficient to overmatch the [Pennsylvania] militia who may be between them and the city" of Philadelphia. Then, with political priorities foremost, Hamilton had also written about this crisis situation: "This renders the situation of Congress extremely precarious if they are not on their guard; my apprehensions for them are great, though it is not improbable they may not be realized."[59]

Knowing that Washington possessed no plan for a decisive stand-up battle to decide Philadelphia's fate if the larger and better-equipped British Army struck, Hamilton's warning was well-founded, because America's capital was vulnerable without protective defensive works and Washington possessed too few men. Therefore, out of necessity, members of Congress fled in an "undignified" manner for York, Pennsylvania, in the state's remote interior. Even Washington was panicked when Captain Lee reported that Hamilton had found a watery grave in the Schuylkill River. He assumed either that the young man could not swim or that the long amount of time underwater indicated that he had been shot. Consequently, when a water-logged Hamilton suddenly showed at Washington's headquarters in the early evening with a wry smile, a celebration erupted in honor of his miraculous escape and good fortune.

However, Hamilton had over-evaluated Howe's abilities. In the end, therefore, Hamilton's warning to Congress was actually premature and garnered criticism from John Adams who fled for his life, because Howe was hardly the aggressive commander as the young officer imagined, despite the golden tactical opportunity presented to him to now capture America's capital. Most importantly for political and psychological reasons that were all-important for an infant nation struggling to survive, Congress was alerted by Hamilton in time. Every Congressman had vacated Philadelphia by the evening of September 19. However, Howe ultimately marched up the Schuylkill away from the city instead of crossing the river as Hamilton expected, wasting more than a week before taking Philadelphia.[60]

With the British and Hessians now hovering near Philadelphia's suburbs, Washington and his headquarters staff worked overtime in a race against time. Because Philadelphia could not to be adequately defended, Washington understood that it was far more important for the army, which was now especially vulnerable after the Brandywine setback, to survive than the capital. Meanwhile,

Washington breathed a sigh of relief that Hamilton had not drowned, and immediately put his lucky chief of staff back to work with a challenging new assignment of importance.

On September 21, Washington ordered Hamilton on another urgent mission that called for "much delicacy and discretion," while giving him "extraordinary powers" at age twenty-two. He was directed to gather as many horses, supplies, and blankets from the Philadelphians, especially the many Tories whose presence made the mission dangerous for Hamilton with Howe's Army now so close to the doomed capital. Collecting such invaluable essentials would help Washington's ill-clad soldiers survive the upcoming winter, especially with the Congress and states having demonstrated an inability to properly fund and supply the army.

Of course, Washington hoped to keep as many horses as possible from falling into the hands of the British, who could then strengthen their cavalry arm to harass a Continental Army that was always short on horsemen who were needed to protect flanks and gather intelligence. Working fast, Hamilton directed Lieutenant Colonel Anthony Walton White, second in charge of the 4th Continental Light Dragoons and the senior officer who remained in a panicky Philadelphia, to round up horses in the city and from the surrounding area. To get the job done, Hamilton supervised around one hundred fifty followers, both infantrymen and cavalrymen. Displaying his humanitarianism even in a crisis situation, Hamilton was judicious and fair in his confiscations. He specified that the horses of poor people who depended on these animals for their livelihood (mostly farmers), horses ridden by transient people in Philadelphia, and those animals used by families fleeing the capital were not to be confiscated.

Lieutenant Colonel White was then directed by Hamilton to remove the collected horse herd to a safe location well beyond Howe's reach. For two days and empowered by Washington's full authority, Hamilton's energetic diligence and hard work allowed him to gather a large amount of much-needed supplies for the army's use this coming winter at Valley Forge, located just northwest of Philadelphia. This can-do young officer had everything, including invaluable munitions, placed aboard boats, which were then dispatched up the Delaware and far from the enemy's reach, while operating right under Howe's nose, when time was of the essence. Therefore, Howe would benefit relatively little in regard to gaining supplies as Philadelphia fell. Most importantly, what Hamilton had been gathered would be utilized by Washington's troops to help to fuel their next offensive operation, the upcoming attack on Germantown in early October 1777. But most of all, had Hamilton not excelled in this crucial mission, Washington feared that "the ruin of the army, and perhaps the ruin of America" might well have resulted.[61]

With insufficient troops and with Howe retaining all of the advantages, Washington had little, if any, real chance of saving Philadelphia, even if he desired. He prudently was not about to risk sacrificing the army—the heart and soul of America's increasingly fragile resistance effort—for a doomed city. On the afternoon of September 21, Howe maneuvered to within a dozen miles of the right of Washington's Army, which was positioned on the Schuylkill to block the next British move: an effective feint that Washington was forced to meet. Washington, therefore, made his anticipated counter move by directing troops to the right. But when night fell and with blazing campfires giving the impression of the night's encampment, Howe turned his army in the opposite direction and crossed over the Schuylkill at Swede's Ford, northwest of Philadelphia, on Washington's left. Thanks to another dazzling tactical maneuver for which Washington had no answer, thousands of redcoats, under the highly capable Cornwallis, then poured across the river without meeting opposition, sealing Philadelphia's fate as Hamilton had long feared.[62]

In a tactical triumph, about half of Howe's Army, with Lord Cornwallis leading the way in a resplendent uniform, marched into Philadelphia without opposition—America's ultimate humiliation—on September 26. Feisty men in Washington's ranks, including Hamilton, were disgruntled by the lack of a determined effort to stop Howe from capturing the capital. But Hamilton was wrong in this regard, with his heightened sense of American pride and nationalism dominating his usual sound reason for once. Most importantly, Washington's Army remained intact to fulfill the more pressing strategic objective in a lengthy war of attrition: simple survival to keep the flame of revolution alive, despite one setback after another. However, with a trick up his sleeve, Washington saw the possibility of a logistical opportunity. He envisioned laying siege to Howe's great prize of Philadelphia, which now had to be supplied over a long distance by water (up Delaware Bay and then the Delaware River), to eventually force the British Army out of the fallen capital.

Hamilton remained optimistic for future success. As he had earlier penned in a letter: "Our own army is continually growing stronger in men and discipline [and] we can maintain our present number . . . while the enemy must dwindle away; and at the end of the summer [1777] the disparity between us will be infinitely great, and facilitate any exertion that may be made to settle the business with them. . . . Our business then is to avoid a General engagement and waste the enemy away by constantly goading their sides, in a desultory way": an astute analysis and smart strategic plan.[63]

Attack on Germantown and the Chew Mansion

Hamilton and the other members of Washington's headquarters were exceptionally busy on October 3, after American fortunes turned for the better, despite Philadelphia's loss. Howe encountered a host of vexing resupply problems in occupying Philadelphia because Washington had blocked the main British route of resupply, the Delaware River. Additionally, reinforcements had recently reached Washington's encampment to swell the army's ranks. But most of all, Howe in his hubris of capturing America's capital and feeling that Washington's Army was impotent, had allowed his army to remain divided in two places, Philadelphia and Germantown, Pennsylvania, instead of concentrating his forces in Philadelphia.

Demonstrating tactical flexibility and almost certainly based partly on Hamilton's strategic and tactical advice about achieving another Trenton-like success, Washington switched over to the tactical offensive with a boldness that gave great credit to his generalship. Indeed, a good tactical opportunity existed, and Washington now audaciously sought to avenge his loss at Brandywine and the fall of America's capital. Even more, if Howe could be taken by surprise at his Germantown headquarters and an unexpected victory could be secured, then his decision to capture Philadelphia might still prove to be a great mistake.

With around eight thousand Continentals, under hard-fighting Generals John Sullivan and Nathanael Greene, and another three thousand militiamen who now benefited from the invaluable supplies that Hamilton had gathered from Philadelphia, Washington planned to deliver a hard-hitting "stroke" at dawn with four columns that were to strike just northwest of Philadelphia and overwhelm Germantown, situated just north of the Schuylkill River, and about half of Howe's Army, before going into winter quarters. Sensing a golden opportunity to suddenly reverse the war's fortunes like the ever-aggressive Hamilton, Washington targeted Howe's vulnerable position at Germantown with a slight advantage in numbers.

Spirits among the revolutionaries were soaring like late summer temperatures, because Washington had just announced that Burgoyne's Army had been defeated by General Gates and his top lieutenants (especially Generals Benedict Arnold and Daniel Morgan) in the depths of the upper Hudson Valley at Freeman's Farm, located near Saratoga, New York, on September 19. Washington also wanted to strike to ensure that the Germantown troops were not ordered by Howe to march north to reinforce Burgoyne, who was in serious trouble in upper New York State. However, Washington developed an overly complex battle-plan of unleashing four columns in a coordinated attack—simultaneously hitting the center and flanks that called for perfect timing to catch the idle Germantown troops by surprise at sunrise on October 4.

Washington's aggressive plan succeeded in the beginning, catching General Howe by surprise and striking hard. With fixed bayonets, the Americans surged through the thick ground fog of early morning, advancing southeast on both sides of the Germantown Road and parallel to the Schuylkill, just to the south, with discipline. A sight rarely seen and to Howe's utter shock, the British troops of Germantown's advanced outposts fled before the unexpected onslaught of the Americans, who swarmed onward with cheers that split the cool October air. An unnerved Howe ordered his troops to retreat before being overwhelmed by the surging American tide of confident troops. But the complexity of Washington's battle-plan and the lack of visibility in the dense fog resulted in confusion and ineffective piecemeal assaults. Washington's volunteer aide John Laurens, riding with Sullivan's advancing column in the center, was struck in the shoulder by a musket ball at the assault's onset. But the wound failed to diminish Lauren's ardor, and he continued to lead troops into the fray. Continuing to charge down both side of the Germantown Road, the onrushing Americans, animated and elated, nearly reached the center of Germantown.

Additional prisoners were scooped up by Washington's fast-moving men. A dramatic victory seemed all but assured until the unexpected happened. After Sullivan's troops had already passed by and pushed toward the center of town, a relative handful of determined Britons took shelter in the formidable mansion of Benjamin Chew (appropriately a loyalist), known as Cliveden. Located on the main road, that ran southeast, to Germantown and built in the 1760s, this imposing stone mansion was shortly transformed into a formidable defensive bastion. Doors and windows were barricaded by more than a hundred British soldiers of half a dozen companies of the 40th Regiment of Foot under a determined Lieutenant Colonel Thomas Musgrave.

Washington committed the tactical mistake of making a time-consuming attempt to reduce the two and a half story mansion by assault instead of pressing home their tactical advantage by continuing to push forward to retain the momentum by pursuing the retiring foe. Meanwhile, Laurens and Hamilton played key roles in organizing desperate attempts to capture the formidable structure filled with veteran redcoats, who blazed away at the attackers.

In a daring effort to torch the Chew Mansion to force the redcoat's surrender, Laurens was hit once again, but this time by a spent ball that struck his right shoulder. His uniform was pierced by other bullets that failed to stop the brave South Carolinian. Laurens' heroics and leadership ability in a key battlefield situation convinced Washington to shortly change his status from volunteer to permanent aide-de-camp. Likewise mounted and in the forefront as usual, Hamilton also had a number of close calls, but escaped injury in the hard-fought battle.[64]

Having learned timeless lessons of history going back to ancient times, the tactically astute Hamilton instinctively knew that it was a fundamental tactical mistake to halt the successful attack in an ill-advised attempt to reduce the formidable mansion. Along with other esteemed members of Washington's staff, Adjutant General Timothy Pickering and other officers, Hamilton immediately understood the extent of his serious tactical blunder. Therefore, they advocated for Washington to simply bypass the obstacle and leave a contingent of troops behind to deal with the Chew Mansion's surrounded defenders who were not going anywhere, while continuing to press the attack to exploit the tactical advantage and momentum.

But the Continental Army's usually wise artillery commander, General Henry Knox, had thought otherwise, and he had been right so often in the past. He had convinced Washington, who again demonstrated indecision in a key battlefield situation that frustrated more aggressive men like Pickering and Hamilton, that he could not afford to leave a defensive bastion in his rear. Washington had belatedly agreed with Knox (who was Hamilton's old commander and firm supporter since the 1776 New York Campaign) ensuring a waste of precious time while on the verge of an impressive success.[65]

Lieutenant Colonel Hamilton's worst fears were confirmed when British troops rallied, after having been allowed a respite. Washington was forced to retreat before noon because of the squandered tactical opportunity, while the bullet-riddled Chew Mansion stood unvanquished and at least seventy-five fallen Americans—a waste of valor and sacrifice—lay around the stone structure, which was impervious even to cannonballs. Like other staff officers, Hamilton had a number of close calls. As Tench Tilghman, commissioned lieutenant colonel since April, wrote in an October 6, 1777 letter to his father about the price paid among Hamilton's closest associates: "two of the Generals family are wounded. Mr. [John] Lawrens [Laurens] of [South] Carolina slight and Mr. Smith of Virginia his leg broke."[66]

Filled with regrets over wasting so much precious time and American lives for nothing, a frustrated Hamilton also blamed the defeat on the "hazy weather," because the fog had early proved to be "a fatal disadvantage" to the attackers' momentum. But the bulldog tenacity of the experienced Britons, especially at the embattled Chew Mansion, had also played a significant role in thwarting Washington's ambitions at Germantown.[67]

After Washington's tactical plan went awry, winter quarters beckoned the Continental Army. Just as during the offensive thrust at Germantown that benefitted from supplies recently collected in the nation's capital, Hamilton's supply of blankets gathered immediately before Philadelphia's fall provided a God-send at the army's winter quarters at Valley Forge which was established on December 19, 1777, as Washington had envisioned. The crucial nature of Hamilton's mission and his success continued to be readily apparent, paying impressive dividends to the army that received so little support from Congress and the states.

The bitter cold winter of 1777–1778 ended campaigning in the tradition of eighteenth century warfare. With the British and Hessians remaining quiet due to harsher weather, Washington now took the opportunity to finally to take necessary measures against a troublesome hidden enemy of America's often-forgotten civil war behind the lines, the Loyalists. The threat to his stationary army at Valley Forge was only too real because so many Loyalists denied Washington supplies, especially clothing and invaluable foodstuffs. Of course, they wanted to sell to the British because of the inflated value of Continental currency. A good many Tories also served as spies, informing the British of the Continental Army's dismal condition and other vulnerabilities. Therefore, Washington was forced to take action to "cleanse" the Morristown area of Tories, who played a role in jeopardizing the Continental Army's survival. First, on January 25, 1778, Washington ordered those inhabitants who had sworn loyalty to the Crown to report to his Valley Forge headquarters near the Schuylkill River, that flowed just to the north, and take an American loyalty oath. Individuals who refused to do so were to be transported into the British lines, officially becoming America's enemies in what was as much of a civil war as a revolution.

Washington was rightly concerned that his harshest directives might be used against him by his political enemies in Congress, who were just waiting for an opportunity to pounce, or by the British as effective propaganda. Therefore, Hamilton served as the author who officially sent out Washington's harsh orders (signed by Hamilton) to military and political authorities. Issued from headquarters located just east of Valley Creek and at the end of the Valley Creek Road, these sterner directives allowed Washington to appear less vindictive to his fellow Americans. Given the green light by Washington, Hamilton ordered harsh measures to cow the Loyalists as a last-ditch solution to a festering problem. Although an idealist and romantic, Hamilton was also tough-minded and no-nonsense when necessary. Of course, these were much-needed stern qualities in wartime, especially a revolution, which allowed Hamilton to often make hard but necessary decisions, especially when the lives of the army and nation were at stake.

In his letter to the New York Committee of Correspondence in Congress, Hamilton advocated a policy to deter additional Americans from becoming active Loyalists: "An execution or two [hanging in a public display], by way of example, would strike terror, and powerfully discourage the wicked practices going on."[68] Caught in the midst of a festering civil war that grew increasingly ugly, Hamilton realized that time was of the essence to purge this strategic area of an omnipresent threat on not only the military, but also the political front. He directed New Jersey's Presbyterian governor, William Livingston, with an air of authority which gave no hint that he was still a relatively low-ranking Continental officer only in his mid-twenties: "It is the ardent wish of His Excellency that no delay might be used in making examples of some of the most atrocious offenders."[69] Just as he was Washington's "trouble-shooter" in all-important matters at headquarters that was located north and northwest of the army's sprawling encampment, Hamilton now "saw the war through the general's eyes," and acted with swift efficiency to solve problems that seemed to offer no solution.[70]

Simultaneously, Hamilton also continued to advise some of America's top politicians and offer solutions to vexing problems. For good reason, he early criticized the weaknesses of New York's new state constitution to the very highly placed men who had created the document, and without asking for his opinion. The egalitarian-minded young man advocated for a more "representative democracy, where the right of election is well-secured and regulated, and the exercise of the legislative, executive and judiciary authorities is vested in select persons, chosen *really* and *nominally* by the people, will in my opinion likely to be happy, regular and durable."[71]

Hamilton saved his greater vehemence for the incompetent and impotent Continental Congress, which possessed no power over the states, yet were responsible for raising and supplying their troops, in failing to effectively manage the war effort: a guarantee that the army continued to suffer from the lack of everything except courage and spunk. In a letter to John Laurens—without exaggeration and with his trademark satirical wit—Hamilton denounced the representative body that caused so much misery to the army's common soldiers, who faithfully fought and died for a fragmented country that had seemingly turned its back on them for selfish reasons: "three-fourths of members of Congress were mortal enemies of talent and three-fourths of the remainder had only contempt for integrity."[72]

Dramatic Victory at Saratoga

Meanwhile, the war significantly changed in the way that Hamilton had predicted, with Burgoyne acting too rashly by over-committing and advancing too far south toward Albany, and that Howe would fail to advance north to meet him. Ironically, few British campaigns in this war had begun so promising, but Hamilton knew better. Located at the south end of Lake Champlain and as mentioned, Fort Ticonderoga had been captured by Burgoyne in early July 1777, after gaining possession of the heights that dominated the masonry fortress.

However, Hamilton was not discouraged by the loss of the mightiest defensive bastion in North America, and only saw this victory as opening the door to an important American success in the future. In consequence, Hamilton had sought to lift the morale of some of America's faint-hearted political leaders who lacked resolve in the face of this new crisis. In a July 13, 1777, letter to his friend John Jay, the upbeat Hamilton wrote, "All is [now] dark beyond conjecture. But we must not be discouraged at a misfortune" even of this magnitude.[73]

Hamilton had little time to bask in his summer successes. In the recent Philadelphia Campaign, for instance, Hamilton had also served as Washington's top diplomat to Congress, where he had good connections, especially the New York Committee of Correspondence. When Washington had been unsure of Howe's opaque intentions, he had finally decided to march north from his Bucks

County, Pennsylvania, headquarters on August 21, after concluding incorrectly that Howe's true objective was to link with Burgoyne. However, a march north into New York would have left Philadelphia vulnerable. Washington had been concerned about the reaction of a nervous Congress. Therefore, he had once again relied upon Hamilton.

The young man from the West Indies had ridden south on a special mission to Congress, carrying Washington's letter of explanation for departing the Philadelphia area. The letter and Hamilton's salesmanship and persuasive ways had accomplished the trick. Congress had allowed Washington to do as he pleased. However, the plan to move north shortly fell apart with startling news that the British fleet was seen located off the New Jersey coast and heading south. Washington's plan then had to be cancelled.

By this time, Lieutenant Colonel Hamilton was gaining recognition by both Washington's friends and enemies who were seeing the significant influence the young man had upon the most important revolutionary leader in the land, an unprecedented and rather remarkable development in itself. In fact, one of Pennsylvania's Congressmen, Benjamin Rush, voiced concern that Washington was being "governed by General Greene, General Knox, and [Lieutenant] Colonel Hamilton, one of his aides, a young man of twenty-one years."[74]

The ambitious plan of Lord George Germain, King George III's American Secretary, to split the colonies (now states) in two had completely fallen apart at this time, as Hamilton had boldly predicted long before. When Howe had made his decision to turn his sights on Philadelphia instead of marching north up the Hudson to link with Burgoyne, "Gentleman Johnny" was stranded on his own amid the untamed New York wilderness. Burgoyne's skills in polite society and having composed his popular London play *The Maid of the Oaks* could not stop thousands of resurgent rebels, especially New Englanders who realized that the enemy's intent was to sever their region from the rest of the colonies. One of Washington's wisest decisions had been to reinforce the northern army with two of the hardest-fighting officers in America, Generals Benedict Arnold and Daniel Morgan. Thanks to the efforts of these two fine leaders, Major General Horatio Gates, who had survived (like Washington) the Braddock fiasco in the Ohio country in July 1755, became an American hero for the victory at Saratoga, although he had been born in England. After having replaced General Schuyler in command of the army's Northern Department, because of the political backlash for Fort Ticonderoga's loss that was at no fault of his own, a mixture of luck and fate allowed "Granny Gates" to win a decisive victory at Saratoga. General Burgoyne surrendered nearly six thousand British, Hessians, and Loyalists in a grassy meadow located on the Hudson's west bank on October 17, 1777, to Americans, whom he had once viewed as "our child[ren]".[75]

Lieutenant Colonel Hamilton was simultaneously cheered by the joyous news of Saratoga and Laurens' official appointment to the "family." At long last and as mentioned, John Laurens, who had been serving as a volunteer aide on Washington's staff since August and was Hamilton's best friend by this time, received his official appointment to the staff on October 6, 1777. Washington's general orders on this day specified that Laurens was "now appointed Aid de Camp [and he] is to be respected and obeyed as such."[76]

Special Mission of Importance to the Northern Army

Hamilton continued to be Washington's invaluable "trouble-shooter," who could seemingly do the impossible, especially when the chances for success were especially slim.[77] In still another solid vote of confidence by relying on the native West Indian's seemingly limitless "political acumen," Washington dispatched Hamilton on a special mission to Albany at the end of November not long after the battle of Germantown. Based on the recent decision made by Washington's council of war, that additional troops were needed to bolster his thinned ranks of Washington's Army for future operations before winter, the young man now became Washington's personal emissary.

However, this was a "thankless [if not impossible] assignment," because the victorious Gates was known for his arrogance and intransigence. Hamilton, the youngest but most gifted and trusted staff member, was assigned to make the attempt to somehow pry "a very considerable part" (three brigades) of Gates' force to provide much-needed reinforcements to Washington's Army around Philadelphia, weakened by he expiration of one-year enlistments.[78]

But in choosing Hamilton for this key assignment, Washington seemed to have forgotten something significant that involved both personal and political considerations: that he had given Hamilton one of his first assignments in March, which had been "to upbraid [Gates] for failing to keep track of" men joining the army to collect a nice bonus and those men would then desert to reenlist in order to secure still another lucrative bounty. In addition, Gates had replaced the New Yorker General Schuyler by artful political maneuvering and gained the support of Congress to remove the Northern Department's commander. Ever-the-politician, Hamilton was solidly in the New York and Schuyler camp. Therefore, Hamilton and Gates were natural enemies on the political front that was as heated as any battlefield front. Under the circumstances, Hamilton's mission to the north seemed doomed to almost certain failure. However, Washington knew that if anyone could succeed, it was his can-do chief of staff.[79]

With Washington's army weak and his reputation sagging after the general's twin setbacks at Brandywine and Germantown, the young man was directed to embark upon the lengthy journey from Washington's headquarters near White Marsh, Pennsylvania, to Albany, New York, to meet with the celebrated victor of Saratoga. Hamilton's assignment was also especially challenging, because Gates' ego (already outsized to begin with long before Saratoga) had been even more inflated by his recent Saratoga success, and his desire to eventually replace Washington. Gates was now at the height of popularity across America.

Ironically, Washington had dispatched some of his finest troops to play a key role Gates' dramatic October victory at Saratoga, and now Washington wanted them back. Preparing the "Hero of Saratoga" for the arrival of Hamilton who was authorized to act as his proxy despite having only a lieutenant colonel's rank, Washington informed Gates on October 30: "I have, by the advice of my Genl Officers, One of my aids, to lay before you a full state of our situation, and that of the Enemy in this Quarter. He is well informed upon the subject, and will deliver my Sentiments upon the plan of Operations, that is now necessary to be pursued [and] From Colo. Hamilton you will have a clear and comprehensive view of things. . . ."[80]

Gates was now America's latest hero, which placed Washington, the old hero of Trenton and Princeton, in the shadow of this English-born general, including in the eyes of many in Congress: another paradox of the overall situation. To guarantee an even more difficult mission for Hamilton, the transplanted Briton was brazenly contemptuous toward Washington, whom he had deemed unworthy to command America's armies. Gates was so arrogant that he had dispatched his official report announcing his Saratoga victory—the most important American success to date for opening the door to foreign intervention from France and Spain—to Congress instead of his military superior, Washington.

Therefore, an incredulous Washington had only belatedly learned of the Saratoga victory from New Englander General Israel Putnam. As if to return the insult that had stung him deeply, Washington had dispatched only a lieutenant colonel on this mission instead of a senior officer, which was normal under military protocol: A fact well known to Gates, who had once served in the British Army. Clearly, Hamilton was at a serious disadvantage for a good many reasons in part because he was now unable to communicate with Washington for new instructions. On his own, Hamilton would have to rely upon all of the tact, cleverness, and diplomatic skill that he could muster to succeed in Washington's vital mission.

On October 30, Hamilton began his journey of almost two hundred thrity-five miles north from Washington's headquarters to Albany. No ordinary endeavor, this was one of Hamilton's most critical and delicate missions of supreme importance. Therefore, Washington granted an inordinate amount of latitude and flexibility. Despite the obstacles, Washington knew that Hamilton, ever the psychologist and analytical genius, at least had a chance to succeed. In a war that was as much political as military, Washington needed to secure a victory in an offensive against Howe to get back into the good graces of Congress and a fickle populace. He was hoping to accomplish against the over-confident British aristocrat what Gates had achieved against Burgoyne, because he was increasingly politically vulnerable without additional laurels. After all, Gates would never have won at Saratoga had not Washington reinforced his army, including with the highly capable General Daniel Morgan. But this fact was of no concern to General Gates.[81]

On the cold day of November 5, with Captain Caleb Gibbs and a small escort of Washington's Life Guards, Hamilton finally reached Gates' headquarters at Albany, after riding around fifty miles a day for five consecutive days. Here, the northern army was encamped in upper New York after the surrender of Burgoyne's entire army. Before reaching Albany, he had stopped at Fishkill, New York, near the Hudson's east bank, and requested that General Israel Putnam hurry two Continental brigades south to reinforce Washington's Army, while also securing a promise from the seasoned New Englander that seven hundred New Jersey militiamen would follow. To assist him in his Albany mission and bestow a measure of authority to the young man, Hamilton now carried the October 30, 1777, letter (tactfully composed by him) from Washington to Gates. In part, the letter read: "I cannot but regret, that a matter of such magnitude and so interesting [decisive victory at Saratoga] in our General Operations, should have reached me" [Washington] from a source other than General Gates, which went against proper military protocol.[82]

However, because the situation was so delicate and complex on multiple levels, Lieutenant Colonel Hamilton needed to first carefully ascertain the exact military situation in New York to determine if General Gates planned to truly utilize the troops for some good purpose or just wanted to willfully withhold his good troops from Washington for purely selfish reasons. If Gates possessed a promising strategic plan, then Hamilton would not make a forceful demand. But if he determined that Gates was selfishly holding troops for himself just to diminish Washington's future chances for success, then Hamilton would attempt to obtain the much-needed reinforcements of three brigades with a stern demand. Hamilton knew that if he was too aggressive then the aristocratic Gates, who was sure to be irritated by a young upstart making demands, would complain loudly to a sympathetic Congress, now literally in the palm of his hand, and cause "serious" difficulties for Washington.

Under these challenging and sensitive circumstances, Washington's orders were so generally vague that Hamilton possessed maximum flexibility to do what he determined was best depending upon the existing situation he faced. Far from Washington's headquarters, the relatively recent immigrant who was less than half General Gates' age was now on his own. Hamilton was determined to fulfill his crucial mission to the best of his ability, however, he would have to first precisely ascertain the overall situation with great care and then make the proper decision based on what he learned firsthand to be true rather than what Gates told him. Quite simply, he would have to determine if it would be best to demand the three brigades that Washington needed or just obtain whatever Gates decided to give him.[83]

At Gates' headquarters, the showdown began between two strong-willed men not born in America and who had known the social sting of illegitimacy, young Hamilton and the gray-haired "Granny Gates." Knowing the wisdom of not pressing too hard to secure the three brigades that Washington desired, Hamilton initially employed a delicate and diplomatic touch. Naturally, Gates first indicated that he could spare none of the three brigades desired by Washington on the premise that Howe might still advance north up the Hudson to sever New England from the rest of the United States (General Burgoyne's old plan), or that he planned to take the offensive. Then, out of necessary, Hamilton applied a firmer touch, emphasizing that Washington needed manpower if Howe attacked.

Gates told Hamilton that he could spare only one brigade, the Massachusetts infantry regiments under Connecticut-born General John Paterson. However,

Hamilton knew better than to now forcefully press for all three brigades with Washington's full authority in such a delicate political-military situation, because of Gates' excessive sensitivity over this issue and his many supporters in Congress. Before leaving headquarters, Hamilton employed "every argument in my power to convince him of the propriety" of sending the brigades for the overall good of the country.

To assist Washington, Hamilton was determined not to take no for an answer. After the meeting, he then went to work, launching his own personal investigation and gaining new information like an experienced detective. What he discovered raised his ire. Hamilton now realized that he had been misled (he believed deliberately lied to and tricked) by the experienced politician-general, because the young man was not aware of either the condition or strength of the northern army's units in the faraway Northern Department.

It turned out that a conniving General Gates had taken full advantage of Hamilton's lack of information as well as his routine expectation of proper gentlemanly behavior. From his investigation, Hamilton learned that Paterson's brigade, which Gates offered, was in overall poor condition and was severely undermanned. With a strength of barely six hundred Massachusetts men, adding Paterson's brigade would do Washington relatively little, if any, good. Hamilton also discovered the true situation that the veteran troops and leaders who Washington needed were not to be utilized by Gates in any offensive operation. It became clear that Gates had no plan of action, and that he just wanted to withhold them from his commander-in-chief. Angered by the cynical deception, Hamilton immediately sat down to write an indignant letter to Gates on the evening of November 5, despite his weariness from the long journey to Albany and the risks of angering the victor of Saratoga. As Hamilton wrote in controlled anger: "By inquiry, I have learned [that the brigade] you propose to send is, by far, the weakest of the three now here, and does not consist of more than 600 rank and file [or about half a full brigade] fit for duty [and] there is a militia regiment with it [whose] term of service . . . is so near expiring, that it would be past by the time the men could arrive" at Washington's Army.[84]

· Then, shocked by having been artfully duped, the twenty-one-year-old Lieutenant Colonel Hamilton made a bold decision. He decided to now play his high card to get what was most needed by Washington: utilizing Washington's name and verbal orders requesting the other two brigades that consisted of more than two thousand Continental troops in total. In a careful and skillfully crafted letter to General Gates that blended tact and proper protocol, he applied Washington's full authority in his request. Hamilton wrote to America's latest most popular hero: "Under these circumstances, I cannot consider it either as compatible with the good of the service or my [verbal] instructions from His Excellency General Washington, to consent, that that brigade [of Massachusetts men under Paterson] be selected from the three [and] I am under the necessity of requiring, by virtue of my orders from him, that one of the others be substituted instead of this [one]. . . . When I preferred your opinion to other considerations, I did not imagine you would pitch upon a brigade little more than half as large as the others; and finding this to be the case I indispensibly owe it to my duty, to desire in His Excellency's name, that another brigade may go instead of the one intended."[85]

General Gates' immediate reaction was absolute shock, mixed with seething anger. This boyish and dapper aide-de-camp, with only a lieutenant colonel's rank, possessed the audacity to use the full weight of Washington's name and high rank (all the leverage that he could muster) to apply the pressure necessary to force Gates against his will to do the right thing for not only Washington but also America. To Gates' mind, the general saw Hamilton's bold actions as an example of far too much power (as Benjamin Rush had denounced) bestowed by Washington to a mere aide, which was highly irregular and in violation of standard protocol. But, of course, Gates had no idea that this boyish-looking officer was no ordinary aide, one who did little more than write letters and carry dispatches on horseback for Washington. Indeed, this young man was no mere clerk at headquarters, but in fact Washington's official chief of staff in the modern sense and primary protector, who knew that Gates hoped to replace Washington. Therefore, Gates' ambitions needed to be thwarted at all costs.

All in all, Hamilton had acted accordingly and well within his jurisdiction in a critical situation of heightened sensitivity. There was nothing out of line in regard to Hamilton's actions, because he was only doing his job as ordered by Washington. Most of all, he was acting in Washington's best interests and that of the army. Clearly, General Gates had underestimated the iron will and determination hidden by the appearance of this slight and slender young man. With confidence and self-assurance from so many past successes, Hamilton had maneuvered like a master chess player in a delicate, highly sensitive situation. Clearly, as on the battlefield, the "Little Lion" had roared a forceful checkmate to the revered general.

The next day on November 6, Hamilton duly reported the delicate political situation to Washington, who was eager to receive the much-needed three brigades. In dealing with Washington's most popular subordinate, Hamilton had faced his most difficult mission to date. More importantly and as always, Hamilton was focused on protecting Washington, especially from his growing number of detractors in Congress, while enhancing his own chances for future success. In a typically thorough and analytical report, Hamilton revealed the judicious utilization of his wise judgment, while ever-mindful of the delicate symbiotic relationship between politics and popular sentiment that lately have worked to Washington's disadvantage: "I felt the importance of strengthening you as much as possible, but on the other hand, I found insuperable inconveniences in acting diametrically opposite to the opinion of a Gentleman, whose successes [Saratoga] have raised him into the highest importance. General Gates has won the intire [*sic*] confidence of the Eastern States; if disposed to do it by addressing himself to the prejudices of the people he would find no difficultly to render [Washington's] measure odious; which it might be said, with plausibility enough to be believed, was calculated to expose them to unnecessary danger, not withstanding their exertions during the campaign had given them the fullest title to repose and security. General Gates has influence and interest elsewhere; he might use it [against Washington], if he pleased, to discredit the measure there [in Congress] also."[86]

In the end, the stubborn Gates caved in to the applied pressure, and informed Hamilton he would send the required two brigades of disciplined Continentals to Washington. A triumphant Hamilton showed he had "finally prevailed" in his satisfied words revealed in his letter to Washington. With his sly humor emerging out of a sense of relief because he had succeeded in defeating Gates' defiant "impudence, his folly and his rascality" that had revealed his selfish ambition at Washington's and America's expense. He reported to Washington that he succeeded (another brilliant performance) in his important mission, because he had applied just the right amount of pressure and leverage, and after "having given General Gates a little more time to recollect himself."[87]

Hamilton's adroit handling of this situation obtained the best troops (two brigades of more than two thousand two hundred Continental soldiers) for Washington to increase his chances for future success, while reducing the possibilities for success of Washington's rival. Hamilton had demonstrated considerable political savvy and prudent decision-making in a most sensitive situation (more political than military) given the ever-intriguing Gates less justifiable reason to loudly complain to his powerful Congressional supporters to cause Washington political damage and make additional enemies for the beleaguered Virginian: a disastrous political situation that could potentially prove fatal to Washington's status and even command position.

A truly thankful Washington gained even more confidence in what Hamilton could accomplish in the future in a seemingly impossible situation, ensuring "their lifelong collaboration" in military-political matters long after the war ended. He fulfilled Washington's wishes and most urgent need for the two brigades with the judicious finesse of a genie unleashed from a bottle, performing his magic that not only befuddled but also outsmarted the most admired general in America. However, a price had to be paid. Hamilton had now made a lifelong enemy of General Gates, who never forgot the little aide who had employed highhandedness to get his way. As could be expected from a natural politician who knew how to play the behind-the-scenes game with consummate skill, a seething Gates wrote two angry letters (only one was sent, however) to Washington that declared that he was "astonished" by Hamilton's actions to get what he (and Washington) wanted, regardless of the England-born general's arguments.

Of course, Hamilton was fully aware that he had made a mortal enemy, because he had outsmarted him. As Hamilton wrote in a September 6, 1780, letter in regard to Gates' animosity, after perhaps the most egotistical generals (on either side) in America relinquished his command in the northern theater to take charge of America's primary Southern Army in an ill-fated bid to save the day in the South: "I am his enemy personally, for unjust and unprovoked attacks upon my character. . . ."[88]

After Hamilton had caught the sly general trying to pawn off an under-manned brigade to his superior in order to keep the best troops for himself and with Gates having met his match to his astonishment, the young man in a lieutenant colonel's uniform was not aware that the incensed Gates had complained in his first draft (not sent to Washington) of the "dictatorial power" employed by "one Aid[e] de Camp sent to an Army three hundred miles distant."[89] But of course, Gates' true target in the larger political chess game was not Hamilton but Washington, who he wanted to replace as commander-in-chief. Therefore, Hamilton's other top priority in his delicate Albany mission was to cause Washington as few future political problems as possible, especially in regard to Congress.

Hamilton was not alone in this crucial guardian angel role. Proving to be a most effective team, the two kindred spirits, Hamilton and Laurens became even more proactive in regard to protecting Washington's reputation against his growing number of enemies in the days ahead. They were destined to play a leading role in eventually thwarting an anti-Washington conspiracy to replace the Virginian, who now so seldom won victories as in his glory days of Trenton and Princeton. From what he had learned in Albany and the Northern Department, Hamilton gave Washington ample warnings about the full extent of Gates' popularity, enhanced political power, and overall sinister designs toward the commander-in-chief, especially in regard to replacing him. From what he had learned about this conspiracy, Hamilton summarized: "I cannot doubt its reality in the most extensive sense."[90]

During the grueling Albany mission, trouble also soon developed for Hamilton when General Israel Putnam reneged on his promise to dispatch his two brigades to Washington. Now more confident after outmaneuvering Gates who could hardly believe that he had been outsmarted by a brash officer who was young enough to have been his son, Hamilton was again forced to use his full authority granted to him by Washington to guarantee that "Old Putnam," who had been fighting Indians before the native West Indian had been born, rushed the two brigades on to Washington.[91]

An outraged Hamilton relied upon the surefire tactic of righteous indignation fused with a direct appeal to Putnam's patriotism while once again employing the full force of Washington's authority: "I am astonished and alarmed beyond measure [that] no step of those I mentioned to you [in Washington's name] has been taken to afford him the aid he absolutely stands in need of [and by] delaying [the reinforcements] which the cause of America is put to the utmost conceivable hazard [and] I tremble at the consequences of the delay."[92]

Out of urgent necessity and having lost all patience with self-serving older generals who refused to take him seriously, Hamilton came down hard on the stubborn Putnam, who detested the aide's demands as much as Gates. Just as General Gates had learned the hard way, so General Putnam had thoroughly underestimated the self-assured officer, and he was about to learn a hard lesson. Clearly, Hamilton was determined to allow no one to thwart his efforts to strengthen Washington's hand in this game against rivals, and this meant that the commander-in-chief needed as many troops as possible to increase his changes for winning victory to gain greater support in Congress and enhance his overall image. In Hamilton's threatening words that got right to the point in no uncertain terms: "How [your recent] noncompliance can be answered to General Washington you can best determine."[93]

But, as in dealing with the hardheaded Gates, Hamilton saved the best for last by directly ordering Putnam to immediately hurry his two Continental brigades to Washington without delay. Then, continuing to adroitly outmaneuver the baffled "Old Put" with the same finesse as in skillfully outmatching General Gates, Hamilton had proven that he possessed an uncanny ability to think ahead of his increasingly indignant opponents of a much higher rank in a fast-paced political game. Knowing how these old generals, especially Gates, maneuvered skillfully behind the scenes to damage reputations and careers in order to place themselves in the most positive light to gain the advantage, he rushed off a letter to Washington to warn him of the exact situation, before the inevitable angry letters from Gates and Putnam grossly distorted the situation. To Washington, Hamilton rightly complained that Putnam had "deranged" the situation and ignored orders "in [Washington's] name" on his shaky premise that he planned to attack New York City and needed the extra manpower. Correctly reading through this man's cynical thinking and his designs, Hamilton emphasized that this so-called plan of the old French and Indian War hero was nothing more than a self-serving excuse.[94]

However, the excessive stress in having to play an endless political game and in having to so forcefully deal with hardheaded French and Indian War–era veterans for Washington's maximum benefit came at a personal price. The overburdened and increasingly weary Hamilton now suffered in health, and most likely in spirit as well. He was unable to make it back to Washington's headquarters. His remaining republican idealism about the nobility and righteousness of brothers in arms battling for America's sacred cause was shaken to the core.

But fortunately for Washington, Hamilton had repeatedly demonstrated that he could also be equally Machiavellian, if forced by necessity, in a complex situation that required boldness on behalf of Washington and America. However, he had been too successful. Consequently, Lieutenant Colonel Hamilton feared that he had exceeded his authority in playing hardball with two senior generals: Another fact that caused anxiety that almost certainly affected his health. Therefore, Hamilton was racked with a high fever, "violent rheumatic pains throughout my body," and overall "very unwell," as he informed Washington on November 11 from New Windsor, Ulster County, New York. Here, on the west bank of the Hudson River and located north of West Point, Hamilton's condition worsened at New Windsor.

Nevertheless, he remained determined to fulfill his mission at any cost, because Washington was in dire need of troops. Emerging from his sickbed and despite his weakened state, he gamely rode the twenty miles south and down the Hudson to Peekskill, on the Hudson's east bank, to hurry Putnam's brigades south to reinforce Washington, passing by West Point on the journey. Hamilton's obsession—orders were orders—to complete his mission resulted in a relapse in late November. He had grown up in the Caribbean, and harsh winter weather was still relatively new to him. Hamilton learned about the risks of overexertion and pushing himself too hard in wintertime. Indeed, he nearly succumbed to an untimely death from this serious bout with rheumatic fever, and Washington almost lost his chief of staff.

Hamilton was bedridden at a private house of a patriotic Irishman named Dennis Kennedy at Peekskill for almost a week during the most serious illness in his life. By Hamilton's side as his guardian and protector, Rhode Island-born Captain Caleb Gibbs, who was from the fishing port of Marblehead, Massachusetts. The captain wrote to Governor George Clinton, of New York and the son of Irish immigrants, that the combined effect of the high fever and chills might well result in Hamilton's death, which almost became a grim reality for the most promising officer on Washington's staff before the end of November. As a concerned John Laurens penned to his father Henry in a December 3, 1777, letter, "Col. Hamilton, who was sent to the northern army to explain the necessity for reinforcements from there, lies dangerously ill on the road."[95]

Indeed, even the gloomy physicians at Peekskill believed that Hamilton was about to die. He lay in bed under close supervision for weeks, including from the faithful Captain Gibbs, who provided good care and fresh food to combat the illness and restore his health. Against the odds, Hamilton slowly began to recover. But it had been a very close call. Clearly, losing Hamilton would have come as a severe blow to Washington, and could have ended the highly effective lifelong political and military team.[96]

An often-overlooked factor had played a role in Hamilton's almost miraculous recovery that lifted his spirits at the right time, while he was overly concerned that he had abused the authority given to him by Washington. He had gotten his way (and Washington's of course) at the expense of the ambitions of Generals Gates and Putnam. Therefore, with great relief, Hamilton read the newly arrived letter from Washington, who rarely bestowed glowing compliments and such a complete vote of confidence, about his recent mission with supreme satisfaction: "I approve entirely all the steps you have taken and have only to wish that the exertions of those [Generals Gates and Putnam] you have had to deal with had kept pace with your zeal and good intentions."[97]

Meanwhile, General Gates and Putnam eagerly awaited news that their upstart irritant, who had caused them embarrassment and humiliation in equal dosages, would succumb to his illness and trouble them no more in the future. When Hamilton finally began to recover from the illness, there was absolutely no joy in Gates' and Putnam's headquarters. With a touch of sarcasm and almost seemingly to hint that a duel of honor might well be in order because of Hamilton's aggressive actions on Washington's behalf, Colonel Hugh Hughes presented the bad news to his friend Gates on December 5, 1777, that Hamilton, "who has been very ill . . . at Peekskill, is out of danger, unless it be from his own sweet temper."[98]

Colonel Hughes's words indicated that Hamilton had almost certainly lost his temper in the face of either Gates or Putnam, or both. But this expressed anger more applied to Putnam than Gates, because the New Englander could inflict far less political damage to Washington than the popular Gates. Clearly, Hamilton's sense of righteous indignation had risen to the fore, when dealing with not only Gates but also with General Putnam, who had been "tongue-lashed" by the bright, fast-talking lieutenant colonel. Hamilton's mastery of language and his argumentative skills had proved too much for "Old Put."[99]

But in truth, the greatest danger had come not from Generals Gates or Putnam, but in fact from Hamilton himself. As mentioned, Hamilton, still weak and sickly, had exerted himself after having learned that Putnam's two Continental brigades on the move to Washington's Army were near mutiny because of the lack of pay as promised. To quell the disturbance that threatened to deprive Washington of these much-needed troops after so much effort, Hamilton had "literally leaped from his sickbed" to solve this new crisis that had so suddenly emerged at Peekskill. He had convinced New York's Governor Clinton, who lived in New Windsor, to release funds to immediately pay the troops, who then continued onward to join Washington.[100]

The entire array of impressive accomplishments of Hamilton's mission to Albany included even a significant step forward in his personal life. In paying a courtesy call during a lull period in his intense discussions and communications with Gates, he had met his future wife, Elizabeth Schuyler, the attractive young second daughter of General Philip Schuyler. Here, he had dined with the former commander of the Northern Department and his family at their exquisite mansion. Hamilton had been impressed by the mansion and the wealth, but far more impressed by the general's pretty daughter.[101]

Lieutenant Colonel Hamilton hoped to return to Washington's "family" at Valley Forge by Christmas. But it was not to be. Worn down from his grueling mission, Hamilton literally collapsed on his journey south from exhaustion near Morristown, New Jersey, before reaching headquarters to the southwest. He was in such bad shape that he was forced to hire a coach to take him some sixty-five miles to the northeast and all the way back to Peekskill.

After recovering some of his strength, Hamilton finally returned to headquarters at Valley Forge, where the army had established winter quarters since December 19, 1777. Hamilton arrived with his health only recently improved, but his spirits returned upon returning to the "family." As could be expected, Hamilton's lengthy illness was troubling to Washington, who rightly worried that he would never see his most indispensable man again. Now appreciating Hamilton more than ever before after his long absence in which the heavy workload and unresolved problems had piled-up at headquarters, Washington realized that whenever "a crisis had occurred [in the past he] could always rely on the diligent Hamilton . . . to help him" in even the most impossible situation.[102]

Indeed, Hamilton had helped Washington far more than even he imagined. A troublemaking Irish-born general named Thomas Conway openly voiced strong anti-Washington opinions to Gates, who had an ally in the festering anti-Washington coalition. Conway's secret anti-Washington letter to General Gates had been revealed that a united front in the army existed against Washington. In a letter to Gates, of which a copy had come into his possession in November 1777 while Hamilton was on his Albany mission, Washington was denounced by Conway, a newly appointed brigadier, as a "weak general [with] bad councilors," meaning: Hamilton most of all. Hamilton early understood the true depths of the so-called Gates-Conway conspiracy, and correctly saw it as Washington's most serious threat.

He, therefore, denounced Conway as the most "villainous calumniator or incendiary" in the land. With the copy of Conway's letter to Gates in hand, Washington wrote to Gates and requested an immediate explanation. Gates attempted to turn the tables on his own traitorous sentiments by falsely declaring that a "spy" and a "thief" (as he wrote to Washington in a December 8 letter) had been in headquarters and had copied the letter from his files, implicating Hamilton during his recent visit. But in truth, Hamilton was then recuperating from his illness in Peekskill.

Still angry at Hamilton for prying so many precious troops from him and getting the best of him by artful maneuvering, General Gates hoped to tarnish Hamilton's reputation. But even this devious strategy backfired, because Gates lost more credibility, especially among conservative Congressmen, like New Yorkers and Hamilton's friends Robert R. Livingston and John Jay, who stood solidly behind Washington. In no small part because Hamilton (along with John Laurens) served as his primary protector, especially against the covert activities of the so-called Conway Cabal in the future, Washington remained the army's commander-in-chief to the war's end.[103]

As the Albany mission demonstrated, Hamilton's Machiavellian qualities and wise decision-making were appreciated by Washington, because this irrepressible young man obtained for him two good combat brigades from Gates's army. This was a crucial addition of manpower, because Washington needed to win another victory to keep rivals at bay. Not only in the role as chief of staff after he returned to headquarters, Hamilton also continued to serve as "Washington's most trusted advisor," political councilor, and "trouble-shooter" in the most crucial matters, both military and political. Revealing the depth of his contributions, he even "was already spouting civics lessons to state governors" with hard-hitting political arguments.[104]

Washington learned that not only were Hamilton's strategic views sound, but also his judgments and insights about high-ranking subordinates. This was especially the case of one of America's most revered heroes of the French and Indian War and the revolution's early days, General Putnam, who had commanded the New York Highlands north of New York City ineffectively. "Old Put" was well past his prime, while a new generation of dynamic younger officers, such as Knox and Greene, had risen to the fore. The October 6, 1777, loss of Forts Montgomery and Clinton on the Hudson exposed Putnam's considerable strategic and tactical failings in this important theater. After the latest episode with Putnam's intransigence over sending the two Continental brigades of reinforcements to Washington, Hamilton (who unknowingly echoed the sentiments of Congress in denouncing Putnam) implored Washington to relieve "Old Put" for the overall good of America's overall war effort. By late March 1778, Putnam was finally relieved of command.[105]

Doing what he felt was necessary, Hamilton had played a role in convincing Washington that the best policy was to remove the incompetent Putnam. Since his service as a young aide from New Jersey, Major Aaron Burr loved Putnam like a father. He had long referred to him as "my good old General."

Hamilton's role in the New England general's fall from grace engendered a life-long hatred from the young New England firebrand. Hamilton was destined to pay a high price for Burr's bitter hatred that never diminished.[106]

But General Gates was only one of many enemies who had set their sights on this gifted "fair-haired boy," because of his considerable clout and his aggressive actions that got so much accomplished for Washington. In this vital role, Hamilton had become Washington's most effective pen, mouthpiece, and protector, which ensured a sharp backlash, including that he exerted too much influence upon the middle-aged general and former planter. Jealousy also ran high among highly placed Americans because Washington had bestowed this precocious young man with an unprecedented amount of his authority.

Therefore, Hamilton emerged as the number one most irresistible target of Gates' circle of cronies and other military and political leaders, including members of Congress such as John and Samuel Adams. Indeed, "the Little Lion was fair game for professional lion-killers in and out of the army; and they had seldom drawn a bead upon a more tempting and—thanks to Hamilton's practice of speaking his mind freely—a more vulnerable target."[107]

But making a good many enemies was the inevitable price that Hamilton paid for performing so skillfully in getting quick results as Washington's trouble-shooter and chief protector; the long list of enemies he accumulated was a direct testament to his amazing success. Therefore, Hamilton fairly basked in his "success in flushing out" those self-serving generals, who sought to replace the commander-in-chief for reasons that had little to do with America's well-being. But even more remarkably, Hamilton's ever-increasing list of achievements and successes never went to his head. He was still easy to work with at headquarters, while continuing to serve Washington and his country at the expense of his personal ambitions and desires for the overall good of the country.[108]

Winter at Valley Forge

As mentioned, Washington had established winter quarters on December 19, 1777, while Hamilton had been absent. The commander-in-chief had decided not to undertake any attempt to recapture Philadelphia, although he remained within striking distance. He knew that Howe's forces were too strong and lack initiative. Therefore, the army's winter position along the Schuylkill was far enough from Philadelphia to be safe while gathering additional strength for next year's spring campaign, and close enough to monitor any future British movements. However, Washington's prudence in deciding to leave Philadelphia free from attack drew a new round of criticism from an increasingly vocal anti-Washington bloc, especially in Congress, and even from former supporters. After the most patriotic presses that had once produced pro-Washington periodicals had been driven out of the city by the British occupation, the Philadelphia press naturally became more critical of Washington, who remained inactive just to the northwest at Valley Forge.

As could be expected, General Gates continued to be increasingly seen as Washington's most worthy replacement, including by Congressional members. In addition, a mounting tide of criticism was directed toward Hamilton. He was now charged with having too much influence over Washington's decision-making and judgment: ironically, this was actually a great advantage for the commander-in-chief rather than a liability. Of course, no one knew of the full extent of Hamilton's broad range of talents and contributions warranting this disproportionate influence like Washington. In an indirect compliment that he delighted knowing about, Hamilton continued to serve as the "favorite culprit" and the most convenient target of a growing number of Washington critics, who sought their revenge on the increasingly detested native West Indian.[109]

The winter encampment at Valley Forge, located along the south bank of the Schuylkill River, was dominated by the toxic mixture of political intrigue, unrest, and gloom. Meanwhile, Philadelphia and New York City—America's two largest cities—continued to be occupied by the British, who enjoyed the comforts of a relatively luxurious winter quarters. Valley Forge, located around twenty miles just northwest of Philadelphia, was a bleak exile by stark comparison. Hamilton continued to perform his duty at the stone house owned by Isaac Potts, the thrifty forge co-owner, who lived in Philadelphia. Potts' summer house served as the home of Washington's military "family." At the intersection of Valley Creek, that ran north, and the east-west flowing Schuylkill River, just to the north, Washington's headquarters was located at the northwestern corner of the Valley Forge encampment. Potts owned the forge that provided war materiel to the Continental Army with William Dewees, a patriot Quaker.

But despite its bleakness and shortages that cost precious lives, Valley Forge was a good strategic position, providing Washington with distinct advantages. Here, Washington could still threaten Howe and his stationary position in Philadelphia, if necessary. Because of the overall dire situation and because his greatest successes—Trenton and Princeton—were in the distant past, Washington's reputation remained under steady attack from Congress, the army, and the press, even before General Gates' October 1777 victory at Saratoga.

After all, America's capital had been lost under Washington's watch, along with his ineffective efforts to stop the advance of the invaders at Brandywine Creek. A growing number of New Englanders in high places wanted Washington replaced. Sectional divisions continued to rise to the fore, with Congress as divided as the army. Serving on the staff as Washington's adjutant general, Colonel Timothy Pickering, a pious New Englander who was an Old Testament warrior, learned of the depth of anti–New England sentiment: just as New Englanders possessed their own regional prejudices. Washington realized that he possessed very few generals, especially Gates and Lee, who he could totally trust. Therefore, he continued to place even more of his faith in his chief of staff in the days ahead, a trust that was well-placed and returned in full.

Meanwhile, spirits steadily sank among America's revolutionaries while more good men died of disease and the British Army continued to occupy warm quarters in the houses of Philadelphia. Washington's men endured the harsh winter without adequate quarters or clothing, especially shoes. The Valley Forge area had been long ago stripped of provisions and supplies. Nearby American farmers continued to readily sell their produce to the British, who paid in hard cash instead of virtually worthless Continental notes. Under the Articles of Confederation (the first United States Constitution) that had been created in mid-November 1777, states were responsible for supplying clothing as well as food to their troops. But the states were unable to transport supplies to Valley Forge. Washington's commissary and supply system was inefficient and corrupt, and the whole logistical structure began to break down in winter's depths. Angered over the corruption, incompetence of the army's commissary department, and selfishness that signed the death warrants of a good many starving and diseased soldiers, Hamilton wrote letters to Congress to secure supplies and provisions. But this was not enough.

Meanwhile, Howe's well-supplied occupiers of Philadelphia mocked Washington's ill-clad rabble, suffering only a short distance away. Morale and discipline of these amateurs in revolution had plummeted to new lows. Hamilton even feared that the army might simply dissolve or never reach the combat capabilities to launch another campaign to defend America. Soldiers lacked everything but stoicism, and Hamilton greatly admired their "unparalleled . . . degree of patience" under such severe adversity. And when new uniforms and shoes were finally issued to Valley Forge, they were too small in size. In December 1777 alone, and the situation worsening into the New Year, nearly three thousand of Washington's nine thousand men were unfit for duty because they lacked clothing and shoes. However, the army's condition would have been far worse at Valley Forge had Hamilton not secured supplies of blankets and clothing for the army before Philadelphia fell, because the "distressed situation of the army for want of blankets and many necessary articles of clothing is truly deplorable," lamented Washington.[110]

By January 1778, meanwhile, Philadelphia newspapers, Congressional members, and revolutionary leaders continued to unleash barrages of criticism about Washington's shortcomings, both real and exaggerated. Generals Gates and Conway of the so-called Conway Cabal, or "this junto," in Washington's words, hoped to undermine his position as the army's commander to force his resignation in disgrace. Rumors were afloat about Washington's possible resignation under the avalanche of criticism, especially after his recent setbacks.

Not long after Hamilton returned to headquarters at the Isaac Potts' House at Valley Forge on January 20, 1778, following his exhaustive Albany mission, Washington finally took action by launching his own defense, after his chief of staff had appraised him of the full extent of the threat: A mini-mutiny of sorts by senior commanders. At Hamilton's urgent urging because of this escalating political maneuvering behind the scenes and the overall dire situation facing the army from internal weaknesses, Washington wisely took the initiative. Along with Hamilton, he knew that the best defense was taking the offensive, and this called for a proactive plan that basically usurped the mission of the Board of War of reorganizing an ill-supplied and ineffective army.

Fortunately, the army's beleaguered commander now relied upon Hamilton. Hamilton especially excelled at this kind of problem solving on an extensive scale. Washington now needed to forcefully answer his growing number of critics with a well-conceived strategic plan for the army's reform and reorganization to enhance overall quality and effectiveness by laying a sturdy foundation for future success in the years ahead. Clearly, in political terms, this was also a masterful means of increasing greater confidence in Washington among the increasingly skeptical Congressional members who had lost faith in the Virginian.[111] Here, in a sixteen-square-foot room with only one stone fireplace in the summerhouse of Isaac Potts, "Lieutenant Colonel Alexander Hamilton, the most talented writer on the general's staff, sharpened his quills, filled his inkpot, and went to work on a document that was aimed not only at rescuing the army but also at defeating the men who were trying to destroy George Washington."[112]

Washington's reputation as a far-sighted commander-in-chief began to be resurrected when the massive document of more than sixteen thousand words, which primarily espoused the many ideas of Hamilton (mostly in his neat handwriting), was prepared for presentation to five members of the Congressional committee on January 29, 1778: essentially a blueprint of guidance that detailed the necessary steps required by the Congress to reorganize the Continental Army that was in need of practically everything, especially a thorough reorganization. Although Hamilton was not the sole author, he was the primary architect and contributor. At Washington's request, general officers (such as the highly capable Major General Greene) made contributions for the remodeling the army. Hamilton incorporated these sound ideas, but primarily relied upon his own many already well-thought-out views into this lengthy comprehensive analysis.

Hamilton's monumental treatise provided the much-needed remedies to improve the army's capabilities and chances of surviving a lengthy war of attrition. With clarity and insight, Hamilton crafted the document for reforming the army, while "devising reforms systematically." Hamilton reworked and transformed the final document with his stylish "serviceable prose."[113] In the end, Hamilton created "nothing less than America's first great state paper" in the history of the United States.[114] As could be expected, a thankful Washington was highly impressed by the breadth of Hamilton's finished document and satisfied with the innovative ideas and solutions that the masterpiece contained. A delighted Washington, therefore, "accepted Hamilton's reformed regulations [for the army] and turned them over to an investigating committee of the Continental Congress" at Valley Forge.[115]

To improve the rapidly worsening situation facing his army, meanwhile, an increasingly frustrated Washington was forced to take more drastic action beyond just listing remedies for Congress to act upon. The amount of supplies at the winter encampment had dwindled to new lows. Hamilton knew that political infighting, or bitter "faction" (denounced by Hamilton as "the monster"), was a primary source of Congress' inefficiency and for America's greatest political problems in general, because so many of its members lacked proper public spirit, and were more focused on personal gain. The absence of basic necessities at Valley Forge led to a spike in not only in desertions, but also hundreds of deaths. In February, Hamilton lamented how the "desertions have been immense," more than he had ever seen before. With so many people involved in profiteering, Washington rightly suspected that theft or black market activities had significantly reduced the volume of the already too-small amount of supplies that managed to eventually reach Valley Forge.

Around mid-February 1778, Washington unleashed his most competent bloodhound and sleuth to sniff out the sources of the troubles. He ordered Hamilton, meticulous and detail-oriented, to conduct an in-depth investigation of the entire winter encampment to ascertain the sources of the logistical and supply problems, especially why newly arrived provisions were not reaching the men in timely fashion or not at all. Hoping to solve the ration shortage crisis, Washington "convened extra meetings of his staff, and kept his aides [including Hamilton] working until late at night as he fired off pleas for food."[116]

On February 13, at the Potts house, Hamilton allowed a flood of his bold and novel ideas to flow smoothly in his problem solving initiatives, while ever-mindful that his repeated requests for supplies were either being ignored or bogged down by tangles of bureaucratic red tape. Hamilton utilized the strategy of adding weight in his condemnation of Congress by employing the aid of New York's Governor George Clinton. In another hard-hitting letter through Gouverneur Morris, Hamilton appealed to Governor Clinton on "a matter [which now] requires the attention of every person of sense and influence [because of the] degeneracy of representation in the great council of America."[117]

An indignant Hamilton again utilized his masterful pen to address the crisis that was leading to the army's gradual and systematic destruction, beginning at Valley Forge: "It is a melancholy truth Sir, and the effects of which we dayly [*sic*] see and feel, that there is not so much wisdom in a certain body, as there ought to be, and as the success of our affairs absolutely demands. Many members of it are no doubt men in every respect, fit for the trust, but his cannot be said of it as a body. Folly, caprice a want of foresight, comprehension and dignity, characterize the general tenor of their actions. . . . Their conduct, with respect to the army especially, is feeble, indecisive, and improvident."[118]

As usual, Hamilton was especially infuriated at these harmful politicians who were motivated far more by self-interest than national interest, doing immeasurable damage to the war effort and nation at large: the antithesis of the duty-minded, stoic "Little Lion" who sacrificed all for the cause and repeatedly risking his life on the battlefield. As he continued in his attack on Congress' seemingly endless failings in his February 13 letter, despite having greeted members of a Congressional delegation who had visited Valley Forge less than a month before in response to the formal recommendations for the army's reorganization: "Their conduct with respect to the army especially is feeble indecisive and improvident—insomuch, that we are reduced to a more terrible situation than you can conceive" at this time.[119]

Blaming state politicians who proved irresponsible in supplying the troops, Hamilton ascertained the fundamental problem of states' rights versus the national priorities: the central weakness of the hastily constructed republican system that was partly leading to America's failed war effort. He saw early on the urgent need of a stronger government to provide for the army and wage war. The states "should have nothing to do with" the army, because this was rightly the role of a central government. The situation was so bad that he was forced to beg Governor Clinton on February 16: "you can perhaps do something towards" the army's relief, because "any assistance, however, trifling in itself, will be of great moment at so critical a juncture." With a mixture of sound logic and sarcasm that presented a broad strategic-political perspective, Hamilton also warned the newly elected governor of New York about the possible dire international consequences: "Realize to yourself the consequences of having a Congress despised at home and aboard. How can the common force be exerted, if the power of collecting it be put in weak foolish and unsteady hands? How can we hope for success in our European negociations [sic], if the nations of Europe have no confidence in the wisdom and vigor, of the great Continental Government?"[120]

Martha Washington arrived at the Valley Forge encampment on February 8, after the one-hundred-thirty-mile trip from Mount Vernon. Spirits lifted among the general's military "family" at headquarters when Martha threw a party for her husband on Sunday February 22, his forty-sixth birthday. Washington's headquarters were especially light-hearted on this evening. As could be expected, "Hamilton was the very life of every party."[121]

A distinguished French philosopher and linguist who had recently arrived in America and Valley Forge, Pierre Etienne Du Ponceau, who now served as the secretary to Baron Friedrich Wilhelm von Steuben, was invited to dine with Washington and his staff. He described his first impressions of Washington's headquarters, when, "We were in a manner domesticated in the family [and] General Washington had three aids: Tench Tilghman, John Laurens, and Alexander Hamilton; Robert Hanson Harrison was his secretary. I soon formed a friendship with Laurens, and Hamilton."[122]

The respected Frenchman, educated at a Benedictine school in France, was impressed by examples of sterling character: "In the midst of our distress . . . Mrs. Washington had the courage to follow her husband in that dreary abode" of Valley Forge.[123] Du Ponceau also described how the Spartan wives of Washington's principal officers, such as Generals Greene and Lord Stirling, "often met at each other's quarters and sometimes at General Washington's [headquarters] where the evening was spent in conversation over a dish of tea or coffee [but] no dancing, card-playing or amusements of any kind except singing."[124]

At his Valley Forge headquarters, Washington continued to dictate a record number of letters and other correspondence. It has been estimated that Harrison and Tilghman wrote more than half of the paperwork generated during an especially hectic six-month period. If so, then Hamilton's almost certainly penned the remainder, or nearly half. But what was most significant about this massive production flowing from Washington's headquarters was the fact that Hamilton accomplished the important work on the most crucial issues on national importance.[125]

As part of the ambitious plan to reform the Continental Army, Washington benefitted from the expertise of a newly arrived foreign volunteer soldier from Prussia. After landing in New England on December 1, 1777, forty-eight-year-old Friedrich Wilhelm von Steuben made his appearance at Valley Forge. Despite the false attachment of the aristocratic "von" (he had gained the title of Freiherr—roughly baron status—while serving as a chamberlain in a minor German court) that denoted the Prussian upper class elite, this seasoned Prussian officer had been schooled in European ways of training and was a faithful follower of Frederick the Great. Like Hamilton before him, he arrived at Washington's headquarters at exactly the right time. Von Steuben saw a disorganized army in an appalling condition. Experience was badly needed to bring improvements to this amateur army, and as a veteran officer with European militaries, including the legendary Prussian Army of Frederick the Great, von Steuben was that man. Ironically, unlike Hamilton, Washington was not initially convinced about von Steuben's worth in part because the Prussian had been endorsed by General Gates, which was sufficient to arouse suspicions. But Hamilton, like Laurens, was enthusiastic about the Prussian, and he worked his magic on Washington, who became a believer.

Incredibly, Washington's Army even lacked a manual of written regulations possessed by every army in Europe. After Washington assigned

Hamilton and Laurens as the Prussian's aides and interpreters because he spoke very little and only poor English except for an occasional "Goddamn" when angered, Hamilton learned from von Steuben about the professional workings of the proficient Prussian staff, where a chief of staff had long advised the monarch in days past. In the Prussian military, von Steuben had been instructed in staff officer duties. With Hamilton's assistance, von Steuben was about to apply to Washington's Army what was now most desperately needed: a professional system of training, tactics, and discipline, following the professional Prussian model.[126]

To ensure a smooth acclimation for von Steuben, Hamilton took the Prussian under his wing, including loaning him money when needed. "With Hamilton acting as interpreter, the Baron made an excellent impression from the first," especially to Washington.[127] Because French was von Steuben's second language after German, Hamilton made sure that his exact words and thoughts were committed to paper. The Prussian "dictated [his] dispositions in the night." Von Steuben wrote out his suggestions for his drill manual in confusing mix of Germanic-French. Then, this rough draft was rewritten in proper French from Hamilton's neat hand and concise understanding of French. Besides the role of translator, Hamilton also served as Von Steuben's editor. Laurens, the only other member of Washington's staff fluent in French besides the native West Indian, assisted Hamilton in this time-consuming effort.

Working together as an excellent team and beyond what could have been achieved by Washington's older staff officers, Hamilton and Laurens completed translating the Prussian's ideas and suggestions into English. They then put Steuben's words into the understandable language of the common soldiers, including many recent immigrants, especially Irish soldiers. Because no printing press was located at Valley Forge, von Steuben's instructions, as clearly written out by Hamilton's hand, were circulated throughout the army. What these young young men of Washington's staff had created was the first manual and set of regulations ever used by the American Army, which was eventually published as the *Regulations for Order and Discipline of the Troops of the United States.*

By March and with the first hints of spring in the air among the rolling hills of Valley Forge above the Schuylkill, thousands of Americans began to drill like Frederick the Great's Prussian soldiers with newly imported Charleville muskets from France to the precise instructions of the "Steuben-Hamilton manual." Finding himself in the middle of everything as usual, Hamilton was one of the first Continental officers to personally drill the troops, divided in groups of one hundred men, and succeeding groups by the dictates of the new manual. All in all, this much-needed army manual was very much of Hamilton's creation. Appreciating how much the Prussian was assisting the army, Hamilton felt considerable affection for the Prussian, perhaps partly because he was also a recent immigrant. Hamilton had even taught von Steuben, at his request because his German and French invectives were not sufficient, a number of English curse words to shower upon the recruits to get them to drill properly. Von Steuben was on his way to gaining a major general's rank early May 1778. Hamilton wrote candidly how the "Baron is a gentleman for whom I have a particular esteem."[128]

With his tasks never-ending at the busy headquarters, Hamilton received another assignment from Washington in March 1778 that was destined to eventually come back to haunt him. He was sent to present Captain Henry "Light Horse" Lee, age twenty-two, with an offer to join the "family." But "Harry" declined what almost any officer would gladly accept. The gifted cavalry commander from the Northern Neck of Virginia, nestled between the Potomac River (on the north) and the Rappahannock River (on the south), chose to remain with his command and his beloved fighting men, which was a more important priority to him than rising higher in rank, status, and prestige. Clearly, like Hamilton, Lee was a true republican soldier who sacrificed his all for his country.[129]

Chapter IV

Washington's Most Erudite Diplomat
to the French and the Battle of Monmouth

By this time, Hamilton's role as chief of staff and chief adviser had become even more important to Washington. Hamilton was "the only man [after Washington] who knew the workings of the army and could deal successfully with Congress" and other officials and generals.[1] Hamilton's abundant skills were now applied to cultivating America's powerful partner in the revolutionary struggle, the French. Hamilton's new role in serving as a diplomat and personal representative of Washington to America's new ally, after France officially recognized the United States in April 1777, was vitally important on multiple levels.

With its survival at stake, America overcame its traditional animosity for its historic Catholic foe since before the French and Indian War. Hamilton possessed a host of qualities that made him a master in the fine art of diplomacy with a powerful European ally. He possessed a well-honed tactfulness, courteous manner, and easy cordiality that was actually more European than American, thanks to having worked with so many Europeans, including Frenchmen, with the mercantile firm in St. Croix. Hamilton was fluent and articulate in the most graceful and courtly French. He had been first gained French from his mother, Rachel. French had long served as the universal international language of European diplomacy and the upper class across Europe, even in Russia. Hamilton's mastery of French was essential in regard to Washington's vital communications with France's leading nobles, generals, counts, and admirals of the upper class elite. Boasting a distinct sophistication amidst an army of rustic and provincial revolutionaries, Hamilton was right at home among Europeans of the highest rank.

Hamilton had been reading and writing in French since age sixteen. Unlike so many Americans, especially New Englanders who possessed bitter memories from the horrors of the French and Indian War, Hamilton had always been open-minded and curious about all things French. As in the case of von Steuben, Hamilton's fluency was invaluable to the overall acclimation process of young Marquis de Lafayette, whose English language skills were poor. Essentially acting as the liaison officer to Lafayette as in the upcoming 1778 Monmouth Campaign, Hamilton had early played a prominent role in allowing the French aristocrat's easy entry into the American army, while also laying an early basis for the key relationship between the young Frenchman and Washington. General Washington was so impressed by Lafayette, who had fought for America before the French Alliance, that he had invited him to join his "family."

During military meetings, conferences, and social events at Valley Forge, Hamilton's work as an erudite translator with a cosmopolitan flair gave visiting French officials, including nobles, a highly favorable first impression of Americans. Hamilton established close and very good relationships with the French officers and leaders (especially Lafayette), who adored him in part for his "delightful manner [and] great sweetness," in one French aristocrat's words. All the while, he broadened his already extensive European knowledge base by acquiring a greater understanding of the French elite. In contrast to his ever-growing admiration for the French, Hamilton held nothing but a deep-seated contempt for British leadership. Mocking Howe's generalship to a Frenchman while revealing the depth of his own strategic insights, Hamilton emphasized: "All that the English need to have done was to blockade our ports. But, thank God, they did nothing of the sort."[2]

Meanwhile, Hamilton's influence continued to grow steadily in overall terms, far beyond the narrow confines of Washington's headquarters, reaching out to military and civilian leaders not only across America but also across the Atlantic. All in all, Hamilton's "sangfroid in observing the French factor in American policy and in advising policymakers of the course that should be taken would have done great credit to the wiliness of Benjamin Franklin" in Paris.[3]

Not long after Lafayette brought the exhilarating news of the French Alliance, Hamilton offered his advice to Congress in order to put America's best face for the allies to see, for sound political and psychological reasons. In a letter to James Duane, he advised Congress about the key points that were necessary to ensure initial good relations with the new ally, while tactically educating the New York Congressman like a sage tutor about the finer qualities of French cultural traits and European diplomatic protocol. Regarding the proud, young aristocrat Lafayette, Hamilton emphasized a number of points that reflected key insights as well as wise council: "The Marquis has a thousand little whims to satisfy; one of these he *will have* me to write to some friend in Congress about. He is desirous of having the Captain of the frigate in which he came complimented; and gives several pretty instances of his punctuality and disinterestedness. He wishes Congress to pass some resolutions of thanks, and to recommend him to their Minister in France, to be recommended to the French Court. . . . The *essential* services the Marquis has rendered America in France, give him claim for all that can be done with propriety."[4]

Of course, Hamilton's vital role as Washington's chief diplomat and translator to the French would not have developed without decisive victory at Saratoga, New York. As Hamilton had predicted and as mentioned, Burgoyne's Army had advanced too far south into hostile territory on its own in its overly ambitious push into New York's depths on October 17, 1777. Because Howe had refused to march or sail north up the Hudson from New York City to unite with Burgoyne, Gates' victory forcing Burgoyne's surrender at Saratoga dramatically changed the war's course. Existing talk of accommodation with the Mother Country ended. The Saratoga success had opened the door for the all-important French Alliance signed in April 1778.

A resurgent France wanted to avenge the loss of Canada in the Seven Years' War (a world war that was known as the French and Indian War in America) and weaken English hegemony in the Americas, especially in the Caribbean and Europe. America's former enemy officially recognized the independence of the United States on February 6, 1778. Then, France declared war on England on June 1, 1778. With the news from Versailles and the King Louis XVI of the new alliance and the Bourbon Pact between France and Spain, Washington, Hamilton, and the "family" celebrated the remarkable diplomatic success. After all, the Declaration of Independence of July 4, 1776 had actually been an urgent call for assistance from France and from Spain to a lesser extent.

Thousands of American soldiers cheered, "Long Live the king of France!" Members of the Continental Congress offered prayers for King Louis XVI and the royal family. Quite literally and as fully realized from the very beginning of America's bold experiment with nationhood, the French Alliance offered the tantalizing best hope of national salvation to America during a lengthy war of attrition. Boston's John Adams, who was dispatched to France despite being unable to speak the language, emphasized how "our alliance with France . . . is a rock upon which we may safely build" in the future.[5]

After rebuilding its military strength, France was now more powerful than England, including in regard to naval affairs. London, therefore, worried about the safety of its lightly defended sugar islands, which were sources of vast wealth that provided a substantial part of the economic foundation for the far-flung empire. However, King George III also saw the war as an opportunity to snatch rich sugar islands in the French West Indies, if sizeable reinforcements were rushed to the Caribbean. These British reinforcements could most readily and quickly be dispatched from nearby America. As hoped by London in a global economic war, capture of the wealthy French sugar islands might wreck the French economy, while rejuvenating the British economy and repaying its sizeable war debt.

Consequently, large numbers of British troops in America were now redirected by London to the Caribbean. Because of the upcoming manpower drain that would dramatically weaken British forces in America, military strategists in London on the Thames River decided to evacuate Philadelphia. Incredibly, America's capital was about to be returned to the rebels without a fight, because shortsighted King George III and his ministers were distracted by the tantalizing prospect of capturing the wealthy French sugar islands that were more profitable than the thirteen colonies. Around five thousand British troops in Philadelphia were designated for the upcoming campaign to capture the French sugar island of St. Lucia. With a clear understanding of economic warfare, Hamilton knew: "The primary motivations of France [was] to enfeeble a hated and powerful rival by breaking in pieces the British Empire."[6]

Naturally, members of Washington's "family" had closely followed these international developments with great interest. In a February 27, 1778, letter to his father, Tench Tilghman took note of the exciting strategic possibilities that existed for France in the Caribbean. Perhaps withholding more concrete information that was known at Washington's headquarters, he wrote about the "uncommon preparations by France, in the West Indies, cannot be for nothing."[7] Now better informed from intelligence that flowed into headquarters, the young Marylander rejoiced that America had gained a new lease on life with the French Alliance, writing to his father on May 31, 1778: "The terms of our Alliance with France are generous. . . . The British Army leave Philad. in a few days and . . . goes first to New York [City], ours of course will be near them—Ten Regiments go to Jamaica—perhaps they may be too late—I shall not be surprised if all the Troops leave the Continent to save the Islands [because] France has ten thousand Men there ready to strike."[8]

Lieutenant Colonel Tilghman's sources of information was reliable, because the French had around ten thousand troops garrisoned on their Caribbean islands and high-ranking British leaders had even contemplated abandoning America altogether to save their vast income-producing sugar islands, especially Jamaica.[9] Likewise agreeing with Tilghman, fellow staff member John Laurens wrote on May 27, 1778, about the real reason for the planned British withdrawal from Philadelphia, "It is certain that a notion prevails among the soldiery that many of them are going to the West Indies. . . ."[10]

Tilghman also emphasized how "ours of course will" follow in the hope of exploiting an opportunity: a view shared by Hamilton, who might have informed the Marylander as much.[11] Clearly, neither Washington nor Hamilton had been caught by surprise of the news of Philadelphia's planned evacuation. Large numbers of Loyalists already had fled the city to the delight of long-suffering patriots. In addition, British and Hessian deserters provided accurate information about what was transpiring. Therefore, numerous reports of the impending evacuation of the British Army steadily poured into Washington's headquarters. Hamilton graciously received talkative Loyalists at headquarters and accumulated the latest intelligence from informants because they faced no penalty or reprisal. Because of the French entry into the war, the importance of securing timely and accurate intelligence became even more pressing at Washington's headquarters. Consequently, Hamilton worked overtime to the point of exhaustion. One Continental officer revealed in a March 26, 1778: "Col. Hamilton is so hurried that he has not yet had time to write to you—He looks like Death!"[12]

While speaking to leading French officers and officials in America, the young man must have felt that he was once again among the commercial and business community of French captains and merchants, with whom he had worked closely as a teenage clerk. In one letter to the Marquis de Barbe-Marbois, Hamilton pleaded with the Marquis in the flowery, but appropriately respectful, manner that was fully expected by the high-ranking French officers of the upper class elite: "Have the goodness to assure the Chevalier . . . of my sincere respect and attachment."[13]

Spring 1778 Mission

A much-hoped for prisoner exchange had been in the works at Washington's headquarters since 1776. Hamilton had been dealing with the sensitive issue in

Washington's name since that time and more extensively since March 1, 1777, since joining the staff, but no agreement had developed because the British refused to recognize American rebels as legitimate belligerents. As a captain of New York artillery, Hamilton had first served on one of the early prisoner exchange mission of General Montgomery's men, who had been captured in the doomed attack on Quebec, in September 1776.

Having gained prior experience from interrogating British and Hessian deserters to gain intelligence, Hamilton was named by Washington to a prisoner exchange mission in March 1778. After at least two thousand five hundred men had died at Valley Forge during the winter, Washington hoped that his premier negotiator and diplomat might break the frustrating stalemate, and opened communications with Howe at Philadelphia. On March 28, Hamilton and three others—Col. Robert Hanson Harrison, Washington's oldest staff officer, Elias Boudinot, and Col. William Grayson a former member of Washington's "family" just before Hamilton's arrival—had been named to the new prisoner exchange commission. At this time, Hamilton's old friend Boudinot now officially served as the commissary general of prisoners. Hamilton was the youngest member of this group. But as usual, he had been handed the lion's share of the responsibility and expectations. Once again and like the mission to General Gates in Albany, Hamilton was Washington's chosen leader of the delicate mission to offer a new proposal for a fair prisoner exchange.

Embarking upon another special mission from Washington's Valley Forge headquarters, Hamilton and his party rode around seventeen miles to Germantown, after crossing from the south side to the Schuylkill River's north side. But since Hamilton's earlier attempt at negotiations for a prisoner exchange on March 30 at Germantown (north of Philadelphia), Pennsylvania, met with frustration, Washington agreed to a second round of negotiations with Howe's representatives. Hamilton was determined to succeed this time, despite being angered by the fact that some members of Congress were against any agreements with the British. Along with Boudinot and Grayson, Hamilton and Harrison rode to the new negotiation site at Newton, Pennsylvania. Located around twenty-four miles northeast of Germantown, the second session of talks resulted in a round trip journey (more than eighty miles) for Hamilton and his followers. Here, Hamilton drafted an agreement for a cartel to exchange prisoners.[14]

After the frustrating conference at Newton on Tuesday April 7, Hamilton and his team of negotiators crossed to the Schuylkill's south side and returned

The first meeting of Captain Alexander Hamilton, then commanding his New York "Provincial Company of Artillery," and General George Washington at Fort Bunker Hill that overlooked New York City and guarded the Hudson River at this strategic point of commanding high ground. Author's collection.

Birthplace of Alexander Hamilton. Here, on January 11, 1755, Hamilton entered the world on the Caribbean island of Nevis. The family moved to nearby St. Croix before Hamilton was a teenager. Author's collection.

Portrait of Alexander Hamilton in uniform. Author's collection.

Portrait of General George Washington in uniform by Rembrandt Peale. Image courtesy of The Athenaeum.

WASHINGTON CROSSING THE DELAWARE.

From the original drawing in possession of the Publisher, for Irving's 'Life of Washington.'

Washington's Army crossing the Delaware River on the night of December 25–26, 1776. Hamilton exerted considerable efforts in getting his New York cannon loaded aboard a ferryboat for the journey across the river in the stormy darkness. Author's collection.

Portrait of Marie-Joseph Paul Yves Gilbert du Motier, Marquis de Lafayette by Joseph Désiré-Court. The close friendship between Hamilton and Lafayette was a key link in helping to strengthen the French alliance and soothing the considerable differences between dissimilar allies. © Direction des Musées de France.

Washington's attack on Trenton on the morning of December 26, 1776. Captain Hamilton led his New York artillery unit with distinction at Trenton. After his guns fired on Trenton's garrison from the commanding heights north of town, he played a key forgotten role that revealed his trademark aggressiveness. Hamilton boldly ordered his cannon down the snowy slope toward the town to inflict greater damage on the reeling Hessian garrison. He was the first American artillery officer to employ his guns effectively as "flying artillery" in an urban combat setting. Author's collection.

The surrender of the Hessians at Trenton, New Jersey, on the morning of December 26, 1776. During a hard-fought engagement in which many American muskets were wet and unable to fire, Captain Hamilton's guns played a leading role in garnering for Washington his first true battlefield success to reverse the tide of the American Revolution. Author's collection.

Tench Tilghman. A native Marylander and distinguished member of Washington's staff. Bright and personable, Tilghman became one of Hamilton's closest companions during the years when they worked together on Washington's staff. Author's collection.

James McHenry. Born in County Antrim, Ulster Province, Ireland, James McHenry was an intelligent physician with a refined sense of humor like Hamilton. McHenry, of Scotch-Irish heritage, was also a recent immigrant to America. Hamilton, a West Indian, and McHenry, an Irishman, became close friends. They enjoyed exchanging jokes and witticisms directed at not only others, but also each other. Author's collection.

General Henry Knox. A former bookstore owner from Boston, Knox was a remarkable self-made man (like Hamilton) and gifted general of outstanding ability. As the commander of Washington's artillery, he early recognized the talents of a young and dynamic commander of a New York artillery unit, Captain Alexander Hamilton. Washington early learned of Hamilton's many leadership skills and abilities from Knox. Author's collection.

The parlor of Washington's headquarters at the Ford Mansion, Morristown, New Jersey. Here, Hamilton socialized after the end of long hours of working at his desk and conferring with Washington.

Washington's headquarters at Valley Forge, Pennsylvania. The team of Washington and Hamilton worked closely together during some of the most trying and difficult times of the American Revolution, including at Valley Forge. Author's collection.

Washington's headquarters at Morristown, New Jersey. Here, Lieutenant Colonel Alexander Hamilton worked by Washington's side at the stately mansion built by Jacob Ford, Jr., after the Continental Army went into winter quarters. Author's collection.

THE BATTLE OF MONMOUTH, NEW JERSEY, ON JUNE 28, 1778.

General Washington and Lieutenant Colonel Hamilton played leading roles in rallying the routed troops of General Charles Lee at the battle of Monmouth Court House, New Jersey, on June 28, 1778. Hamilton's spirited performance in helping to save day was described as a "frenzy of valor" even by his arch enemy, General Lee.

Robert Hanson Harrison was a longtime member of George Washington's personal staff known as the "family." A former Virginia attorney, Harrison became one of Washington's first staff members. He served Washington with distinction from November 1775 to the spring of 1781. Author's collection.

Elizabeth Schuyler Hamilton in all her glory as revealed in this 1787 portrait by artist Ralph Earl. In the enchanting Elizabeth (also called Betsey and Eliza), who was well known for many admirable qualities, Hamilton gained not only an ideal wife but also a worthy companion. Elizabeth was devoted to Hamilton, who she outlived by more than half a century, and never lost her love for him. Elizabeth Schuyler Hamilton lived to nearly the age of 100. Courtesy of the Museum of the City of New York. Image courtesy of The Athenaeum.

Philip Schuyler was elected to the Continental Congress in 1775 and then gained the lofty rank of major general in the Continental Army. Although a member of the aristocratic elite, Major General Schuyler fully accepted Hamilton into his family and as the husband of his dark-eyed second daughter Elizabeth. Author's collection.

Known as the Pastures, this magnificent brick mansion at Albany, New York, was the home of Major General Philip Schuyler. At this house, located on a commanding bluff that overlooked the Hudson River, Hamilton found his greatest personal fulfillment with the general's daughter, whom he married in December 1780, and a warm family setting that he had long lacked in his native Caribbean. Author's collection.

to Valley Forge. Hamilton had acted with the full authority as Washington's personal representative, demanding a prisoner exchange endorsed by the British government and not an individual commander. On Wednesday April 15, 1778, as the head commissioner of prisoner exchange, Hamilton wrote his official report to the commander-in-chief. The British commissioners had opened the talks by declaring that any prisoner exchange treaty would be binding only between Washington's and Howe's commands: England refused to recognize Americans as soldiers of a legitimate nation due equal recognition and rights. Therefore, as the Britons had emphasized, this treaty, if signed, would be "of a personal nature, founded on the mutual confidence and honor of the contracting Generals," Washington and Howe.[15]

Leaving out no detail, the ever-meticulous Hamilton emphasized to Washington, "In answer, we assigned them our reasons at large, for thinking there was a material defect, in their powers, which must render any Treaty, we could form, nugatory and unequal. . . . The Commissioners from General Howe [then] intimated an impropriety in treating with us, on a national ground, in a contest of such a nature as the present [Washington and his men were rebels], which might imply an acknowlegement inconsistent with their claims. We observed to them, that if there was any inconsistency at all, it would operate equally against the forming a cartel, on any principle whatever, and against the whole business of exchange [and] that a clause should be admitted into the cartel, declaring, that no expressions contained in it, should be construed to affect the political claims of either country, in any thing, not directly necessary to the due and faithful observance of the Treaty. . . ."[16]

Despite Hamilton's negotiating skills, Howe refused to revise the wording or conditions of his prisoner exchange commission. In conclusion, Hamilton reported with regret to Washington on April 15: "We are sorry the views of General Sir William Howe were so far different from yours as to render them impracticable. Your powers to us were the standard, by which we were to judge of the sufficiency of his. The former are founded on the broad basis of national faith; the latter, on the narrow one of private faith. A dissimilarity, in so material a point, appeared to us a solid, and on our part, an insuperable objection. We considered the formation of a Treaty, by which such momentous concerns would be affected, with no other sanction, than the personal honor and interest of an individual—not only as incompatible with our commission; but as repugnant to reason, to the nature of the business, and to common usage, in similar cases. A Treaty so formed would, in our conception, be merely nominal, or at best of temporary operation, certainly ceasing with personal command—liable, at any time, to be violated by public authority, without the imputation of public dishonor, and highly derogatory to the dignity of these United States."[17]

Of course, Hamilton's reservations about formulating a prisoner exchange treaty between commanders instead of between nations (England, of course, refused to recognize the United States as an independent nation since this was a rebellion that could not be granted legitimate status) were well-founded, because Howe was about to be replaced by General Henry Clinton, Howe's second in command. Howe resigned in part because of the lack of reinforcements from England, knowing that the overall chances for success in America had dwindled dramatically, after the French Alliance and with the West Indies (sugar was the most profitable commodity because of the insatiable demands of European consumers) became more strategically important in London's eyes.[18]

Hamilton had done his best, but congressional interference and bungling also played a role in sabotaging a possible permanent agreement, until his last initiative when a prisoner exchange deal was finally on the verge of being struck. Congress had violated articles of the agreement for Burgoyne's surrender at Saratoga in October 1777, which Hamilton condemned because of the "system of infidelity" of Congress. Negating Hamilton's earlier efforts, these violations only increased his disgust with Congress, whose folly had "put off an exchange perhaps forever" to guarantee the deaths of countless American prisoners, as he bitterly lamented earlier in the year. Worst of all, some Congressional members not only were against Hamilton's efforts, but also hoped to see negotiations fail so that Howe and the British could be blamed. In a letter to Governor Clinton, a disgusted Hamilton concluded: "It is thought to be bad policy to go into an exchange. But admitting this to be true, it is much worse policy [as undertaken by Congress] to commit such frequent breaches of faith and ruin our national character."[19]

By his trademark dogged persistence and hard negotiating, Hamilton eventually broke through the deadlock. In May 1778, Howe finally agreed to exchange nearly eight hundred prisoners. Hamilton was delegated by Washington to monitor proceedings to ensure that the exchange process flowed smoothly.[20] Now that Hamilton had succeeded and "that a general prisoner exchange [including no more American captives imprisoned in England or the Caribbean] appeared imminent, Hamilton [continued his] prominent role [as] Washington's most trusted deputy."[21]

When Valley Forge erupted in celebration in the first week of May 1778 as the official news of the French Alliance was read to the troops from Washington's May 6 general orders, Hamilton remained quiet and consumed by his own thoughts.[22] In fact, he was now worried, while seemingly everyone else was celebrating the good news. Knowing human nature and the folly that stemmed from it only too well from his careful readings of history, this savvy natural psychologist and expert on human nature was concerned that the news of this remarkable alliance with this European powerhouse would make the revolutionaries too overconfident and, hence, more vulnerable in the end. Therefore, while other Americans believed that the war was now all but won at long last, Hamilton was concerned that the opposite might in fact be the case. In this regard, he was once again correct. Ironically, Hamilton also might have felt uneasy because of a planned strike by the Queen's Rangers (Loyalists), whose commander was familiar with the home that housed Washington's headquarters.

Hamilton wrote still another one of his many prophetic letters, which alerted General Greene—who had been so enchanted with the extensive range of the native West Indian's military knowledge and intelligence upon their first meeting in the war's early days—of his worst fears. The young man emphasized that the new French Alliance should not "justify the least relaxation" of America's war efforts, which should "be continued in their fullest vigor." If not, then the consequences, Hamilton feared with sage insight, well "might be fatal."[23]

Dramatic Showdown at Monmouth Court House

On June 18, 1778, and after occupying America's capital for nine months, the last of Sir Henry Clinton's army of around ten thousand British and Hessian troops finally departed Philadelphia. Clinton was correctly worried that the arrival of an approaching French fleet would unite with Washington's Army to entrap him along the Schuylkill. Consequently, with flintlocks on shoulders, around nine thousand of Clinton's soldiers marched out of the infant republic's first capital and headed northeast for the east coast and New York City. The British Fleet already had sailed from the "City of Brotherly Love," taking many panicked Loyalists with them. As Hamilton now envisioned with clarity, Clinton's Army, burdened by its lengthy baggage train and lowered morale after departing the great prize of Philadelphia, was becoming increasingly vulnerable. Hard marching and scorching summer weather shortly made the already too-lengthy enemy column more vulnerable by straggling and desertions.[24]

With the British Army moving across unfamiliar country, a good opportunity finally existed for Washington to strike a blow. Hamilton's strategic sense and political instincts were right on target in this regard: Washington needed a success for not only military but also domestic and political reasons. Like few other officers, Hamilton now viewed Clinton's withdrawal to New York as an unprecedented tactical opportunity to deliver a punishing blow with the British and Hessians soldiers far away from Philadelphia's confines. With the enemy now forced to march overland toward the coast across the sun-baked fields and woodlands because the existence of the French fleet made transportation by waters too risky, Hamilton thought expressly in offensive terms. Once again demonstrating a clairvoyant-like ability in strategic matters like in regard to the Saratoga Campaign, he even envisioned that Clinton's withdrawal might present the golden opportunity to strike a punishing blow and perhaps even win the war.

As usual, Lieutenant Colonel Hamilton's views were shortly openly voiced and at the highest levels. When Washington called a commanders' conference on June 17, he asked Hamilton to prepare the most pressing question to the Virginians' top lieutenants about the possibility of launching a strike. Hamilton was shocked by the ultra-conservative consensus of the army's leading Continental generals, who believed that it was simply too risky to follow Clinton's Army. Convinced that American soldiers could never stand-up (much less defeat) to well-trained British regulars when they turned back to meet any rearward threat, England-born General Charles Lee was the leading voice not only against an attack but also against a vigorous pursuit of Clinton. Articulate and impassioned, the experienced Lee easily made converts of most of Washington's generals, who viewed Philadelphia's evacuation as a sufficient victory for America in itself: the return of the nation's capital without a fight. Only General Anthony Wayne advocated the kind of aggressiveness that Hamilton believed was now necessary to exploit an opportunity.[25]

For sound political and military reasons and following Hamilton's early advice, Washington decided to follow Clinton's long withdrawal northeast toward New York City. With an advanced force, Lee was dispatched in pursuit on June 18. Then, on June 19, after a half-year respite, the Continental Army's troops marched out of Valley Forge with a new confidence, after von Steuben's tireless efforts and intensive training of the troops.

Riding at Washington's side along with other staff members, Hamilton galloped into a new campaign and another long-awaited opportunity to engage in combat, while the confident army of revolutionaries headed northeastward with renewed optimism. Early in this new campaign, Hamilton even found time to employ his well-honed skills in flirting with "a pretty, full-faced, youthful, playful lass," after stopping for the night at a private home in Doylestown, Pennsylvania, located about thirty miles north of Philadelphia. But neither the lengthy romance for the future nor brief carnal interlude for the night materialized much to Hamilton's regret, because duty inconveniently called. Washington shortly dispatched his ever-energetic chief of staff with a troop of cavalry northeastward to scout up ahead and gather intelligence. Washington needed to know the location and condition of Clinton's Army, especially if any good tactical opportunity existed to strike a blow, as Hamilton emphasized with enthusiasm.

Leading the advance, Lee and his forces crossed the Delaware River on June 20. Washington held another council of war on June 24 to discuss strategy and tactics. After his return from another reconnaissance mission over the New Jersey countryside, Hamilton officially served as secretary at the council. He diligently took the minutes with his usual care, but was also serving as an advisor to Washington at the meeting. During these conferences, Lieutenant Colonel Hamilton offered his bold advice and opinions to older men of much higher rank, and it had little to do with the pervasive caution among senior commanders. Once again, he was showing that he was no average staff officer before the army's senior generals. As Hamilton had written to the American people that revealed his axiom of an aggressive officer who knew what was necessary for victory: "there is hardly anything more prejudicial than excessive caution. . . ."[26]

Washington asked his generals if they should now "hazard a general action." He wanted to know if a general assault should be launched, or if only a portion of the army should attack the British column, if a good tactical opportunity was presented. General Lee continued to emphasize that Clinton should be allowed to proceed on his northeast withdrawal unmolested for the entire ninety miles to the coast and New York City. A number of general officers agreed, partly because of Lee's masterful eloquence, but not Lafayette (to Hamilton's delight), Anthony Wayne, or Nathanael Greene. In a compromise and in overriding the consensus, therefore, Washington decided to only detach one thousand five hundred troops to pursue Clinton in the hope of unleashing a partial attack on his rear guard, if a favorable tactical opportunity arose. Lieutenant Colonel Tench Tilghman was as encouraged as Hamilton by this time. As he had recently penned to his father on June 22 that partly revealed the tactical opportunity fully realized and articulated by Hamilton: "The British Army makes very slow marches thro' Jersey [and the] Desertion from them is enormous. Two hundred [of them] have come in since yesterday morning and the numbers [of British and Hessian deserters] in Jersey are very great."[27]

Meanwhile, Lieutenant Colonel Hamilton continued to be not only shocked but also disgusted by the rise of negative developments, especially the lack of fighting spirit among most of Washington's generals, who refused to see the good opportunity that he so easily perceived. After all, he had advocated an attack on the British Army to Gouverneur Morris as early as September 1 not long after the enemy had disembarked from the Chesapeake and advanced on Philadelphia from the south. Hamilton continued to feel confident for success, sensing a golden opportunity lay in New Jersey along the route to New York City. He, therefore, strongly denounced Lee's histrionics at the commanders' conference and overall "conduct with respect to the command of this corps was truly childish."[28]

In a letter to Elias Boudinot, Hamilton summarized the turn of events that angered him because he sensed an unprecedented tactical opportunity—an entire British Army in retreat—slipping away: "When we came to Hopewell Township [New Jersey], the General unluckily called a council of war, the result of which would have done honor to the most honorab[le] society of mid-wives, and to them only. The purport was, that we should keep up a vain parade of annoying them by detachment [and] in persuance of this idea, a detachment of 1500 men was sent off under General [Charles] Scot[t] to join the other troops near the enemy's lines. General Lee was *primum mobile* of this sage plan; and was even opposed to sending so considerable a force. . . ."[29]

Taking into account all dimensions of the struggle, young Hamilton possessed a larger and comprehensive strategic view that was as much political, moral, and psychological as military. Hamilton, consequently, viewed the act of striking at Clinton's withdrawing army on New Jersey soil southwest of New York City as a matter of "fortune and honor" in regard to the new nation's and army's image, as he wrote to Lafayette, who thought like Hamilton in this regard.[30]

The night after the conference, General Greene wrote Washington a confidential letter that stated his disagreement (like the ever-combative General Wayne) with the consensus that advocated caution. Instead, he advocated for a larger force to be designated to strike Clinton's rear guard. Greene also emphasized that the main army should be ready for a general engagement, just in case the British turned to strike back when they were most likely to do if threatened. Greene's views coincided with Washington's own and, of course, those of Hamilton. Therefore, changing his mind to go against the pro-caution consensus in a decision that displayed tactical flexibility, Washington increased the advance force assigned to hitting Clinton's rear, if an opportunity was presented, to four thousand five hundred men, sending "Mad" Anthony Wayne's and Lafayette's troops in pursuit.[31]

Serving as a liaison officer that provided assistance to the inexperienced, young Lafayette, Hamilton was assigned to Lafayette and his advancing column, after a more determined Washington "ordered the Marquis forward," in his words, in a northeastward pursuit.[32] With his fluency in French and excellent relationship with the young nobleman, Hamilton conferred with Lafayette in the Marquis's native language, amusing homespun American onlookers, especially uneducated soldiers from the backwoods. Desiring to deliver the enemy a crushing blow, an animated Hamilton, flush with excitement and adrenaline, was eager for the challenge. Despite having suffered a leg wound at Brandywine, Lafayette was equally adamant as his young friend from the West Indies.

Hamilton as Hard-Riding Reconnaissance Officer

To serve not only Washington but also his good friend Lafayette, Hamilton was now in his element. Unchained from the desk job and endless paperwork, Hamilton relished the challenges and opportunities of active campaigning. An unleashed Hamilton rode like the wind through the New Jersey countryside, galloping ahead of Lafayette's column to ascertain any tactical weaknesses in British Army's rear, after conferring with the young Frenchman. Clearly, and as so often in the past, Washington was relying heavily on Hamilton's astute tactical sense and good judgment. From the period of June 25 to June 28 "Hamilton was [about to be] everywhere, acting as the eyes and ears of Lafayette and Washington [and] his written intelligence reports were models, giving necessary information without an unnecessary word," as Washington desired.[33]

Hamilton hoped to secure as much accurate intelligence as possible, but the scorching weather and unfamiliar terrain posed difficulties from the beginning. At Robins Tavern, which was located eight miles from the Negro Run, Indian Run, and Doctors Creek area at Allentown in Monmouth County,

New Jersey, Hamilton halted his reconnaissance mission out of weariness in the intense heat. He finally found spare time to send his written intelligence report (earlier reconnaissance reports had been verbally communicated) to Washington. Here, at noon on June 26, Hamilton described the logistical crisis among Washington's advancing troops: "Our reason for halting is the extreme distress of the troops for want of provisions [and] General Wayne's detachment is almost starving and seem both unwilling and unable to march further 'till they are supplied. If we do not receive an immediate supply, the whole purpose of our detachment must be frustrated. This morning we missed doing any thing from a deficiency of intelligence."[34]

Having acted with his usual alacrity, Hamilton had already taken urgent steps to organize and improve the army's deplorable intelligence capabilities, especially now in the presence of a superior opponent. As Lieutenant Colonel Hamilton explained in his timely report to Washington while far in the army's advance: "On my arrival at Cranbury [Middlesex County, New Jersey] yesterday evening, I proceeded . . . to take measures for cooperating with the different parts of the detachment and to find what was doing to procure intelligence. I found every precaution was neglected—no horse [cavalry] was near the enemy, or could be heard of 'till late in the morning; so that before we could send out parties [of cavalry] and get the necessary information, they were in full march and as they have marched pretty expeditiously we should not be able to come up with them during the march of this day; if we did not suffer the impediment we do on the score of provisions."[35]

Then, leaving behind a situation that he improved upon, Hamilton continued to ride ahead to ascertain vital intelligence about the enemy's weaknesses. He learned that Clinton's troops were marching briskly under the sweltering New Jersey sun and suffering severely in consequence. Such timely intelligence about the enemy's vulnerabilities was important for Washington's decision to advance closer to the British Army. Hamilton continued in his report: "If the army will countenance us we may do something clever."[36]

Ascertained from his observations of the British Army's rear, Hamilton's accurate reports continued to convince Washington that a tactical opportunity existed, which, of course, was the vital information that he needed. Agreeing with Hamilton, who had been a dissenting voice among his conservative generals, Washington began to realize that he might well be able to deliver a punishing blow.[37] Dispatched by Washington, Hamilton and

Lafayette reached Lee's column to confer with the army's most haughty general who had been born in England. They attempted to persuade Lee to hand over his forward elements to the Frenchman, because Lee was reticent to serve as Washington's second-in-command since he disagreed with the plan of action. But Lee refused to relinquish what he considered a post of honor, pulling rank by right of seniority. Consequently, Lee now led the entire advance corps of nearly five thousand men northeastward as Washington's most senior officer.[38]

Most of all, Hamilton was eager to find the best tactical opportunity for the unleashing of an attack, if the right tactical vulnerability was presented. With telescope in hand during his ongoing reconnaissance to provide Washington with timely intelligence, Hamilton surveyed the lengthy column of weary soldiers in red (British soldiers) and blue (Hessians), and an immense baggage train that extended for more than ten miles. In gathering the most up-to-date intelligence, he sometimes approached so close to Clinton's withdrawing army that he found himself in harm's way. As a survivor of Washington's miserable withdrawal through New Jersey during the fall of 1776 when America's fortunes had sagged to new lows, Hamilton also wanted a measure of payback.

In addition, he was motivated to prove Lee wrong about his strong opinions and strategy, because it was known that this cantankerous general detested Washington and mocked Hamilton's and von Steuben's longtime efforts to professionalize the army. Like many others, General Lee held Hamilton in contempt because of his youth, lowly background, and success by Washington's side. Even more, Lee's dissenting voice now presented still another challenge to Washington's authority, generalship, and strategic reasoning, not long after Hamilton had helped to expose Gates and the so-called Conway Cabal. For such reasons, Hamilton wanted Washington to win the victory that would prove Lee wrong and thoroughly discredit Lee and his tactical views. Therefore, eager to ascertain the right opportunity for his boss to strike a blow, Hamilton explained to Washington in his June 26 report of Clinton's lack of resolve that bestowed a distinct tactical advantage to the pursuers: "We feel our personal honor as well as the honor of the army and the good of the service interested and are heartily desirous to attempt whatever the disposition of our men will second and prudence authorise [and] it is evident the enemy wish to avoid not to engage us."[39]

Like an experienced intelligence officer far to the front because the Virginian, now anxiously waiting the most recent intelligence, was basing his fluid plans upon the timely information from him, Hamilton continued to keep Washington closely appraised of Clinton's movements and his troops' overall condition. Even more than any previous time, Washington now needed timely intelligence before unleashing his troops to strike at the most opportune point, after "stressing that even a half hour would make a difference" in regard to receiving timely intelligence: a requirement that Hamilton tried hard to fulfill.[40] Therefore, Hamilton continued to perform his vital reconnaissance missions, including at night, while staying in the saddle for long hours, riding far and wide, and delivering daily intelligence reports to Washington.[41]

For two successive nights, Lieutenant Colonel Hamilton rode even farther ahead with a cavalry escort for protection, reaching a point in front of Clinton's army to ascertain vulnerabilities. Hamilton continued to note how Clinton hoped to avoid any kind of confrontation with his pursuers, desiring only to reach New York City to the northeast: an attitude that made Clinton and his army less combat ready and more vulnerable. The tireless lieutenant colonel, who displayed considerable stamina in the saddle, made two other important discoveries. While in an advantageous position before the lengthy British column, he learned that the advancing Americans at New Brunswick, New Jersey, to the north were now positioned across the route of Clinton's withdrawal.

Most importantly, Hamilton also discovered that Clinton had cleverly maneuvered solely to escape pursuit, changing the direction of his march. After reconfirming this fact with a final observation to avoid any possible error in judgment, Hamilton dispatched a rider back to inform Washington and another courier to tell Lafayette that Clinton was now pushing directly toward Monmouth Court House, just northeast of Princeton and south of Brunswick: evidence that the enemy was now attempting to reach Sandy Hook on the northeast Jersey coast, where the British Navy could then transport the army to New York City just to the north.

Besides providing this invaluable intelligence that informed Washington's of Clinton's route of withdrawal, Hamilton also continued to serve as a highly effective liaison officer, while distributing timely intelligence to the advance elements of Washington's Army, especially Lafayette's column. Hamilton also advised Lafayette to hurriedly march to Cranbury, New Jersey, around sixty miles northeast of Philadelphia, to maneuver closer to the British Army's vulnerable rear.[42] Based on Hamilton's accurate intelligence, Washington force-marched his troops to Cranbury to maneuver within striking distance of Clinton's rear, despite the pouring rain and muddy roads that slowed their pursuit.[43]

When Washington learned that Clinton had stopped at Allentown, New Jersey, he wanted to know why. Consequently, he dispatched Hamilton to investigate and ascertain the latest tactical developments before him. Hamilton wrote another revealing intelligence report to Washington: "Their march today has been very judiciously conducted—their baggage in front [and all protected by a strong] rear guard [under Cornwallis] of 1,000 men about 400 paces from the main body. To attack them in this situation, without being supported by the whole army, would be folly in the extreme."[44]

Nevertheless, Hamilton still felt that a good tactical opportunity existed to strike a blow, if Lafayette was ordered forward, toward Monmouth Court House. Based upon Hamilton's latest intelligence, therefore, Washington now realized that the entire army needed to advance to support Lee's advanced elements to exploit any newly presented tactical opportunity, and ordered his troops to Cranbury, which they reached on June 26.[45]

Meanwhile, Aaron Burr also advanced in Lord Stirling's column in its pursuit of Clinton's Army during its long march to New York City. With an ego nearly the size of General Lee's which was rather remarkable in itself, Burr was one of the army's youngest majors. He had won a name for himself at snowy Quebec in the ill-fated attack on the last day of 1775. While in the vanguard of General Richard Montgomery's assault column, Burr survived the fatal cannon-blast of canister at close range that cut down America's first general to die in battle. The diminutive Burr risked his life in a desperate attempt to retrieve Montgomery's body. Hamilton admired Burr's heroics in Canada that had become well known through the army.

General Lee and young Burr possessed a shared a mutual contempt for Washington. Burr admired General Lee, who denounced Washington as "not fit to command a sergeant's guard," almost as much as fatherly General Israel Putnam. Hamilton hated Lee as much as Lee detested Washington, labeling him as "a driveler" in the military arts. Born in Newark, New Jersey, Burr by now had just secured the same rank (lieutenant colonel) as Hamilton. Ironically, Hamilton and Burr were very much alike, which was another reason why they eventually evolved into mortal enemies: scholarly intellectuals (including history lovers) who were also dynamic men of action, highly competent, multitalented (including in conducting intelligence work), aggressive, and tactically astute on the battlefield.

In addition, the two remarkable young men were ambitious and about the same age, build, and height. Like Hamilton, who was described as "a mere sapling" even as late as the battle of Princeton, Burr was also considered a mere "boy" when they first "drew their swords" at the revolution's beginning. After learning of the young man's Quebec heroics in a wintery hell, Washington had invited Burr to join his staff. But Burr shortly departed to serve as Putnam's staff officer, embarking upon a much different career and destiny.

Because of health issues stemming primarily from the Monmouth Campaign's rigors and a long-existing animosity toward Washington, whom he blamed for not promoting him, this was destined to be Burr's final campaign. After the battle of Monmouth, he retired his officer's commission. Meanwhile, in contrast to Burr whose military career ended at age twenty-three, Hamilton's own career was guaranteed to ascend ever-higher and last far longer.[46]

On June 27, after the bulk of General Clinton's Army had halted in and around Monmouth Court House, a small village of around thirty buildings, Clinton ordered his exhausted troops to rest before pushing on northeast toward the safety of the New Jersey coast, just below New York City.[47] Meanwhile, Hamilton was riding far ahead before Lafayette's column in his relentless attempt to ascertain just the right tactical opportunity to deliver a fatal blow to Clinton's Army. Fairly lusting at the sight, Hamilton described what he fully believed was exactly the right tactical opportunity when, "The advanced corps came up with the enemy[']s rear a mile or two beyond the [Monmouth] court House; I saw the enemy drawn up, and am persuaded there were not a thousand men; their front from different accounts was then ten miles off [which was a most] favourable . . . situation" for success.[48]

On June 27, Washington, Hamilton, and Lafayette met at Englishtown amid the rich farmlands of east central New Jersey. Dust-covered and weary from four long days in the saddle, Hamilton notified Washington that Lee was approaching near to Clinton's stationary rearguard at Monmouth Court House just to the southeast. Hamilton suggested a bold plan for Washington to entrap Clinton's rearguard and cut them off from the main force: order his right wing to advance and outflank the enemy's isolated rearguard while sending the left wing, under Hamilton, to reinforce Lee in advance. Washington agreed with Hamilton's daring tactical plan. But General Lee's controversial actions, if not outright sabotage as some people came to believe, on June 28 were about to ensure that Hamilton's ambitious plan that might have resulted in victory, was never carried out.[49]

While Hamilton's aggressive instincts continued to rise to the fore, this was certainly not the case in regard to General Lee. Despite his loud boasting at seemingly every opportunity, especially at councils of war, Lee was in over his head as the commander of the advance on June 28, after having been ordered by Washington (as suggested by Hamilton) to attack in the early morning, if he determined that the British were not too strong. When Washington had first learned (perhaps from Hamilton, dispatched to scout the situation) on the morning of June 28 that Clinton's troops were once again in motion to continue their retreat, he ordered Lee, through aide Richard Kidder Meade, one of Hamilton's best friends, to strike a blow. General Lee proved more of a conceited loud talker than a real fighter as Hamilton already fully realized to his disgust. Despite having read Washington's orders to not unleash a full-fledged attack, but only skirmish with Clinton's forces to allow time for Washington and the main army to advance and reinforce him, Lee still remained tentative and hesitant.

Clinton's rear guard was under the very capable Lord Cornwallis, but this was not what deterred Lee. The seeds of disaster were early sown because Lee had failed to coordinate his advance and even inform his subordinates of his plans. But most of all, Lee had no real interest in adhering to Washington's orders, having no desire to strike as Lafayette had earlier feared. The unfamiliar terrain also befuddled Lee, who became even more tentative in consequence. This was especially the case because Lee had failed to gather intelligence about the nature of the ground before him: A gaping void that Hamilton attempted to fill by acquiring intelligence and then hurriedly distributing the information to the advance elements of Washington's Army and headquarters to enlighten the commander-in-chief.

Hamilton was also ordered to make sure that Lee was following orders and to ascertain developments at the front. Then, an increasingly anxious Washington also dispatched John Laurens and James McHenry, the most recent member of the "family," forward to reconnoiter and gather intelligence in the direction of Monmouth Court House to determine if all was progressing according to his plan. To link with Lee's advance force, Washington then pushed the main column forward toward this obscure courthouse seemingly in the middle of nowhere.

Like Hamilton, Washington found a discouraging situation in Lee's vanguard. Lee's movements were not only haphazard, but also careless in the sunbaked fields and pine barrens, ensuring disunity and potential danger for the advance force that had been ordered to strike. Finally, Lee seemed about to unleash an attack as ordered by Washington on the previous night. Hamilton then rode back and informed Washington around noon that Lee's attack was at last about to commence, but Hamilton ascertained a tactical problem. Seeing a serious weakness, Hamilton then proposed to Washington to shift Greene's troops south to cover a road to protect the army's right flank. While Washington contemplated the wisdom of Hamilton's proposed tactics (which were correct because securing high ground on the right flank was all-important) and upon hearing several cannon boom from the vicinity of Monmouth Court House, Washington then ordered Richard Kidder Meade, the fastest rider of the "family," to the front to report of the most recent developments.

Washington also dispatched Hamilton back to Lee's command to report any progress in compliance with his orders to strike. Washington was concerned because no sound of fighting was heard, which meant that Lee had not struck as ordered. However, Hamilton discovered to his shock that Lee's right was threatened by a flanking party, and these American troops were falling back hardly before they had engaged the enemy. Riding rapidly to relay the vital information, Hamilton quickly appraised Lee of the looming danger, and implored Lee to stop the retrograde movement. Lee then ordered Hamilton to ride to Lafayette and inform him to strengthen the vulnerable right flank, before it was too late. Hamilton then turned rearward, and rode back to Washington, who had just learned from General Henry Knox that Lee's troops were in confusion and that a reversal now seemed possible.

Meanwhile, an escalation of gunfire erupted in Lee's front. With Hamilton now by his side, Washington spurred his horse down the road to reach Lee's advanced position and ascertain the most recent tactical developments himself. The commander-in-chief and Hamilton were stunned to discover that large numbers of Lee's troops were withdrawing before the advance of Clinton's most able top lieutenant, Cornwallis. The redeployment on the right led to a shift rearward, which convinced some of Lee's commanders that the general had ordered a withdrawal, and they pulled back. Lee's offensive plan had quickly fallen to pieces.

With Clinton's main force in close support and providing reinforcements, Cornwallis now planned to smash Lee's advance force before the arrival of the rest of Washington's Army. Sickened by the sight, Hamilton was astounded when "we found the troops retiring in the greatest disorder and the enemy pressing their rear." After all, Lee had been ordered by Washington to attack a vulnerable rearguard of an overextended column in the midst of lengthy and exhausted withdrawal, and the loudest braggart in the Continental Army was now in retreat, after having failed to exploit the advantage.

Hardly believing his eyes, Washington was angered by what looked like still another embarrassing defeat hardly before the battle began. Larger numbers of retreating American troops were encountered by Washington, who had expected to see Lee's men attacking and exploiting the tactical opportunity. Incredibly, Lee had failed to report to headquarters anything about these shocking developments, especially his unauthorized withdrawal. Therefore, Washington was incensed when he finally encountered Lee. The Virginian hotly requested to know "the meaning of his disorder and confusion" to a surprised Lee, who had never heard such forceful language coming from an incensed Washington. Feeling the sting of Washington's temper for the first time, that seemed even hotter than the one-hundred-degree New Jersey heat, Lee blurted out stammering words and then made ineffective excuses. It was clear to Washington and Hamilton that Lee had lost control of not only the developing battle situation, but also his men and himself in a battlefield situation.[50]

Besides Washington, no one was more stunned than Hamilton by the fast-paced tactical developments that had so suddenly turned against American fortunes. After all, Hamilton had only recently ascertained what looked to be certain tactical possibilities for success. Indeed, Lieutenant Colonel Hamilton had first spied the tactical opportunity of striking Clinton's isolated rearguard that had been ordered to guard the lengthy baggage train, of around one thousand five hundred wagons a dozen miles in length, which moved at a snail's pace under the blazing sun. Clearly, this vulnerable British-Hessian column provided an opportunity to inflict significant damage. But now Hamilton was astounded by the shocking realization that "our advanced corps [under Lee] got into a general confused retreat [just north of Monmouth Court House] and even route [*sic*] would hardly be too strong an expression. Not a word of all this was officially communicated to the General [Washington]" by Lee.[51]

Hamilton's Early Role in Saving the Day

With his fighting blood up and hoping to rally the troops streaming rearward, Hamilton rode into the midst of the crisis situation on his gray horse even before Washington's arrival. He was attempting to rally Lee's withdrawing men amid the confusion. With his saber drawn and hoping to prevent another defeat that now seemed inevitable, Hamilton swore to Lee, "I will stay and we will all die here on the spot!"[52] Knowing that the situation was desperate, Hamilton had also yelled: "I will stay here with you, my dear General, and die with you; let us all die here rather than retreat."[53]

Whatever Hamilton's exact words in this crisis situation, these diehard sentiments had astounded (like Washington's later harsh words) the less determined Lee, who was more proficient at backdoor politics and looking more after his own safety than leading troops in battle. Lee later paid an indirect compliment to Hamilton's spirited performance in rallying the troops on a commanding ridge on the north side of the West Ravine just northwest of Monmouth Court House, which offered an ideal position to make a defensive stand: an astute tactical evaluation first suggested by Tench Tilghman. Impressed by what he saw, even the English-born general admitted how Hamilton's frantic actions on this battlefield to stem the tide and help to save the day were distinguished by "a sort of frenzy for valor." Clearly, Hamilton provided timely service in ascertaining early on that a defensive stand just southeast of the little Freehold Meeting House and inspirational leadership were now needed atop the ridge, before it was too late.[54]

Washington's Finest Hour

With most of Lee's four-thousand-man command falling back and as mentioned, Hamilton had rejoined Washington to be by the general's side. An excited Robert Hanson Harrison then rode up to Washington, Hamilton, and other aides, including Dr. James McHenry (the only person added to his staff in 1778) and Tench Tilghman, with the shocking news that sizeable numbers of British troops, now only fifteen minutes away, were now advancing with fixed bayonets and increased momentum. On his finest day, Washington played the leading role in rallying Lee's shaken troops, who had withdrawn around two miles, now deploying them in excellent defensive positions on the north side of West Ravine. Assisted by his aides, he then formed Lafayette's and Wayne's troops on this good defensive ground to meet the onslaught.

Meanwhile, Hamilton continued to rally troops, even reverting back to his old captain of artillery role, while being seemingly everywhere at once. With so many of Lee's troops having fallen back, he hastily supervised the

alignment of one of Colonel Eleazer Oswald's batteries on high ground abve
the West Ravine to meet Cornwallis' attack from the east. Then, fearing the
loss of these guns, Hamilton also hurriedly rallied a retiring brigade of New
Jersey and Rhode Island Continentals and then rallied them on good ground.
With sword in hand and shouting orders, he led them forward to protect the
row of blazing guns. Most importantly, Hamilton now knew what was most
needed to stabilize the front: an attack, which was always the best form of
defense, which he now not only ordered but also led to ensure the safety of the
guns. Therefore—after herculean efforts by Washington, who was at his best,
and Hamilton and other staff officers, especially Laurens—the Americans were
finally ready to greet the advancing British lines with a solid defense along the
north side of West Ravine. With the Americans standing firm for the first time
all day, a slugfest developed for most of this afternoon amid the fields of summer, while the firing of guns grew to a roar.

As never before, Hamilton felt a sense of awe at the sight of Washington
rising magnificently up to his supreme challenge in the crisis situation and literally saving the day. He wrote how he "never saw the general to such an advantage [and] his coolness and firmness were admirable [because] he instantly
took measures for checking the enemy's advance, and giving time for the army,
which was very near, to form and make a proper disposition" to meet the
advancing redcoats.[55]

As penned in a July 5 letter, Hamilton never forgot how an animated
Washington "rode back and had the troops formed on a very advantageous
piece of ground [and] America owes a great deal to General Washington for
this day's work; a general route [sic] dismay and disgrace would have attended
the whole army in any other hands but his. By his own good sense and fortitude
he turned the fate of the day."[56]

Like so many others, aide Dr. James McHenry was also greatly impressed
when Washington "unfolded surprising abilities which produced uncommon
effects."[57] Hamilton (like Laurens) also saw one of his finest days at Monmouth.
In a letter written by McHenry, Washington's newest aide-de-camp, could
hardly believe his eyes in watching the frantic efforts of Hamilton in action: "I
am happy to have it in my power to mention the merit of your friend Hamilton.
He was incessant in his endeavors during the whole day—in reconnoitering the
enemy, and in rallying and charging. But whether he or Col. Laurens deserves
most of our commendation, is somewhat doubtful—both had their horses shot

under them, and both exhibited singular proofs of bravery. They seemed to court death under our doubtful circumstances, and triumphed over it as the face of war changed in our favor."[58]

Hamilton's "Heat and Effervescence"

Indeed, Hamilton came into his own in the ultimate crisis situation and inspired large numbers of troops, both officers and enlisted men, to stand firm around him, when the army's very life was at stake. Clinton had reinforced Cornwallis' attackers until they outnumbered the Americans. He not only aligned infantry and artillery in good defensive positions, but also led units in a least two desperate attacks to play a key role in stopping Cornwallis' determined advance with a daring that caused one aide to believe the Hamilton seemed "to court death" in his desperation to reverse the tide. Even more, he had early warned Washington to secure the high ground on the vulnerable right flank, which could not be turned with an ample number of Greene's troops and guns on Combs Hill. Hamilton was not even hurt after his "old gray horse" fell atop him when shot. This was not a sufficient enough setback to deter Hamilton's fighting spirit or efforts to prevail against the meancing tide of advancing red-coats. One observer never forgot Hamilton's "singular proofs of bravery."[59]

Clearly, the old fighting spirit of the New York State artillery captain came out of the young lieutenant colonel during the day-long (the revolution's long-est) battle of Monmouth, after this hard-fought fight evolved into an artillery exchange under the broiling sun of one of the year's hottest days. After Rhode Island soldiers freed Hamilton from the heavy weight of his wounded horse, he rejoiced at the sight of General Knox's booming cannon. Knox was also highly impressed by Hamilton's "head and effervescence" on June 28. However, the painful injury from his horse's fall kept Hamilton out of the remainder of action that day.

But characteristically, he refused to leave the field and seek medical atten-tion. In a dusty blue uniform drenched in sweat and suffering from heat exhaustion after having fought this day without a hat (evidently having fallen off while riding or leading the attack), Hamilton was then propped up on the trunk of a tree under the shade to recuperate, while the struggle raged on with renewed intensity.

Here, in stubborn fashion, he was determined to stand his ground with drawn saber, when the redcoat formations advanced ever-closer. Hamilton ignored the pain from the fall and the increasing danger, as the escalating roar of the American artillery and the loud cheering of fast-working American gunners sounded like music to his ears. He must have been reminded of when his own New York cannon had played leading roles earlier in the war. Ever the artilleryman, Hamilton penned with admiration how Knox's gunners "acquitted themselves most charmingly."[60] In a letter, Hamilton also praised "General Greene & Lord Stirling [William Alexander who] rendered very essential service, and did themselves great honor."[61]

Hamilton was lucky to have survived what some onlookers thought must have been a death wish that hot June day. While riding back and forth over the grassy plain swept by projectiles, Hamilton had numerous close brushes, especially while leading desperate attacks against Cornwallis's seasoned regulars, in an effort to blunt the enemy's momentum and buy time for Washington's men to rally. Two of Washington's aides-de-camp were wounded at Monmouth: John Fitzgerald and John Laurens. Because of the South Carolinian's bravery and "youthful lust for combat" Hamilton almost lost his best friend, who rejoiced at the "considerable slaughter of the British Grenadiers."[62]

In close-quarter combat, Laurens' horse was shot from under him, and he suffered a slight wound. But as usual, Laurens ignored the injury to continue fighting, while doing what he loved best.[63] With a growing sense of pride in Washington's soldiers who had so gamely stood up hour after hour to the toughest British regulars in a fierce fight, Hamilton wrote with pride how "we beat the enemy and killed and wounded at least a thousand of their best troops."[64]

Clearly, thanks in no small part to Hamilton's contributions in working closely with von Steuben, the endless drilling and discipline imposed upon the young soldiers of liberty at Valley Forge had paid impressive dividends at Monmouth. After the lengthy battle of June 28, Hamilton gained an even greater awareness about the importance of proper instruction and training, because he had never "known or conceived the value of military education" among the men and officers of Washington's Army.[65] He marveled how, "The behavior of the officers and men in general was such as could not easily be surpassed. Our troops, after the first impulse of the mismanagement [of General Lee], behaved with more spirit and moved with greater order than the British troops."[66]

Despite having missed "the finest opportunity America ever possessed," in Hamilton's words, for delivering a knockout blow to Clinton's Army before it reached New York City, Hamilton was still very proud of the performance of the American fighting man, who had stood up magnificently to the best troops that Britain had to offer. Although he had emphasized to a friend in a letter, "You know my way of thinking about the army and that I am not apt to flatter it," Hamilton had changed his mind. He now admired this spunky army more than ever before. Indeed, retaining possession of the hard-fought field after Clinton's men marched away after having been severely bloodied, Washington's troops finally reversed the casualty ratio, inflicting four times more than losses (more than one thousand in total) on their opponent than they themselves suffered. But Hamilton was angry, especially at General Lee's bungling, feeling that an opportunity had slipped away and three hundred sixty Americans had died in vain.[67]

As the most "impulsive swashbuckling" young officers on Washington's staff, Hamilton and Laurens had especially distinguished themselves. In a July 2, 1778, letter to his father, Laurens, who had scouted (like Hamilton) ahead during a reconnaissance with von Steuben before the battle, was now jubilant about what Washington and his "family," especially Hamilton, had accomplished against the odds: a hard-earned moral victory at Monmouth by pulling out a most improbable success from the jaws of defeat, after the Gods of War had so suddenly turned against them. One of the best-educated young men in America, Laurens wrote: "The merit of restoring the day, is due to the General. . . . My three brother aids gained themselves great applause by their activity and bravery, while the three secretaries acted as military men on this occasion, and proved themselves as worthy to wield the sword as the pen."[68]

Lieutenant Colonel Hamilton's distinguished actions on June 28 at Monmouth drew high praise throughout the army, including from his old commander General Knox and, of course, his fellow staff officers.[69] In a letter to Hamilton's friend Elias Boudinot, James McHenry praised: "Hammy [who] was incessant in his endeavors during the whole day. . . . rallying and charging," until it seemed that Hamilton "court[ed] death."[70] Cavalryman "Light Horse Harry" Lee long recalled Hamilton's "paroxysms of bravery" on this day, when so much hung in the balance. With his characteristic modesty, Hamilton described his stirring performance at Monmouth in only a few words, writing how he "got my horse wounded and myself much hurt by a fall."[71]

Ironically, Hamilton failed to garner the recognition that he deserved because of his own excessive modesty, believing it to be the proper behavior for a true gentleman to not boast of accomplishments. In his official battle-report to Congress, Washington included Hamilton's inspirational and timely role in helping to save the day, bestowing well-deserved recognition. Doing what was unprecedented in the Continental Army's history, Hamilton requested that Washington's glowing words of recognition of him be removed from his report "from the motives of delicacy."[72] But for his impressive performance during a crisis situation, Hamilton was satisfied that he garnered much "praise of Continental Army officers [because] not only had he proposed troop dispositions to both Washington and Lee but also, by his skillful use of American artillery, had prevented the routed vanguard from being overrun."[73]

Revealing his great admiration for the Virginian who symbolized the revolution like no other man in America, Hamilton continued to lavishly praise General Washington for his splendid performance, while criticizing Lee's "silly and pitiful" generalship at Monmouth. He was rightly convinced that "a general rout, dismay, and disgrace would have attended the whole army in other hands but his."[74] But Hamilton was not basking in accolades about his almost manic-heroic performance at Monmouth that engendered a sense of awe among amazed observers, who never forgot the impressive sight. Instead of obsessing about his own significant accomplishments, he was fairly raging over the missed opportunity of inflicting a mortal wound upon Clinton's Army. As he wrote to Elias Boudinot, now a New Jersey delegate in Congress, on July 5, Hamilton allowed his sense of outrage to freely flow, as if his letter was somehow almost therapeutic to this diehard revolutionary who had almost sacrificed himself at Monmouth for the greater good: "I can hardly persuade myself to be in good humour with success so far inferior to what we, in all probability should have had, had not the finest opportunity America ever possessed been fooled away by a man, in whom she has placed a large share of the most ill judged confidence."[75]

Quite naturally under the circumstances, Hamilton turned his considerable wrath upon the bungling General Lee. Like Washington, Hamilton and Laurens rightly believed that Lee was responsible for the army's close brush with disaster at Monmouth. Lee's "silly" conduct was so atrocious that Hamilton was convinced that he might even be a traitor, who had deliberately allowed the enemy to advance unopposed and failed to restore order, after ordering a retreat against Washington's orders. Hamilton unleashed his fury upon Lee, writing to Boudinot, "This man is either a driveler in the business of soldiership or something worse [and I will] let you fully into the silly and pitiful game he has been playing. . . ."[76]

Because of Hamilton's severe criticism of Lee (officially and in private) that included that "his conduct was monstrous and unpardonable," the general mockingly denounced Washington's most can-do staff officer as nothing more than "The Boy" and a "son of a bitch."[77] General Lee sought to formally apologize for Monmouth in a letter to Washington, who simply ignored the missive. Realizing that he was being blamed for the near fiasco at Monmouth, Lee knew that the growing political and personal campaign against him to protect Washington's reputation had been "instigated by some of those dirty earwigs [primarily Hamilton and Laurens] who will forever insinuate themselves near persons in high office."[78]

An angry General Lee criticized Hamilton for being one of the principals of the "idolatrous Sett of Toad-Eaters," (a direct hint about the French-speaking Hamilton and Laurens being Francophiles) who had long performed Washington's dirty work (as General Gates, and then General Putnam, had recently learned from Hamilton's mission to Albany) for him like true disciples: a true accusation and a backhanded compliment to the top officer of the "family." Indeed, they had already played a leading role in waging a masterful campaign (Hamilton through his "eloquent pen" and Laurens through his father, who was the president of Congress), against Gates, because of his desire to replace Washington. And as Hamilton saw it, Lee was one of the co-conspirators who had aligned with Gates.[79]

Hamilton possessed an uncanny ability and distinct knack for making mortal enemies, regardless of rank or social standing. His sharp words, strong opinions, biting wit, and, most of all, his increasing number of successes were guaranteed to create an ever-growing list of personal foes. Already, rumors were spreading among angry New England officers about Hamilton's illegitimate birth and lowly Caribbean past to mock his pretensions as a proper officer and gentleman, one so highly revered and respected at Washington's headquarters. Most of all, a good many highly placed men, military and civilian, eagerly looked for opportunities "to bring the cocky little [lieutenant] colonel down" a notch or two.[80]

General Charles Lee on Trial

Ironically, Hamilton's goal was much the same concerning General Lee. He wanted to bring Lee down a notch or two, because he viewed Lee's actions at Monmouth as a deliberate behavior to deny Washington a victory thus hastening the day when he would be unceremoniously removed from command by Congress. Hamilton saw a conspiracy against Washington, and this had to be crushed at all costs.

An indignant Lee, whom Washington had placed under arrest much to Hamilton's delight, requested a court-martial to clear his name, after having suffered the humiliation of being removed from command on the battlefield. Washington granted his request. To ensure that Washington's generalship was not blamed for the near disaster at Monmouth and proper censure fell where it was rightly due, Hamilton and Laurens, the two young romantic idealists, were the "star witnesses" for the prosecution. Here, at New Brunswick, New Jersey, they presented the most damaging testimony to Lee's reputation during the July–August court-martial trial. Lee's court-martial was headed by Hamilton's old friend Lord Stirling (General William Alexander), in whose brigade the New York battery of the native West Indian had advanced on Trenton during the early morning hours of December 26, 1776. Still bruised from when his wounded war horse fell on him at Monmouth, Hamilton presented damning testimony on July 4 (symbolically the second anniversary of the Declaration of Independence) and July 13 that made him now mortal enemies among General Lee's friends.

All the while, a young officer nearly as dynamic as Hamilton, Aaron Burr sat silently during the tense proceedings, while seething in rage as the outspoken West Indian's words emphasized how Lee had done nothing to stop the retreat, even after having been ordered by Washington to do so. The New Englander angrily stared at the Hamilton with ill intent. Washington's most egotistical general was especially incensed that he was under attack by two staff officers, who were young enough to have been his own sons: a factor (along with them having lesser rank and Washington's ear and complete trust) that had also angered General Gates in regard to Hamilton's past mission to Albany. Lee correctly saw Hamilton as the beside-the-scene mastermind, who worked cleverly overtime and with considerable energy (both were the case) to damage his reputation and protect Washington's reputation: basically, this was part of his job as chief of staff. With Hamilton leading the charge as at Monmouth where the bullets had flown the thickest, to make sure that Lee's anti-Washington accusations were ignored and soon forgotten not only by Congress but also by the nation and the American people before the anti-Washington movement could gain more momentum, the court-martial dealt harshly with Lee.

Even during the court-martial when Lee cross examined Hamilton, he was not prepared for the force of the young man's well-chosen and on-target words like a prosecuting attorney, including the startling implication that the general's mental state seemed to border on the unhinged. Clearly, like General Gates before him back in Albany, Lee had met his match in Hamilton, who correctly saw Gates and Lee as acting together to unseat Washington. Such rivals to Washington's position of commander-in-chief had to be eliminated, and this called for thoroughly discrediting them in public. If not previously, this experienced general and master of political maneuvering was now beginning to recognize the true depth of Hamilton's analytical mind, which had cleverly orchestrated the very scenario that eventually led to Lee's ultimate downfall.

In the end, General Lee was found guilty on several charges, especially in conducting a "disorderly retreat," as Hamilton had so forcefully emphasized. He was then suspended by the court for one year. Lee appealed his case to Congress. But by this time, Congress already had been early influenced by Hamilton's and Laurens' stealthy initiatives and tireless efforts behind the scenes, including well-composed anti-Lee letters, which sabotaged criticism of the pro-Lee/anti-Washington camp. Congress, therefore, upheld the court's verdict, which was almost as much of a victory for Hamilton as Washington on the political front, where the fighting was waged as fiercely as on any battlefield.[81]

Most importantly, Hamilton had played the leading role in eliminating General Lee as a rival to Washington, solidifying his position and making it much more secure. No longer would subordinate generals openly criticize and challenge Washington's position as in the past. As carefully planned, Hamilton had made a highly visible example of General Lee, and it would not be lost on others in the future. Washington's role as the leader of America's armies was now more secure than ever before. Once again, this young chief of staff had accomplished his all-important mission with a brilliant effectiveness.

As revealed during the court-martial, Hamilton's contempt for Lee earned him the bitter hatred of the incensed general and his devoted followers, including Aaron Burr, and for ample good reason. Hamilton's effort to knock General Lee down to size was an impressive performance. Before senior officers and in order to thoroughly discredit this rival to Washington, he had thoroughly denounced the general, many years his senior in age and military experience, while even "pontificating to a veteran general [during cross examination] on the ideal mental state of a field commander."[82]

A Lull

Meanwhile, after having escaped from Washington's attempt to deliver a powerful blow to his rear guard at Monmouth, Clinton and his army safely reached New York City. A relatively quiet period now settled over Washington's theater of operations. British policy was now focused on consolidating its position in North America in order to mount an offensive in Hamilton's native West Indies to capture the French sugar islands that represented so much wealth. Meanwhile, after playing the leading role in eliminating the threat of General Lee, Hamilton went back work at Washington's headquarters at New Brunswick, where the Americans had recently celebrated the second anniversary of the Declaration of Independence's signing with a parade and a ball. In his finest uniform and now fully healed, Hamilton made his usual splendid showing at the ball. Both on and off the dance floor while musicians played and the wine flowed, he continued to attract the young ladies, especially the pretty ones, with his charm, wit, and graceful style. In turn, he continued his tradition of gravitating toward the prettiest women, playing his part as a diehard ladies' man, continuing to charm the females who fell under his spell.

Later in July 1778, Washington's Army moved from New Brunswick and headed to Paramus, Bergen County, New Jersey, around forty-five miles northeast of Morristown. After he lost his favorite gray horse at Monmouth, Hamilton had gathered scarce funds with difficulty (inflation continued to thoroughly erode continental currency values) to purchase a mare. Compared to Washington's staff officers from wealthy families, Hamilton possessed the least resources and he was still a bachelor. Consequently, without his own family or a family through marriage, he primarily existed on a lieutenant colonel's meager pay. He had few friends outside of the Washington's staff, and he no longer had ties with his old college chums from King's College. But Hamilton was no stranger to being alone, and he was frugal by nature. At least Hamilton did not have to pay for meals because he ate the fare at headquarters. Hamilton's new horse was left behind, when the army moved out from New Brunswick. Feeling the loss of his horse, Hamilton traveled to Paramus by wagon.

After he and his staff visited Passaic (Paterson) Falls, Paterson, New Jersey, Washington initially established his new headquarters at the home of a Mrs. Watkins. Washington later accepted the invitation to move his headquarters nearby to a larger house known as "The Hermitage" with his staff. This was the stately home of Mrs. Theodosia Prevost. She was the widow of a British officer who had recently died in the West Indies.

During this period, Hamilton grew closer to the personable Scotch-Irish Dr. James McHenry, a north Ireland immigrant to America's shores and a committed revolutionary like Hamilton. A transplanted Marylander who had been well-educated in Dublin, he never lost his distinctive Irish ways that included a compassionate and poetic heart. He had been captured with his Pennsylvania battalion at Fort Washington in mid-November 1776, when the large garrison surrendered in one of the greatest fiascos of the ill-fated New York Campaign. Dr. McHenry had then continued to administer to injured and sick Maryland soldiers in the hell of the British prison. Thankfully, before he could succumb to the high attrition rate from disease like so many others, McHenry had been exchanged in early March 1778.

McHenry was the newly appointed assistant secretary on Washington's staff, serving since early May 1778, the first physician assigned to the staff, indicating that Washington may have had some concerns, about the health of his staff and himself. After all, Washington knew that he could not afford to lose the absolutely indispensable Hamilton, his "most confidential aide," in his words. The gregarious Irishman then became a member of Lafayette's staff near the conclusion of 1780. McHenry possessed wry Irish wit and a keen sense of humor, qualities fully appreciated by Hamilton, who could match the best witticisms that flowed with ease from the good doctor.

Dr. James McHenry had been born on November 16, 1753, at Ballymena, a market town connected to the linen industry and located on the River Braid in County Antrim, Province of Ulster, north Ireland. A Presbyterian of strong faith and whose Irish cultural ways were more conservative than those of Hamilton, who reflected the more freewheeling ways and lax morals of the Caribbean's Creole society, McHenry was a free spirit with "an easy and cheerful temper," that was typically Irish. He was especially struck by his young friend's uncanny ability to attract women of all sorts and means, from the lower to the upper class. Like other men with less romantic skills, charm, and ardent natures, McHenry became jealous in watching Hamilton's easy way with women of all ages and backgrounds.

The dashing Hamilton, blessed with a boyish handsomeness that was heightened by his neat blue uniform, was always the favorite with "the local farm girls," wrote an astounded McHenry, who marveled at the West Indian's well-honed skills. At the town of Doylestown, Bucks County, Pennsylvania, and about twenty-seven miles north of Philadelphia, when on the march to the showdown at Monmouth Court House, McHenry had been attracted to a pretty Quaker girl. Knowing that the girl's strong religious faith might be the only possible obstacle that could stop the ever-ardent Hamilton from making still another easy conquest, McHenry wrote with smug satisfaction and wry delight, "Hamilton thou shalt not tread on this ground."[83]

So strong was Hamilton's appeal to a wide variety of women that McHenry was "never so taken back" by a most surprising realization that shocked him, while staying at the Doylestown tavern for the night. At that time, the "pretty milk maids" paid more attention to a handsome drummer boy of Washington's elite bodyguard, the "Life Guard" under Captain Caleb Gibbs, rather than the "swashbuckling Hamilton" for once: a rarity duly noted by the astonished Scotch-Irish physician in his diary.[84]

Hamilton and McHenry became such close friends that the physician affectionately addressed him as, "My dear Hammy." Hamilton's best friend, the ambitious South Carolinian Laurens, also called him "Hammy."[85] Clearly, as their letters revealed, Hamilton's closest and best friends were members of Washington's little military "family." Just as Hamilton teased his friends, especially Robert Hanson Harrison, the good-humored McHenry whom Hamilton called "Mac," often returned the favor at seemingly every good opportunity. With Hamilton having digestion problems, McHenry recommended a proper diet, and then took the opportunity to poke fun: "Never go beyond three glasses [of wine.] . . . You will then be your own counselor in diet for the man who has had ten years experience in eating and its consequences is a fool if he does not know how to choose his dishes better than his Doctor." Teasing Hamilton about his love for fine wine—like Washington and other staff officers—served at balls and at the dinner table (an ample amount of wine was always available at the main meal at headquarters) and especially during social events, McHenry reminded him that "When you indulge in wine let [it] be sparingly" unlike so often in the past.

On another occasion, as McHenry often reminded him, Hamilton drank too much wine in either leading the customary rounds of festive toasts at a social gathering at Washington's headquarters, or because of the less likely possibility of adhering to the day's accepted medical belief that wine helped to prevent smallpox. Of course, the Irish physician was also part of this merriment at headquarters after the day's work had been completed, with Hamilton and McHenry occasionally joining together in song ("those fine sounds," in Hamilton's words, that rang through Washington's headquarters) to enliven the evenings. The "doctor" McHenry prescribed the traditional cure of a regular "table of diet" for relief of "Hammy," which he hoped had the additional benefit of "having a tendency also to correct your wit."[86]

No one's wit at headquarters was sharper than that of Hamilton, although McHenry, whose own Irish wit was well-honed and possessed a fine cutting edge, competed with enthusiastic vigor with his good friend in a competition that he could not win. More importantly, McHenry fully understood Hamilton's supreme importance to Washington, because the young man's "advice in many instances (a fact known to myself) had aided our chief in giving to the [military] machine that perfection to which it had arrived previously to the close of the revolutionary war."[87]

The French Navy Arrives

After the battle of Monmouth, near the end of one of the hottest Junes on record, spirits among the troops in Washington's encampment lifted with the July 14, 1778, news by letter received by Washington of the much-belated arrival of the French fleet of a dozen ships and nearly half a dozen frigates. This development—long emphasized by American diplomats as the key to victory—that suddenly bestowed naval superiority to the allies occurred on July 11 near Sandy Hook, New Jersey, the outer approaches to New York City on the south. Here, the Sandy Hook channel led east to the Atlantic and New York harbor to the north.

Just north of Sandy Hook in defensive positions at New York City, Staten Island, and Long Island, Clinton's defensive positions now appeared threatened by heavily armed French warships. Having been informed by Congress of the French fleet's arrival after an eighty-seven-day voyage that was more than twice as long as expected, Washington ordered John Laurens to ride south from Paramus to confer with the fleet's vice admiral and Lafayette's distant relative, Count Charles Henri-Theodat d'Estaing, about the overall strategic situation, now that naval superiority had been obtained: should an allied offensive be launched against New York City or Newport, Rhode Island?

Meanwhile, the French admiral was indecisive, and remained in position at Sandy Hook. The French fleet was anchored outside New York harbor just below (slightly southeast of) Sandy Hook, and threatening New York City. Meanwhile, Clinton drew his troops to New York City in time, and Admiral Richard Howe set a line of his warships in defensive positions to protect the harbor. The admiral prepared for the anticipated French naval attack, with warships carrying eight hundred fifty guns to capture New York City.

For the express purpose of conferring with d'Estaing and to assist Laurens after his hard-hitting testimony at the General Charles Lee court martial, Hamilton was then shortly dispatched by Washington to also ride south from Paramus and join the South Carolinian to once again link up a most dynamic team of two young staff officers, who both spoke fluent French. Washington wisely chose Hamilton to be present to officially greet the admiral in his name. To provide nautical information about local waters to the French who were still unfamiliar with America's waterways, Hamilton led a party of captains and pilots, who knew the area's treacherous waters.

After reaching the French fleet in mid-July near an estuary, protected from the Atlantic on its eastern side by a barrier peninsula that extended north to become Sandy Hook, (known as the Shrewsberry River, that flowed just south of Sandy Hook), Hamilton and Laurens secured additional local pilots, with more thorough knowledge of the area's waters. Such experienced men were needed to guide the French fleet safely past the expansive sand bars that were located just off Sandy Hook and to safely gain the channel leading to New York Harbor. One of these sand bars extended well north of the northern point of the so-called hook that jutted north toward New York City, offering only a narrow passage close to the New Jersey shore. Just north of Sandy Hook, the Narrows was situated between the northeastern end of Staten Island and south-western end of Long Island, just south of New York Harbor at the lower end of the Hudson River.

The debonair Hamilton now became a regular feature on Admiral d'Estaing's magnificent flagship, the *Languedoc*. Here, as if conferring in a stylish townhouse along the Seine in Paris, he spoke his flawless French with the highly respected admiral of noble blood. In the future, Hamilton continued his key liaison role between Washington and d'Estaing, while cementing relationships and good feelings between allies, with his skillful handling of the complexities of delicate communications, proper customs, and protocol of which few Americans were knowledgeable.

But other problems soon developed for Hamilton and Laurens. The American pilots, old and recently enlisted to help, balked at their assigned duties. They were to have guided the French vessels through Sandy Hook's tricky waters that were easily navigated by the smaller British ships. Consequently, these pilots concluded that they would not be able to pass the French ships over the dangerous sand bars, where the large ships would be grounded. To develop a solution, d'Estaing himself conducted a reconnaissance along the Skrewsbury River, digging a canal to avoid and bypass the sandbars. Clearly, these waters proved more challenging than anyone, including Hamilton, had expected. On July 16, 1778, Laurens "ran great risk of being drowned" in attempting to reach the admiral's flagship. Comte d'Estaing had only made a tentative approach to enter New York harbor, and then the row of British warships and the dangers of the sandbars caused him to lose his nerve on July 22.

Because of the difficulties and on the advice of Washington as proposed by Congress and as articulated to the French admiral by Hamilton, an alternative strategic solution was shortly developed out of necessity, given the disadvantageous circumstances. As desired by Congress and Washington, d'Estaing then decided to focus on the secondary target to the north instead of New York City: the frustrated French vice admiral sailed his fleet to Newport, Rhode Island. The Newport Campaign was about to begin.[88]

Significantly, after welcoming him to America, Hamilton (like Laurens but to a lesser degree) had made a lasting favorable impression on the French admiral: a prerequisite for laying a sound foundation and solidifying the new alliance, especially the naval arm, which was now the key to victory. As the aristocratic d'Estaing, a member of France's elite, later wrote in a confidential letter to Washington, revealing his admiration for his youngest staff officer: "I entreat you not to confide the secret to any person, except [Lt.] Colonel Hamilton. His talents and his personal qualities have secured to him for ever my esteem, my confidence and my friendship."[89]

After having conferred with the French admiral and carrying the proposal from Congress to initiate the Newport Campaign, Hamilton then returned north to Paramus. Here, he resumed his chief of staff duties with "the family" at headquarters. But Hamilton was once again on the move in the fall during still another assignment. Thereafter, Hamilton served the primary liaison officer, translator, emissary, and diplomat and messenger to a lesser degree between Washington and the French admiral.

While at Fredericksburg, Virginia, on the Rappahannock River north of Richmond, a thoughtful Hamilton reflected on the past campaign, including its missed opportunities. He also simultaneously looked forward to the possibilities of the upcoming 1779 campaign with his usual positive outlook for future success. In a letter to his New York City friend Major General Alexander

McDougall, a French and Indian War veteran who had migrated with his family at age six from Scotland, Hamilton displayed the depth of his broad geopolitical insight in regard to the relationship between the military and economic situation: "It is a question very undecided in my mind whether the enemy will evacuate or not. Reasoning *a priori* the arguments seem to be strongest for it, from the exhausted state of the British resources, the naked condition of their dominions every where, and the possibility of a Spanish War. But on the other hand naval superiority must do a great deal in the business. This, I think, considering all things appears clearly enough to be on the side of Britain. . . . The preserving posts in these States will greatly distress our trade and give security to the British West India trade. They will also cover the West Indies, and restrain any operations of ours against the British dominions on the Continent."[90]

As so often in the past, Lieutenant Colonel Hamilton's analysis was typically keen and on target. His years of working for Kortright and Cruger at Christianstead on St. Croix had early bestowed upon Hamilton a solid education and hands-on experience about economics and trade. But now, Hamilton's already extensive knowledge had grown from his endless self-education of reading late at night. No officer of Washington's officer corps concentrated more on educating himself about the complexities of economics and fiscal matters than Hamilton. In his November 8, 1778, letter to McDougall, he continued to bestow sage economic and strategic advice: "These considerations and the depreciated state of our currency, will be strong inducements [for the British] to keep New York and Rhode Island, if not with a view to conquest with a view to temporary advantages, and making better terms in the future negotiation. . . ."[91]

Hamilton was increasingly upset about America's deteriorating economic situation, especially inflation which sapped the young republic's strength and vitality, steadily eroding the war effort. In October and November 1778, he once again turned his pen against the widespread corruption in high places. In the pages of the *New-York Journal* and using the pen name of "Publius," he rebuked Maryland Congressman Samuel Chase for using his insider knowledge about the arrival of the French fleet for him and his cronies to reap nice profits: buying up surplus flour, which then more than doubled in price because of its impending sale to the French, to corner the lucrative market. However, Hamilton turned his primary focus in searching for a solution to the escalating fiscal crisis, understanding the economic aspects of warfare. Hamilton bemoaned the sad state of American finances that insidiously eroded the economic foundations of infant republic and the overall war effort, because, "The depreciation of our Currency really casts a gloom on our prospects."[92]

Meanwhile, another harsh winter soon descended upon the land, the fourth since America's struggle for liberty began and long after the first defiant shots had rang out on Lexington Green on the warm morning of April 19, 1775. To assist an important French friend, Hamilton made a polite effort to gain additional warmth for d'Estaing's aide-de-camp at the first cold snap, revealing his mastery of a necessary step when presented with an awkward situation: Andre Michel Victor, Marquis de "Chouin the French Gentleman who lives at [Washington's] Head Quarters informs he has heard you [evidently a lady friend] had a bear-skin which you would part with; and requests me to inquire if it is so—I told him I thought it very improbable you should have any but what you wanted for your own; but for his satisfaction would inquire how the matter stands."[93]

November 1778 brought not only colder weather, but also a significant change to Washington's staff. Laurens' dream finally came true when he gained a field commission. On November 5, 1778, Congress resolved that Washington present Laurens—who fairly lusted for action and martial distinction like Hamilton—with a line command in the field "whenever opportunity shall offer."[94]

As during the previous winter, Washington established his winter quarters on December 11, 1778, near Middlebrook. Located in a chain of the Watchung Mountains that provided a good high ground defensive position, this was a strategic location that allowed Washington to better safeguard New Jersey.[95] But all was not quiet and serene in Washington's encampment. Not content in only battling a seemingly invincible foe, the Americans were fighting among themselves as usual. General Lee's summer 1778 court of inquiry had only hardened the lines between pro-Lee and pro-Washington camps: a mini-war existing within a larger conflict of a relatively little-known political war behind the scenes. Of course, Hamilton, who was the ultimate villain to Lee and his cronies, was caught in the tempest, because of his magnificent defense of Washington and his reputation to continue his aggressive fight—General Gates had been the first foe as witnessed during the Albany mission—against the commander-in-chief's rivals.

To strike back against the effective letter-writing campaign of Hamilton and Laurens (along with Tilghman and McHenry to a lesser degree) who had testified against him as lead witnesses in the prosecution, an angry Lee waged his political war with his usual malicious intent. He launched his own vigorous propaganda campaign against Washington, including damaging stories that were circulated through Congress and even printed in the Philadelphia newspaper, *Pennsylvania Packet*, in December. In his article, Lee savagely attacked Washington's generalship, character, and judgment: an assault that could not go unchallenged by the ever-protective members of Washington's faithful staff.

Like Hamilton, Laurens was incensed by the personal assault on their beloved commander-in-chief. Laurens requested Hamilton to turn his powerful (or poison, in the view of his opponents) pen in a rebuttal, but for once the native West Indian was hesitant, perhaps because he had already exposed his strong opinions during the court-martial. More likely, however, Hamilton saw no need for unleashing a writing campaign because Lee might shortly be eliminated from the scene altogether. And, of course, he did not want to risk exposing himself. Indeed, the hot-headed South Carolinian had concluded that a more forceful rebuttal was required to settle this matter once and for all. Not even the approaching Yuletide Season or the merriment of another popular dance assembly quelled the internal turmoil among the American officer corps.

Encouraged by Hamilton who proved that he for once now believed that the pistol was mightier than the pen, Laurens decided to take more forceful action. Hamilton's best friend challenged Lee to a duel after the publication of the general's article about Washington incompetence to justify his controversial actions and failings at Monmouth. Most of all, Laurens wanted "forever to silence" General Lee, to most effectively eliminate this rival to Washington: a desire warmly supported by Hamilton. Laurens naturally chose his best friend Hamilton as his second.

Only recently, Hamilton had already adroitly sidestepped a clever attempt by Lee's aide-de-camp, Major John Skey Eustace, to provoke a duel by insulting him and leveling the charge of untruthfulness (perjury) in his testimony against Lee during the court-martial. But Hamilton was too smart to take the bait. He wisely kept his West Indian temper and sharp tongue under control in this delicate situation, having no desire to risk sacrificing his life for nothing.

An Officers' Duel Just Outside Philadelphia

On the dueling ground of Point No Point, located at the edge of woodlands four miles south of Philadelphia, at 3:30 p.m. on December 23, 1778, General Lee and Colonel Laurens faced each other to settle their differences, which were most of all about Washington's reputation. Fearing the worst for his friend during the customary ritual that dictated movements, Hamilton watched as Laurens and Lee approached to within only half a dozen paces of each other. Both men fired almost simultaneously, and seemingly missed their respective targets in their eagerness to dispatch a hated opponent. Laurens was busily reloading his pistol for the second shot, when Lee suddenly declared that he was hit. Laurens, Hamilton and his friend Major Evan Edwards, Lee's second, advanced to assist Lee.

However, they ended their concern when Lee stated that the wound (the lead ball just grazed the skin on his right side) was not as serious as first thought. Proving that he was no coward, the English-born general then proposed a second exchange of fire. But Hamilton and Edwards "warmly opposed" the idea. However, determined to demonstrate his courage and vindicate himself, Lee again requested a second fire. Laurens, whose emotions had gotten the better of him, instantly agreed to General Lee's proposal. Knowing that Lee was an experienced duelist and a very good shot, unlike his hot-headed friend who was known to be more dominated by passion than reason in regard to his own life, Hamilton then turned to present Lee with a well-conceived argument calculated to conclude the duel.[96]

Hamilton hurriedly emphasized that this affair of honor was now technically settled after the first exchange in the hope of eliminating the second. Thinking fast, "Col. Hamilton observed, that unless the General was influenced by motives of personal enmity, he did not think the affair ought to be pursued any further; but as General Lee seemed to persist" in a second exchange. Edwards agreed with Hamilton. After Lee said that he would abide by whatever Hamilton and Edwards decided, this so-called gentlemen's affair was finally settled with the reputations of the duelists intact. At almost the last second, Hamilton succeeded in stopping the duel and perhaps saving his friend's life, while keeping the honor of both men intact.[97]

On Christmas Eve and relieved that his best friend from South Carolina was not a corpse as Lee so fervently desired, Hamilton (like Edwards) wrote an official report about the duel to halt the spreading of lies that were directed at damaging Washington's reputation for political reasons and selfish ambitions.[98] Machiavellian and always at the center of thwarting any effort directed at destroying Washington's reputation, Hamilton might have orchestrated the duel by his trademark backdoor maneuvering. In the words of historian Gregory D. Massey: "Hamilton, who encouraged [von] Steuben to pursue a duel with Lee, probably also urged Laurens to tender a challenge" to the caustic general, who hated the two young officers with an unbridled passion.[99]

Preserving Washington's Reputation

Even more importantly, with Generals Lee, Gates, and Conway thoroughly discredited and no longer posing threats to the reputation and future of the commander-in-chief, Hamilton and Laurens had effectively saved Washington's reputation by veiled threats, public and private exposures, backdoor initiatives to Congress, and weapons (pistol and pen). Hamilton (and Laurens to a lesser degree) helped to guarantee that the stoic Virginian remained firmly entrenched as the army's commander to the war's end. Providing an invaluable service for America at a crucial time, these two "young men helped to eliminate from the scene the troublesome Generals Conway and his so-called cabal and Lee, and, to a lesser extent, also succeeded in shoving aside Horatio Gates [and] Washington faced no further serious challenges to his authority and prestige."[100]

Year after year, Hamilton continued to lead the way in protecting Washington and his reputation when under heavy criticism, doing whatever he felt was necessary to sustain the Virginian's symbolic status and lofty stature. In this crucial regard, Hamilton continued to serve as Washington's ever-vigilant chief protector and guardian angel. He realized that "America owes a great deal to General Washington for this day[']s work" most recently at Monmouth and elsewhere.[101]

For the always-busy Hamilton, the time passed quickly at Washington's headquarters at the John Wallace House at Middlebrook, New Jersey, north of New York City. Hamilton continued to serve not only as the chief political officer and advisor for Washington, but also as a traditional chief of staff in the modern sense. As in the past, Hamilton's political brilliance often continued to exceed even the commander-in-chief's lofty expectations, because the astute native West Indian knew that America's and the army's difficulties were primarily rooted in America's dysfunctional political realm. The young man's enlightened views that offered sound and well-conceived solutions continued to be similarly appreciated by members of Congress. Hamilton, consequently, met with Congressional committees on a regular basis, bestowing advice and guidance on seemingly all matters.[102]

When the Continental Congress requested that Washington journey to Philadelphia and appear in person to discuss strategic plans for the upcoming 1779 campaign, Hamilton was again at the forefront during the key political mission. Along with General Greene, Washington made sure that Hamilton, who already had wisely advised Greene (Washington's top lieutenant), was by his side to advise the almost always-difficult Congressional members on the most sensitive military and political matters. In addition, Washington brought the other trusty members of his staff from Middlebrook to Philadelphia: Laurens, Meade, Harrison, and Tilghman, who formed a dynamic team that performed well under Hamilton's guidance, per Washington's directions.[103]

Despite now staying in America's cosmopolitan capital where flashy Tory women of wealth still wore their hair in the latest London style as if to mock homespun patriotic women of more modest means, it was all work and no play for Hamilton during the six-week stay in Philadelphia. As Tilghman penned in a letter to James McHenry, who remained at the army's winter encampment: "I suppose you think we must be by this time so wedded to sweet Philadelphia that it will break our hearts to leave it. Far from it [because now] we anxiously await the moment that gives us liberty to return to humble Middlebrook. Philadelphia may answer very well for a man with his pockets well lined, whose pursuit is idleness and dissipation. But to us, it is intolerable. . . ."[104]

Watching Congress function so feebly and reconfirming the observation that America's destiny was in the hands of incapable and corrupt politicians was like a tonic. What Hamilton saw inspired him to concentrate more on remedies that were largely economic, because the nation's ruling body could not raise and collect the revenues that were necessary for not only the army's but also the republic's survival. Therefore, he placed more faith in the French Alliance, feeling that only Europeans might save Americans from themselves.

When Hamilton was not serving on a special mission or project for Washington, a typical winter day at headquarters after the February return from Philadelphia was anything but uneventful for Washington's staff members. Washington eased the heavy burden of responsibility and heavy workload on staff members, especially Hamilton, with a festive dinner. In his journal, physician James Thacher described on Friday, February 26, 1779, how "his excellency the commander-in-chief has long been in the practice of inviting a certain number of officers to dine at this table every day. It is not to be supposed that his excellency can be made acquainted with every officer by name. . . . Yesterday I accompanied Major Cavil to head-quarters, and had the honor of being numbered among the guests at the table of his excellency. . . . The table was elegantly furnished, and the provisions ample, but not abounding in superfluities. The civilities of the table were performed by Colonel Hamilton and the other gentlemen of the family. . . ."[105]

All the while, Hamilton as usual presented a gregarious and exuberant exterior that hid a no-nonsense attitude, scholar-like seriousness, and tough-mindedness. Not to mention his roving eye for the prettiest ladies present, Hamilton's pleasant personality and winning ways seemed to present a contradiction in regard to one of the most analytical and penetrating minds among the Continental Army's officer corps. Along with his advanced political and economic views of an innovative nature that challenged conventional wisdom, Hamilton's strategic, political, and economic insights remained keen and on target year after year. In March 1779 and like his earlier judgments, Hamilton correctly predicted British strategic designs and London's new plan for winning the war: turning focus away from Washington's Army and a frustrating strategic stalemate in an embattled mid-Atlantic theater, in order to strike at the more vulnerable Southern theater of operations, where greater opportunities for success existed.[106]

Invaluable French Allies

A host of greater challenges and more important roles lay in store for Hamilton in the new year of 1779. With the French Alliance and because of his mastery of the French language and protocol Hamilton continued to serve as Washington's chief representative, emissary, and diplomat to the French, both army and navy, which was sent to America in staggered stages. Many of these upper class leaders were well-connected to the French king, Louis XVI. Not knowing the French language or culture—unlike the erudite Hamilton who felt perfectively at ease among the French elite—Washington was incapable to accomplishing what Hamilton so often achieved among these high-ranking French aristocrats. These men of power and influence in the French military and society greatly admired the dashing young man in part because he was so open-minded and un-American in many fundamental ways.

Despite the vital importance of the alliance upon which America's life now depended, Hamilton's role in regard to influencing the Gallic newcomers has been generally underestimated and underappreciated by historians. But in truth, Hamilton's crucial role with the French ally was vitally important on multiple levels that were necessary to maintain the overall health and strength of the inherently unstable alliance. While Benjamin Franklin served as America's envoy on the Atlantic's east side in France since 1776, Hamilton unofficially played a comparably significant representative role to the French on the ocean's west side, while serving as Washington's principal liaison officer to the French. This mission was crucial, because Hamilton correctly realized that America could only win this war, if the French played a much larger role, especially in regard to naval support.

Even the wealthiest and most snobbish French noble, who looked upon Americans as little more than New World heathens from the backwoods, was impressed by the sophisticated, ever-gracious Hamilton, a natural diplomat who demonstrated rare qualities of a European-like tact and charm combined with a graceful skill. But while Franklin was hampered by only a rudimentary knowledge of French, Hamilton spoke a highly refined and flowery French with the eloquence of a lifetime resident of Paris, Bordeaux, or Marseille. Equally important, Hamilton was more open-minded toward the French, their Gallic culture, and seemingly mysterious ways than almost every American officer in the Continental Army (especially French and Indian War veterans who still harbored old grudges), including even his better-educated but less cosmopolitan friend from a Deep South planter culture, John Laurens.[107]

Hamilton's early life in the multicultural West Indies, where France possessed its string of precious sugar islands, especially St. Domingue (today's Haiti), fluency in French, and familiarity with French cultural and societal ways paid immeasurable dividends for America. Therefore, as mentioned, Hamilton was the ideal choice to have served as the chief representative, liaison officer, and diplomat between Washington and the new French allies for an extended period. Hamilton's easy cultivation of upper class French leaders was notable at a time when American prejudices toward Catholics (deeply rooted in Protestantism and anti-Catholic stereotypes, hatred of the Papacy, a lengthy history of religious wars with Catholic France in Europe, and the recent Seven Years' War) had been long dominated thought in America.

Like Hamilton, Franklin was concerned that America's longtime prejudices toward France might prove fatal to the most important relationship and partnership in the republic's short lifetime. Fortunately for America and its new alliance, Hamilton was not hampered by any hint of anti-France sentiments, especially those prejudices of New England, and especially French and Indian War veterans of all classes, a fact greatly appreciated by these ultrasensitive and proud French army and navy leaders in America. Consequently, Hamilton became a skilled arbitrator in the art of soothing ruffled feathers between French officers, who were aristocrats and often looked down upon homespun provincials, and American officers, who were incensed by the excessive arrogance.[108]

Quite unlike Hamilton, Washington had once hated and almost certainly killed French soldiers as a young man during the French and Indian War. Giving vent to a sense of righteous indignation, Washington emphasized in a 1754 letter (written just before Hamilton was born) how he and his fellow Virginians fought against "the invasion of a usurping enemy, our Majesty's property, his dignity, and land."[109]

Hamilton was a shining exception to the "blind prejudice" of so many Americans against the French, and Washington fully realized that this key distinction was all-important. However, in the pervasive Protestant tradition in which he was raised (his father's Presbyterianism and his mother's Huguenot background), Hamilton exhibited a small bias toward Catholic priests, but this prejudice was more rhetorical and humor-based than actual fact. Displaying a broad-mindedness about religion that was rare in his day, Hamilton poked fun at religious men of different faiths with equal zeal. Even John Jay, Hamilton's New York friend and patron, grew weary of the French Alliance and exhibited strong anti-Catholic prejudice that he could not shake off. Like so many other Americans, Jay was ever-mindful of how England had once sheltered his persecuted Huguenot ancestors from the religious hostility of an intolerant Catholic France. In contrast, Hamilton predicted that "Europe will save us in spite of ourselves."[110]

Meanwhile, behind the scenes and as throughout the past, Hamilton continued to work tirelessly in attempting to do all in his power to enhance the army's capabilities. More recently, he had convinced Congress to immediately increase the army's strength. Hamilton had barraged Congress with well-thought-out letters that implored the strengthening of Washington's Army so that the French would see an ally worthy of their own high sacrifice. Explaining Hamilton's typical no-holds-barred approach in his determination to get results, this enhancement of the army's thinned ranks was now absolutely necessary because in his insightful words: "The fate of America is perhaps suspended on the issue; if we are found unprepared, it must disgrace us [and result in the] defeating the good intentions of our allies, and losing the happiest opportunity we ever have had to save ourselves."[111]

Most importantly, from the perspective of well-educated French Enlightenment intellectuals who also aspired to a bright, new liberal day for monarchy-dominated Europe in the future, Hamilton served as the ideal representative to present a dignified romantic image of this new republican man who nobly struggled against monarchical abuses to live up to the cherished egalitarian principles of the Age of Enlightenment. Hamilton's role was especially crucial because the heady euphoria stemming from the exciting news of the French Alliance had quickly faded across America. Relations between the allies were destined to plummet almost immediately, leading to disillusionment. Thanks in part to mutual prejudices that existed between former enemies, this widening disconnect between new allies was partly fueled by stereotypes about French Catholics. America's provincial realities shattered the heady idealism of a united brotherhood, fostering French disillusionment about their new ally.

After sailing into the port of Newport, Rhode Island, Admiral d'Estaing had sent a representative (his aide-de-camp) to Washington's headquarters, while Washington had dispatched Laurens and Hamilton to Admiral d'Estaing's headquarters aboard his flagship, the ninety-gun *Languedoc*. Guaranteeing a formidable diplomatic team for men so young but so promising, Laurens's and Hamilton's fluency in French made Washington's difficult job much easier from beginning to end. After the planned allied offensive to capture New York City had fizzled, Comte d'Estaing planned to exploit his command of the sea by engaging the smaller British fleet outside Newport, Rhode Island, and unite with American land forces for a combined attack. The proposed land-sea effort against Newport was the first time that Americans and Frenchmen cooperated together. However, General John Sullivan's forces were too weak to overwhelm the British garrison of around five thousand troops, because they consisted of mostly ill-prepared New England militia.

In addition, the "most dreadful" storm before mid-August and lack of cooperation between the new allies combined to result in a failed offensive effort, including d'Estaing's striking at the British fleet, after sailing out of Newport to avoid entrapment in the harbor. With his fleet battered by British cannonballs from warships as well as the raging storm, the admiral's ships limped back to Newport. Worried that the powerful British fleet was about to arrive to break the siege, and threatened by the sudden arrival of British reinforcements from Halifax, Nova Scotia, d'Estaing then did what was most unexpected by the Americans.

After a council of war met and instead of continuing the siege with Sullivan, he set sail south to refit his warships in Boston. What the French admiral left behind were ugly recriminations and ill-feeling between French and Americans that threatened the alliance (even Laurens—of Huguenot heritage and acting as Washington's liaison officer—delivered "a solemn protest," but also deplored America's anti-French prejudice). Determined to combat the escalating anti-French sentiment rising in America and the army, Hamilton remained France's greatest supporter, and especially during this crisis situation, when faith in the French ally reached a new low.

Unfortunately, the old prejudices and stereotypes between the allies continued to rise to the surface—one of the reasons Washington had wisely sent his Hamilton-Laurens diplomatic team to d'Estaing's headquarters to head off any such threats to the alliance. After refitting in Boston, a decision that outraged General Sullivan who felt that he had been abandoned, the French admiral then sailed off to the Caribbean's warm waters to protect the valuable sugar islands that funneled so much money into the French economy. The close coordination that had been expected between allies to reap decisive victory over a common foe had quickly faded away.

Angry Americans believed that the opportunity to capture Newport had been needlessly thrown away by the French. America's revolutionaries now mocked the French for their hasty departure. After all, were not French Catholics effeminate cowards and frog eaters, according to popular Protestant stereotypes that went back long before the French and Indian War? Serious trouble had developed in Boston before the admiral sailed away, as angry mobs of enraged Americans waged anti-French riots, killing one French officer. This strong anti-French backlash caused Washington to regret the mounting intolerance rooted largely in ignorance. Likewise, Hamilton was distraught at the weaknesses inherent with the fragile alliance, because, as he wrote with certitude and strategic insight on June 30, 1780, if "we are saved France and Spain must save us."[112]

Influenced by their own lofty sense of cultural superiority (largely justified when contrasted with the provincial colonists far removed from the dynamic centers of Europe's cultured sophistication), the French were equally disillusioned with their new ally. From the European point of view, the French saw the Americans as ungrateful country bumpkins (ironically, much like the popular British perspective of Americans) and incompetent, undisciplined soldiers, especially Sullivan's raw Rhode Island militiamen. The New Englanders' anti-French bias was deep-seated, because of New England's bloody history in having long battled French Canadians and their Indian allies, especially the Abenaki of St. Francis, Canada. The French also held contempt for America's regulars (Continentals) and the backbone of the resistance effort, including top officers. Again, Hamilton was a shining exception to the general rule, garnering respect from high-ranking French officers, including General Lafayette who when united with Laurens and Hamilton formed the so-called merry "gay trio." One French officer was shocked to discover that the Americans were "English as regards Frenchmen." And the mere concept of a superiority (based on class, education, and wealth) assumed by proud American officers was endlessly mocked by cultured French officers. For ample good reason, the sophisticated French military and political elite naturally saw these pretentious New World "proper gentlemen" as decidedly inferior in every possible way. Clearly, mutual cultural shocks between the vastly different allies had early rocked the flimsy foundation of the fledgling alliance of convenience. All in all, "the divide between the two worlds" seemed beyond repair.[113]

In consequence, the timely and disproportionate role of Hamilton, who was the darling of French leaders from General Lafayette to Admiral d'Estaing, was crucial in helping to bridge this ever-widening schism. He was especially motivated because he knew that this war would be lost without the French. Unlike native-born Americans who were burdened with provincial views and ancient stereotypes, Hamilton was able to more clearly see complex situations without prejudice and from a broader perspective that included an appreciation of French prerogatives. At conferences among New England officers, Lafayette was infuriated by casual anti-d'Estaing comments and other anti-French sentiments. After disparaging remarks about French military men and the Gallic nation, Lafayette felt so personally insulted that he seriously contemplated the issuing of challenges to duel offending American officers, including generals. In a letter to Hamilton, Lafayette was angered at having been "personally [now] put in the position of hearing the name of France spoken without respect, and perhaps with disdain, by a herd of Yankees from New England."[114]

New Hampshire's General Sullivan, a roughhewn officer of Scotch-Irish descent and strong passions, was almost certainly the primary target of Lafayette's wrath, because he was the chief offender. Washington and

Hamilton, therefore, became increasingly concerned about the future of the seemingly disintegrating alliance. Making a gross political mistake, Sullivan took the outlandish step of openly denouncing the French for having abandoned the United States in his official orders. With the alliance more splintered with each passing day, Hamilton accomplished all that he could to prevent a permanent fissure between the allies, when close cooperation was absolutely necessary for any chance of achieving decisive victory, as the young man had long emphasized and repeatedly emphasized.

To mollify the French, especially Lafayette, Hamilton (only a lieutenant colonel) shrewdly advocated a sharp reprimand of General Sullivan from Congress. By doing so, he hoped to win greater favor for America among the increasingly disgruntled French, whose sensitivities about matters of honor and national pride in the European aristocratic tradition were excessive to say the least by American standards, as Hamilton fully realized. Consequently, Hamilton quite correctly condemned General Sullivan's actions as "the summit of Folly" with so much at stake.[115]

For good reason, Hamilton also criticized Sullivan for "the stigmatizing [of] an ally in public orders and one with whom we mean to continue in amity was certainly a piece of absurdity without parallel."[116] A close friend of Lafayette who was only slightly younger than himself, Hamilton was the most invaluable and truest friend of the French in Washington's Army, because he so fully appreciated their value and worth at every level. As Hamilton explained to New Jersey Congressman Elias Boudinot, of French Huguenot heritage, in a letter from Washington's headquarters at White Plains, New York, on September 8, 1778, in advising on Congress' proper course in regard to the severely strained relationship between allies: "The French expect the state will reprobate the conduct of their General [Sullivan], and by that means, make atonement for the stain he has attempted to bring upon French honor. Something of this kind seems necessary and will in all likelihood be expected by the Court of France; but the manner of doing it suggests a question of great delicacy and difficulty, which I find myself unable to solve."[117]

Intimately understanding the French point-of-view and cultural sensitivities like few others, Hamilton was not guilty of exaggeration when he emphasized to the Protestant Congressman, who had no knowledge of the French but plenty of old prejudices, that the situation called for "great delicacy." He, therefore, offered additional judicious advice to Congress that was right on target: "The temper with which General Sullivan was actuated was too analogous to that which appeared in the generality of those concerned with him in the expedition, and to the sentiments prevailing among the people. Though men of discression will feel the impropriety of his conduct; yet there are too many who will be ready to make a common cause with him against any attempt of the public authority to convince him of his presumption, unless the business is managed with great address and circumspection. The credit universally given him for a happy and well conducted retreat, will strengthen the sentiments in his favour, and give an air of cruelty to any species of disgrace, which might be thrown upon a man, who will be thought rather to deserve the esteem and applause of his country. To know how to strike the proper sting will require more skill, than I am master of; but I would offer the general hint, that there should be a proper mixture of the *sweet* and *bitter* in the potion which may be administered."[118] Adhering to Hamilton's sound advice that was as timely as it was important under a delicate situation when the stakes were especially high, Congress took wise action accordingly, seeking to minimize the damage caused by Sullivan's angry words as much as possible.[119]

Consequently, Hamilton's September 8, 1778, letter was remarkable in a variety of ways. The young man's letter to the Continental Congress, the highest and most dysfunctional authority in the land, revealed his deep thinking and sharp political sense, sensitivity (especially cultural terms), and tact toward America's most important foreign ally. He presented sound advice to a respected Congressman about the proper course that America's ruling body should take in an extremely sensitive situation upon which so much depended in regard to the vital alliance and America's future.[120]

Most importantly, exactly when most needed at a turning point moment between allies, Hamilton made lasting favorable impressions and contributions that considerably raised the esteem of Americans in the eyes of the elite French officer corps and the Gallic commanders at the head of naval and land forces. Later, one French officer recalled, "I had expected to see in this democratic camp [of Washington's Army] unkempt soldiers and officers without training, all republicans devoid of that urbanity so common in our old civilized counties. . . . The generals, their aides-de-camp and the other officers evinced in their behavior and their speech noble and decent manners. . . ."[121] Hamilton stood out as the foremost of these impressive American officers.

Chapter V

Hamilton's Most Audacious Proposal

Unlike most of his fellow staff officers (except the twenty-three year old Laurens who hailed from one of South Carolina's leading slave-owning families)—and even Washington who was one of America's largest slave owners—Hamilton hated slavery. He had no personal connections to the institution since departing St. Croix. As romantic idealists, these two kindred spirits—one from the Deep South and the other from the Caribbean—were diehard abolitionists, representing the rise of young men deeply influenced by Age of Enlightenment ideology. Therefore, both Hamilton and Laurens freely expressed their enlightened opinions about this forbidden subject, and were guaranteed to receive a sharp backlash. Significantly, however, Hamilton's enlightened views about slavery were shared with a new and more liberal generation of progressive French government and military leaders, like his good friend Lafayette. Hamilton embraced the egalitarian faith that a true "Whig [patriot] abhors the very idea of slavery, let the colour or complexion of a slave be what it may [because] He is a friend of liberty, and a supporter of the rights of mankind. . . ."[1]

Hamilton had seen slavery's horrors at first-hand in the Caribbean, which no doubt created disturbing memories and perhaps a sense of guilt about slavery that still haunted him, partly because his mother Rachel had inherited slaves. On St. Croix, he had come to know Ajax—a servant given him by his mother—as a fellow human being and friend. As the teenage clerk and then temporary manager of the firm of Kortright and Cruger for half a year, Hamilton had occasionally worked in the slave trade that fueled the company's profits. Part of his job had been to supervise the sales of slaves transported to the company from West Africa. The mercantile business in Christiansted, St. Croix, sold slaves in "Cruger's Yard," as advertised the sale of three hundred "Prime Slaves" (around the same number owned by Washington at the revolution's beginning) on January 23, 1771. These unfortunate men, women, and children had been "imported from the Windward Coast of Africa." This unsavory, if not horrific, experience, including witnessing the selling of slaves on the auction block, informed Hamilton's understanding of human nature's darker side that served him well as Washington's chief of staff in multiple fields of endeavor. The cruelty of slavery had played a part in early making him a diehard cynic.[2]

Quite unlike his Virginia-born boss, Hamilton, a non-slave owner, was enlightened, liberal, and progressive to a degree that was rare for the day. However, to be fair, the war's stern demands and harsh realities brought a change in Washington's thinking about slavery. Ironically, slaves had been officially prohibited from serving as soldiers in America's armies until manpower shortages altered the policy. But while a number of Northern states allowed blacks to serve in the military, the South continued to bar enlistment, because of what the example represented to slaves.

General Washington became more enlightened partly because of the faithful service of his slave Billy Lee, as well as the presence of hundreds of African American soldiers who served in the Continental Army. Billy Lee was a regular feature at Washington's headquarters. He remained by the general's side during most of the war, and throughout Hamilton's service at headquarters.

What has been often overlooked was the fact that Hamilton (and Laurens to a lesser degree) played a leading, but forgotten, role in Washington's gradual conversion toward more enlightened sensibilities toward the antiquated concept of human bondage. After all, no anti-slavery voice (and a respected one at that) and personal influence were more of a constant presence for a longer period upon the Virginia planter than his closest confidant Hamilton. Never before had Washington been around a more progressive and liberal-thinking individual, who was the antithesis of a typical provincial.[3] Indeed, Washington "spent practically all of his time" with Hamilton, and this had a significant impact upon his thinking, including about slavery.[4]

Despite being the privileged son of a large Deep South slave-owning family, John Laurens possessed a passion for "my black project": the employment of black soldiers to fight for liberty in his native South Carolina, where they were in fact prohibited from serving. Every inch the abolitionist as Laurens, Hamilton was the other leading player in this ambitious "black project," which they viewed as an asset to winning the war. Representing the youngest generation of revolutionaries, Hamilton and Laurens embraced a set of true republican principles that existed on a higher moral level beyond mere revolutionary rhetoric. Consequently, in developing and promoting this bold plan for blacks to fight for America and gain their freedom, these two remarkable young men united their enlightened ideas to lead the charge against the curse of slavery, hoping to elevate the struggle "to a higher [moral] plane."[5]

The need for black troops to fight for America became more obvious when America's fortunes took a turn for the South, beginning with the fall of Savannah, Georgia, on December 29, 1778, and with South Carolina—Charleston was next—under severe threat. From Washington's headquarters at Middlebrook, New Jersey, on March 14, 1779, and while John Laurens had returned to his home state of South Carolina to defend his homeland after resigning from Washington's staff, Hamilton sat down to reveal his enlightened progressivism in matters of race for not only the good of his country, but also for the overall welfare of enslaved people. Laurens hoped to convince the Congressmen in Philadelphia to accept an audacious plan for the creation of black battalions (from two to four) to serve in the Continental Army. To support Laurens's bold plan, Hamilton wrote his remarkable letter to be delivered by the South Carolinian to John Jay, the new president of the Continental Congress and his New York friend. Combining humanitarianism with urgent military and political priorities, Hamilton's letter contained the boldest pro-black fighting men proposal to date, thus laying before Congress the possibility of elevating this people's revolution to a higher moral plane and enhance its overall chances for success and winning the war.

Clearly, in matters of race, the open-minded Hamilton and Laurens looked at the world quite differently from their older generation of revolutionaries, including Washington. At this time when the war's outcome was still in doubt, England's primary strategic focus was on conquering the South, and America desperately needed manpower, especially in the Southern theater of operations, Laurens and Hamilton worked together as an effective team on their most progressive project of immense potential. They sought to address two pressing and vital concerns of the war in the South that needed to be solved for enhance the possibilities for winning the war. Firstly, America's crucial manpower shortage across the lightly populated South because so many Loyalists were Southerners. Secondly, the disturbing and stark contradiction of Americans battling for liberty while allowing the institution of slavery to not only exist but also flourish in their midst, thus mocking the loftiest Age of Enlightenment ideologies and revolutionary principles. By early 1779, these two idealistic young officers were the leading advocates of a bold plan for securing much-needed manpower (black soldiers) in a lengthy war of attrition, and fulfilling the republic's noblest humanitarian ambitions and pressing wartime requirements.

In ideological and especially moral terms in regard to slavery, they believed that the infant republic should live up to its most enlightened core principles, as emphasized by Thomas Jefferson in the Declaration of Independence—that all men "were created equal." Laurens planned to deliver Hamilton's March 14, 1779, letter in person to John Jay and Congress, because they believed that this was nothing less than a timely bid to save America, before it was too late.

To set the stage to enhance the proposal's acceptance, Hamilton had also made an accurate and intelligent assessment of the war situation in the South. At the army's seasonal encampment (since 1777) of Middlebrook, Bridgewater Township, New Jersey, where the army wintered after the battle of Monmouth, Hamilton had been deeply troubled. Most of all, he was worried that the pulse of America's increasingly fragile life was fast fading away, because of economic, political, and manpower concerns that seemed to have no solutions. He hoped to provide a much-needed remedy to a vexing strategic situation that he correctly saw as disastrous in the South. Here, at Washington's headquarters at the William Wallace House, located northeast of Trenton, Hamilton finished writing his letter at his wooden desk. He predicted a dire fate for American fortunes in the South, if the pervasive racial prejudice was not overcome for a more united front.[6]

As early as February 2, 1778, Laurens had emphasized in a letter to his father of the many obstacles, including "a monstrous popular prejudice," that confronted the ambitious "scheme" of black soldiers fighting for America's and their liberty on Southern soil. However, Laurens was undaunted of the daunting extent of the formidable racial and cultural barriers because of his "perseverance, aided by the countenance of a few virtuous men," especially his kindred spirit on Washington's staff.[7] Hamilton was the foremost of these "virtuous men," and the two zealous staff officers worked together with unbridled enthusiasm on their joint pet project in early 1779 to bring a new birth of freedom to America, if accepted.[8]

In no uncertain terms to Jay on March 14, 1779, the ever-strategic minded Hamilton emphasized how at this time, "Extraordinary exigencies demand extraordinary means [because] I fear this Southern business will become a very grave one."[9] On this mid-March day at Middlebrook when he accurately foresaw even greater disasters ahead in the Southern theater, Hamilton warned the president of the Continental Congress, Jay, with his typical candor: "While I am on the subject of Southern affairs, you will excuse the liberty I take in saying, that I do not think measures sufficiently vigorous are pursing for our defense in that quarter," because of far too much reliance on militia.[10]

In no uncertain terms, Hamilton emphasized his much-needed solution to the South's military and manpower crisis to the president of the Continental Congress. Enlisting slaves in Continental service to fight for their own freedom and America's liberty on Southern soil was truly a revolutionary policy and readily available possible solution to a dire strategic situation that was bound to become far worse. This young man from the West Indies, whose societies and economies were based on slavery, explained the details of his and Laurens's "project, which I think, in the present situation of affairs there, is a very good one and deserves every kind of support and encouragement. This is to raise two, three, or four battalions of negroes; with the assistance of the government of that state [South Carolina], by contributions from the owners in proportion to the number they possess [and Lauren] wishes to have it recommended by Congress to the state; and, as an inducement, that they would engage to take those battalions into Continental pay. It appears to me, that an expedient of this kind, in the present state of Southern affairs, is the most rational, that can be adopted, and promises very important advantages. Indeed, I hardly can see how a sufficient force can be collected in that quarter without it; and the enemy's operations there are growing infinitely serious and formidable."[11]

Of course, Hamilton's inflammatory and ultra-sensitive views (arguably the day's most racially enlightened and forward-thinking about race) challenged the central foundations of the South's entrenched aristocratic society and its value system that rested on racial superiority. Even more, the South's economy and profitable cash crops were all based on slavery. Therefore, the mere mention of freeing slaves was the most forbidden possible subject across the South. But Hamilton went even further, expounding upon enlightened concepts that were considered social and racial heresy by the slave-owning South. Rejecting the existing racial stereotypes as too foolish to be seriously entertained on any level, he articulated a case for black equality that was partly based upon what he had in the Caribbean, including having seen well-trained black militiamen who protected St. Croix with their lives. As he continued to expressed to Jay with considerable insight about race based on first-hand experience: "I have not the least doubt, that negroes will make very excellent soldiers, with proper management. . . . It is a maxim with some military judges, that with sensible officers [and] soldiers can hardly be more stupid. . . . I mention this, because I frequently hear it objected to the scheme of embodying negroes that they are too stupid to make soldiers. This is so far from appearing to me a valid objection that I think their want of cultivation (for their natural faculties are probably as good as ours) joined to that habit of subordination which they require from a life of servitude, will make them sooner to become soldiers than our white inhabitants."[12]

Clearly, these were some of the most unconventional and boldest ideas ever offered by Hamilton or any American revolutionary in uniform, especially a young officer serving on Washington's staff. Of course, these enlightened racial views were in direct opposition to those of many conservative Founding Fathers, especially those who hailed from the South. In striking contrast, Hamilton believed that blacks possessed ample intelligence, and that they might even make better soldiers than whites, especially when serving in the Southern theater, thus overturning some of the most basic and widely accepted racial stereotypes.[13]

Despite knowing that he risked alienating America's political elite, in a true profile in courage that has too often been ignored by generations of historians, Hamilton emphasized the practicality of the ambitious plan to Congress with the bold conviction of a true believer: "I foresee that this project will have to combat much opposition from prejudice and self-interest. The contempt that we have been taught to entertain for the blacks, makes us fancy many things that are founded neither in reason nor experience; and an unwillingness to part with property of so valuable a kind will furnish a thousand arguments to show the impracticability or pernicious tendency of a scheme which requires such a sacrifice. But it should be considered that if we do not make use of them in this way, the enemy probably will; and that the best way to counteract the temptations they will hold out will be to offer them ourselves. An essential part of the plan is to give them their freedom with their muskets. This will secure their fidelity, animate their courage, and I believe will have a good influence upon those who remain, by opening a door to their emancipation."[14]

Hamilton advocated freedom for slaves if they faithfully fought for America in black combat units led by white officers, to save the South from subjugation in England's determined bid to sever this strategic region from the North, and reverse the war's fortunes. In regard to the day's most radical concept of "opening a door to their emancipation" and revealing that he was a true son of the Age of Enlightenment by combining egalitarian thought with a commonsense practicality to advocate a novel military solution to a serious crisis, Hamilton concluded: "This circumstance, I confess, has no small weight in inducing me to wish the success of the project; for the dictates of humanity and true policy equally interest me in favor of this unfortunate class of men."[15]

United with his kindred spirit Laurens, Hamilton's bold call to Congress for the use of black troops in the South "for the dictates of humanity" and America was not meaningless rhetoric, but a practical (not to mention moral) solution that solved a host of pressing problems that almost led to the conquest of the South in the upcoming years. In addition, Hamilton and Laurens sought to emplace a policy for bestowing freedom to blacks to match an enlightened British policy: a timely countermeasure that would have enhanced the chances of not only surviving but also perhaps even winning the war in the South, where the war was going to be decided in the end.[16]

As his actions throughout the Revolutionary War demonstrated, especially in regard to his appeal to incorporate black soldiers into the Continental Army, Hamilton sincerely "believed that he [had] dedicated his life to ideas that were intended for the betterment of society as a whole."[17]

Most significantly and as mentioned, Hamilton was not proposing the use of blacks for Southern service in the short-term militia, which was entirely unsuitable for a lengthy war of attrition. Instead of untrained and poorly led militiamen who were unable to stand up to British regulars on the battlefield, these transplanted Africans were to serve as long-term Continental soldiers, essentially regulars who benefitted greatly from extended training and battle experience: The true key to sustaining a lengthy war of attrition against a regular army of well-trained soldiers.[18]

Clearly, Hamilton was championing a far-sighted plan that offered to solve the South's pressing military manpower shortage and reverse the war's fortunes in that strategic theater. After all, the situation was about to grow far worse with the May 1780 capture of Charleston and its large garrison, including of thousands of Continental soldiers: one of the lowest ebbs for American fortunes in the South. This innovative plan destined to be laid before Congress was the centerpiece of the most enlightened and practical thinking of the dynamic team of Hamilton and Laurens, who were brothers as much on the battlefield—mostly recently at Monmouth—as in the ideological realm. Appropriately, once reaching the capital of Philadelphia after a lengthy ride, Laurens handed Hamilton's well-written document to the president of Congress for proper consideration by America's leading political body in the land.[19]

Impressed by Hamilton's insightful document that might well save the South from subjugation and with the possibility of reversing the war's course in the South, the Continental Congress then recommended on March 29, 1779, that South Carolina and Georgia "take measures immediately for raising three thousand able-bodied negroes" in separate battalions (regiments) led by white officers. Freedom would be bestowed to these slaves after their faithful service in battling for liberty—their own and that of the infant republic.[20]

In a letter to his father, Laurens emphasized how his and Hamilton's efforts had produced a "plan for serving my country and the oppressed negro race" at the same time: a remarkable document in military and moral terms.[21] Not fearful of alienating Congress and angering highly placed Southern officers and politicians who were sure to be offended by the mere suggestion of black equality, Hamilton and Laurens risked their reputations and career for the greater national good, but had boldly forged ahead nevertheless. As could be expected, the plan was far too radical for acceptance by the South Carolina government. Incredibly, South Carolina's leaders preferred defeat to racial equality.

Significantly, Hamilton and Laurens saw the novel solution of using black soldiers at a time when white resistance effort was in the process of sagging to new lows, because of the South's large number of Loyalists, a situation that would grow even worse in the days ahead. As an enthusiastic Laurens penned in the same letter to his father on February 2, 1778: "A well chosen body of 5,000 black men, properly officer'd, to act as light troops, in addition to our present establishment, might give us decisive success in the next campaign."[22]

Clearly, instead of just offering lip service and rhetoric, Hamilton and Laurens were fully prepared to fight for what they believed was right, both on and off the battlefield, despite the great risks. These two young officers were true examples of profiles in courage. In Hamilton's words to Laurens: "We have fought side by side to make America free. . . . "[23] But along with his good ideas about the best way to reform the army and freely speaking his mind as usual, Hamilton's radical proposal about utilizing black soldiers (the South's largest manpower pool when white soldiers were lacking) made him even more of a hated man, especially from slave-owning Southerners and upper class Congressmen. After all, such respected men of wealth and prestige had an alternate plan: South Carolina and Virginia, Washington's home state, eventually offered slaves as bounties for the enlistment of white soldiers.

As could be expected, some politicians were already angry at Hamilton for his sharp, but well-deserved, criticisms of Congress that continued over an extended period of time. New England Congressmen and officers were also upset by Hamilton's perceived high-handed actions in the past toward their chosen favorites, Generals Gates and Putnam. From a letter by a concerned Lieutenant Colonel John Brooks, Hamilton learned that Congressman Charles Dana had denounced Hamilton in a Philadelphia coffeehouse for advocating throwing Congress out of office to gain personal power for himself: an ugly false rumor that he openly voiced in public. Hamilton wrote to Dana to seek the source of the malicious rumor, tracing it to a Congregational minister in Massachusetts, William Gordon. Angry New Englanders, military and civilian, united with Southern Congressmen in their hated of Washington's golden boy, who had become a polarizing figure in both the American military and in main political body in no small part because of his string of successes.

And, of course, Hamilton was never shy about voicing his strong opinions and innovative views that featured a distinctive "Little Lion" boldness in the face of misplaced convention and mindless opposition, regardless of how highly placed. In consequence and realizing how easy it was to stir up a hornet's nest, Hamilton wrote on September 12, 1780, a typical candid and heartfelt letter to Laurens, whom he worried he would never see again because he knew that the South Carolinian would be reckless on Southern battlefields, where the nation's destiny was about to be decided: "You are almost as detested as an accomplice with the administration. I am losing character my friend, because I am not over complaisant to the spirit of clamour, so that I am in a fair way to be out with every body. With one set, I am considered as a friend to military pretensions, however exorbitant, with another as a man, who secured by my situation from the sharing of distress of the army, am inclined to treat it lightly. The truth is I am an unlucky honest man, that speak my sentiments to all and with emphasis."[24]

Despite all that he had accomplished since even before the war's beginning, Hamilton continued to feel that he was unlucky in his military career because he was not now serving at the front in dramatic fashion as at Monmouth, where he had distinguished himself in helping to save the day. While working tirelessly at his desk at Washington's headquarters, he continued to lust for action and the opportunity to play a larger role on the battlefield. In a June 1779 letter to Maryland's Colonel Otho Howard Williams, who had made a name for himself as an excellent leader in Colonel William Smallwood's Maryland Regiment and a friend of Welsh descent, Hamilton's deep feelings and ambitions were revealed. After Washington had moved the army to West Point,

New York, on the Hudson River, Hamilton wrote down words that betrayed a great deal about himself: "Mind your eye, my dear boy, and if you have an opportunity, fight damned hard!"[25]

Indeed, Lieutenant Colonel Hamilton possessed good reason to be envious of his Maryland friend, because he still badly wanted to return to a field command. In part, his radical proposal to have African American soldiers fight for America and their own freedom was also a political maneuver calculated "to out flank Washington" in order to win a field command, perhaps gain a commission to join Laurens in South Carolina, where their ambitious pet project was to have been implemented. But, of course, Washington refused to change his mind, because Hamilton was simply too valuable to let go. Ironically, in many ways a victim of his own successes and growing reputation, Hamilton remained the leader of his staff, working at his desk with stoic resignation instead of leading a charge on the battlefield as on that glorious day at Monmouth.[26]

Late Summer and Fall, 1779

Hamilton's erudite and enlightened views continued to carry considerable weight in multiple arenas that revealed his broad knowledge, ranging from the strategic to government affairs. As he penned in a September 7, 1779, letter to James Duane, Hamilton correctly believed that the British strategy was about to switch "from conquest to pacification" in the South. Lieutenant Colonel Hamilton offered sound advice to Major General Nathanael Greene, who was Washington's most reliable top lieutenant. In a September 10, 1779, letter, Hamilton made key points not lost on the capable Greene: "I really do not think it would be an advisable measure to detach a brigade . . . it would hardly be prudent to lessen our force. . . . But my principal objection rises from my considering a compliance rather as a bad precedent; if you yield to the importunity of one state [Connecticut's governor, Jonathan Trumbull, requested reinforcements], you must not only do the same to others in similar circumstances but you encourage that importunity and ultimately multiply your embarrassments."[27]

Hamilton also continued to focus on deciphering the nuances of British strategy, after gathering and analyzing intelligence. On September 11, 1779, from West Point, Hamilton put down his thoughts about the overall strategic situation. Writing to John Laurens, he believed that he had ascertained British intentions, especially in regard to the vulnerable Southern states: "Negotiation not conquest will then be [England's strategic] object; the acquisition of two or three of the Southern states would be the counter ballance to the loss of her [sugar] islands [in the West Indies], give credit in Europe, facilitate honorable pacification or procure it. The plan of operations, I suppose in that case would be this—to evacuate Rhode Island, leave a garrison of eight thousand men for the defence of New York and its dependencies, detach five thousand to the West Indies to assist in garrisoning their remaining islands, and then they will have five thousand to send to the Southward" to conquer the South.[28]

At Washington's Morristown headquarters, it continued to be one of Hamilton's primary jobs to decipher intelligence and advise Washington. Hamilton laid out his sound strategic reasoning to Laurens, in a September 11 letter: the British "plan here suggested, you will perhaps think with me is not the worst the enemy could adopt in their present circumstances. Its goodness is perhaps the strongest reason against its being undertaken; but they may blunder upon the right way for once, and we ought to be upon our guard."[29] As in the past, Hamilton was eager to exploit any tactical opening presented by a British blunder or weakness.

Meanwhile, naval developments began to play a larger role in the war by the late summer and early fall of 1779. While a British fleet sailed into New York Harbor, America turned its eyes toward the French fleet under Admiral Count d'Estaing, which had assisted the disastrous allied assault on Savannah, Georgia, in October 1779. Washington hoped that d'Estaing would sail north for the launching of a joint allied operation against New York City during the narrow window of opportunity that time presented, after the French fleet's service in Southern waters and before returning to the Caribbean for the winter. The French fleet was expected to appear in Philadelphia, after sailing northwest up Delaware Bay.

Therefore, Washington handed Hamilton another special mission of importance: proceed immediately to Philadelphia by way of the New Jersey coast to intercept the French admiral, and convince him of the wisdom of a joint operation against New York City. Hamilton's flawless French was essential for communications and clear understanding among allies of precise strategic and tactical details that so often separated victor from loser. Gaining no news from d'Estaing and his fleet, Hamilton and French Brigadier General Louis Du Portial, who earlier had been sent secretly by the French Government to assist Washington's Army, rode forth on their new mission to Great Egg Harbor, southeast New Jersey, about forty miles southeast of Philadelphia.

Here, on the windswept Jersey coast, the two officers anxiously scanned the Atlantic's distant horizon in the hope of sighting the French fleet's arrival. On October 26, Hamilton wrote his first report to Washington from forlorn "Egg Harbor Landing": "We propose to remain till the arrival of the Count [d'Estaing], till intelligence from him decides the inutility of a longer stay or 'till we receive your Excellency's orders of recall. We have now a better relation to the different points in which we are interested and have taken the necessary precautions to gain the earliest notice of whatever happens. . . ."[30]

Compared to lively Philadelphia, which flaunted republican virtues as well as vices as represented by fast women on the make, Hamilton and Du Portial felt that they had been exiled to what seemed to be a futile mission on the cold New Jersey coast. Day after day, the two officers, who communicated with each other in exquisite French, continued to scan the horizon in the hope of catching sight of the tall masts of warships. In the same missive, Hamilton also reported to Washington, "By recent information we find that so late as the fourth of this month [October] the Count was yet to open his batteries against the enemy at Savannah. The time that will probably intervene between this and their final reduction . . . and his arrival on this [eastern] coast may we fear exhaust the season too much to permit the cooperation to which our mission relates. We do not however despair; for if the Count has been fully successful to the Southward [Savannah], and should shortly arrive which may be the case, the enterprise may possibly still go on."[31]

For what seemed like an eternity, Hamilton and Du Portial continued to search in vain for signs of the French fleet's arrival. From their lonely coastal outpost on November 8 while enduring the cold weather of winter's early descent upon the lengthy New Jersey coast, Hamilton then reported to Washington: "We have received no late advices from the Southward, which confirms us in the ideas of our last" report on October 26.[32] Three days later, a discouraged Hamilton wrote to Lieutenant Colonel John Taylor and lamented, "I am getting sick & can't say more."[33]

Unfortunately for Hamilton's mission, Admiral d'Estaing was not sailing north for Philadelphia as Washington desired. Instead the aristocratic French admiral was sailing southeast back to safeguard the valuable sugar islands of the French West Indies, even when the siege of Savannah was still ongoing, following the repulse of the allied offensive effort.[34]

After his futile mission on the lonely and cold coast, Hamilton and the French general returned to Washington's headquarters at Morristown. As usual, Hamilton was still consumed by his desire to win battlefield distinction, which was a true passion: A very personal quest bordering on obsession that never ended for the ambitious young man. In a strange way, Hamilton seemingly could only feel validation as a man and as a soldier, if he earned recognition on the battlefield. Hamilton already had proven his courage and leadership ability on past battlefields, but even this widespread acclaim, including from Washington and other generals, was not sufficient to satisfy his insatiable desire. Therefore, Hamilton continued to speak privately with Washington about his desire of gaining a field command, presenting his most convincing arguments—but to no avail.

Hoping to take advantage of an existing opportunity, Hamilton then focused his efforts on securing a command for the proposed expedition to Staten Island, New York, as he described in the same letter: "When the expedition to Staten Island was afoot, a favourable one seemed to offer. There was a [infantry] battalion without a field officer, the command of which, I thought, as it was accidental, might be given to me without inconvenience."[35]

To increase his chances of securing the field commission, Hamilton smartly utilized the added advantage of a solid endorsement from Lafayette, who was essentially Washington's surrogate son. However, Hamilton's carefully calculated bid to secure release from headquarters was not enough to sway Washington and change his mind. Quite sensibly under the circumstances, Washington continued to refuse to let Hamilton depart from his military "family," because he was just too valuable in almost too many ways to count. Therefore, Washington informed Lafayette—not Hamilton which was in accordance to the rules of proper military protocol—of his final decision. As a frustrated Hamilton explained gloomily in his letter: "I made an application for it [command of the available infantry battalion] through the Marquis, who informed me of your refusal. . . ."[36]

Lieutenant Colonel Hamilton had good reason to feel a deepening sense of frustration during this period. The Marquis de Lafayette and General Greene already had attempted to "liberate" him from Washington's headquarters by nominating Hamilton for the coveted position of the Continental Army's adjutant general. With some justification, Washington employed the excuse that Hamilton's rank of only lieutenant colonel was too low for either this position or an appointment to a field command. Of course, the most obvious solution in both cases was for Washington to simply bestow this well-deserved promotion to colonel (long overdue and very much deserved) that the Virginian *never* gave

Hamilton, despite his lengthy list of accomplishments and even Lafayette's personal efforts to assist his friend in this regard.[37]

A frustrated Lafayette, who believed like Hamilton that "insurrection is [for the oppressed] the most sacred of the rights and the most indispensable of duties," was not only perplexed, but also angered at Washington's iron determination to keep Hamilton sequestered on his staff.[38] Demonstrating wisdom in regard to his own responsibilities and duties, Washington was not about to release the best staff officer, only age twenty-four, that he had ever possessed, and almost certainly ever to have in his career as commander-in-chief of America's armies.

Winter 1779–1780

The conclusion of the campaign of 1779—the fourth year of the war—in Washington's sector proved to be still another frustrating stalemate. The once-bright optimism stemming from the first news of the French Alliance and possibility of quick success had evaporated in America by this time. Bright visions of decisive victory had faded away from the American people and the republic's fighting men, lingering only as a distant memory in faded past. During the winter of 1779–1780 when British strategists directed their main offensive effort at the strategic port of Charleston, Washington was encamped in winter quarters at Morristown under the dark and snowy skies of still another bleak December. Here, several miles southwest of the small village of Jockey Hollow, and nestled amidst the hardwood forests of a mountainous region three miles southwest of Morristown, the log cabins of a sprawling winter quarters—the second winter encampment at Morristown—served as home for threadbare and ill-supplied soldiers of liberty.[39]

During this winter of discontent and after Washington's refusals, Hamilton feared that the battle of Monmouth had been his last chance to win battlefield recognition. After all, that late June 1778 battle was the last major clash in the middle states, before the war had shifted to the South as the principal theater of operations. Overworked and professionally frustrated, Hamilton was overcome by a dark gloom that coincided with the wintry dreariness. His personal distaste for serving endlessly at a headquarters desk was demoralizing. The young man also felt discouraged by the failure of the ambitious Laurens-Hamilton plan for slaves to fight for America to bolster its thin manpower reserves. In a sad and prophetic letter to Laurens, Hamilton penned with a sense of fatalism:

"I wish its success, but my hopes are very feeble [because] Prejudice and private interest will be antagonists too powerful for public spirit and public good."[40]

At times, the ghosts of Hamilton's tragic past in the Caribbean began to trouble the young man of seemingly endless promise, especially during relatively quiet periods and wintertime. The frantic pace of Hamilton's daily existence as Washington's chief of staff usually allowed him to stay ahead and outrun his demons, but not forever. His dark past finally caught up with Hamilton. During the winter of 1779–1780 at Morristown, Washington and his staff were housed in the English colonial style mansion, painted white with stylish green trim, owned by the widow of Jacob Ford, a former judge. Here, located several miles from the army's main encampment at Jockey Hollow, Hamilton endured the harshest winter that he had ever experienced in his life.

After his seemingly endless duties were completed, Hamilton slept in an upstairs bedroom of the mansion with his two best friends, McHenry and Tilghman. Especially demoralizing was the fact that he possessed fond memories of the Caribbean's omnipresent warmth, while this brutal winter was one of the worst yet seen in the eighteenth century. Nothing previously experienced by Hamilton prepared him for this wintry hell of Morristown. Washington's winter encampment was literally buried in a blanket of heavy snows—up to six feet on one occasion—for lengthy periods.[41]

Harboring warm memories of the bright sunshine of his native Caribbean homeland, Hamilton's spirits continued to be affected by the dark skies and the snow piled high outside Washington's headquarters. Hamilton's sunny disposition and spirits were battered by the gusts of icy winds and heavy snowfall, which was compounded by his underlying personal and professional frustrations. Consequently, Hamilton's obsession with somehow securing an opportunity for gaining an independent command and battlefield recognition only deepened, while enduring the excessive workload and wintry gloom that seemed to have no end. Without family, connections, or fortune that fueled a sense that he was alone and still battling not only the British but also the world, Lieutenant Colonel Hamilton knew that making a name for himself could only happen for him by earning distinction on the battlefield. The young man's soaring ambition was too great and his mind too broad to settle happily for a desk job in Washington's giant shadow to obscure the breath of his achievements. As he realized, Hamilton had already accomplished enough for Washington and America to have garnered a promotion not only to a full colonel's rank but also perhaps even a brigadier general's commission by this time.

On January 8, 1780, Hamilton confided his creeping personal anguish in a letter to his best friend Laurens, now serving in South Carolina. After he refused the prestigious position offered by Congress by unanimous choice as Franklin's secretary in Paris, the debonair South Carolinian (not temperamentally suited for patience, tact, and delicate diplomacy) had attempted to gain a release for his West Indian friend from the relative seclusion and isolation of Washington's staff. This coveted diplomatic posting was a true plum position. Instead of taking the prized position because of his disinclination for serving in a diplomatic role far from his beloved South Carolina, he instead recommended Hamilton to Congress for the prestigious position.

However, Hamilton, who fairly lusted at such a golden opportunity to truly shine, had no support in Congress (as lamented Laurens in a letter to Hamilton), thanks to his strong criticism of the governing body's seemingly endless past failures to support the army and his well-known clashes and openly voiced disgust for Congress's favored generals, Gates and Lee. Many Americans also still looked unfavorably upon Hamilton, because he had not been born in America, and hailed from no leading American family of high social standing. Hamilton's role as Washington's leading defender also made him a marked man to the Virginian's haters and self-serving politicians in Congress. These Congressmen had no idea of the true extent of Hamilton's gifts that made him the ideal choice as the new French envoy, and allowed pettiness and prejudice to cloud their judgment: ironically, the very failings that had been long denounced by Hamilton

In his letter, Hamilton poured forth a flood of his deepest feelings: "Believe me my D[ea]r Laurens I am not insensible of the first mark of our affection in recommending me to your friends [in Congress] for a certain commission. . . . Not one of the four in nomination but would stand a better chance than myself; and yet my vanity tells me they do not all merit a preference. But I am a stranger in this country. I have no property [land or slaves] here, no connexions [therefore] I have strongly sollicited to go to the Southward [Southern theater of operations]. It could not be refused; but arguments have been used to dissuade me from it, which however little weight they may have had in my judgment gave law to my feelings."[42]

Hamilton's spirits sank to new lows after he failed to secure the coveted envoy position as Franklin's secretary in Paris, the eighteenth century's cultural epicenter. Additionally, the knowledge of having so many influential enemies in high places in the military and political realms, especially Congress, was also unsettling and boded ill for his future. Becoming gradually more alienated by the overall vexing situation, Hamilton was ever-conscious of the bitter irony of continuing to risk his life battling for a new nation's liberty when he was still "a stranger in this country" by his own gloomy admission of a common perception and prejudice that he could never change: A situation to his considerable detriment, but to Washington's and his staff's maximum benefit.[43]

During this cheerless winter at dreary Morristown, Hamilton's sense of optimism continued to erode, and demons raised their ugly heads. He even began to lose some of his romantic spirit by the harsh realities of a betrayed people's revolution that he saw all around him, lamenting in a letter with growing disillusionment that, "We do not live in the days of chivalry."[44] The double frustration of failing to secure either diplomatic service in France or obtaining a field command was devastating to the ambitious Hamilton, whose many achievements for Washington and America seem to have been ignored. He felt mired in thankless obscurity under Washington's lengthy shadow and in an unsavory ultra-political environment at the highest levels, especially Congress, where an ever-increasing number of cunning and clever enemies lurked like jackals in the dark shadows to exploit any first misstep. For good reason, General Charles Lee denounced such Congressmen as nothing more than "cattle," and Hamilton hated their overall "degeneracy." For once, Hamilton and Lee were in perfect agreement.[45]

Revealing his growing disillusionment with the corruption and lack of virtue among his fellow revolutionaries, especially Congressmen because of the "alarming and dangerous" decline in their overall quality, Hamilton then emphasized in his distressing letter to Laurens, barely a week after the New Year's arrival: "I am chagrined and unhappy but I submit. In short, Laurens I am disgusted with every thing in this world but yourself and *very* few more honest fellows and I have no other wish than as soon as possible to make a brilliant exist."[46]

Indeed, what the increasingly disgruntled, if not depressed, Hamilton was saying—as fully understood by Laurens who had similar sentiments—was that he was now flirting with the relatively comforting thought of suffering a martyr's death on the battlefield as a final release from his inner torment. To Hamilton's way of thinking, a heroic demise on the field of strife would be a noble sacrifice, releasing him from his personal misery and leaving a distinguished legacy for all time, if America eventually won its struggle for life. In another letter to Laurens, the disillusioned young man expressed discouragement over the death of the black soldier project, because he fully realized its importance: "Every [hope and desire] of this kind my friend is an idle dream [in part because] there is no virtue in America."[47]

And because of the incompetence and neglect of Congress, whose consistent failures and lack of effectiveness had led to the deaths of so many good common men of true character and quality, Hamilton became embittered about the personal tragedies that he saw around him. Because the overall situation became more desperate for America with each passing day, Hamilton, like Washington, continued to be convinced that a stronger government was the only solution for saving the army and the war effort, admitting: "I hate Congress." Thoroughly disgusted by the failings of Congress—a case of many good men having gone bad from swollen egos, greed, and corruption—as well as with political infighting within the army, especially the ever-ambitious officer corps where men were at each other's throats, Hamilton admitted: "We begin to hate the country for its neglect of us [and] the country begin to hate us for our oppressions of them."[48]

However, Hamilton became more of his old self with the advent of social activities that broke some of Morristown's monotony and raised his spirits in his darkest hour. The robust Washington, an imposing physical specimen that towered over the slight Hamilton, enjoyed dancing as much as fox hunting and riding across Mount Vernon's Tidewater lands along the Potomac River. Therefore, to lift morale among his officer corps and overburdened staff members, the commander-in-chief once again established the popular dancing assembly that consisted of thirty-four officers, including Hamilton. As a free-wheeling Virginian light on his feet when the fiddles played lively tunes and the rum and wine flowed freely, Washington, performed with great agility like a younger man despite his hulking size. He especially enjoyed the *Virginia Reel*, almost as much as Hamilton.

Of course, the young man from Nevis and St. Croix had long embraced the dance and musical traditions of West Indian Creole society. When a pretty lady was in his arms, the lithe Hamilton acquired the reputation as the best dancer on Washington's staff of dashing young men. With the local girls of the appropriate class (more upper class than middle class) providing suitable dance partners and possible paramours, these dances and drinking, sometimes to excess typical of a wartime environment when fighting men were far from home, occasionally continued to as late as 2:00 a.m. Of course and as usual,

Hamilton and other "family" members were always present at these festive occasions, making the most of the opportunity that provided a much-needed relief and relaxation to compensate for their heavy daily workload.

On at least one occasion perhaps when the fiddlers were playing the popular "A Successful Campaign," (that in the minds of young men like Hamilton translated into bedroom conquests at such heady times that swirled around nocturnal social activites) alert staff officers, including Hamilton, immediately intervened to "to smooth things over" for their commander-in-chief in an incident that caught everyone's attention. Washington's dainty dance partner shouted at the stout Virginian, who was known for his physical strength and imposing figure, "If you do not let go of my hand, I will tear out your eyes. . . ." As if suddenly outflanked by superior numbers of redcoats on the battlefield, Washington quickly vanished from the embarrassing scene on the dance floor. Then, the vigilant Hamilton immediately stepped in to restore harmony and merriment to present the façade that nothing had happened.[49]

As usual Hamilton focused upon the prettiest girls at social events at Washington's headquarters or the headquarters of generals at Morristown. Martha Washington's sly tomcat analogy for the prowling Hamilton was actually a backhanded compliment, as Hamilton seemed determined to win every lady's heart for sport, ego-enhancement, and amusement. Resplendent in his finest blue uniform of a lieutenant colonel, he was destined to gain renown for having danced with wife of General Nathanael Greene, who did not dance because a limp, for three hours, while observers marveled at the marathon that went a bit beyond socially accepted conduct.[50] Hamilton's romantic ambitions eventually centered on a Morristown brunette beauty named Cornelia Lott.[51] He initially appeared to be genuinely love struck with Cornelia to a degree that astounded his fellow staff officers, who had always seen exactly the reverse situation. An incredulous fellow staff member Lieutenant Colonel Samuel Blachley Webb, a cynic like Hamilton, wrote a humorous rhyme in tribute to this most surprising development that shocked the entire staff. The opening question of his humorous rhyme mocked the possibility of true love and perhaps even marriage: "To [Lieutenant] Colonel Hamilton": "What, bend the stubborn knee at last, Confess the days of wisdom past?"[52]

In keeping with his freewheeling style in his well-played game of love, Hamilton's infatuation with the young New Jersey lady proved fleeting as the cynics had predicted. Hamilton's comrades confused his unusually ardent efforts in the art of seduction with more noble and much higher-elevated sentiments, which was not the case. After all, Webb had mused with unconcealed delight: "Now [Hamilton] feels the inexorable dart / And yields Cornelia all his heart!" But Hamilton became bored after too easily conquering Cornelia's heart and evidently bedding her with his usual seemingly effortless ease, perhaps because she expected too much from him, such as marriage. After all, Hamilton had long spouted the axiom that a true soldier should have no wife, because he should be married only to the military. Focusing on a new and better romantic opportunity after leaving poor Cornelia behind, Hamilton quickly turned his sights on Polly, who was another one of the fashionable ladies who made the circuit of social activities at headquarters. With astonishing rapidity during this January of 1780, the dashing Hamilton, whose looks were almost closer to pretty than handsome, then "broke her heart too."[53] Living up to his ladies' man reputation that made him the talk and envy of headquarters, Hamilton was well known "for his cavalry-like advances on the latest feminine arrival in camp."[54]

Along with success on the romantic front, Hamilton's spirits rose with the prospect of action—the best tonic to relieve his frustrations and restore his optimism, after the swirl of social activities. Washington now planned a rare winter attack: an unexpected raid that was sure to catch the enemy by surprise. As just before his remarkable Trenton success on the day after Christmas 1776, Washington now needed another such incredible victory for political as much as military reasons. Almost certainly with Hamilton's assistance, Washington, therefore, chose Staten Island as the target. As in Washington's first true battlefield victory at snowy Trenton, General Knox was chosen to play the leading role with his artillery arm.

Displaying his trademark sound military judgment, Hamilton tactfully criticized his old superior's estimation of the number of cannon needed to succeed in his ambitious mission, which called for hauling the artillery on sleighs a lengthy distance over a snowy landscape. Hamilton took the esteemed Knox to task for allowing too few artillery pieces and too little ammunition for the planned assault to succeed. Critiquing Washington's highly competent and top commander of the army's artillery arm, Hamilton questioned the talented New Englander's well-known good judgment and tactical sense. As the ever-analytical Hamilton reported with his trademark honesty to Washington in his concise evaluation of the possible success of the proposed assault: "It appears to me the quantity of ammunition proposed by General Knox for the artillery is inefficient. A larger consumption may be necessary—the stone house [on Staten Island] in which the enemy may attempt to defend themselves may be obstinate, and we should have it in our power by the severity and duration of our fire, to bring them to reason" and surrender.[55]

As so often in the past, Washington agreed with Hamilton's sound recommendations. He consequently ordered Knox to take additional artillery pieces on his mission. However, Knox's attempt to catch the enemy by surprise at his defensive position on Staten Island ended in a dismal failure, verifying Hamilton's harsh critique and insightful arguments. Almost as if doing some of the tactical thinking for the commander-in-chief, especially when it came to the use of artillery because of his past experience as a New York battery commander, Hamilton's criticism was a direct attempt to convince Washington to cancel this difficult and overly ambitious operation in the dead of winter, because of the opposing garrison's strength, Staten Island's strong defenses, and the very slim possibility of catching the enemy by surprise.[56]

As mentioned, it was not all work and no play at Washington's headquarters amid the snows of Morristown. In early 1780, the Marquis de Chastellux described a memorable scene at Washington's headquarters one evening after cold blackness descended early and all work was finally put aside for the day. The aristocratic Frenchman wrote how the dinner at headquarters resembled a festive social event among the close-knit "family," which was full of life, especially with Hamilton leading the way as usual: "General Washington usually continues eating for two hours, toasting and conversing all the time . . . there were then no strangers [present in the room], and nobody remained by the General's family. The supper was composed of three or four light dishes [and] a few bottles of good claret and madeira were placed on the table [and] being a French officer . . . I accommodate myself very well to the English mode of *toasting* [and] I observed that there was more solemnity in the toasts at dinner: there were several ceremonious ones; the others were suggested by the General, and given out by his aides-de-camp, who performed the honours of the table at dinner; for one of them is every day seated at the bottom of the table, near the General, to serve the company, and distribute the bottles. The toasts in the evening were given by Colonel Hamilton, without order or ceremony."[57] As usual, Hamilton presided over the formal dinners and social activities at Washington's headquarters, which resembled state dinners attended by French and American political and military leaders. All the while, Hamilton continued to be the "life of every party."[58]

Washington's nighttime social activities at the Morristown winter encampment acted as a tonic to lift the spirits of the young men, including Hamilton, of his "family." Hamilton developed what might be described as passing relationships with "many young women," but nothing serious for one who played the field among the ladies with a vigorous finesse. As during the previous winter, the burdensome workload at headquarters weighed as heavily on Washington as on Hamilton, fraying nerves and leading to exhaustion.

Sure to restore the general's spirits as in the past, Martha departed Mount Vernon in mid-December 1779 in the hope of reaching army headquarters and her husband by Christmas. But the heavy snows stranded Martha in Philadelphia. Washington dispatched one of his trusty aides-de-camp, perhaps Hamilton but more likely McHenry or Tilghman, to retrieve Martha from the nation's capital in a horse-drawn sleigh. To make extra room at the crowded headquarters after Martha's arrival—and while Theodosia Ford, the widow of Judge Jacob Ford, still managed her own personal household at the Ford Mansion—Washington went to extra lengths to provide appropriate accommodations for his staff. He soon ordered the construction of three buildings to be located behind the stately two-story mansion, which would include an office for his staff, a stable for horses, and a separate kitchen for his "family." At the newly built log office, Hamilton performed his chief-of-staff duties with his usual vigor and competence.[59]

But after all of the brilliant conversations, witty jokes, dancing, and drinking, Hamilton, overburdened with work, again lapsed into one of his periodic dark moods. To Laurens as usual, Hamilton poured out his heart and mounting frustrations and gloom. The whirlwind of the Cornelia Lott and Polly affairs had only caused greater disillusionment about the fickleness of love and life, providing Hamilton with very little in what he was looking for in a relationship.

Hamilton and other staff members continued to enjoy the "dancing assembly," when the pretty and stylish daughters of leading patriot families enlivened the cold nights at Morristown. But this was only a merry façade that only continued to disguise Hamilton's inner frustration and disillusionment with America and its people, who reaped a profit at the army's expense. Fortunately for Hamilton at perhaps his darkest hour on this dreary winter of 1780, a quite remarkable young woman suddenly made her appearance at the Morristown headquarters, and his life would never be the same thereafter.

A Dream Comes True with a General's Pretty Daughter

Twenty-two-year-old Elizabeth Schuyler (called either Betsey or Eliza alternately by Hamilton), the spirited and attractive second daughter of Major

General Philip Schuyler, made her appearance at Morristown. After arriving at the sprawling winter quarters by military escort for protection, the good-natured young woman was in camp to visit her aunt, Mrs. John Cochran who lived near Morristown, while her parents journeyed to Philadelphia, where her father served in Congress. The Schuyler family's summer home in Saratoga in upper New York State had been burned down by General Burgoyne's invaders, before they surrendered in October 1777.

Not looking for love, Betsey had journeyed to Morristown to visit family. She came with letters of personal introduction to Washington and von Steuben from her father. However, her father hoped that Betsey, a lively brunette with a zest for life, might enjoy herself by joining with other young people at the popular dance assembly at Washington's headquarters. General Schuyler's sister Gertrude had married Dr. John Cochran, who was Washington's personal physician and the surgeon-general of the Continental Army. Cochran's parents were Irish immigrants from Ulster Province, north Ireland. The Cockrans were now staying in the Morristown home of Dr. Jabez Campfield, whose residence was located only a quarter mile—fortunately for Hamilton—down the little, dirt road from Washington's headquarters at the Ford Mansion.

Most of Washington's staff officers could hardly believe their eyes at the sight of the stylish young woman when she suddenly appeared at headquarters. But no eyes were wider than those of Hamilton, whose standards for the ideal wife were exceptionally, if not unrealistically, high. A tomboy and nature lover, Betsey was indeed a very special young lady, as Hamilton had first duly noted during his fall 1777 Albany mission when he had had first met her upon visiting the General Schuyler home overlooking the Hudson. Memories of what had interested him about the more common Cornelia and Polly instantly faded until they were nonexistent.

As could be expected, and despite (or because of) their class differences and dissimilar backgrounds, Hamilton aggressively pursued Betsey beginning in early February 1780, and not long after his previous two romantic dalliances that had been for fun. Under Hamilton's vigorous charm offensive and aggressive pursuit that would not have been acceptable under the usual social norms, she was unable to resist the gentlemanly and intelligent young officer, who was besotted with the general's daughter until she became an obsession. Hamilton was now enchanted with Betsey's "fine black eyes" that fairly sparkled, when talking to the native West Indian. In overcoming the wide social gap between the relatively recent immigrant and one of the wealthiest families in New York,

Hamilton's longtime role on Washington's staff now paid its greatest dividend in his personal life.

Always excessively driven and goal-oriented, he was focused on obtaining his romantic goal that was not a fleeting one this time. Hamilton's visits to the Campfield house became a nightly routine. Becoming inseparable, the young couple attended the dinners, dances, and balls at Washington's headquarters and those of other generals at Morristown. George and Martha Washington were enchanted by the whirlwind romance of the handsome couple. Hamilton's notoriously wandering eye strayed no longer to everyone's astonishment: the pretty young woman described by Tilghman as "the little saint" tamed the rakish spirit, lustful ways, and fickleness of a former playboy, who had broken many hearts along the way. After a whirlwind romance since coming together as one in February, the two were engaged in March, when he was twenty-five and his beloved native New Yorker was twenty-two. They planned for "a brilliant marriage" in the autumn, which was much longer than desired by the ever-ardent Hamilton, who nonetheless abided by General Schuyler's wishes.[60]

In true analytical fashion, Hamilton seemed almost amused, if not somewhat perplexed, about how the sheer transformative power of love had completely muddled his logical judgment and changed his notorious fickle ways with pretty women. Suddenly, in returning one night from visiting Betsey and with lovemaking still on his mind, he uncharacteristically forgot the password when stopped by the headquarters guard, when caused much personal embarrassment. Most of all, Hamilton was amazed how even the most artful of seducers among the men of Washington's staff had been seduced himself by the intelligent, classy Betsey, who was a charmer and spoke French to his great delight. Cynical, perhaps too worldly, and holding a generally low opinion of human nature that had long fueled his desire "to keep my happiness independent of the caprice of others," Hamilton was taking a great risk in personal terms by making himself vulnerable by choosing to love another person with all his heart: A vulnerability that he had carefully avoided with considerable success in the past.

Indeed, Hamilton's balanced analytical nature, axioms about how to live life, and cool intellect had been completely thrown out of whack by the emotional depth of his burning love. But fortunately, he had made a wise choice. The young man's love was returned in full by this lively woman from one of New York's most respected families. A member of the Dutch Reformed Church that reflected New York's early heritage, she was loving, unassuming, spiritual, and down to earth: qualities that served to more securely ground the mercurial Hamilton, who had been long hurled about like a sailing ship by life's unpredictable storms. As a somewhat perplexed Hamilton wrote to Betsey in attempting to explain the love that consumed him like a powerful intoxicant: "I am too much in love to be either reasonable or witty [and] I feel in the extreme; and when I attempt to speak of my feelings I rave. Love is a sort of insanity and everything I write savors strongly of it."[61]

In a letter to his best friend John Laurens who was battling for liberty in the South, Hamilton made light of his so suddenly lost status as a dashing ladies' man (only recently so highly prized), whose numerous nocturnal encounters and conquests had long had been the talk among higher-ranking officers in the army: "I confess my sins. I am guilty. Next fall [marriage] completes my doom. I give up my liberty to Miss Schuyler [who] is a good-hearted girl who I am sure will never play the termagant."[62]

After the snows finally faded from the Morristown area, Washington and Hamilton worked overtime in addressing a host of problems and in making preparations for the new spring campaign. Continuing to perform as an unbeatable leadership team in the confines of headquarters, Washington and Hamilton continued working to convince the ever-inefficient Congress to adequately provide for the long-suffering army of revolutionaries who were losing their idealism and faith in the struggle that seemed to have no end. Therefore, as during the previous winter, Washington requested a committee to spend some time at the Morristown encampment to view the army's deplorable conditions, in the hope of prompting remedies and solutions. To apply pressure on Congress to act decisively rather than talk, Washington naturally chose his master diplomat Hamilton to get things accomplished as so often in the past. With his usual zeal, Hamilton now conducted "most of the public courting" of the Continental Congress that was so necessary for the upcoming campaign.[63]

One modern historian explained why Washington continued to depend upon Hamilton like no other officer in the Continental Army: "First, the loquacious aide was a far better writer than the general. He was expected to weave literary magic and he did, peppering targeted [Congressional] delegates such as James Duane with letters that outlined an army at wit's end: 'For God's sake, my dear sir, engage Congress to adopt [a committee]. . . . We have not a moment to lose,' Hamilton wrote in his usual breathless style."[64]

In a steady stream of correspondence, Hamilton continued to serve as the sharp point of Washington's political and diplomatic spear, which tactfully pierced through the tangles of red tape and incompetence of politicians to reap excellent results as it did in out-foxing the wily General Gates. Hamilton's carefully calculated diplomatic style and artful maneuvering to apply subtle pressure continued to pay dividends for Washington. On this occasion, he garnered more authority for Washington, which the commander-in-chief could not legally request because of separation of powers and military protocol, by way of a committee from a Congress that was historically obsessive about not relinquishing any power to the military because of the old fear of standing armies. By stealthily garnering additional authority from Congress to ensure his army's well being, if not survival, in the days ahead, "Washington had Hamilton do his work for him."[65] Therefore, Washington's request for a committee was fully approved by Congress, which even selected the three individuals whom he had first suggested as members to serve. In the end, these committee members delivered a report to Congress that Washington "might have written himself."[66]

Spring 1780

The arrival of spring 1780 brought other new responsibilities to the already overburdened Hamilton. Much to his personal agony and only weeks after cementing the most important personal relationship of his life with plans to wed, he was forced to place his romance with Betsey on hold, when Washington ordered him and two officers to proceed from Morristown to Perth Amboy, New Jersey, during the second week of March 1780. This special assignment called for conferring with British officers in the hope of securing the exchange of American prisoners. Riding his favorite horse, Hamilton journeyed southeast from Morristown to Perth Amboy on the coast. Hamilton was not delighted about a lonely mission that took him around twenty-five miles from Betsey. While riding away from the winter encampment of Morristown and Betsey, Hamilton might well have regretted ever having become a soldier.

Detesting Perth Amboy's loneliness, Hamilton's spirits plummeted in a miserable exile. He naturally worried that Betsey, who continued to attend the dance assembly at headquarters to enjoy the company of gallant and handsome officers on the dance floor, might find someone else of higher social standing and wealth in keeping with her elevated status. Therefore, the lovesick Hamilton wrote to Betsey on St. Patrick's Day, March 17, 1780, "every moment of my stay here becomes more and more irksome; but I hope two or three days will put an end to it. Col. [Samuel Blachley] Webb tells me you have sent for a carriage to go to Philadelphia. If you should set out before I return have the goodness to leave a line informing me how long you expect to be there [and] though it will be a tax upon my love to part with you so long, I wish you to see that city before you return. . . . Only let me entreat you to endeavour not to stay there longer than the amusements of the place interest you, in complaisance to friends; for you must always remember your best friend is where I am. . . ."[67]

For the first time, Lieutenant Colonel Hamilton was so obsessed with his new love that he even put aside—but only briefly—official army business matters, because of his passionate letter writing to Betsey: "It is now half an hour past our time of meeting. I must bid you adieu. Adieu my charmer; take care of your self and love your Hamilton as well as he does you."[68] His good friend Captain Richard Kidder Meade took Hamilton's letter to Betsey as part of a clever initiative developed by the still cynical young man, who was still not comfortable with completely trusting his heart that might betray him. After all, Hamilton was new to the challenges of a serious love match, which presented fresh dilemmas to his analytical mind now clouded by strong emotion. Hamilton, proving less confident in love than in playing the field when "I have plagues enough" without taking on "that *greatest of all*" (marriage) and with personal insecurities (thanks to his Caribbean past) rising to the fore, was hoping to gauge Betsey's true heart in his long absence to end his lingering doubts that nagged at him.

After all, Betsey's social status was far above that of the lowly young immigrant who had only recently (1773) come to America's shores. Therefore, this stealthy detective work was calculated to ascertain if Betsey might be turning her eyes toward another handsome and dashing suitor in a resplendent officer's uniform. Clearly, Hamilton was still very much the intelligence officer in search of answers to perplexing mysteries, but now of the heart. In a letter that revealed his sense of relief, Hamilton later admitted how Meade "had the kindness to tell me that you received my [last] letter with marks of joy and that you retired with eagerness to read it. 'Tis from circumstances like these we best discover the true sentiments of the heart."[69]

General Philip Schuyler and his good, but stern and pious, Dutch wife, Catherine Van Rensselaer-Schuyler, departed Philadelphia to visit Hamilton, after his return to headquarters, and to officially entertain his hasty proposal to marry their daughter: a customary formality of high society. In fact, Schuyler already greatly admired Hamilton from previous meetings, including at his home when Washington's chief of staff had journeyed to Albany on his turbulent Gates mission. Hamilton easily overcame all of the natural social concerns of this wealthy aristocrat, who conversed in French with him and shared other common interests. Schuyler had also voted for Hamilton to serve in America's diplomatic mission as envoy in France.

Unleashing a typical charm campaign of which he was a master, the tactically astute Hamilton already had cultivated Betsey's mother with his sincere letters to win her support for the hand of "your amiable daughter," as he emphasized in one letter. Indeed, with the same skill as in dealing with haughty Congressmen, upper class officers, or French officials, he had prudently forwarded the letter of Betsey's acceptance to her mother in Albany and diplomatically thanked Mrs. Schuyler for her early and full "acceptance" of him as a future son-in-law. On Saturday April 8, 1780, in a formal letter from General Schuyler, Hamilton learned that the parents formally approved the match seemingly made in heaven. He even referred to his son-in-law as "my beloved Hamilton," as revealed in a letter to Betsey. Schuyler later stated that "Hamilton did honor to the Schuyler family." Hamilton and Betsey initially were to be married in late autumn of 1780. In a letter to Laurens, Hamilton revealed how Betsey "is rather handsome, and has every other requisite of the exterior to make a lover happy."[70]

On Wednesday April 19 and after Betsey departed with her father to Philadelphia, where he served as the New York delegate in Congress, Washington's encampment at Morristown was enlivened by the arrival of additional distinguished visitors. Anne-Cesar, Chevalier de la Luzerne, the newly appointed French Minister and Ambassador to America (1779–1784), and other French officials, along with Spanish diplomat Don Juan de Miralles, were received with an official formality carefully orchestrated by Hamilton. Most importantly, the diplomat's special mission was to ascertain if Washington indeed commanded a revolutionary army with genuine war-waging capabilities, before France would officially dispatch thousands of troops and warships to America.

Therefore, Washington and Hamilton had prepared the army to present its finest appearance, because America's destiny lay partly on the extent of the good impression made upon these distinguished visitors. Washington's soldiers were aligned in neat ranks, while inspected by the French and Spanish diplomats. Then, on the village green of Morristown, American troops marched in review past the officials with discipline and to the martial airs of fife and drum. Lengthy conferences and dinners followed between the foreign diplomats and

Washington, while Hamilton stood close by his side as an interpreter. The commander-in-chief again depended on Hamilton to do and say exactly the right things in the formal European style of the upper class and in the most diplomatic manner, according to the proper social and official protocol expected by the respected representatives.

As in the past, Hamilton and his fluent French were key factors in garnering a highly favorable impressions from these officials, who had to be won over to save America. During such official missions, Hamilton's well-honed interpersonal and diplomatic skills were fully appreciated by the hypersensitive French and Spanish diplomats, who expected proper deference and protocol befitting the court of King Louis XVI. The French impressions of Hamilton were universal: "He united with dignity and feeling, and much force and decision, delightful manners, great sweetness, and was infinitely agreeable" to one and all.[71]

Prophetically, as early as the summer of 1777 and before the battle of Saratoga, Hamilton already had envisioned with clarity the distinct possibilities of foreign intervention. Emphasizing what was the true key to decisive victory in America, he wrote with hopeful optimism, "All the European maritime powers [especially France] are interested for the defeat of the British arms in America . . . . "[72]

Therefore, thanks in part to what these diplomats saw of Washington's Army at Morristown, the overall prospects for future cooperation improved significantly in May 1780, when Lafayette brought the best possible news to Washington's headquarters: Louis XVI and his ministers had decided that a French war fleet and troops were to be permanently assigned to the American theater of operations. Even now the fleet, with fifteen thousand French troops, was sailing toward America from the West Indies, as reported by Lafayette, who officially served as the French liaison officer between the French and Americans. In consequence, Washington's chief liaison officer of his staff, Hamilton, rightly felt a sense of accomplishment. Indeed, Hamilton had earlier emphasized to Lafayette that the American revolutionaries must be aided by a French expeditionary force: an all-important initiative that Lafayette had in turn emphasized to the court of Louis XVI at Versailles.[73]

Ever the diplomat, Hamilton also advised James Duane, an influential member of Congress, about what steps were necessary by Congress to properly prepare for the arrival of the French allies on American soil. In a plea for Congress to take urgent action in a May 1780 letter in which Hamilton's offered sound advice: "This [letter] will be handed you by the Marquis [Lafayette], who brings us very important intelligence. The General [Washington] communicated the substance of it in a private letter to you, and proposes a measure which all deem essential. For God's sake, my dear sir, engage Congress to adopt it, and come to a speedy decision. We have not a moment to lose. Were we to improve every instant of the interval, we should have too little time for what we have to do. The expected succor may arrive in the beginning of June, in all probability it will not be later than the middle. In the last case we have not a month to make our preparations in, and in this short period we must collect men, form [ammunition] magazines, and do a thousand things of as much difficulty as importance. The propriety of the measure proposed is so obvious, that an hour ought to decide it, and if any new members are to come, they ought to set out instantly with all expedition for head quarters. Allow me, my dear sir, to give us a hint. The General will often be glad to consult the committee on particular points, but it will be inexpedient that he should be obliged to do it oftener than he thinks proper or any peculiar case may require. Their powers should be formed accordingly. It is the essence of many military operations, that they should be trusted to as few as possible. . . . Again, my dear sir, I must entreat you to use the spur of the present occasion. The fate of America is perhaps suspended on the issue; if we are found unprepared, it must disgrace us in the eyes of all Europe, besides defeating the good intentions of our allies, and losing the happiest opportunity we ever have had to save ourselves."[74]

Meanwhile, by late spring 1780, the enemy was once again on the move with the arrival of warmer weather and the ending of the rainy season. A British-Hessian expeditionary force under Baron von Knyphausen, the best Hessian commander in America, landed near Elizabethtown, New Jersey, after departing Staten Island. Washington dispatched Hamilton to investigate the threat's seriousness and overall tactical situation. Hamilton needed to ascertain if the enemy's movement was only an isolated raid or the spearhead of a major advance. After scouting the area with care and obtaining as much intelligence as possible, Hamilton sat down with his inkwell and quill pen to write his report to Washington.

Of course, Hamilton became familiar with the sight of these blue-uniformed German troops when Colonel Johann Gottlieb Rall's German brigade was systematically eliminated by Washington's surprise attack at the battle of Trenton, where Hamilton had won distinction as a New York artillery commander. From a point "Near Springfield," New Jersey, Hamilton wrote a typically thorough report on June 8, 1780: "I have seen the enemy; those in view I calculate at about three thousand; there may be and probably enough are others out of sight. . . . Different conjectures may be made. The present movement may be calculated to draw us down and betray us into an action. They may have desisted from their intention of passing till night for fear of our falling upon their rear. I believe this is the case; for as they have but few boats it would certainly be a delicate manoeuvre to cross in our face. We are taking measures to watch their motions to night as closely as possible. An incessant but *very light* skirmishing."[75]

However, the threat of a possible British-Hessian advance on Morristown was thwarted by the rising of the New Jersey militia at the battle of Springfield, in northern New Jersey, on June 23, 1780. The clash of arms ended the enemy's ambitions for pushing through northeastern New Jersey to strike Washington's encampment. After providing valuable intelligence, Hamilton rode back to Morristown to resume his duties at Washington's headquarters. But he was seething with disgust by what he had seen in regard to the belated and over-all feeble defense of American soil. In a confidential June 30, 1780, letter to Laurens in which he criticized the lack of spirited resistance, this ultra "born nationalist" angrily denounced how "our countrymen have all the folly of the ass and all the passiveness of the sheep in their compositions . . . the conduct of the states is enough most pitiful that can be imagined. Would you believe it—a German baron [von Knyphausen who had led Hessian troops since the 1776 New York Campaign] at the head of five thousand men, in the month of June insulted and defied the main American army with the Commander in Chief at their head with impunity, and made them tremble for the security of their magazines forty miles in the country."[76] The tactically astute Hamilton even pointed his finger at Washington for not marching forth to confront von Knyphausen's small expeditionary force and crushing the vulnerable command in its exposed position.

By the time of summer's arrival, Betsey was back at the family home in Albany on the Hudson. With his love far away, Hamilton's spirits sank in consequence. From the town of Preakness, New Jersey, in early July Hamilton wrote an impassioned letter to Betsey: "I love you more and more every hour [because your shining qualities] place you in my estimation above all the rest of your sex." He then signed his letter, "Yrs. my Angel with inviolable Affection. Alex Hamilton."[77]

Only a couple of days later on July 6 from a private residence of an American colonel in Bergen County, New Jersey, Hamilton wrote another revealing letter to his future wife: "Here we are my love in a house of great hospitality—in a country of plenty—a buxom girl under the same roof—pleasing expectations of a successful campaign—and every thing to make a soldier happy, who is not in love and absent from his mistress. As this is my case I cannot be happy. . . . I alleviate the pain of absence by looking forward to that delightful period which gives us to each other forever."[78] Later, Hamilton complained of the infrequency of Betsey's letters, causing him to write: "For God's sake My Dear Betsy try to write me oftener. . . ."[79]

But thoughts of achieving battlefield distinction were never lost to Hamilton. He still looked for any assignment to a field command to escape the drudgery at Washington's headquarters, tied to a desk and paperwork without end. Hamilton's burning love for Betsey only seemed to paradoxically fuel an equally ardent desire to see action and win battlefield recognition. Lafayette had proposed an attack on New York City. Hamilton was delighted by Lafayette's offensive-mindedness, and the two friends continued to share the same tactical and strategic ambitions.

The wealthy port city on the Hudson was now more vulnerable because large numbers of the finest British troops had been shipped south to the Caribbean and to operations in the Southern theater. Viewed as an assault in political and psychological terms, Hamilton knew that a victory by American arms would encourage the French, when they needed encouragement about their homespun allies' combat prowess. Hamilton also envisioned the liberation of New York City to relieve the abuses and oppressions—as he learned from his intelligence network—inflicted upon its long-suffering patriots by Loyalists and redcoats.

On July 9, 1780, Hamilton wrote a letter to Brigadier General Knox and requested "to know the number of heavy cannon we might bring into an operation against New York." From Preakness, on July 20, 1780, Hamilton wrote to the young French secretary of the diplomatic mission in Philadelphia, deliberately overstating the combat prowess and capabilities of Washington's Army, but more importantly emphasizing that the key to decisive victory in this war was sea superiority. "New York [City] in all probability will be our object; if we can have a naval superiority, I shall not doubt our success; if we have not the event will be very precarious; and in success the advantages infinitely less. The enemy will save a great part of their army; stores & their shipping of course will be safe, and the whole may fall upon some other part where we may be vulnerable."[80]

Clearly, Hamilton was acting not only as a diplomat, strategist, and politician, but also as an effective propagandist for America as during the prewar days, when he had preached the wisdom of revolution to Americans who had needed to be convinced. As he continued in his letter: "I shall take occasion to assure you that it appears clear . . . that with a superiority by land and sea you can infallibly possess the port of New York, and by siege or blockade, reduce the whole fleet and army. What will be done or can be done to secure an object of such magnitude, I cannot judge; only of this I am confident that your [French] court [in Versailles] will do every thing possible. The proofs she has already given would make it ingratitude to doubt her future intentions."[81]

Disappointed that the much-anticipated allied campaign to capture New York City was thwarted by the arrival of a British fleet under Admiral Thomas Graves, and displaying a wry sense of humor about once again having been frustrated from having gained no opportunity for achieving battlefield recognition, Hamilton revealed his strategic thoughts to Betsey in an August 1780 letter written from the little crossroads town of Teaneck, south-central New Jersey: "Though, I am not sanguine in expecting it, I am not without hopes this Winter will produce a peace and then you must submit to the mortification of enjoying more domestic happiness and less fame. . . . The affairs in England are in so bad a plight that if no fortunate events attend her this campaign, it would seem impossible for her to proceed in the war. But she is an obstinate old dame, and seems determined to ruin her whole family, rather than to let Miss America go on flirting it with her new lovers, with whom, as giddy young girls often do, she eloped in contempt of her mother[']s authority."[82]

All the while, Hamilton remained focused on finding solutions for America's many ills, especially those of the army. Hamilton now advocated a badly needed reform to save the army before it was too late. In a September 6, 1780, letter from Bergen County, New Jersey, Hamilton implored James Duane, a leading New York politician who appreciated the young man's advice, that a major change to enhance the army's capabilities was urgently needed, after learning of the shocking news of the August 16, 1780, destruction of America's primary Southern Army in the steamy pine forests of Camden, South Carolina: "I have heard since of Gates defeat, a very good comment on the necessity of changing our system. . . ."[83]

As mentioned, General Gates had long remained a bitter enemy of Hamilton. He had falsely charged Hamilton with covertly copying an anti-Washington letter from General Thomas Conway, which had been allegedly taken from his files at Gates' headquarters by Washington's sleuthing point man, when he was in the room alone during his successful autumn 1777 mission to secure reinforcements from Gates. Therefore, what was "an apparent attempt to destroy both Hamilton and Washington" by savaging their reputations, Gates had indignantly informed Washington and Congress that Hamilton, during a visit to see Betsey in Albany, had "*stealingly* copied" his private correspondence.[84]

Hamilton, consequently, enjoyed a smug satisfaction in learning of Gates' downfall at Camden. With his trademark sarcasm unleashed on the detested Gates, who had deserted his army and fled the Camden battlefield and rode a great distance (sixty-five miles) to ensure his safety that he valued above all else, Hamilton asked Duane with obvious contempt: "What think you of the conduct of this great man? . . . Did ever any one hear of such a disposition or such a flight? His best troops placed on the side strongest by nature, his worst, on that weakest by nature, and his attack made with these. 'Tis impossible to give a more complete picture of military absurdity. It is equally against the maxims of war, and common sense. . . . But was there ever an instance of a General running away as Gates has done from his whole army? And was there ever so precipitous a flight? One hundred and eighty miles in three days and a half. It does admirable credit to the activity of a man at his time of life. But it disgraces the General and the Soldiers."[85]

During September 1780, Hamilton continued to be frustrated with the endless political infighting, lack of patriotic spirit, and the widespread corruption that had long deprived the neglected Continental Army of precious supplies and all manner of support. As he lamented bitterly to Laurens, who had been assigned to the Southern theater of operations, on September 12, of the worsening situation, while revealing his thwarted ambitions of winning an independent command: "you can hardly conceive in how dreadful a situation we are [in]. The army, in the course of the present month, has received only four or five days rations of meal, and we really know not of any adequate form of relief in future [so therefore] the officers are out of humour. . . . I hate Congress—I hate the army—I hate the world—I hate myself. The whole is a mass of fools and knaves; I could almost except you and [Richard Kidder] Meade."[86]

As this letter revealed, Meade and Hamilton remained close friends, especially after Laurens' departure to serve in his native South Carolina. As from the beginning, Hamilton's friendship with staff members was based upon mutual respect as the men were members of "the family" and brothers-in-arms. While throwing himself into his work with typical zeal to overcome the pain of separation from Betsey throughout the summer of 1780, and impatiently awaiting his wedding day in the fall, Hamilton continued to make his usual disproportionate contributions on multiple levels. He continued to serve as the "thoroughly political officer" who met and exchanged ideas with leading state politicians and Congressional members, especially when they visited Washington's encampments on fact-finding missions.[87]

All the while, Hamilton maintained the key role of serving as Washington's hammer, striking hard at any entrenched and politically based intransigence to either make an important point, force an issue, or secure what was most needed for the army of revolutionaries, who lacked everything but stoicism and spunk. Hamilton repeatedly accomplished what Washington was unable to achieve, because of the Virginian's lofty image and symbolic position as commander-in-chief that made him unable to act as forcefully as his opportunistic chief of staff, who had been given free rein in consequence. Hamilton was so busy that he hardly had time to write Betsey. At the end of one letter to her, he lamented, "I would go on, but the General summons me to ride."[88]

In late September 1780, James Duane, an influential Congressman who had so often appreciated Hamilton's wisdom, visited Washington's headquarters. Looking for solutions to endless problems that continued to plague America's war effort and diminish the army's already limited capabilities, Duane spoke at length with Hamilton. Duane knew that Hamilton's analytical thinking about the principal maladies that negatively affected the new nation and army (both of which were on the brink of collapse) offered intelligent solutions. Thanks to his in-depth study of the complexities of history, politics, and economics, Hamilton possessed the rare ability to draw the most useful examples from his vast readings and then incorporate them to create intelligent solutions to seemingly insurmountable problems. Therefore, Duane specifically requested that Hamilton present his solutions in writing about "the defects of our present system, and the changes necessary to save us from ruin."[89]

Hamilton was a self-educated authority on America's most pressing problems in regard to finance, logistics, politics, soldiers' pay, economics, government, and recruitment. Indeed, few individuals in America were as expert on so many subjects of importance during this crucial period in America's lifetime. Hamilton also employed life lessons gained from his extensive knowledge about human nature drawn from personal experience, especially from his days in the Caribbean. Consequently and as Duane fully expected, what Hamilton wrote was anything but a mere routine or mundane summarization, but rather a masterful, lengthy treatise displaying a brilliant analysis that offered innovative solutions to the republic's most vexing problems. Quite simply, Hamilton took full advantage of this opportunity to set forth a plan in great detail to revise the ineffective Articles of Confederation (at the future Constitutional Convention after the war) to create a more powerful Congress guaranteed to get results, especially for a stronger republic and army.

But Hamilton's brilliant analysis as revealed to Duane was actually nothing new from Hamilton, because he had evolved into America's foremost thinker in regard to developing solutions. Earlier in the year, for instance, Hamilton had written an anonymous letter (more than six thousand words) to a Congressman that proposed economic solutions to America's ills, especially in regard to its inflated currency. Never losing his cynicism or realism in this case, which was only additionally reinforced by what he saw in the selfish behavior Americans, including Congressmen, in this faltering war effort, Hamilton knew that people were "governed more by passion and prejudice than any enlightened sense of their interests"; the currency had depreciated so much because of a general "want of confidence." Therefore, in demonstrating a "staggering precocity," Hamilton proposed bold measures—a twelve-point plan—to restore this shattered confidence, which included an entirely reformed financial system, one including a substantial foreign loan and a central bank.[90]

Hamilton's letter to Congressman Duane was the most impressive document written by him in 1780. On September 3, 1780, and with America's novel republican experiment and its long-neglected army falling apart at the seams, Hamilton put his extensive accumulation of thoroughly developed ideas about how to save the nation not only on, but also off the battlefield. Here, at an obscure place appropriately called Liberty Poll, New Jersey, Hamilton revealed the depth of his expansive thoughts and ideas about the best possible remedies to America's faltering war effort and ineffective government that was still ill-prepared for a lengthy war's challenges. First and foremost, Hamilton proposed scrapping the still-not-ratified Articles of Confederation in its entirety, because its states' rights priorities were destroying the war effort and tearing apart the weak fabric of the nation.

Consequently, this precocious young man advocated starting anew by creating a stronger and more centralized government to ensure adequate national (versus the highly ineffective state) support for the army and a successful resistance effort, especially for a lengthy war of attrition. To cure the infant nation's long list of ills, especially near bankruptcy, Hamilton also proposed to give more economic authority to Congress for collecting revenues, especially from the sale of western lands and taxes on existing property, in order to generate the necessary funds necessary to maintain, pay, and supply regulars (long-term troops) of a standing army.

The current disastrous policy of printing money fueled a dangerous level of inflation because Congress did not have the power to raise and collect funds. Hamilton already had been taking steps to reorganize and improve the army during the last three years while serving as Washington's chief of staff, and he now continued to develop brilliant solutions to a host of seemingly unsolvable problems that plagued the nation and the overall war effort.[91] Thanks to his self-education and experiences in the Caribbean and America, what Hamilton wrote with considerable insight revealed that he had succeeded in thoroughly "mastering the great topics of political economy: finance, taxation, banking, and commerce [and] it was a project destined to have a profound impact on his adopted nation."[92]

The army's endless suffering and the deaths of far too many soldiers from the evils of corruption, neglect, and folly, especially during the winters at Valley Forge and Morristown, fueled Hamilton's urgency for reform. To Hamilton's disgust, and in reconfirmation of his deeply entrenched cynicism, even much-needed supplies had been deliberately withheld from the army to drive up prices to increase profit margins by opportunistic "pests of society," in Washington's words. Unable to control his temper in this regard, the angry commander-in-chief believed that hanging was the best remedy. Hating these unscrupulous individuals who were almost as deadly to America's fortunes as the enemy, Hamilton turned his righteous wrath upon those selfish opportunists who always put America's interests last.

Based upon his careful reading of the day's leading scholarly works combined with a stream of his own innovative ideas, Hamilton's solutions were all-encompassing. Hamilton proposed remedies for the seemingly endless abuses, especially of the most fatal inflationary variety because of excessive printing of Continental currency (now practically worthless) by the Congress and state governments, while the British occupiers possessed the advantage in competing for supplies by paying with the English pound, which remained stable in part because of Bank of England that Hamilton used as a model for reform.

After Howe occupied Philadelphia, Hamilton had early realized this disastrous cause-and-effect relationship that led to a severe depreciation of Continental currency and an erosion of war-waging capabilities of the seemingly ill-fated revolutionary army: "'Tis by introducing order into our finances [and thereby] in a position to continue the war—not by temporary, violent, and unnatural efforts to bring it to a decisive issue [on the battlefield], that we will, in reality, bring it to a speedy and successful one."[93]

As early as 1779 and most forcefully articulated in 1780, Hamilton correctly emphasized that America's only salvation now lay in creating a strong national government, which equated to a stronger army.[94] He concluded to Congressman Duane how the government's principal failings could be permanently remedied if "we should blend the advantages of a monarchy and of a republic in a happy and beneficial union": the central premise that led to the creation of the Constitution (ratified after the war) and the modern American nation.[95]

In an October 12, 1780, letter to Isaac Sears, who was a former leader of New York City's Sons of Liberty, Hamilton explained his military solution to save America, before it was too late: "We must, above all things, have an army for the war, and an establishment that will interest the officers in the service. . . . All those who love their country ought to exert their influence in the states where they reside . . . . The enemy will conquer us by degrees during the intervals of our weakness. . . . My fears are high, my hopes low."[96]

Like America itself, the Schuyler family, including Betsey, also benefitted from Hamilton's wisdom that had been now directed at reforming not only the government but also the economic system. When the British, Tories and their Indian allies surged down Lake Champlain in October 1780, General Schuyler wrote to Hamilton to request assistance. Thanks to Hamilton's timely efforts, several regiments were hurriedly dispatched north to Schuyler's aid. One officer carried separate letters from Hamilton to the general and his daughter. Clearly, the can-do Hamilton continued to pay dividends to the Schuyler family.[97]

While laboring day and night at headquarters and proving that he was less of the true ladies' man in terms of overall confidence that he had originally fancied, Hamilton continued to be occasionally consumed by occasional dark thoughts about the love of his life, Betsey. This was a striking paradox because Hamilton was at the zenith of his success as Washington's invaluable chief of staff and had never been held in higher esteem by so many American leaders because of his brilliant "high-level strategy papers and comprehensive blueprints for government," in Ron Chernow's words, and the economy. In an October 27, 1780, letter to Betsey from Preakness, he confessed his fear that was now more haunting to him than facing enemy bayonets and bullets, revealing his deep-seated insecurities rooted in the tragedies of his Caribbean past: "I had a charming dream two or three nights ago. I thought I had just arrived at Albany and found you asleep on a green near the house, and beside you . . . stood a Gentleman. . . . As you may imagine, I reproached him with his presumption and asserted my claim. He insisted on a prior right; and the dispute grew heated [but then] you flew into my arms and decided the contention with a kiss. I was so delighted that I immediately waked, and lay the rest of the night exulting in my good fortune."[98]

Meanwhile, two of Washington's aides, including Lieutenant Colonel Richard Kidder Meade, departed the "military" and returned to Virginia to marry their loves, shouldering Hamilton with additional staff duties. In consequence, Lieutenant Colonel Hamilton became even more indispensable to Washington during this period. Therefore, Hamilton was unable to gain a furlough to visit Betsey for an extended period. Hamilton, torn between duty and his fiancée, felt the pain of separation, because as he had written to Betsey, in an honest assessment of his most admirable qualities: "I have a good head, but thank God he has given me a good heart."[99]

Ironically, on the same day that Hamilton wrote his October 27 letter to Betsey, Lieutenant Colonel Robert Hanson Harrison was writing his own letter from Philadelphia. Harrison's letter contained information of considerable strategic importance in regard to future military developments, including in regard to the future military career of Lieutenant Colonel Hamilton: "The delegates [from the South] think the situation of [Earl] Cornwallis [who had advanced a great distance from South Carolina to Virginia and far from reinforcements] delicate, and that by management, and a proper application and use of force there, the late check given [Major Patrick] Ferguson [and his force of Loyalists at Kings Mountain, South Carolina, on October 7, 1780] might be improved into the Earl's total defeat [but] this, I fear, is too much to hope [and give] my love to the lads of the family."[100] Fate and destiny were already beckoning Hamilton toward the Southern theater of operations.

Chapter VI

Rising Even Higher in Washington's Esteem

Year after year, Hamilton continued to serve as Washington's top political, diplomatic, advisory, and intelligence officer, including as the first chief of staff in the modern sense in the history of the America's army. Hamilton's multiple roles, including as Washington's chief intelligence officer, most trusted advisor and primary liaison officer to the French, caused Washington's dependence upon him to steadily grow until it became excessive.[1] Hamilton's masterful intelligence work revealed the Gates-Conway-Lee conspiracy that had been calculated to replace the commander-in-chief. Year after year, he continued to communicate with American spy networks, especially in New York City, including efforts to uncover British spies. Hamilton not only early alerted Washington of this danger at the highest levels, but also played a large role in ensuring that the Virginian did not lose his position as the army's head, because of his and other staff officer's timely preemptive actions.[2]

Most important of all, Hamilton continued to serve "Washington faithfully as an incredibly skilled chief of staff [and therefore the commander-in-chief] wanted him to stay right where he was, where Washington believed he could do the most good for the army."[3] As Washington's trusty chief protector and guardian who knew how to eliminate threats, Hamilton had been so effective in countering attempts to replace Washington that Gates was convinced that "the entire plot against him [was] masterminded by Alexander Hamilton."[4]

After having grown closer to him than any other member of his "family," especially since the two men were constantly around each other at headquarters and in the field, Washington even perceived Hamilton's greatest weakness—ambition—in a favorable light. As Washington explained after the war: "That he is ambitious I readily grant [but his motivations and behavior were] of that laudable kind which prompts a man to excel in whatever he takes in hand."[5]

Despite all that he had achieved as the leader of Washington's staff, Hamilton never wavered from his long-elusive goal of obtaining an assignment to active field command. But Hamilton had been consistently (but politely and according to proper protocol) refused by the commander-in-chief in his relentless quest to attain what Laurens had accomplished in leaving the "family" to serve in the field and his native South Carolina. Washington always emphasized the young man's indispensability to thwart Hamilton's consuming ambition. With his frustration growing month after month, Hamilton became worried. He again feared at one point that he had gone too far in crossing the line of proper protocol in requesting active command too aggressively.

After the last refusal, Hamilton wrote back to Washington in the hope of soothing what might have been ruffled feathers by emphasizing that the field command which he so passionately desired was simply not that important after all. Thinking ahead as usual and keeping in mind that another opportunity to gain a field command might eventually arise, Hamilton was also concerned that he might have significantly reduced his future chances of receiving a choice assignment. Hamilton rationalized to Washington: "These are my pretensions, at this advanced period of the war, to be employed in the only way, which my situation admits [and] I am capable of wishing to obtain any objective of importance."[6]

But Hamilton's most determined bid in order to force Washington's hand and escape the "military" was played out near the end of November 1780. He desired to play an active role in Washington's proposed plan for an expedition, in conjunction with Lafayette, which was to be launched to capture Staten Island. Of course, Lafayette wanted his good friend Hamilton by his side in this offensive operation. To increase Hamilton's chances for success in his quest to gain a permanent release from Washington's staff, Lafayette offered to review his letter to Washington and make suggestions for improvement.

As Hamilton penned an ever-so-tactful letter to Washington from Passaic Falls, New Jersey, on November 22, 1780: "Sometime last fall when I spoke to your Excellency about going to the Southward, I explained to you candidly my feelings with respect to military reputation, and how much it was my object to act a conspicuous part in some enterprise that might perhaps raise my character as a soldier above mediocrity. You were so good as to say you would be glad to furnish me with an occasion. When the expedition to Staten Island was on foot a favourable one seemed to offer . . . I made an application for it though the Marquis [Lafayette], who informed me of your refusal on two principles—one that giving me a whole battalion might be a subject of dissatisfaction, the other that if an accident should have to me, in the present state of your family, you would be embarrassed for the necessary assistance. The project [attack on New York City] you now have in contemplation affords another opportunity. I have a variety of reasons that press me to desire ardently to have it in my power to improve it. . . . I take this method of making the request to avoid the embarrassment of a personal explanation; I shall only add that however much I have the matter at heart, I wish your Excellency intirely [sic] to consult your own inclination; and not from a disposition to oblige me, to do any thing, that may be disagreeable to you."[7]

By any measure, this was a remarkable letter and admission by Hamilton. Despite all that he had accomplished in this war, Hamilton still felt that he had something meaningful to prove, but more to himself than anyone else. Nevertheless, Hamilton had expressed to Washington exactly what had long nagged at his moral conscience and unsettled his sense of emotional and psychological well-being to fill a void that not even Betsey was able to fill: a very personal issue that the young man still held dear to his heart, "my character as a soldier." More than anything else, Hamilton desired to achieve "my object to act a conspicuous part in some enterprise that might perhaps so raise my character as a soldier above mediocrity," which meant reassignment from Washington's staff to active command of infantry in the field during active campaigning.[8]

Even when carefully asking Washington for a coveted position as diplomatically as possible under delicate circumstances, Hamilton gently took the revered commander-in-chief to task in reminding him about his initial indication that he would grant his heartfelt request: "You were so good as to say you would be glad to furnish me with an occasion" to prove himself on the battlefield, on separating from the "family."[9]

By emphasizing Washington's prior verbal commitment to hold his commander to his word, Hamilton was of course attempting to force Washington's hand by emphasizing a point of honor. Even more, he was literally pleading for the long-awaited assignment to lead his own command, if only a single regiment, on the battlefield. Hamilton utilized a clever psychological ploy in the hope of making Washington more directly accountable in regard to this sensitive subject. By this means, he hoped to gain a new assignment in order "to avoid the embarrassment" of missing the opportunity to play a leading role in New York City's capture. He could not bear the thought of having to explain to friends (now including General Schuyler and his family) why he had been passed over for an active command in an important new campaign.[10]

As Lieutenant Hamilton explained in his November 22, 1780, letter: "I take the liberty to observe, that the command may now be proportioned to my rank, and that the second objection [used by Washington to deny Hamilton the opportunity to lead an infantry battalion in the fall of 1779] ceases to operate, as during the period of establishing our winter quarters, there will be a suspension of material business. . . . My command may consist of one hundred and fifty or two hundred men. . . ."[11]

Hamilton not only proposed the command that he should take and its composition, but also its strategic objective. Situated on lower Manhattan Island, the earthen heptagonal-shaped bastion—formerly Fort Bunker Hill which had been defended by him and his New York artillerymen in the summer of 1776—was situated atop Bayard's Hill. A strategic point, this high elevation overlooked the Hudson and New York City.[12] Hamilton could hardly contain his enthusiasm at the mere thought of leading an infantry battalion in an important charge during a climactic battle for possession of America's largest and most strategic city. Even more, he felt that Providence had finally come to his assistance because he knew his target so well, enhancing his chances of gaining a field command, or so he thought. Hamilton had become well acquainted with William Bayard, although a Loyalist, when this highly motivated artillery captain and his New York gunners had held Fort Bunker Hill on the Bayard family property before the battle of Long Island in late August 1776.[13]

As Hamilton continued in his November 22, 1780, letter: "The primary idea may be, if circumstances permit, to attempt with my detachment Byard's [sic] Hill. Should we undertake it, I should prefer it to any thing else, both for the brilliancy of the attempt in itself, and the decisive consequences of which its success would be productive. If we arrive too late to make eligible [then] my corps may form the van of one of the other attacks, and Byard's [sic] Hill will be a pretext for my being employed in the affair, on a supposition of my knowing the ground. . . . "[14] What was truly incredible about Hamilton's bold words to Washington was that he proposed to be in the very vanguard of the assault upon Bayard's Hill or any other attack on any defensive point around New York City that Washington deemed the most vital and strategic: hence, the most powerful and most dangerous.

Clearly, the "Little Lion" was roaring in an outspoken manner to Washington as to the Congressmen who he had long advised on government, political, and financial matters that urgently needed to be addressed. Despite his impending marriage, Hamilton was practically begging Washington to be allowed to lead the charge in what might well be the war's most important attack. Consequently, this was the ideal tactical and strategic situation that Hamilton viewed as his long-sought opportunity "to act a conspicuous part . . . to raise my character as a soldier above mediocrity."[15] In concluding his November 22, 1780, letter to the army's commander and hoping that Washington might feel grateful for all that he had accomplished for him as chief of staff year after year, Hamilton then added how Washington's acceptance of his request would "make me singularly happy if your wishes correspond with mine."[16]

To additionally enhance Hamilton's chances to make his great dream come true, Lafayette was to present Hamilton's letter and personally plead his case to Washington. The young French aristocrat advocated strong support for his friend's tactical plan. Six days after Hamilton wrote his missive to Washington, Lafayette sent a flattering letter to Hamilton from Paramus, Bergen County, northern New Jersey, on November 28, 1780. Lafayette was optimistic that Hamilton's ambitions would be finally fulfilled this time. As the Frenchman wrote in agreement with Hamilton's rationale on this matter that was so important to him: "you deserve from [Washington] the preference; that your advantages are the greatest; I speak of a co-operation; of your being in the family; and conclude, that on every public and private account, I advise him to take you [and] I know the General's friendship and gratitude for you, my dear Hamilton; both are greater than you perhaps imagine. I am sure he needs only to be told that something will suit you, and when he thinks he can do it, he certainly will. Before this campaign I was your friend, and very intimate friend [and] since my second voyage [to America] my sentiment has increased. . . . "[17]

As this letter revealed, Hamilton could not have had a better advocate than the French nobleman, who was so highly revered by Washington. As mentioned, Hamilton had formed solid relationships and strong connections with a number of leading French officers besides Lafayette, maintaining regular communications with them and strengthening the bonds between allies as throughout the past. One highly impressed French nobleman described him as "firm and [in all matters] decided [and] frank and martial."[18]

But Hamilton's hope of winning the distinguished honor of leading the assault on New York City at the head of an infantry battalion evaporated as suddenly as it had appeared. In the end, Washington "altered his mind," in Lafayette's words, to dash the ambitions of his dear friend. Quite simply and as in the past, Washington could not now afford to lose his chief of staff, because of his great value. A victim of his own successes, Hamilton received the bad news from Lafayette's December 9, 1780, letter, The frustrated young man would seemingly never escape Washington's giant shadow and chief of staff position that had become a trap, if not a Faustian Bargain of sorts.[19]

Lafayette explained in his letter upon meeting with Washington how he had "made a verbal application in my own name [and] I can't express to you, my dear friend, how sorry an disappointed I felt when I knew from him, the General, that (greatly in consequence of our advice,) he had settled the whole matter [in favor of another officer] I confess, I became warmer on the occasion than you would have perhaps wished me to be. . . ."[20]

But in the same December 9, 1780, letter, Lafayette offered significant consolation to the crestfallen Hamilton, who had missed his coveted opportunity to lead the assault on New York City. Lafayette informed his friend of some good news in a timely compensation: "Congress seem resolved that an *Envoy be sent in the way you wish*, and this was yesterday [December 8] determined in the house. Next Monday [December 11] the gentleman will be elected. I have already spoken to many [Congressional] members;—I know of a number of voices that will be for you [therefore] I think you ought to hold yourself in readiness, and in case you are called for, come with all possible speed; for you must go immediately [to France and] If you go, my dear sir, I shall give you all public and private knowledge about Europe I am possession of. Besides many private letters, that may introduce you to my friends, I intend giving you the *key* of the [French] cabinet, as well as of the societies which influence them, In a word, my good friend, any thing in my power shall be entirely yours."[21]

Lafayette, who was Hamilton's greatest French supporter, along with his fellow officers, thanks partly to his unfailing pro-French support especially after the Newport Expedition fiasco, was convinced that Hamilton (nominated by General John Sullivan) was about to become the new French envoy to serve in Paris as a secretary under Benjamin Franklin. With his fluency in French, sophistication, and well-honed diplomatic skills, Hamilton was an ideal choice, especially in regard to securing the French loan.

Long knowing that this war could not be won without a significant French contribution on multiple levels, Hamilton had long emphasized that a French loan was necessary for America's successful war effort and he had first proposed the vital financial-political mission to France for this express purpose. Lafayette and Hamilton had long served as a natural team for this important initiative. As mentioned, Hamilton had already carefully orchestrated that distinct possibility upon which the fate of America depended. He had earlier nominated Lafayette to Congress for the envoy position to the Court of Versailles on the mission to secure additional assistance from France. If Lafayette gained the position, then he would take Hamilton with him to France as his right hand man, liberating him from Washington's staff, if everything went according to plan.

But Lafayette instead set his sights on active command in the Southern theater, and Washington naturally ordered his favorite Frenchman south to the southern theater of operations. Then, Lafayette recommended to Congress that Hamilton would be the right man to take his place as envoy. However, Hamilton correctly gave himself little chance for winning the prestigious appointment to an exciting diplomatic role in France, because he had few connections or supporters in Congress and, of course, too many old enemies: the high price paid for having so many enemies in Congress and being considered a recent immigrant to America. As Hamilton had informed Laurens in a September 12, 1780, letter about his many foes who were steadily on the increase, because some people believed that he was a close "friend to military pretensions, however exorbitant," which evidently meant a general's rank or perhaps more.[22]

But the appointment to the French mission never came also because Hamilton kindly deferred unanimously to Laurens, revealing the depth of their friendship. John's father, Henry Laurens, had been captured by the British while journeying to France. The distinguished former president of the Continental Congress was now imprisoned in the infamous Tower of London. If Laurens became the French envoy, then he would be in a position to win his father's release. Ironically, Congress had originally requested Laurens as the French envoy. But Laurens had emphasized that Hamilton would make a better choice, which was certainly true. For reasons that were more political than circumspect, however Congress had wanted Laurens as their man in France, and the politicians got their wish.

Therefore, the less-qualified Laurens became the "special envoy" to France in December 1780. Although the mission had slipped from his grasp, Hamilton played a role in improving Laurens' overall chances for a successful diplomatic effort on the Atlantic's other side: "The importance of giving a correct view of the state of affairs at this juncture, suggested to Hamilton the idea of a special letter of instructions [carried by Laurens], in addition to that which had been given to the envoy by congress, being addressed to him by General

Washington, which, in the opinion of La Fayette, it was supposed would add additional weight to his representations [and] this important duty was delegated to Hamilton by Washington. . . ."[23]

Indeed, a gracious and wise personal gesture that masked his deep disappointment in not securing the coveted envoy position, Hamilton's glowing letter (in French) of introduction that lavishly praised Laurens to the French foreign minister at the court of Versailles helped to make the South Carolinian's vital mission a more successful one in the end. One secret of Hamilton's success in life (personal and professional) was to overlook setbacks and forge ahead with renewed vigor to accomplish even more impressive achievements. After the Camden, South Carolina, fiasco on August 16, 1780, for instance, Hamilton had written to Betsey, "This misfortune affects me less than others because it is not in my temper to repine at evils that are past but to endeavor to draw good out of them. . . ."[24]

Meanwhile, as if to compensate for unhappiness in his professional life at a time when he felt trapped as the leading member of Washington's staff, Hamilton's personal life continued on the upswing. His intense passion, if not obsession, for Betsey was equal to his ardor for gaining an infantry command. Despite his relatively recent immigrant status and lack of social standing or wealth that seemed to mock his high standing with Washington's staff, all of the aristocratic Schuyler family, including Betsey's older and married sister Angelica, whom some people took to be Hamilton's lover and not Eliza because of the intensity of their chemistry, was entirely smitten with Hamilton. At Schuyler's magnificent yellow-brick mansion that overlooked the Hudson, he was eager to marry Betsey Schuyler and become united with one of America's leading families.

Because of the shortage of "family" members at his headquarters, Washington was unable to allow Hamilton to take leave for his own wedding, which was then put off out of necessity until December 1780. Hamilton's reaction has not been recorded, perhaps for ample good reason. Ironically, not unlike Washington himself when he had married one of the wealthiest widows in Virginia, Hamilton had moved seamlessly into one of America's great aristocratic families with the same skill as leading his men and maneuvering the guns of his New York Battery, heading Washington's staff, and performing with distinction on the battlefield.

It was virtually impossible for a recent immigrant and illegitimate son to achieve such a swift and sweeping social advancement of a magnitude seldom seen in colonial America. A testament to his own outstanding abilities as the leader of Washington's staff and his winning personal ways, Hamilton was fully accepted by these members of an American aristocracy that was obsessively concerned about pedigree and lineages. General Schuyler's family was part of the New York Dutch elite of the Hudson River country. A good judge of character, the general even advised his son to model himself after the seemingly spotless Hamilton, whose most positive qualities never shined brighter than when he was in the midst of the Schuyler family, partly because he had no family of his own. In his personal and professional life, Hamilton continued to astound observers by his seemingly effortless rise to lofty heights that were simply unattainable to other men, especially of his age and background.[25]

In fact professionally and personally, Hamilton's rise had been too rapid and meteoric to not have gone to his head, especially for someone in their mid-twenties. His dramatic advances in military and civilian spheres certainly affected Hamilton, but only to a limited degree. By early 1781, Hamilton had changed considerably from the wide-eyed youth who had first stepped off the ship in Boston harbor as a stranger in a new land in 1773. Nevertheless, even at this time, Hamilton's past and its demons were not far behind him, despite all that he had accomplished for Washington, the Continental Army, and America. Heady from his recent advance up the social ladder to reach dizzying heights, Hamilton's already healthy ego had grown because so many of his achievements, personal and professional, were truly outsized. However, he still remained firmly grounded in part because of his humble upbringing in the faraway Caribbean in a life that now seemed from a bygone age. America and the war had provided Hamilton with the opportunities for an astonishing rebirth, and he had taken full advantage of what became available to him for the first time in his life.

Additional Frustrated Ambitions

By this time, seemingly everything in Hamilton's life was on the rise, except his stagnant military career. Although still serving as the respected head of the Virginian's military "family," Hamilton's ambitions as a military officer, who possessed a wide range of tactical and strategic insights, remained entirely unfulfilled. He was still "a man of action," as he had demonstrated throughout the New York Campaign, at the Raritan River, and in the battles of Trenton, Princeton, and Monmouth. Hamilton had always excelled during the most challenging situations, rising to the occasion again and again. Even while performing the more mundane staff officer duties at his desk at Washington's headquarters, Hamilton occasionally allowed himself the luxury of dreaming about the missed opportunities if he had continued in active service and never joined Washington's staff on March 1, 1777. Never one to doubt his abilities but for good reason, he was convinced that he would have garnered a general's rank, which was probably true. Such nagging thoughts swirled through Hamilton's mind on dreary nights to his frustration, if not torment, when his periodic dark moods and a sense of loneliness allowed him to believe that his talents as a combat officer had been wasted.

While working long hours at his wooden desk before piles of paperwork, Hamilton never forgot the flow of adrenaline, the excitement of battle, and the ecstasy of victory from past battlefields, where he had distinguished himself. In a paradox that continued to haunt him at Washington's headquarters, the most vexing frustration in Hamilton's life was failing to garner an active field command. Ironically, only one man stood in the way of the fulfillment of Hamilton's last remaining military ambition and this was the individual whom he had faithfully assisted the most year after year: Washington.[26] In this sense because he was desk-bound like a prisoner, there was some half-truth in Hamilton's humor-laden words to Betsey that his love for her had caused his swift personal evolution "from a soldier metamorphosed into a puny lover."[27]

In a striking paradox, Hamilton was still very much like the young man who was destined to kill him in the most famous duel in American history in the summer of 1804, Aaron Burr. Born in Newark, New Jersey, in early February 1756, Burr had excelled as a favored member of General Gates' staff.[28] After having decided not to follow his parents' wishes to enter the ministry, Burr had elected instead to answer his country's call. At only age nineteen, he had first won recognition for bravery and leadership ability during the doomed attempt to capture Quebec on the last day of December, 1775. Burr had then served in a temporary position on Washington's staff until late June 1776 when he joined the staff of General Putnam as aide-de-camp. But like Hamilton, Burr had desired to play a more active role well beyond duty on a general's staff, including Washington's military "family." Partly because of his "dislike" for the autocratic ways and perhaps the temper of the commander-in-chief, Burr had "wanted to leave Washington's staff even before he met the general."[29] But unlike Hamilton, Burr's ambition had been fulfilled, escaping the general's staff to follow his own destiny. His long-awaited promotion to active command

and gaining a lieutenant colonel's rank in a New York Continental Regiment came in late June 1777.[30]

Because of his thwarted ambitions that revealed his paradoxical nature, Hamilton reached his personal low point during the winter of 1779–1780.[31] Nothing more bothered Hamilton than the central dilemma and contradicions of his military life. With monotonous regularity, Washington made his usual case of why Hamilton should remain on his staff, which was entirely true: The young man was simply too valuable to let go. Who could possibly replace Hamilton? Of course, Washington already knew the answer. Indeed, by this time, Hamilton had become Washington's "alter ego" in an unbeatable team and absolutely invaluable on multiple levels. But Washington's relied-upon rationale had been used for so long that the thoroughly frustrated Hamilton now viewed it with disdain. He was devastated by the refusal to be allowed to embark upon duty in the Southern theater where Laurens now served, qualified American leadership was sorely lacking, and opportunities abounded for officers of promise.

Perhaps Washington, who knew him in a fatherly way and possessed strong paternal instincts, continued to refuse Hamilton the active service that he so passionately craved because Washington very likely did not want to live with the guilt if Hamilton, his favorite of the "family," was released from headquarters and killed in battle. Ironically, after departing Washington's staff, Laurens possessed the same idealized concept of a heroic death and eventually met this tragic fate in a small, needless fight of no consequence in a remote backwater region of his native South Carolina.[32]

Whenever he found time to take his mind off his work at headquarters and his ever-growing sense of frustration, Hamilton's thoughts focused on Betsey. After they were engaged in March 1780, Hamilton looked forward to the marriage before the year's end.[33] In some amazement, Lieutenant Colonel Tench Tilghman wrote to his brother on May 12, 1780, from Morristown, describing Hamilton's love for Elizabeth (Betsey) in part due to her "lovely form" and "a mind still more lovely," (in Hamilton's words), while hardly believing the native West Indian's romantic fate because of his abundant past successes as a seductive bachelor: "Hamilton is a gone man, and I am too old for his substitute [as a dashing ladies man]—She had better look out for herself and not put her trust in Man. She need not be jealous of the little Saint—She is gone to Pennsylvania and has no other impressions than those of regard for a very pretty good tempered Girl, the daughter of one of my valuable acquaintances."[34]

Like so many others, Tilghman was still impressed by Hamilton's past successes with the ladies, but now his carefree bachelor days of bedroom conquests were over. Hamilton's youthful romanticism and idealistic obsession with a heroic death of the battlefield also faded away as his love for Betsey grew. In his own words from a letter that revealed a startling confession that might have saved Hamilton's life in the end: "I was once determined to let my existence and American liberty end together [in dramatic fashion on a distant battlefield but now] My Betsey has given me a motive to outlive my pride."[35]

In fact, Lieutenant Colonel Tilghman knew a good deal about Hamilton's future wife. The young Marylander was almost as smitten by her as his close friend, who had shown absolutely no caution in his ardent pursuit of Betsey. In late August 1775, Tilghman recounted his first meeting with Hamilton's future wife in a journal: "A Brunette with the most good natured lively dark eyes that I ever saw, which threw a beam of good tempter and benevolence over her whole Countenance [and] Mr. [William] Livingston informed me that I was not mistaken in my Conjecture for that she was the finest tempered Girl in the World."[36]

Hamilton was indeed a "gone man," expressing thanks for her "tenderness toward me." However, paradoxically, he still occasionally allowed dark thoughts to intervene into a life of remarkable achievements in only a few years. As he wrote to Laurens on September 12, 1780, and not long before his marriage, Hamilton even felt sorry for himself in the depths of a bout with his reoccurring depression, because of the long-lasting backlash garnered from enemies for speaking too candidly, including influential men in Congress: "The truth is [that] I am an unlucky honest man that speaks my sentiments to all and with emphasis. . . ."[37]

While Hamilton's personal life reached an all-time zenith, America's fortunes continued to flounder and sag from the endless internal dissension that tore at the fabric of a fragile nationalism. Paradoxically, additional revolutionaries began to rise up against the revolution. Anger among Washington's disgruntled soldiers reached new heights because of these crucial failings of the weak decentralized national and state governments and the bungling of Congressional and state leaders that led to a long list of failures to supply the army with adequate food, clothing, and pay. The suffering in the ranks created radicals among the angry Pennsylvania Continentals, and then New Jersey Continentals. This rising tide of hostility toward the ineffective Articles of

Confederation government grew steadily in the ranks just as it had long swelled inside Lieutenant Colonel Alexander Hamilton.

Rumors circulated in September 1780 that some leading officers were trying to convince Washington to "assume dictatorial authority," and the influential Hamilton was seen as the primary culprit. These concerns mounted until Nathanael Greene had to personally assure the chief executive of Pennsylvania, Joseph Reed (Washington's early staff officer who turned against him in favor of General Lee), that he obtained Hamilton's personal word and promise that no such plan had been formulated at Washington's headquarters. Clearly, some highly placed individuals, enemies who were well aware of a young mastermind working tirelessly behind the scenes, believed that Hamilton's ambitions might well be the hidden force behind such mischief.[38]

Benedict Arnold's Treachery

Like a few other generals, especially Gates, Lee, and Putnam, Hamilton had given General Benedict Arnold ample reason to detest him. Washington had long employed Hamilton to lead the way in the always-sensitive dealing with the mercurial and talented general, who had been a magnificent battlefield commander in the past.[39]

Lieutenant Colonel Hamilton had last seen Arnold, whom he respected for his distinguished combat role in winning the day at Saratoga where General Gates (instead of a more deserving Arnold) reaped the glory, immediately after the Hartford, Connecticut, summit between Washington and Lieutenant General Jean-Baptiste-Donatien de Vimeur, Comte de Rochambeau at the beginning of the third week of September. This was the first meeting between the two leaders that Hamilton had long prodded a reluctant Washington to undertake. With his broad knowledge about the French, Hamilton offered Washington instructions about how to act and even the best argument to take in regard to doing whatever he could to ensure that a French fleet reached American waters. Here, besides acting as interpreter and writing down the summit's proceedings along with Lafayette in regard to both capacities, Hamilton played a role in strengthening ties between allies, developing solutions for a more workable relationship in the future. The two leaders discussed defending Newport, and targeting New York City for capture—always Washington's favorite topic as if to wipe out the stain of losing the city in the disastrous 1776 Campaign. Most importantly, the two generals agreed that French naval superior was the key to any future success. At the conclusion of the conference, Hamilton and Lafayette then penned requests for additional French troops and funds, while also making clear copies of the detailed report about the proceedings at Hartford.

Along with an escort of nineteen elite cavalrymen, Washington, Hamilton, Robert Hanson Harrison, Lafayette and his aide James McHenry (formerly Washington's faithful aide), and Knox rode toward West Point, and stayed at an inn on the night of September 24. General Washington dispatched Hamilton and McHenry to ride ahead with the baggage the fifteen miles to West Point early on next morning to inform General Arnold of Washington's impending arrival. They then planned to visit West Point on the morning of September 25. Knowing its strategic importance, Washington considered West Point "the key to America." One of America's best fighting generals who had been cut down twice while exhibiting inspired leadership on the battlefield, including at Saratoga, Arnold had by now commanded the strategic defensive bastion of West Point since the summer of 1780. Washington planned to confer with the Connecticut-born general on the situation at West Point, and inspect the bastion that dominated the high ground overlooking the Hudson.

However, at Arnold's headquarters located at the Beverly Robinson House (the owner now served as a colonel of a Loyalist regiment in New York City) located on the east bank of the Hudson just opposite and downriver from West Point, Washington was unable to find the mercurial general. At breakfast, Hamilton and McHenry had talked to Arnold, just before he received a secret letter that told him how the plot to turn over West Point to the British had been exposed.

With the game now over because of co-conspirator Major John André's capture by New York militiamen who had found incriminating papers hidden in his boot, Arnold had immediately ridden off to escape just before Washington arrived. Naturally, Hamilton and McHenry were puzzled by General Arnold's sudden departure that violated protocol. Here, Washington arrived and ate breakfast without Arnold present. After eating, Washington conducted his inspection of the defenses of West Point, while Hamilton remained at Arnold's headquarters to finish his assigned paperwork and perhaps even to enjoy the considerable charms of the ravishing beauty who was Arnold's wife, Margaret "Peggy" Shippen-Arnold. Closer to Hamilton's age than her husband who was two decades older than her, Peggy hailed from a leading Loyalist family of Philadelphia.

But what Washington found was more shocking: West Point's defenses were incomplete and the garrison unready if the British launched an attack. Arnold, of course, had deliberately allowed the defenses to fall into disarray. Ironically, during the Quebec Campaign of 1775–1776, Major Aaron Burr had viewed the first hint of moral flaws in Arnold's character, and he did not like what he saw. After learning that André had been captured, Arnold had realized that he was about to be exposed for his plot to hand over the defensive bastion of West Point to the British, and had flown the nest by escaping to a British ship.[40]

Upon learning of Arnold's treachery after Hamilton handed him a packet of letters that revealed the ugly truth, Washington, knowing that Arnold was one of the army's best fighting generals, was speechless. In fact, Washington "never had sustained such a shock, but he gave no indication of distress of mind. He merely made it plain that he wished to be alone with Hamilton and Harrison."[41]

In a letter to Betsey on September 25, Hamilton wrote that when he learned of the stunning development "that shocked me more than any thing I have met with—the discovery of a treason of the deepest dyes. The object was to sacrifice West Point [because] General Arnold had sold himself of [Major John] André for this purpose."[42] Even more and although unrealized by Hamilton, Washington and his entire staff, including the native West Indian, were to have been captured along with West Point. When the conspiracy was discovered "Arnold, hearing of it being detected, immediately fled to the enemy [and wrote Hamilton] I went in pursuit" of the old hero of Saratoga.[43]

Along with McHenry, Hamilton met with frustration in his pursuit, after riding down the Hudson's east bank for around a dozen miles to Verplanck's Ferry in the vain hope of capturing Arnold. In a hastily written note to Washington from Verplanck's Ferry, New York, Hamilton explained, "We are too late [because] Arnold went by water to the *Vulture*," the appropriately named British warship that saved America's greatest traitor. Thinking fast in a crisis situation, Hamilton then offered wise council to Washington, while also having the wherewithal of quickly taking the initiative to save West Point, if the British suddenly moved against the strategic bastion perched above the Hudson as expected: "I shall write to General Greene advising him . . . to be in readiness to march and even to detach a brigade this way [because] it is possible Arnold has made such dispositions with the garrison as may tempt the enemy in [West Point's] present weakness to make the stroke this night and it seems prudent to be providing against it. I shall endeavor to find [Colonel Return Jonathan] Meigs and request him to march to the garrison and shall make some arrangements here. I hope Your Excellency will approve these steps as there may be no time to be lost."[44]

Then, to General Greene at Orangetown, New Jersey, Hamilton wrote a note to explain this "blackest treason [because] West Point was to have been the sacrifice, all dispositions have been made for the purpose and 'tis possible, tho' not probable, tonight may still see the execution [since] The wind is fair" for a British naval attack and I "advise your putting the army under marching orders and detaching a brigade this way."[45] Hamilton was almost acting like a commander-in-chief in wisely issuing orders and even making adroit suggestions to a senior general on the fly in a crisis situation, when time was of the essence.

Even more and on his own initiative, the fast-thinking Hamilton demonstrated prudence in immediately ordering a Connecticut regiment to march to West Point to reinforce the weak garrison in the hope of saving one of the most strategic points in America. Upon his return from the unsuccessful mission to capture Arnold, Hamilton then handed Washington a recently arrived letter from Arnold that explained his treason and emphasized that his pretty wife was blameless. The first explanation was far more honest than the second.

Here, at the Robinson house, Hamilton fell victim to the skilled acting performance of Arnold's pretty wife, Peggy. This very clever woman proclaimed her lack of knowledge of Arnold's sinister plot, which was certainly not the case. She played the right emotional cards to make her words more believable to men of honor. Hamilton's sympathy for the helpless fell prey to her splendid acting performance that would have probably made her a star in today's popular Broadway play *Hamilton*.

As Hamilton, who was reminded of his own father's abandonment of his mother Rachel and the family on St. Croix in regard to Peggy's distressed situation after Arnold escaped to leave her alone, wrote in his September 25 letter: "We have every reason to believe she was intirely [sic] unacquainted with the plan [and] Her sufferings were so eloquent that I wished myself her brother, to have a right to become her defender. . . . Could I forgive Arnold for sacrificing his honor reputation and duty I could not forgive him for acting a part that must have forfieted [sic] the esteem of so fine a woman. At present she almost forgets his crime in his misfortune, and her horror at the guilt of the traitor is lost in her love of the man. But a virtuous mind cannot long esteem a base one, and time will make her despise, if it cannot make her hate."[46]

Having become a victim to Peggy's wiles like Washington and Lafayette, Hamilton was also captivated by Major John André's charms and elegant manner like so many others: ironically like his own beloved Betsey in her not-so-innocent past. Betsey's first love had been the handsome British officer, who wore his long black hair in a stylish queue, only five years before. He had briefly stayed at the Schuyler mansion at Albany when under house arrest. The musical and poetic British spy, Arnold's chief covert contact in the plot, had been caught in civilian attire. He impressed Hamilton so favorably, from several visits, that he took André's letter—a desperate plea requesting a soldier's proper death by firing squad instead of hanging—to Washington. Hamilton put aside his personal concerns in regard to Betsey's first romance with the skilled English lady-killer in order to do what he felt was morally right. He saw the dashing major as only a liaison officer in passing communications between British leadership and Arnold. Therefore, Hamilton believed the major was not technically a spy. Because of his unfortunate past in the Caribbean, Hamilton's compassion and actions revealed his longtime leniency toward people in unfortunate circumstances, including prisoners-of-war.

But since André had been captured in civilian clothing instead of a major's uniform and while using the name of John Anderson, Washington remained strict and inflexible on this matter. Consequently, the commander-in-chief ignored Hamilton's heartfelt initiative that urged the fulfillment of André's request to be shot rather than hang like a fellow officer and gentleman. Hamilton penned in a heartfelt letter to his future wife on October 2, 1780: "I urged a compliance with André's request to be shot and I do not think it would have had an ill effect; but some people [Washington] are only sensible to motives of policy, and sometimes from a narrow disposition mistake it. When André's tale comes to be told, and present resentment over, the refusing him the privilege of choosing the manner of death will be branded with too much obduracy. . . . I confess to you I had the weakness to value the esteem of a *dying* man; because I reverenced his merit."[47]

A week and a half after André was hanged like a criminal instead of an officer when he was in fact the adjutant general of the British Army and one of General Henry Clinton's closest associates, a saddened Hamilton wrote a tortured letter to his best friend, John Laurens, on October 11, 1780. Noting the central paradox of Major André's life almost as if he had seen himself in the heart and soul of this doomed young Englishman, who was blessed with so many sterling qualities as an officer and as a man: "There was something singularly interesting in the character and fortunes of André. To an excellent understanding well improved by education and travel, he united a peculiar elegance of mind and manners, and the advantage of a pleasing person. . . . But in the height of his career, flushed with new hope from the execution of a project the most beneficial to his party he was at once precipitated from the summit [and he then] saw all the expectations of his ambition blasted and himself ruined" in the end.[48]

Especially after having visited the ill-fated Englishman several times in his last hours, Hamilton was long haunted by the agonizing image of André going to his death with a stoic grace that brought universal admiration, before swinging in the air. In the same letter to Laurens, Hamilton described the tragic scene that long nagged at his conscience: "In going to the place of execution, he bowed familiarly as he went along to all those with whom he had been acquainted in his confinement. A smile of complacency expressed the serene fortitude of his mind. Arrived at the fatal spot, he asked with some emotion, must I *die* in this manner?"[49]

After he was informed that his manner of execution was "unavoidable," Major André had calmly gone to his death with a heroic resignation. In Hamilton's words, André "springing upon the cart performed the last offices to himself with a composure that excited the admiration and melted the hearts of the beholders. Upon being told the final moment was at hand, and asked if he had any thing to say, he answered: 'nothing, but to request you will witness to the world, that I die like a brave man,'"[50]

Clearly, in part because the doomed major had tightened the noose around his neck to assist the nervous hangman and blindfolded himself before amazed observers, Hamilton was deeply moved by the demise of the cultured Englishman, who had won his admiration and his future wife's heart before him. Therefore, the searing memory of the smiling young Briton bravely going to his death haunted Hamilton for the rest of his life. André's grisly execution (a slow strangulation) also tormented Hamilton's future wife, who had loved (and perhaps still loved him) the graceful Englishman blessed with so many gifts except luck. André's death sent Betsey into a deep depression that took some of the romantic bloom off (at least initially) the idyllic relationship with Hamilton for the first time. Hamilton was thankful to have escaped Arnold's plot for West Point's capture which would have meant his own captivity, including Washington and his staff. As he penned in an October 11, 1780, letter to Laurens: "our happy escape from the mischief with which this treason was big."[51]

After André's execution, the dynamics in the relationship between Hamilton and Washington changed. Hamilton could never totally forgive Washington for ignoring his desperate plea for fulfill André's final request to die like a soldier by firing squad instead of like a common criminal or thieving pirate at a gaudy public hanging before a jeering crowd of onlookers. Washington's inflexibility and "rigid justice" and "hard hearted policy" in Hamilton's words, had sent the major to his death.

This rift between the commander and his chief of staff caused by André's hanging was deep. Hamilton was now even more determined to leave Washington's family once and for all. Therefore, not long after Major André's death, he applied for the coveted adjutant general position left when Colonel Alexander Scammell, who had served as one of Washington's staff officers during the New York Campaign and was fated to be killed in the Yorktown Campaign, resigned. The possibility of securing this prized position for Hamilton increased with Generals Greene's and Lafayette's recommendations to Washington. Washington eventually informed the two generals that he could not appoint an officer with a lieutenant colonel's rank to the position of adjutant general, since Scammell held the rank of colonel. After receiving General Greene's November 19, 1780, recommendation of Hamilton, Washington explained his decision in a letter: "Without knowing that Colo. Hamilton ever had an Eye to the Office of Adjt. General, I did, upon the application of Colo. Scammell to resign it, recommend Genl. Hand for reasons which may occur to you. . . . It would have been disagreeable therefore to the present Sub-Inspectors, some of them whom are full Colonels, to have had a Lt. Colo. put over them."[52]

Ironically, after Arnold's defection and the distance between the energetic chief of staff and his increasingly autocratic boss grew because of André's hanging, Washington became even more dependent upon Hamilton to fill the void left by one of his best generals. Meanwhile, Betsey and Hamilton continued to make marriage preparations, despite the native West Indian cautioning his wife that she might end up "a poor man's wife," because of the uncertainty of the future since he was determined not to rely on Schuyler family money. But despite bouts of resurfacing cynicism, including toward women in general, Hamilton was sufficiently wise to know that Betsey was "one of the exceptions" to the rule. Hamilton praised her "good hearted" nature and "sweet softness" that had so thoroughly captured his heart. He also marveled in a letter to her: "You are certainly a little sorceress and have bewitched me, for you have made me disrelish everything that used to please me."[53]

Hoping to rescue the gifted young man from his headquarters exile, General Sullivan also had attempted to rescue Hamilton from his frustrating dilemma. Like so many others, Sullivan knew that Hamilton possessed a brilliant mind that should be best utilized in high office. Therefore, a possibility for a new position opened when Congress created the executive departments of War, Finance, Marine, and Foreign Affairs. On January 29, 1780, and from Philadelphia while representing New Hampshire in Congress, Sullivan considered nominating Hamilton for the minister of finance, indirectly emphasizing that Hamilton's financial talents and economic expertise by diplomatically asking Washington what he thought of "Colo. Hamilton as a Financier."[54] Robert Morris was in line for the position however, which eventually caused Sullivan to drop Hamilton's nomination.

A Dashing Bachelor No More

As if to compensate for this frustrated ambition of failing to obtain independent field command, Hamilton's other all-consuming dream was about to finally true on December 14, 1780. In late November, Hamilton left Washington's headquarters on his first leave and not on any official business in more than three and a half years as a staff officer: another indication of his supreme importance to Washington, who seemed determined to squeeze every last ounce of talent out of the young man until there was nothing left. Departing Washington's headquarters in late November when the army was idle in winter quarters, Hamilton finally had an opportunity to leave the military "family" for an extended period, and rode north with his good friend Colonel James McHenry toward Albany at a brisk pace. McHenry, the best man, filled in for the absence of Hamilton's father, James Hamilton, Sr., and his older brother, James, Jr. Both of Alexander's closest remaining relatives were still in the Caribbean, and unable to attend the wedding in Albany. Significantly, Hamilton continued to harbor no resentments toward his father, James, Sr., for having abandoned the family, having invited him to attend the wedding on what he viewed as the most important day of his life.

But the snowfall of still another harsh winter impeded Hamilton's progress durng the lengthy journey to Albany. Only because General Schuyler's sleigh easily negotiated the snowy terrain leading up to the heights, the two close friends finally reached Schuyler's showcase three-story home located atop the bluff overlooking the Hudson. In Laurens's absence, Hamilton was delighted to have his good friend "Mac" now by his side. Here, in the huge second floor hallway at the brick Georgian mansion, distinguished by six massive columns and a wide porch, known as "the Pastures," Hamilton's great dream of a magnificent wedding with "his saucy little charmer" finally came true. Here, in the parlor, the twenty-five-year-old lieutenant colonel married Betsey, age twenty-three, eleven days before Christmas.

During the wedding ceremony at home in the tradition of the Dutch Reformed Church, McHenry was given a starring role, because he stood in to represent the groom's family. Ironically, this gifted Irishman, who had long marveled at Hamilton's romantic agility with the ladies, recited an original romantic poem. This poem included an affectionate "dear Ham," that he had written by the versatile McHenry specially for this memorable occasion. The happy couple then spent their honeymoon at the two-story Schuyler mansion which overlooked Albany.[55]

While enjoying his honeymoon at "the Pastures," including during the Christmas Season, and a well-deserved rest away from the hectic pace of the loads of paperwork at Washington's headquarters, Hamilton took time to write a humorous critique to the good-natured "Mac" about his poem. As Hamilton penned with his usual touch of humor combined with sincerity: "The piece is a good one. . . . It has wit, which you know is a rare thing. . . . You know I have often told you, you write prose well but had no genius for poetry. I retract."[56]

During this six-week honeymoon period in Albany, four leading French officers from Lieutenant General Jean-Baptiste-Donatien de Vimeur, Comte de Rochambeau's command paid their respects to General Schuyler and Hamilton, including the Marquis de Chastellux. Not about to live off the lavish wealth of his wife's family out of his sense of honor and due to pride as he had repeatedly informed Betsey, Hamilton had already contemplated resuming his legal studies once the war ended in America's favor. Thinking ahead and knowing that he might be hung by the British if America lost this war, Hamilton reflected upon relocating in a distant place "more favourable to human rights"—Geneva, Switzerland. In his journal, the debonair French officer Marquis de Chastellux wrote about his memorable visit to the home of the Schuyler family patriarch: "I had besides given the rendezvous to Colonel Hamilton, who had just married another of his daughters. . . . General Schuyler's family was composed of Mrs. Hamilton, his second daughter, who has a mild agreeable countenance."[57]

As mentioned and despite the huge social gap that existed between Hamilton and his new father-in-law, General Schuyler, could not have been more pleased with the match. As he revealed to Hamilton, who had returned to Washington's headquarters from Albany, in a January 25, 1781, letter: "You cannot, my dear sir, be more happy at the connexion [*sic*] you have made with my family, than I am. Until the child of a parent has made a judicious choice, his heart is in continual anxiety; but this anxiety was removed on the moment I discovered it was you on whom she had placed her affections [and] I am pleased with every instance of delicacy in those who are so dear to me."[58]

After hiring a guide to lead him south from Albany through rough country, including mountainous terrain covered in snow, Hamilton was now very much of a changed man when he returned to Washington's headquarters at New Windsor, New York, with his thoughts consumed by his new wife of a rare sweetness and "tenderness" that fairly radiated from her in early January 1781. The wedding, the warm, welcoming Schuyler family, and the bright prospects of a new life made the playing the old subservient role—already something that he wanted badly to escape for some time—harder to play at headquarters than ever before.

Meanwhile, the close relationship between Martha Washington and Elizabeth Schuyler (Betsey) Hamilton, who had shortly joined her husband and now visited Washington's headquarters on a daily basis, brought new life and vigor to headquarters. The newlyweds had rented a house in New Windsor. The first "home" of Alexander and Betsey was located not far from Washington's headquarters. Washington's New Windsor headquarters had been established in a two-story and "rather handsome" Dutch farmhouse located on the west bank of the Hudson River and just south of Newburgh, New York, and north of West Point. From the beginning, Hamilton's wife was a "great favorite" with Washington, who enjoyed socializing and dancing with the attractive, young woman of Dutch ancestry also known as Eliza, and with the members of his military "family" of hardworking officers.

In a January 21, 1781, letter from Washington's headquarters, Hamilton revealed that he was a happy man, after having married the woman of his dreams. In this letter to Betsey's older sister, Margarita (known as Peggy) Schuyler, Hamilton admitted that he was "a fanatic in love." Even in writing about love and marriage, Hamilton turned philosophical, while basking in his good fortune of having married a remarkable woman. He proclaimed how love was "a very good thing when their stars unite two people who are fit for each other, who have souls capable of relishing the sweets of friendship, and sensibilities. . . . But it's a dog of life when two dissonant tempers meet, and 'tis ten to one but this is the case."[59]

Revealing more of his brilliance when combined with his well-developed sense of humor that so often shined through his personal correspondence to men and women, Hamilton then teased Margarita by advising her how, "I join her [Betsey] in advising you to marry, I add be cautious in the choice. Get a man of sense, not ugly enough to be pointed at—with some good nature—a few grains of feeling—a little taste—a little imagination—above all a good deal of decision to keep you in order; for that, I foresee will be no easy task. If you can find one with all these qualities, willing to marry you, marry him as soon as you please. I must tell you in confidence that I think I have been very fortunate."[60]

Stiff New Challenges of 1781

While the year of 1781 saw America's fortunes sink to dismal lows, Hamilton's personal fortunes continued to rise, and he felt thankful for all his blessings. Although the memories of the missed opportunities of 1780, including a coveted position as the minister to Russia still lingered, he felt satisfaction in the fact that Congress had adopted some of his economic proposals for strengthening the government to meet pressing wartime requirements in the future.

Harsh winter weather led to epidemics of disease and desertion that took hundreds of young American soldiers from the ranks. Shortages in provisions and supplies continued to reduce the army's capabilities that were already low. As usual, the Articles of Confederation government that Hamilton detested with such passion, was unable to adequately supply their troops. And the weak government and Washington still lacked the necessary power to get the necessary results from the states.

Even the most patriotic men lost faith, beginning with Washington's Pennsylvania Continentals, who suffered severely for shortages in rations, clothing, and pay. These were no ordinary fighting men, but some of Washington's premier troops. The cancer of mutiny then spread through the ranks, contaminating the Continental troops of the New Jersey Line in early 1781. The army was threatened with dissolution. The key to thwarting the rising tide of mutiny was an early and forceful response. The ever-astute Hamilton realized as much, demonstrating once that he knew how to handle almost any crisis that suddenly developed. Like Washington, Hamilton knew that the only solution to the epidemic of mutinies was "to compel them to unconditional submission," as he ordered one colonel. Written by Hamilton during the first three months of 1780, Washington's desperate letters to state authorities to send supplies to their troops had brought no results. Most importantly, Washington quickly crushed the immediate threat of the mutinies, as Hamilton had advocated, with ringleaders forfeiting their lives. In a February 4, 1781, letter to Laurens, Hamilton emphasized the successful formula to the crushing of mutinies: "we uncivilly compelled them to an unconditional surrender and hanged their most incendiary leaders."[61]

Knowing that the inherent weaknesses of decentralized government and incompetence were the root of the never-ending problem, Hamilton had in the previous year (1780) proposed a plan to address the army's deplorable situation, especially in regard to the lack of essential supplies for the long-suffering soldiers. He had sent a letter that contained his well-thought-out remedies to General Schuyler. In a February 5, 1781, letter, the senior New York general agreed with Hamilton's tough solutions musing, "What might not our soldiery be brought to, if properly fed, paid, and clothed?"[62]

Hardly writing as the father-in-law of a much younger man, General Schuyler informed Hamilton that the well-conceived "plan you mention for supplying the armies in America, I should be exceedingly be happy to see attempted [and] in the course of the last year [1780], I proposed it repeatedly to individual members, who generally approved, and once or twice took occasion to mention it to congress [and] I am persuaded, if it was adopted, that a saving, at present almost inconceivable, would be induced, and an order and economy in the public expenditures [and] would eradicate the fears which too generally prevail, that we shall sink under the enormous weight of our expenses."[63]

Hamilton now enjoyed familial support not only from Betsey (Elizabeth, or Eliza, Schuyler Hamilton) at the army's winter quarters but also from senior generals: Washington, Greene, and Schuyler. He no longer lamented that "I am a stranger in this country, I have . . . no connexions" or family in America.[64] But the heavy burden of headquarters work kept him far away from Albany and the Schuyler family, which was a deepening source of regret because he had begun to transfer his most familial feelings away from Washington's military "family" and to a true family of his own by this time.

By early 1781 and despite all that he had accomplished year after year, Hamilton was still a frustrated young man in regard to his lofty military ambitions. All his aspirations to gain independent command and to distinguish himself on the battlefield continued to be thwarted. Hamilton, therefore, believed that he was at a professional dead end, with no prospects to make a name for himself on the field of strife. Even his chief of staff position was an almost secret job behind closed headquarters doors that relatively few people, other than Washington and his staff, understood or appreciated. A fatalistic Hamilton concluded with disgust how even "the stars fight against" me.[65]

But a brilliant mind continued to conceive new ideas and make contributions behind the scenes. The American people never realized that within the period of only a year, a young man only recently from a small, tropical island that they had never heard about and in the middle of nowhere amid the expansive Caribbean had "produced three plans for saving country."[66] He continued to be focused on how not to lose this war, because the Congress still lacked the authority and powers "for calling forth the resources of the country," as he lamented. As if these achievements were not enough, Hamilton also had been focused on reforming and "reorganizing the army, [which he had] been doing for three years."[67]

In January 1781 to confer with Washington before crossing the Atlantic on his envoy mission, the new French envoy, John Laurens, arrived at the New Windsor headquarters. Here, Hamilton and his best friend were reunited once again in a joyous reunion. On January 15, Hamilton went to work on still another important project. Based on the Washington–Laurens meetings, he carefully drafted a well-thought-out statement about America's capabilities for reaping a decisive victory. This was a brilliant summarization with a key purpose, providing Laurens with the fundamental argument to present to the French ministry to secure greater support, especially from the French Navy, to achieve the key to decisive victory: naval superiority.[68]

Lieutenant Colonel Hamilton continued to do all that he could to enhance Laurens' chances for success in dealing with the country's aristocratic elite in Paris and in the court of King Louis XVI, because so much was at stake for America. Knowing that his best friend's temperament was contrary to the delicate and careful diplomacy necessary in dealing with the French elite at the highest levels, especially the king's court, Hamilton tactically provided sage advice to Laurens like a seasoned international diplomat, after first singing Laurens' praises to soften truthful words that the young South Carolinian needed to hear: "In the frankness of friendship allow me to suggest to you one apprehension. It is the honest warmth of your temper. A politician My Dear friend must be at all times supple—he must often dissemble [and] I suspect that the French Ministry will try your temper; but you must not suffer them to provoke it [and] When you wish to show the deficiency of the

French Administration, do it indirectly by exposing the advantages of measures not taken rather than by a direct criticism of those taken. When you express your fears of consequences have the tone of lamentation rather than of menace [and] take every proper occasion of showing the advantages of the revolution to France without however seeming to insist upon them."[69]

Meanwhile, Hamilton remained upbeat about a successful summer of 1781 campaign on the horizon. As he penned to Francois Barbe-Marbois, who was the first secretary of the French ambassador Luzerne, on February 7, 1781, how the "Eastern States are really making great exertions towards the next campaign."[70] Two days later, Hamilton was focused on a new mission to Newport, Rhode Island, with Washington to meet with French leaders. Therefore, out of necessity, he made a special request of a former member of Washington's "family" and now the army's adjutant general, Colonel Timothy Pickering of New England: "The bad condition of my horses and the scarcity of forage in Camp induced me to leave them at Saratoga. . . . I am shortly to make a journey with the General to [Newport] Rhode Island for which I want horses. I therefore request the favour of you to furnish me with a couple of the best Continental horses [one for riding and one for carrying personal belongings] that can be found."[71] However, the trip to Newport for Washington to confer with the Comte de Rochambeau and other French leaders, in which he was to have served as interpreter, was cancelled by Washington until March 2, 1781.[72]

On February 15 in another letter to Pickering less than a week later, Hamilton was focused on important matters for coordinating the upcoming campaign: "the General directs you with the enclosed dispatch for Count De Rochambeau [who had replaced Admiral d'Estaing in overall command of French forces in America but was ordered by the French Government to serve under Washington for obvious political reasons] very early in the morning with the most positive directions concerning [the upcoming] expedition—It is of great importance that it would arrive to him as quickly as possible [and] be so good to enclose the letter for the Duke De Lauzun to your Deputy at Hartford with directions to deliver it immediately into the Duke's own hand—the two for [two other leading French officers] to your Deputy at New Port with the same directives each to its proper owner—If you have no deputy, send them to some friend—They are its seems of a very confidential nature."[73]

As in regard to so many other missed opportunities, Lieutenant Colonel Hamilton still regretted not having secured the coveted position of the army's adjutant general. After all, Lafayette and Greene had endorsed Hamilton for the position, and the chances seemed good at the beginning. But in the end, Washington appointed Irish-born General Edward Hand, a former officer of a Royal Irish regiment which had been stationed in America before the American Revolution and one of Washington's best senior officers, on February 1781: still another development that raised the level of Hamilton's frustration. When Hand became Washington's last adjutant general, Hamilton was not easily "reconciled to it." [74]

Inevitable Clash of Wills with Washington: February 16, 1781

Fate itself seemingly was about to intervene on Hamilton's behalf. On February 18, 1781, Hamilton began to write a letter that was literally a bombshell to his father-in-law in Albany: "I am no longer a member of the General's family. This information will surprise you and the manner of the change will surprise you more."[75]

The inevitable, long-overdue personal clash between Hamilton and Washington had splintered the close-knit military "family" and a dynamic team that had functioned effectively for nearly four years. For a wide variety of reasons,, this development was actually only a matter of time because of differences between them that had grown over time: liberal versus conservative; progressive versus traditional; the widening generational divides between the autocratic, older man's Virginia planter style and the younger man who possessed a host of cosmopolitan qualities; the commander-in-chief decision that resulted in Major André's hanging instead of shooting him like a soldier; Hamilton's social elevation and greater outside support with his recent marriage; having long felt the string of Washington's "ill-humor" as Hamilton called it; and the young man's hatred of all forms of subservience. But most of all, Hamilton had long quite correctly expected that Washington would reward him with command of a brigade for field duty and action, because of all that he had accomplished for the commander-in-chief for years.

After all and from the very beginning, Washington and Hamilton could not have been more different. The young "brash immigrant" with a dark past contrasted sharply with the older, respected aristocratic member of the colonial elite. But Hamilton was no longer a mere upstart, but one of America's leading intellectuals and political and economic minds and admired by the highest-ranking French officers in America, but he had been frustrated from moving forward to higher positions by the man he had assisted the most year after year. Clearly, for Hamilton, it was time for a change because he had significantly changed, especially after all that he had accomplished for not only Washington but also America.

As usual by early 1780, the greatest divide that still existed between Hamilton's relentless ambition to move on with his military career to purse an opportunity to distinguish himself on the battlefield, and the equally stubborn Washington in his repeated refusal to let Hamilton go. To be fair, it was hardly Washington's fault because of Hamilton's irreplaceable value as a principal advisor, alter ego, and chief of staff, who seemingly always had the right answer to the most complex questions in regard not only to the army but also the nation.

In addition and despite all that he had accomplished for him, Washington continued to be autocratic and paternalistic toward Hamilton not only because he had long managed slaves at Mount Vernon with typical upper-class ease, but also because he had no son of his own. At some point, he might have looked upon Hamilton almost like a surrogate son, but more like an illegitimate one compared to his true father-son relationship like he enjoyed with Lafayette. Although Hamilton was in fact illegitimate, he needed no father figure because of his independent nature and headedness. He, consequently, had long remained relatively reserved in his personal feelings for Washington since beginning his work at headquarters.

Hamilton, therefore, still saw their longtime partnership as primarily a formal working relationship. Any other kind personal relationship that involved deep emotions, especially as a surrogate son, in a busy work environment that required for a very businesslike setting, would have hampered overall efficiency. Consequently, they had worked successfully together as a highly effective team in a businesslike and professional manner year after year. Hamilton, blessed with endless energy and the well-honed work ethnic inherited from his mother, was always all-business when it came to work.

After all that he had accomplished both inside and outside of his blue uniform and after nearly four years, Hamilton had even more good reason to fundamentally reject the basic premise of a relatively low subordinate status at headquarters, because he still hated such positions and was now much more of military and social equal to the commander-in-chief thanks to his recent marriage. From the beginning, Hamilton especially detested all forms of subservience, which reminded him of his Caribbean impoverishment and working in St. Croix for little pay and even less recognition. Despite possessing a great ability to do so, he still refused to fawn upon Washington (or anyone else) like so many Continental officers, who shamelessly curried favor for promotion and to boost their egos.

Clearly, a showdown between the two men had been brewing for an extended period. As mentioned, Hamilton was a dynamic man of action and a proven battlefield leader. Therefore, Hamilton's frustration had continued to grow over the years, gradually building up and becoming intolerable for him by early 1781. This situation had taken a toll on Hamilton's good nature, sense of dedication to Washington, and perhaps even his physical health. Smoldering with an increasing amount of resentment that he carefully concealed by his trademark smile and elegant manners—that so impressed the French elite—so as not to interfere with the smooth-working process of headquarters, Hamilton felt that he was being unfairly and rather cynically kept down simply to serve Washington in a subservient role. He believed that he was being deliberately restricted from reaching his full potential to solely benefit Washington, who refused to even promote Hamilton after years of exemplary service. The frustrated young man was not alone in his harsh conclusions about Washington's selfish motivations that might have even betrayed a degree of jealousy. His friends, including Lafayette, Greene, Sullivan, and Laurens, agreed with Hamilton's worst suspicions that he was being deliberately thwarted and held back from achieving his true potential. Consequently, these respected leaders had sought to obtain a transfer for Hamilton to another elevated position that almost everyone, but Washington, felt that he had earned and certainly deserved.

Especially troubling to Hamilton to increase his frustration, Washington was not an easy boss to interact with, especially over an extended period in cramped quarters. He had a tendency to take out his anger on staff members without a hint of gentlemanly grace. After only six weeks, Major Aaron Burr had departed Washington's "family" never to return, because of the difficulty in working for the ever-demanding Virginian, who bossed staff officers around not unlike slaves at Mount Vernon. Hamilton encountered the same difficulties, including a lack of "good temper" in Hamilton's words. Nevertheless, year after year, the young man persevered in a most challenging environment at headquarters, while serving under Washington's giant shadow. He quietly performed with enthusiasm and great skill whatever duty was assigned to him without complaint, biting his tongue and doing his duty to the best of his ability.

Hamilton's life always had been a long struggle to rise above his lowly, humiliating Caribbean past to gain proper recognition that was rightfully due to him. In the self-made man tradition, he had overcome every obstacle that had been unfairly placed in his path by an inequitable, class-based society. And now the most revered man (another wealthy and privileged aristocrat) in America stood squarely in his way, thwarting his ambition and advancement, despite all of his hard work and sacrifice. Ironically, the revolution's and army's very foundation was based on the concept of a meritocracy in which individuals of all ranks could excel and rise up because of what they accomplished rather than what was arbitrarily and unfairly dictated by their wealth and social background as in Europe.

Incredibly, Hamilton now retained the same relatively low rank of lieutenant colonel as when he first joined Washington's "family" in early 1777. Of course, this was a special sore point, because he was barred from more prestigious and better positions that required higher rank. If anyone in the Continental Army deserved a colonel's rank or higher, it was Washington's hardworking chief of staff. A thankful Napoleon wisely bestowed well-deserved recognition by promoting his brilliant chief of staff, the incomparable Louis Alexandre Berthier, to the highest military rank, marshal, in May 1804. As essentially the professional head of the French Army, Berthier provided an unparalleled amount of invaluable service to Napoleon, as his chief of staff and for the Grande Armée during its most legendary campaigns.

Proving endlessly frustrating, if not infuriating, to the young man who might have wondered if being from the West Indies had partly resulted in this unfortunate situation for him, Washington had always employed the same excuse of Hamilton's low rank as a reason for not allowing him to depart the "family" and to command a combat unit in the field. Hamilton ruefully now looked back upon "Harry" Lee's decision not to join Washington's staff in March 1778, when offered by himself on Washington's behalf, because this independent-minded Virginia cavalryman desired to remain with his men in the field.

Like his growing resentment, if not exasperation, Hamilton's grievances were not only long-existing, but also had been recently magnified by the incredible success in his personal life. Ironically, both of these remarkable men were correct in their mutually inflexible positions: Washington needed to retain Hamilton as his invaluable chief of staff, and he was wise enough not to risk losing such a gifted young officer, while Hamilton only wanted his talents to soar higher and to reach their true potential, especially after nearly four years of faithful service to the commander in chief.[76] Every inch of a fighter and knowing that he could make a valuable contribution on the field, Hamilton still longed to once again hear "the charming sound of bullets," in his own words, on the battlefield.[77]

A lifelong obsession that was partly a byproduct of his lowly upbringing and dysfunctional past, Hamilton's ambition still consumed and motivated him. As written in his earliest surviving letter written on November 11, 1769, Hamilton had expressed his innermost and most dominant sentiments to his good friend Edward "Ned" Stevens, who had been educated at King's College like Hamilton: "my Ambition is [so] prevalent that I contemn the grov'ling and condition of a Clerk or the like, to which my Fortune &c. condemns me and would willingly risk my life tho' not my Character to exalt my Station. . . . I wish there was a War."[78]

Lieutenant Colonel Hamilton's deepest feelings had not changed from that November less than a decade ago, which in substance contradicted the very spirit of Washington's March 1, 1777, general orders that announced his appointment as aide-de-camp at headquarters "to the Commander in Chief" of the Continental Army.[79] Here, at Washington's New Windsor headquarters at the Dutch-style home of William Ellison and from where the general could monitor enemy developments in the strategic Hudson River corridor just above strategic West Point, Hamilton was still fairly fuming over Washington's strict inflexibility that casually dismissed his urgent pleas to prevent Major André's hanging.[80]

Now in the steady process of deteriorating, this long-term relationship between the older commander-in-chief, in his late forties and still a provincial product of the value systems of an insular Virginia planter class world, and his young, erudite chief of staff, was a most complex one in personal terms. Hamilton, who was raised without a father, never bonded in a father-son way to his boss. Hamilton's independent-mindedness and lofty ambitions eliminated that possibility, and by way of his own choice. Therefore, year after year, he had respectfully kept his distance in emotional terms. Having been raised without a father who was killed in battling for France on European soil, Lafayette became Washington's surrogate son instead of Hamilton to satisfy the Virginian's psychological and emotional needs in this regard, because Martha had been unable to give him a son.

The psychological cost of guaranteeing a continued smooth functioning of official duties at headquarters was simply becoming too high of a personal price for Hamilton to pay, because the relationship had evolved into an increasingly unhealthy, if not dysfunctional, one for the young man. Tension long had been mounting in what had now become very much of an "edgy" relationship, with Hamilton gradually becoming ever more exasperated.

Despite his youth, a stoic Hamilton had always controlled his emotions and thwarted desires for the overall fulfillment of larger national objectives beyond his own personal concerns and ambitions for years. However, he was unable to fully master the combined effect of his warrior ethos and idealistic ambitions, which he viewed as "my weakness," that caused him to always aspire higher. Most of all by this time, Hamilton had grown tired of serving as Washington's right-hand man without promotion, gratitude, or recognition, while occasionally experiencing the wrath of his "irritable temper." He had become especially weary of the same old frustrating routine game—that insulted his intelligence--of "constantly imploring Washington for more battle duty [and] Washington usually responded by telling him he was too valuable a confidant and strategist to expose to the enemy's muskets. It was rejection by praise, and Hamilton hated it [but] he kept asking [and] Washington kept turning him down. And so it went, back and forth" over an extended period of time.[81]

Another reason also existed to partly explain the all-but-inevitable clash between two strong-willed and forceful personalities at the New Windsor headquarters, which has been long overlooked by generations of historians: Hamilton's abolitionist views. Washington well knew of Hamilton's efforts to enlist slave-soldiers into the Continental Army for service in the South and refused to endorse the bold Hamilton-Laurens plan that might have prevented disaster in the Southern theater. Their strongly opposing views about slavery also complicated their relationship. Unlike Washington, Hamilton shared the same abolitionist views as the enlightened French military leaders serving on American soil. Despite being one of the largest slave owners in Virginia and to be fair, Washington had moderated his hardcore views about slavery since the war's beginning, partly due to Hamilton's more progressive and liberal influence. As sent to Congress in early 1779, Hamilton's written views about racial equality shocked, if not appalled, most Southerners, and almost certainly including Washington, who either heard about or read the document.[82]

Clearly, some of the most deeply ingrained elements of Hamilton's personality and core belief system were eventually bound to clash with Washington's aristocratic and provincial attitudes that were typical of the Virginia ruling class. Now called "His Excellency" by one and all, Washington lived by a long-established traditional code about how to treat subordinates, including the members of his staff, regardless of how accomplished, including his own chief of staff. Symbolically, and certainly not lost to Hamilton who hated slavery with a passion, Washington referred to Mount Vernon's slaves by the same name as his staff officers: "family."[83] For such reasons, for "three years I have felt no friendship for him and have professed none," later wrote Hamilton to General Schuyler, who served as a true father figure (his father-in-law) to him rather than Washington.[84]

As could be expected and especially in crisis situations, Washington's occasional eruption of temper made the overall environment at headquarters tense and nerve-racking for the over-worked Hamilton and other staff officers. A young Washington had been especially prone to emotional outbursts, and these had most often now occurred during stressful periods as commander-in-chief over the years. Here, at the New Windsor headquarters, Hamilton was about to see another sudden outburst of Washington's temper—that very few people ever saw—directed at his favorite staff officer.[85]

In this sense and far more than has been generally recognized, Washington's "family" was somewhat of a dysfunctional in personal—rather than professional—terms at headquarters. Now Hamilton finally knew what a true family was like with the Schuylers, understanding the warmth of positive family dynamics and mutual respect. Although Hamilton was not fully aware of this fact when he first joined the "family" on March 1, 1777, Washington's outward "coldness" and callous dealings with officers under him often came at the expense of the sensitivities and self-esteem of others, including his chief of staff. Reflecting his experience as the hard-driving micro-manger of hundreds of workers (enslaved black and free whites) at Mount Vernon, Washington found it difficult to bond with others, especially in his elevated role as "His Excellency," including staff members, who addressed him by this lofty title.[86] In consequence and by any measure, it "was a touchy business [because] working closely with Washington [which] was no fun."[87]

By this time, Hamilton had also lost some respect for Washington not only as an officer and a gentleman (especially because of Major André's hanging and, of course, the displays of temper) but also as a military commander, especially in regard to strategy and tactics. Colonel Timothy Pickering, Washington's adjutant, was also critical of Washington's poor tactical performance that paved the way to the 1777 reversals at Brandywine and Germantown. As expressed in his letters to friends and wife, Hamilton unleashed "a stream of mature comments on just how the war should be fought," including that Washington should "behave as boldly as he himself would."[88] While Hamilton supported Washington in every possible way at headquarters, he nevertheless could not deny the increasing amount of evidence and clear undeniable examples, which caused greater "doubts about the quality of his mind" as the army's commander.[89]

This upcoming clash of personalities at the New Windsor headquarters, where the heavy workload was especially irksome because the "family" now consisted of only Hamilton and Tilghman, who had not fully recovered from an illness, resulted from other factors as well. At this time, Washington felt a sense of frustration not like Hamilton. The equally overworked Virginian was also in some physical pain from teeth problems and swollen gums. Under tremendous strain in awaiting news about the French fleet in the West Indies that he hoped would be ordered to America's waters, Washington was increasingly embittered by the weight of excessive burdens, criticism (fair and unfair) directed at him, and America's faltering resistance effort that seemed to have no solution. The Continental Army seemed nearly in its death throes, and Washington would almost certainly be hung if this war was lost. For a host of reasons, Washington was at his wit's end during this period, while under the stress of a heavy load of pressing wartime demands and responsibilities. Therefore, at his New Windsor headquarters by mid-February 1781, Washington was himself simmering like a powder keg. Only a small spark was now needed to cause an eruption.[90]

Likewise, under the considerable weight of his own burdens as chief of staff responsibilities and only one of two officers on duty in a much-reduced staff during this busy period, Hamilton was also on edge like Washington. In a letter to James McHenry, Hamilton lamented, "At present there is besides myself only Tilghman, who is just recovering from a fit of illness, the consequence of too close application to business."[91]

In addition, Hamilton was naturally unhappy about his personal exile from Albany and extended family that he loved. Then, fueling additional frustration and resentment, Washington refused to allow Hamilton even a few days of leave to visit Albany. He sorely missed the loving warmth of the Schuyler family, during the long hours of thankless work in the "gilded cage" of Washington's headquarters, which was located in an uncomfortably small house in this gloomy, one-horse town along the Hudson.

Even Washington complained about "the very confined quarters" at New Windsor headquarters, where Hamilton's workload often kept him up to the midnight hour. He and Washington had worked till that late hour on the night of February 15. And next morning's duties called very early. By this time, Hamilton felt that working for Washington was a classic Faustian bargain. As mentioned, Hamilton had never wavered in this ambition to aspire higher than a desk position on a general's staff, and now this burning desire seemingly haunted his every thought. When the war had been young, the twenty-one-year-old Hamilton had refused the coveted positions on the staffs of two generals, Greene and Lord Stirling, for the very reasons that now plagued him.[92] In Hamilton's own words that explained a sentiment that never left him: "I always disliked the office of an Aide de Camp [and therefore] I refused to serve in the capacity with two Major General's at an early period of the war."[93]

In this regard, Hamilton's deepest inclinations had not been altered in any way. What was most remarkable was the fact that Hamilton had served on Washington's staff not only for so long, but also so capably in a situation that he detested. Perhaps his dysfunctional past had been a factor that partly explained why Hamilton endured such an extended period as Washington's right-hand man, while ignoring the negative factors that had steadily grown in number. But since joining Washington's staff on March 1, 1777, at Morristown, he had matured, gaining confidence and growing into his own as never before. Clearly, his increasing distaste for headquarters duty became more poignant because Hamilton's personal life was now in complete harmonious order and set in place for future happiness, after his easy entry into one of America's leading families that thought of him as their own.[94]

As mentioned, Lieutenant Colonel Hamilton was now more aware of the differences between Washington and General Schuyler, his beloved father-in-law with whom he had forged the closest bond. Therefore, despite the Virginian's proper gentleman code, Washington had always been far too autocratic for Hamilton's ultra-egalitarianism and sense of fair play. Clearly, this was an increasingly negative and unhealthy relationship that Hamilton needed to escape for his own good and future welfare. Revealing one aspect of working under Washington's huge shadow, Surgeon Thacher, a New Englander now familiar with the Virginian's elite behavior and intimidating ways, candidly admitted in his journal how Washington "is feared even when silent. . . ."[95]

Hamilton explained why he had long so faithfully served Washington so long at the expense of his own desires and ambitions: "His popularity has often been essential to the safety of America. . . . These considerations [rather than personal] have influenced my past conduct respecting him" and in supporting Washington for nearly four years.[96] He admitted that he had early discovered that some of the best things said about Washington were "unfounded." In his own words and much to his surprise, Hamilton had early discovered that Washington "was neither remarkable for delicacy nor good temper."[97]

By mid-February 1781 the perceived slights (both real and imagined) and instances of bad temper demonstrated by Washington became almost impossible to endure any longer for Hamilton. After all that he had accomplished for the commander-in-chief, Hamilton felt increasingly uneasy by the harsh realization that Washington was unappreciative and ungrateful for deliberately keeping him on his staff for so long without a promotion or any promise of a well-deserved advancement. Perhaps something that he never wanted to admit, Hamilton now accepted the hard truth that Washington had "disappointed him at every turn": the very antithesis of what Hamilton had faithfully accomplished for his demanding and temperamental boss.[98]

As mentioned, Washington and Hamilton were exhausted from overwork and late hours at headquarters. Hamilton had been laboring late the previous night in translating Washington's thoughts into French for important dispatches that were about to be sent to their French leaders at Newport, Rhode Island. Therefore, both Washington and his hard-working chief of staff had been up late (perhaps even past midnight) the previous night, Thursday, February 15. Then, without sufficient sleep, the two men were up early on his early Friday morning that promised seemingly endless hours of dreary work without a break. In some ways and despite all that he had achieved, Hamilton must have felt that he was still a teenager laboring for Nicholas Cruger back at Christiansted, St. Croix.

Washington accidently met Hamilton on the wooden staircase at headquarters, where the commander's room was located on the second floor of the Dutch farmhouse on the Hudson, when the young man was going downstairs. Hamilton had just finished writing at length, and perhaps experienced a weary pen hand. In a curt manner, Washington "told me he wanted to speak to me [and] I answered I would wait upon him immediately," but first had to deliver his official "pressing" order of army business (a missive directed to the army's commissary department) to Tilghman who was working in a downstairs room. Upon attempting to return to Washington at the stop of the stairs as requested after delivering these urgent papers in a businesslike manner to the native Marylander, Hamilton then encountered the Marquis de Lafayette in the hallway.

Here, the two close friends exchanged the traditional pleasantries and courtesies, including the kissing of cheeks, in the accepted upper class French manner of greeting and affection, which was generally longer than according to American custom. Then, "we conversed together about a minute on a matter of business," wrote Hamilton. Lafayette and Hamilton were united by not only by a deep respect and friendship, but also corresponding military ambitions. Hamilton had hoped to lead light infantry troops under General Lafayette in the proposed attack on New York City. After his brief chat, Hamilton then shortly departed from Lafayette's presence "in a manner [that seemed too] abrupt" to both men in order to return to Washington. Feeling that Washington had long selfishly thwarted Hamilton's long-overdue advancement and released from his staff, Lafayette had long sympathized with Hamilton's quandary. Therefore, the sympathetic French general had attempted in vain to have the young man assigned elsewhere, but to no avail.

In the true Virginia planter tradition, almost as if he had beckoned a lowly white domestic, recent Irish immigrant, or a slave at Mount Vernon for an urgent task at hand, Washington expected that Hamilton should promptly report to him without hesitation and not two minutes later in Hamilton's time estimation. Consequently, the awaiting Washington, now impatiently pacing back and forth at the head of the stairs, was upset. Perhaps he was reminded of his own lack of sophistication and education in hearing the animated conversation between Lafayette (Washington's true surrogate son not Hamilton) and Hamilton, which was spoken in a melodic and elegant French that he was unable to understand. Washington incorrectly thought that ten minutes had passed before Hamilton finally reported to him. Washington was already fuming because of Hamilton's relatively short delay in having accidently encountered Lafayette downstairs and exchanged greetings in the customary French manner and then briefly spoke on business matters.[99]

In his lengthy letter of explanation to General Schuyler to explain the incident, Hamilton then related, "Instead of finding the General as usual in his room [on the second floor], I met him at the head of the stairs, where accosting me in a very angry tone, 'Col. Hamilton (said he), you have kept me waiting at the head of the stairs these ten minutes. I must tell you Sir you treat me with disrespect.' I replied without petulancy, but with decision 'I am not conscious of it Sir, but since you have thought it necessary to tell me so we part' [and] 'Very well Sir (said he) if it be your choice,' or something to this effect and we separated."[100]

As in the past, Washington had spoken angrily to his young chief of staff like a "drill sergeant" to a lowly private on the parade ground. Washington was shocked by Hamilton's curt response that revealed a changed man. Hamilton had been first surprised by Washington's animated comment, but he had given his boss a far greater surprise by standing up to him so boldly, which had not been seen in the past. Indeed, since taking command of the army, no one in uniform (or at Mount Vernon for that matter, except perhaps Martha on occasion) had ever dared to talk to Washington in such an openly defiant manner.

But clearly Hamilton, only age twenty-six, had grown by leaps and bounds during the war years: a fact that even Washington had been forced to now realize. As Hamilton continued to inform his father-in-law: "I sincerely believe my absence which gave so much umbrage did not last two minutes. In less than an hour, Tilghman came to me [in Hamilton's downstairs room] in the Generals name assuring me of his great confidence in my abilities, integrity usefulness &c and of his desire in a candid conversation to heal a difference which could not have happened but in a moment of passion."[101]

Displaying strength of character and knowing that he had insulted the young man without thinking about the repercussions of his sharp words as in the past, Washington hoped to reconcile and salvage this most vital of relationships by simply overlooking the matter entirely as if it never happened, because he needed Hamilton so badly. Feeling a sense of regret for his emotional outburst, Washington was not holding any resentment or grudge at what could be viewed as disrespectful behavior toward "His Excellency," the revered commander-in-chief of America's armies, by an officer that was young enough to be his son. But Hamilton, feeling unappreciated and unrecognized after all that he had accomplished for Washington and America year after year (ironically, some of the same kind of reasons that had caused Arnold to recently turn traitor), would have none of it. This was Lieutenant Colonel Hamilton's own personal Rubicon and there was now no going back, because "I have not been in the wrong." Displaying moral courage and strength of will, he turned his back on Washington's almost immediate proposal to reconcile differences.

Hamilton did not have to think twice in regard to his final decision, because this was the turning point for him and a long-awaited one. In his own words: "I requested Mr. Tilghman to tell him, 1. that I had taken my resolution in a manner not to be revoked" and that Washington's proposed meeting of reconciliation, which Hamilton refused, was entirely unnecessary at this point.[102] Hamilton was correct in his determination not to be swayed from his final decision to depart Washington's staff. Washington later admitted that he was "the Agressor [*sic*]," and, therefore, had "quickly repented the Insult."[103]

Although the iron-willed Hamilton refused to budge, he offered a solution to this delicate situation that was unprecedented in the history of Washington's staff: "that though determined to leave the family the same principles which had kept me so long in it would continue to direct my conduct towards him when out of it [and] that however I did not wish to distress him or the public business, by quitting him before he could derive other assistance [especially in regard to the French language to continue Washington's correspondence with America's ally] by the return of some of the Gentleman who were absent" from his "family" and "that in the mean time it depended on him to let our behaviour to each other be the same as if nothing had happened."[104]

Now fully realizing exactly how serious this seemingly once-insignificant matter was to his young chief of staff, Washington relented. He accepted Hamilton's conditions that brought a temporary resolution to the impasse, easing the heightened tension that had reached a boiling point. Hamilton wrote how Washington "consented to decline the conversation and thanked me for my offer of continuing my aid, in the manner I had mentioned. Thus we stand" at this time.[105]

Clearly, Washington had learned once again that Hamilton was driven by a fierce determination and will that was hidden behind the exquisitely mannered and highly polished facade that had never once previously cracked until this regrettable incident at New Windsor. What was now obvious was that once Hamilton made up his mind, "no one could stop him," not even General Washington and his well-known strength of will.[106]

But in truth, Hamilton's intransigence about reconciling with Washington was so strong that something much deeper was actually in play. Almost certainly, after all of his faithful service as chief of staff for nearly four years, Hamilton had actually played a clever hand in a masterful and complex chess game. He was hoping that Washington, whose anger had immediately subsided as Hamilton knew would be the case, might feel sufficiently guilty over his ill-tempered treatment of his most important staff member that the Virginian might finally relent and give him what he desired at the first opportune time: active field command.[107]

Hamilton explained in the same letter to General Schuyler of the true source of the unfortunate dispute (which revealed two hot tempers and strong wills), because it was also about the significant differences in these complex personalities between the two dynamic military men: "I always disliked the office of an Aide de Camp as having in it a kind of personal dependence [but] Infected . . . with the enthusiasm of the times, an idea of the Generals character which experience soon taught me to be unfounded overcame my scruples and induced me to *accept his invitation* to enter into his family. I believe you know the place I held in The Generals confidence and councils of which will make it the most extraordinary to you to learn that for the three years past I have felt no friendship for him and have professed none. The truth is our own dispositions are the opposites of each other & the pride of my temper would not suffer me to profess what I did not feel. Indeed when advances of this kind have been made to me on his part they were received in a manner that showed at least I had no inclination to court them, and that I wished to stand rather upon a footing of military confidence than of private attachment."[108]

Clearly, this feisty "'Little Lion' stood in no awe of other lions, and his admiration for their prowess was always tempered by the conviction that he was the equal of the best [and he certainly was not] content merely to share in another's reflected glory."[109] Therefore, Hamilton "would not be found among those who burned incense at the shrine of the so-called great man."[110] Providing some personal relief, Hamilton could now dismiss any lingering thoughts—as he was so often charged by his enemies—of being "too much Washington's lackey."[111] Once he learned of the incident at the New Windsor headquarters, Lafayette attempted to mend the rift and damage. He wrote to Washington: "From the very first moment, I exerted every means in my power to prevent a separation which I knew was not agreeable to Your Excellency."[112]

In a letter to his good friend James "Mac" McHenry, Hamilton explained his firm stance that could not be altered by friend, family, or his wife, writing more candidly (they were still good friends) than to General Schuyler for a good many valid reasons: "I pledge my honor to you that he [Washington] will find me inflexible. He shall for once at least repent his ill-humor. Without a shadow of reason and on the slightest ground, he charged me in the most affrontive manner with treating him with disrespect."[113] Having decided to no longer feel the sting of Washington's temper and to labor without recognition in the commander-in-chief's shadow, Hamilton had been treated with disrespect that had been the final straw for him.

Despite this unfortunate incident at New Windsor and most importantly, Hamilton never lost his faith in Washington and what he meant to America's fragile life in the midst of struggle. The deep bonds forged between the two men in battles and adversities were too deep and strong to be broken by this relatively minor incident. Therefore, Hamilton continued to be Washington's diehard supporter, who could never "think of quitting the army during the war." He had early realized that for the young republic and its army to prevail in this life-and-death struggle, Washington needed to continue his projection as a popular hero and a powerful republican symbol. Therefore, to the very end of his life, Hamilton never wavered in his firm support for Washington, who likewise never relinquished his faith and sense of loyalty to the native West Indian. Revealing his heartfelt sentiments and a loyalty that never died, Hamilton wrote to his father-in-law in his February 18, 1781, letter, only two days after this altercation: "The General is a very honest man. His competitors have slender abilities and less integrity. . . . I think it is necessary he should be supported" for the overall good of the army and America.[114]

Interestingly, Hamilton had described himself as an "honest man" in a September 12, 1780, letter, and the two men—one a Virginian and the other a West Indian—from such dissimilar backgrounds shared strong characters and an undying love for America as fierce nationalists: a permanent bond between Washington and Hamilton that held firm for the rest of their lives.[115] To the former physician who learned more of the young man's most innermost thoughts other than John Laurens, Lieutenant Colonel Hamilton emphasized to "Mac" McHenry how he was not to mention anything about the incident except to closest friends to avoid rumors and scandal that might damage Washington's reputation, which would not be good for America's fortunes: "I shall continue to support a popularity [of Washington] that has been essential [and] is still useful" to America.[116]

Gracious under the circumstances, Hamilton's promise to continue to provide dedicated support and assistance to Washington was quite unlike Adjutant General Joseph Reed, a cunning New Jersey lawyer who had sided with the General Lee camp. As Washington's most revered staff officer in 1776, Reed had betrayed the trusting Virginian, who had considered him a dear friend to the very end. Although he tried, Reed was never able to reestablish his friendship with Washington like Hamilton. In striking contrast to Reed and just as he held no grudges or ill feelings toward the father who had abandoned him and the family, Hamilton maintained his loyalty to Washington from beginning to end and long after their New Windsor spat, when the two continued to work closely together to drive Washington's presidency in order to guarantee greater national harmony and a long life for the republic. In the end, therefore,

Hamilton remained forever true to his core beliefs and commitments, never betraying himself, Washington, or America.[117]

During the war years and as he informed Betsey (Elizabeth Schuler Hamilton), Hamilton sought to convince his father, James Hamilton, Sr., to relocate from the Caribbean to America to reunite what was left of his little family. He had also invited him to attend his wedding in Albany, but it was not possible for James to make the long journey from the Caribbean, especially in wartime. Unlike his son, James was a British citizen. In much the same way, Hamilton held no grudge toward the "Father of his Country."[118]

As promised, Hamilton continued to faithfully serve Washington week after week, after the clash of personalities on that ill-fated Friday at New Windsor, February 16, 1781. As before, he maintained a formal, business-like relationship with Washington, performing up to his usual high standards of excellence and sense of commitment as if nothing had ever happened between the two. For the all-important business of America and army operations and as both men fully realized, it was essential for Hamilton to continue to serve in multiple roles, especially in regard to communicating with the French allies: a key point that he had emphasized by General Schuyler, who knew that Hamilton's absence would damage the vital French alliance, because of his close contacts and friendships with French army, the diplomatic corps, and naval leaders.

Shortly before the tempers of the two men of different generations erupted when least expected, Hamilton devoted himself to political matters on both sides of the Atlantic. As Washington's chief liaison officer and emissary to the French, he corresponded with the secretary of the French legation in Philadelphia, Francois de Barbe-Marbois, in regard to sensitive military-political matters of importance. Ratified by the states in 1781, the Articles of Confederation—the new national government formed half a decade after the Declaration of Independence's signing but which was far too states'-rights oriented for effectiveness, especially in regard to the war effort—was officially ratified in the hope of remedying a host of national ills. But Hamilton, like Washington who of course was a fellow diehard nationalist, understood how thoroughly that the Articles of Confederation had guaranteed a notoriously weak national government and army. Hamilton communicated to his French friend in the honest and intimate terms that made him so trusted among the allies: "The first step to reformation as well in an administration as in an individual is to be sensible of our faults. This begins to be our case [because] we are so accustomed to doing right by halves, and spoiling a good intention in the execution, that I always wait to see the end of our public arrangements before I venture to expect good or ill from them [but he was concerned that this new government might will prove] unequal to the exigencies of the war or to the preservation of the union hereafter."[119]

Around six weeks after the heated incident at the New Windsor headquarters and waiting patiently for Washington to replace him with a new member of the "family," Hamilton made another attempt to force Washington's hand to obtain a field command. Hamilton departed the New Windsor encampment with wife Betsey. He then moved into a rented house at DePeyster's Point, which was located across the Hudson from the army's encampment around New Windsor on the west bank. Hamilton's service as the leading member of the "family" was over, which was the fulfillment of the young man's hopes of moving on to bigger and better things.[120]

During the spring of 1781, with now more time on his hands away from headquarters for the first time since March 1, 1777, Hamilton wrote half a dozen "Continentalist" (Washington was also a "Continentalist") essays for the *New-York Packet*, in New York City. Overflowing with the usual innovative ideas and novel concepts of merit about correcting the "WANT OF POWER IN CONGRESS," Hamilton continued to do what he did best: offer sound solutions to the many complex national problems that continued to plague America, especially its weak economy, and government that was unable to adequately support its weak republican armies in the field. As he had long emphasized, a stronger government was the only solution to curing America's seemingly endless ills, including the "prejudices of the particular states," as an equally astute Washington also believed was the remedy.[121]

But, to his great delight, Hamilton's brilliant writings ended when he officially received command of a light infantry battalion of Lafayette's light division at the end of July 1781. But the achievement of this longtime ambition had not been easy even up until at the last minute. To force Washington's hand out of a sense of absolute desperation, he had no choice but to send his officer's commission to the commander-in-chief to formally resign, if he was not given an active command. Hamilton had waged still another hard-fought battle of maneuver behind the scenes and won. But within only a few months, Hamilton faced his greatest battle challenge in consequence, and as he had long hoped and prayed.

Glory Won at Yorktown

The day that Alexander Hamilton had long awaited and dreamed about for so long finally became a reality on October 14, 1781. At long last, Lieutenant Colonel Hamilton was now at the head of his own crack infantry command of Lafayette's light division at the most crucial phase of the most important battle of the war. The allied forces of Washington and Rochambeau had marched south and all the way from their combined encampment in New York to entrap an entire British-Hessian-Loyalist army at Yorktown after the French fleet had gained naval superiority. Here, near the southern end of the Virginia Peninsula, Hamilton carefully planned the daring assault on strategic Redoubt Number Ten. Along with nearby Redoubt Number Nine, this key defensive position anchored the left flank of General Charles Cornwallis' defensive line, which surrounded the little Virginia tobacco port of Yorktown.

Sealing his fate, Cornwallis had made the great mistake of trusting the assurances of his superior, General Henry Clinton, which caused him to wait for the promised reinforcements from New York City that never came. Therefore, Yorktown had been besieged by the united French-American Army and pounded by a massive array of artillery (more than one hundred fifty field pieces), including French siege guns. But to close the vise on Cornwallis during this classic European siege, Redoubt Number Ten and the adjacent Redoubt Number Nine must first be captured by infantry assault to seal the garrison's and Yorktown's fate. These two redoubts had to be overwhelmed for the completion of the second parallel of defenses ever closer to Cornwallis' main defensive line to force Cornwallis' surrender.

With saber in hand, and shouting encouragement while bullets whizzed by him, not long after the sun had set in the low-lying Virginia Tidewater, Hamilton led the bayonet charge on the strategic redoubt. He had decided to attack instead of waiting for sappers to clear away obstacles that protected the approach to Redoubt Number Ten. Hamilton correctly calculated that wasting any time for the sappers to complete their work would not only cost attackers' lives but also jeopardize the overall chances for success in this attack over deadly open ground.

Consequently, because of his tactical astuteness, Hamilton and his men overran this strategic point in only six minutes, after hand-to-hand combat in which the native West Indian had a number of close calls. Meanwhile, his old friend John Laurens led another infantry battalion, under Hamilton's overall direction, that simultaneously attacked into the rear of Redoubt Number Ten to seal the doom of the strategic position. Along withNumber Nine that was located around five hundred yards from Redoubt Number Ten that was captured by the French, Hamilton's capture of strategic Redoubt Number Ten played a large role in forcing Lord Cornwallis' to surrender his entire army.

At long last, Hamilton had won the battlefield glory that he had long sought after having become Washington's chief of staff, achieving an amazing success in the most important battle of the American Revolution: The crucial victory in the Virginia Tidewater that convinced London that this war could not be won. Today ironically, nothing remains of Hamilton's original Redoubt Number Ten, after having been eroded by more than two centuries of coastal rains and the relentless pounding of the York River's waves.

Because of the longtime focus on Hamilton's well-known contributions to America and in strengthening its government and economy after the war to lay the central foundation for the rise of a superpower by the twentieth century, the young man's most important role during the war has been the most overlooked and unappreciated for generations: Alexander Hamilton's longtime vital role as Washington's chief of staff that cemented a remarkable symbiotic relationship and partnership that developed at headquarters, which was one of the forgotten keys that separated victor from loser during the American Revolution. Young Alexander Hamilton's Revolution was finally now over. He had been lucky to survive America's struggle for liberty, after so many close calls on numerous battlefields.

Conclusion

No one more fully appreciated Alexander Hamilton and his many achievements, both on and off the battlefield, toward achieving decisive victory for America than General George Washington. For more than four years, the close working relationship between Washington and Hamilton was a generally forgotten key partnership and dynamic leadership team that played an important role in winning America's ultimate victory in the end. Together these two men of divergent backgrounds created one of the most effective winning teams of the American Revolution. Indeed, "No person worked so closely with George Washington throughout the years of war and nation building than Alexander Hamilton, and this historic relationship saw Washington and Hamilton in accord on the great issues of their day."[1]

Most importantly, Hamilton was not only Washington's first and only chief of staff in the modern sense, but also the first chief of staff in the history of the United States military. As with his decision to make General Nathanael Greene his top lieutenant and then wisely assigning him to command the Southern theater of operations in 1780, Washington's decision to appoint Hamilton to his staff in a staff officer position that evolved into his chief of staff was a true "stroke of genius." Indeed, this decision paid immense dividends for most of the war, making him a more capable military commander on multiple levels. From the beginning, no one was better or more adept at translating Washington's ideas into practical plans for his top lieutenants to execute on the battlefield and in the art of diplomacy, especially with the French allies, than Hamilton. While serving under Washington's long shadow, Hamilton was one of the forgotten secrets of the Virginian's overall effectiveness as the army's commander for an extended period: Ironically, a too often overlooked success story of the American Revolution.[2]

Nevertheless, Hamilton's long list of significant wartime contributions (military, diplomatic, economic, and political) have been tarnished by his enemies, including some of America's most powerful men, including Founding Fathers, especially Jefferson. Creating long-lasting negative stereotypes rooted in the hatreds and jealousies (which began in wartime) that rose to the fore during postwar politics, these very personal and politically based assaults on Hamilton's character (including even the most ridiculous charge of his alleged un-Americanism) severely damaged the legacy of his many wartime accomplishments to his day. This was a character assassination from mostly self-serving and agenda-driven politicians who had never fought on the battlefield. They unleashed their venom on Hamilton, as if their political target had never made such a significant and disproportionate role in saving America's life during the revolution's darkest days.

What Hamilton's many personal enemies seemed to have forgotten were his efforts in successfully protecting Washington from removal from command and salvaging his increasingly maligned reputation, while serving as his "favorite aide-de-camp" and invaluable chief of staff year after year. Even more, what Hamilton's haters also conveniently overlooked were his extensive efforts toward the creation of a strong, professional military to replace the weak militia-based system that almost early caused America's demise in the war years, including the establishment of a military academy (West Point). These sturdy national foundations and core strengths later served America and the world well in facing the threats of Fascism and Communism in the twentieth century and Terrorism in the twenty-first century. In war and peace, the dynamic partnership of Washington and Hamilton (the most highly effective leadership team of the American Revolution) was truly one that helped to change the course of not only American but also world history.[3]

Like Washington and from beginning to end, Hamilton was a diehard nationalist, and they both saw stronger government as America's only solution in war and peace. This central foundation cemented their close bond during the war years and afterward, especially in Washington's presidency. As usual, Hamilton said it best: "We must secure our union on solid foundations." Along with fellow nationalist Washington who never lost his faith in the promise of America, he was one of the leading advocates for the scrapping of the weak Articles of Confederation that had only helped to pave the way to the young republic's ruin. Therefore, Hamilton played a vital role in convincing Washington to come out of retirement to lead the Constitutional Convention to end of political folly of the Articles of Confederation and then become the first president of the United States of America in order to unify a divided nation and its squabbling politicians, when the infant republic lay on the verge of dissolution From beginning to end, few people were more of a truly diehard American and nationalistic than this gifted immigrant from the Caribbean, who was criticized by being un-American. This sad legacy was one of the great ironies in American history.

Unfortunately, Hamilton had a special talent for making enemies in extremely high places. Therefore, during an intensive political war that he could not win, the personal attacks of the Anti-Federalists on Hamilton's reputation left him exhausted and depressed, especially after Washington's sudden death at Mount Vernon in December 1799: the old winning team and partnership that had functioned so well from 1777 to 1781 was no more. An increasingly disillusioned Hamilton wondered at the bitter irony of being so widely denounced by his fellow Americans, after having long faithfully served America's best interests during the infant nation's struggle for life. Nevertheless, Hamilton found himself under almost greater pressure and assault on American soil than even the men of Lord Charles Cornwallis' Army at Yorktown in October 1781. His political and personal foes succeeded in transforming this remarkable man of boundless faith and hope in the greatness of America's future into a tormented soul.

Given his long list of military accomplishments from Trenton to Yorktown and especially as Washington's invaluable chief of staff, Hamilton was haunted by dark feelings of a certain sense of betrayal by his fellow Americans. Struck by the nagging paradox that seemed almost as cruelly unfair as John Laurens' needless death in an ill-advised charge in a remote South Carolina backwater during a late August 1782 skirmish of no importance whatsoever, Hamilton felt persecuted by the cycle of injustices and haunting paradoxes stemming from this "base world." Therefore, a world-weary Hamilton lamented without exaggeration only two years before he was fatally cut down by a pistol shot fired by Aaron Burr: "Mine is an odd destiny. Perhaps no man in the U[nited] States has sacrificed or done more for the present Constitution than myself. . . . Yet I have the murmur of its friends no less than the curses of its foes. What can I do better than withdraw from the scene? Every day proves to me more and more that this American world was not made for me."[4]

Ironically, these were almost the identical haunting words—but for different reasons—that he had penned to his best friend John Laurens in a January 8, 1780, letter: "I feel I am not fit for this terrestreal Country."[5] Then, barely nine months later for only trying to do what was right for preserving America's life by emphasizing the gross failures of Congress partly as an attempt to save the Continental Army, Hamilton also confided to Laurens how "you are almost detested [as much as I] as an accomplice with the administration."[6] In the same September 12, 1780, letter, Hamilton wrote that "I hate the world," in part because of so many personal and political enemies, military and civilian, that he had gained only because he had always put America's interests first and had succeeded in so many endeavors on America's behalf.[7]

On February 13, 1783, a frustrated Hamilton wrote another candid letter to Washington, as though he was still serving as the general's chief of staff on an active campaign or a tented encampment: "Flattering myself that your knowledge of me will induce you to receive my observations I make . . . in regard to the public good [therefore] I take the liberty to suggest my ideas to you on some matters of delicacy and importance . . . there has not been a period of the war which called more for wisdom and decision for Congress. Unfortunately for us we are a body not governed by reason or forthright[ness] but by circumstances."[8]

Hamilton's gloomy realization that America was not for him was only tragically reinforced when his beloved first son, nineteen-year-old Philip Hamilton, was killed in a needless duel that resulted from attacks on his father's maligned reputation: "the most afflicting [blow] of my life," wrote the grieving father, who had received a mortal wound to his soul. Hamilton had advised him not to fire a shot at his lawyer opponent, whose sharp tongue had so viciously lashed at his father's character without mercy. A graduate of Columbia College (King's College) where his father had been educated, Philip was doomed to an ill fate that abruptly ended a most promising life. Philip had been in the womb of his young wife Betsey when Hamilton had risked his life in leading the daring charge that overwhelmed Redoubt Number Ten at Yorktown. What tormented Alexander Hamilton the most was the nagging thought that Philip was fatally wounded in a duel to defend his father's good name against outrageous slander. When the teenage Philip, who had been named after his mother's father General Philip Schuyler, died shortly after a dueling pistol's bullet cut him down on November 23, 1801, at Weehawken, New Jersey, his father's once unbreakable spirit suffered a severe blow with the handsome young man's death. Hamilton was devastated by the tragic loss of his son's life that resulted in a traumatic blow from which he never recovered, experiencing the most grievous pain that any parent could feel in losing his beloved child.

Therefore, Hamilton was never the same after the tragic death of his dark-haired son who was so promising and so much like his father. Only three years later, Hamilton himself died in the same tragic manner and for the same hollow reasons as his beloved "Little Phil," while standing on the same fatal patch of dueling ground on New Jersey soil. Equally ironic, the soil of New Jersey, the so-called "crossroads of the revolution," was where Hamilton had so often earlier risked his life and led his New York "Provincial Company of Artillery" with distinction during Washington's surprising winter victories at Trenton and Princeton, where enemy bullets and cannonballs had miraculously failed to strike him. Before the final showdown at Yorktown, Hamilton had won his greatest military fame on battlefields in the Garden State, including at Monmouth Court House in the summer of 1778.[9]

If only Hamilton had acted on his best personal instincts to depart the United States for a new life in his native Caribbean, then such a decision would have saved him from the fatal duel that ended his life before age fifty. In the cruelest paradox, Hamilton's worst foreboding about meeting a tragic end on American soil—although not on a battlefield where everlasting glory would have been forthcoming—was ultimately fulfilled, following his son's tragic demise at age nineteen. As he had long feared, it was this perplexing "American world" that led to the untimely tragic deaths of both father and son on Weehawken's fatal dueling grounds. In a strange way, it was what this fractious republic had become, as distinct from his lofty, idealized virtuous vision of a model republic based on Age of Enlightenment ideologies, which was ultimately as much responsible for Alexander Hamilton's death as the well-aimed shot from a former member of Washington's staff.

All in all, Hamilton's rise in America had been meteoric, making his fall at Weehawken even more tragic. In the heady glow of his Yorktown success in mid-October 1781 that won the army's admiration and America's gratitude, Hamilton never forgot how he had ridden back to Betsey, when she was expecting their first child, Philip (born on January 22, 1782). It was the happiest and most fulfilling time of his young life when only the brightest of futures beckoned. A hopeful immigrant who had migrated to America and to a strange land with no money in his pocket or hardly knowing a soul, he had beaten the odds and defied all probability by accomplishing far more than anyone had imagined possible on his own abilities.

Hamilton had fulfilled his loftiest ambitions, becoming an authentic American war hero who had won glory not only at Yorktown but also on the battlefields of 1776–1778. With a high level of tactical skill and bravery, Hamilton had made a name for himself throughout the army as a resourceful battlefield commander, who rose to the challenge when the crisis was greatest.[10] But while his family life had become extremely satisfying after the war, he still grappled with the demons of the past. In a letter to his brother James

Hamilton, Jr., now living on the island of St. Thomas in the Caribbean, in June 1785, he asked almost pathetically: "what has become of our dear father? It is an age since I have heard" from him.[11]

Alexander Hamilton's postwar image as a Founding Father eventually earned him a permanent place in the American popular memory, but ironically at the high price of obscuring his crucial Revolutionary War contributions as Washington's brilliant chief of staff. Thanks to his efforts as the nation's first Secretary of the Treasury in Washington's Administration (because the Washington and Hamilton friendship and partnership were renewed after the infamous New Windsor, New York, incident on February 16, 1781) to promote the Constitution, a stronger centralized government, a more powerful military, and a modern financial system for boundless future growth, especially industrial, Hamilton played a leading role in creating the modern United States that rose to prominence on the world stage in the twentieth century.

In fact, like no other Founding Father, Hamilton was most responsible for setting the young American nation on the correct road to future superpower status. Nevertheless, Hamilton became the most tarnished Founding Father in no small part because he was Jefferson's eternal enemy. Indeed, the marble bust display of Hamilton at Monticello was little more than a display trophy of the crucifying Anti-Federals, who had waged their political warfare with no mercy.

But unlike so many others during the American Revolution, Hamilton never lost his faith in America and its bright, shining future: the dream of America that had lifted him up and gave him opportunities to excel. Many vivid memories of struggling for liberty beside his comrades never dissipated from his heart and mind as Hamilton grew older and wealthier after the war: crossing the ice-clogged Delaware River on a stormy December night and transporting his New York cannon safely across the river in the cold blackness; his New York artillery pieces roaring from the snowy heights that overlooked Trenton and punishing the Hessian garrison; helping to reverse the tide of the hard-fought battle at Monmouth by helping to stem a rout and then leading counterattacks; and orchestrating the daring nighttime assault that overwhelmed Redoubt Number Ten on October 14, 1781, to ensure the surrender of an entire British-Hessian-Loyalist Army during America's most decisive victory. No matter what happened to him in life, Hamilton most of all cherished the fond memories of what he had accomplished in leading his brave light infantrymen onward in capturing Redoubt Number Ten that changed the course of not only American history but also world history.

Hamilton's outspokenness and directness in speaking his mind continued to make him new enemies in the years after the war. This situation was just a continuation of when he had served as the boyish-looking Washington's chief of staff and principal protector of the general's much-derided reputation, when his outspokenness—especially against the incompetence of an ineffective Congress that had long caused the army so much suffering and deaths—earned him countless enemies in high places, including leading generals and politicians. But Hamilton had managed to escape their wrath because he was Washington's right-hand-man.

However, Hamilton became more vulnerable after Washington ended his service as a two-term president. His political foes fully exploited the opportunity when Hamilton's criticisms about Vice President Aaron Burr's lack of character and morality were printed in newspapers. Hamilton refused to take back anything that he said, because he sincerely believed it was true, which was the case. He, therefore, accepted Burr's challenge to settle their differences in an affair of honor. On the early morning of July 11, 1804, on the Hudson's west bank at Weehawken, Bergen County, New Jersey, Hamilton faced Vice President Burr. For Hamilton, this confrontation was still another issue of personal honor as during the war years. Ironically, Burr had briefly served as Washington's aide-de-camp, but these once-close bonds of a revolutionary brotherhood were no more by this time. As on the hard-fought fields of Trenton, Princeton, and Monmouth in New Jersey from 1776 to 1778, Hamilton was no stranger in facing death or the possibility of shortly meeting his Maker from hostile fire.

Before meeting Burr with a matching pair of smoothbore flintlock pistols, Hamilton wrote that he was morally and philosophically opposed to dueling to settle personal differences. Therefore, he was determined to freely "expose [his] own life" instead of "taking the life of another" human being, even a bitter enemy. Nevertheless, as he had been Washington's "Little Lion" in serving at headquarters and on the battlefield, Hamilton faced Burr with his usual courage on the dueling grounds just outside Philadelphia at exceptionally close range. As previously planned and relying on the power of reason rather than passion that was the very cornerstone of his being since before the American Revolution, Hamilton wasted his first shot in the reasonable gentleman's expectation that Burr would do the same to settle this matter of honor with customary dignity to satisfy both parties.

But still recalling Hamilton's scathing testimony against his beloved commander General Charles Lee about his performance at the battle of Monmouth

Court House during the general's court martial proceedings in 1778, Burr had other ideas about the precise definition of honor. Unlike Hamilton, therefore, he allowed his strong passion to overrule his reason, violating the native West Indian's most sacred personal principle. The many varied successes of Hamilton's past—especially in preserving Washington's reputation and position—had now come back to haunt him at this moment, when he found himself suddenly staring down the barrel of Burr's dueling pistol. Unlike Hamilton, Burr was not about to forget and forgive. Clearly, there was no reasonable settlement of differences between gentlemen as Hamilton anticipated and fully expected. Hamilton might now have regretted having lost his former cynicism that had served him so well during the American Revolution.

No one knows Hamilton's last thoughts when he saw Burr taking careful aim at him just before he fired his fatal shot which was the final betrayal of his misplaced faith in his fellow human beings. Consequently, perhaps a look of astonishment must have appeared on Hamilton's mature but still handsome face, because of the shattering of his life's last illusion when Burr squeezed the trigger. But immediately before he was hit by Burr's .54 caliber bullet, Hamilton might have became stoically reconciled to his tragic fate which was the bitterest of ironies: dying needlessly like his best friend John Laurens in a meaningless South Carolina skirmish and his own promising son in a meaningless duel of honor in which there was no real honor—two of America's best and brightest. Just before he was struck by Burr's lead bullet, then perhaps Hamilton merely accepted the haunting realization that it seemed as if the lives of America's most virtuous men, literally the best and brightest, had to end tragically. If so, then he might have understood how he now somehow had to suffer the same sad fate as Laurens and his own son.

After having served for years with distinction as Washington's chief of staff and on America's battlefield's from New York to Virginia, Hamilton died at age forty-seven with a measure of peace for all that he had accomplished for America and Washington on July 12, 1804. He left behind a grieving widow and their children. Ironically, after having had so many close calls during the war, he had received his fatal wound from an England-made weapon in peacetime.

Ironically, few people, if any, at the time remembered that he had played leading roles in saving Washington's position as commander-in-chief or had served as chief of staff for years. In the end, one of America's brightest shining lights was extinguished on a day that was as hot as on his native Nevis and St. Croix so far away. His final journey in a coffin, topped with his hat and sword, of mahogany (a beautiful wood long exported from his native West Indies) was a slow funeral procession to the south side of the graveyard of Trinity Church on Broadway in Lower Manhattan, New York City, to be buried near his beloved son Philip on July 14, 1804.

Before he had breathed his last in New York City, Hamilton might have thought back of when he had so proudly worn an officer's blue uniform as a republican soldier during a sacred struggle for an infant nation's freedom: Washington's chief of staff when he worked year after year as part of a highly effective leadership team with America's "father" in a special relationship of vital importance when the dignified commander-in-chief was "an Aegis very essential to me" wrote Hamilton; helping to save the day by rallying panic-stricken troops under a blazing New Jersey sun at Monmouth; providing years of wise advice (military, political, logistical, diplomatic, and economic) to America's top civilian and military leaders, especially Washington; enduring Morristown's and Valley Forge's harshest winters that he had ever experienced because he had recently immigrated from the Caribbean; the close friendships and camaraderie between him and his fellow esteemed members of Washington's little "family" of promising young officers; raising the spirits of Washington and his staff members with his sense of humor and unsurpassed wit during the revolution's darkest days; embracing the idealistic promise of America with all his heart and soul; doing all in his power—mental, moral, and physical—so that America ultimately prevailed during its desperate struggle for life; never losing his faith in the great republican dream and egalitarian vision of a brighter future not only for the American people, but also for all mankind; the breathtaking sight, illuminated by the yellow-red flashes of musketry, the flowing "Stars and Stripes" planted atop Redoubt Number Ten to signify one of the war's most important victories; and the personal satisfaction in all that he had accomplished for Washington and in having played so many key roles during America's struggle for survival.

Ironically, when Hamilton was fatally cut down by the pistol shot fired by Burr, no Founding Father (after Washington) had accomplished more both on and off the battlefield to ensure America's ultimate victory than the one who had the most inauspicious start in life and the most difficult life from beginning to end. Nevertheless, he was still looked upon by many Americans, especially his many enemies, as nothing more than a detested "foreigner" who was undeserving of the revered name of American. But without Hamilton and his contributions, there might be no America today. Indeed, when Hamilton died in New York City, his faith of a bright future for America did not die with him, because he left behind enduring political, military, and economic legacies that lived on: His ever-lasting gifts to America and generations of Americans, including those yet unborn.[12]

Hamilton had left his permanent mark on the peoples' republic in the most significant and fundamental ways. America would never be the same again, thanks to Hamilton's many invaluable contributions in war and peace. From beginning to end, he was a shining star and innovative, bold freethinker, who was well ahead of his time. As demonstrated by his actions and words not long after his arrival on America's shores, this hopeful, young immigrant from the West Indies was actually more truly American than most Americans, when he was shot down without mercy by Burr.

With his trademark open-minded thinking unencumbered by ancient rules and prejudices (regional or national), Hamilton stood on moral principle to go against conventional and traditional thought with his most radical proposal in conjunction with John Laurens: boldly advocating the use of black troops to fight for America in order to replenish the army's limited manpower in the South more than a century and a half before African Americans were officially incorporated into an integrated United States military in the post-World War Two period. Hamilton's early promotion of black soldiers and his strong abolitionist views, including as a founder of the New York Manumission Society after the war, did not sit well with the aristocratic Virginia elite, especially slave-owners.

From the obscure depths of a lowly exile on a remote Caribbean island—a mere speck in a turquoise sea—without a bright future and from a broken family, Hamilton's meteoric rise on American soil as a self-made man and visionary was nothing short of miraculous. Against all odds, Hamilton persevered through the hard times and setbacks not of his own making to come out a better man and an authentic American war hero, while greatly benefitting America in war and peace to ensure that the republic became a stronger nation.

But no single wartime role was more important to America's fortunes than that of Washington's brilliant chief of staff and chief adviser, when he forged a truly "unbeatable" team with the commander-in-chief. The intellectual and assiduous Hamilton was the model chief of staff, establishing a template for the modern chief of staff in America's military establishment today. As the brilliant Louis-Alexandre Berthier (who had served with French forces at Yorktown and Hamilton might have talked to him) was to Napoleon as a longtime chief of staff, so Hamilton was the same guiding force to Washington year after year. Napoleon wisely understood the supreme importance of a chief of staff that was performed so well by Berthier (he became one of Napoleon's twenty-six marshals), and Washington likewise benefited greatly from Hamilton's multi-faceted contributions in his capacity. In the end, it was no accident or coincidence that Napoleon lost at Waterloo because he was without Berthier. In still another strange twist of fate, Berthier was destined to die as tragically and prematurely like Hamilton, falling from a building onto a cobblestone street under mysterious circumstances.

On multiple levels, no Founding Father other than Washington made more significant wartime contributions to American victory from 1776 to 1781 than one of the youngest and brightest shining stars of the Continental Army. Hamilton's arrival in the colonies in 1773 and not long before the American Revolution's beginning was still another sign from above that America's cause was indeed blessed by a kind "Providence [which] is for some wise purpose," as Washington believed to his dying day.[13]

Because he knew this undeniable truth better than anyone else, Washington paid a rare tribute, although considerably understated by him, to Hamilton: "There are few men to be found, of his age, who has a more general knowledge than he possesses; and none, whose soul is more firmly engaged in the cause, or who exceeds him in probity and sterling virtue."[14] Unsurprisingly, Washington forgot to mention how in the course of Hamilton's intelligence gathering and backdoor maneuvering to save the position of General Washington, he changed the course of not only the American Revolution but also American history.[15]

In the end, perhaps Colonel Timothy Pickering, Washington's trusty adjutant, said it best: "During the long series of years, in war and peace, Washington enjoyed the advantages of Hamilton's eminent talents, integrity and felicity, and these qualities fixed [Hamilton forever] in [Washington's] confidence to the last hour of his life."[16] Nevertheless, after the war, "few men would remember redoubt 10" and how it fell on the night of October 14, 1871, and the supreme importance of its capture by Hamilton, however.[17]

In a significant understatement, Washington was unable to find exactly the right words to fully convey what Hamilton truly meant to him from 1777 to 1781, while performing as his sage chief of staff, who had seemingly always bestowed wise advice and invaluable council, until the commander-in-chief became heavily, if not utterly, dependent on the young man. Even if Washington had found the proper words to describe the importance of Hamilton's multiple roles over such a lengthy period during the turning point moments of the American Revolution, most Americans of the day (and including today) simply would not have believed the truth about how such a young officer born of humble origins in the West Indies could have possibly so extensively benefitted one of the wealthiest men in America in so many ways year after year by his sparkling brilliance.

However, Washington's actions spoke louder than his words. Continuing the close teamwork of a dynamic partnership that had been cemented during the war years, Washington chose Hamilton as his Secretary of the Treasury when he became the first president of the United States. Even more, Hamilton was most responsible for first convincing a reluctant Washington come out of retirement at Mount Vernon to unite a badly splintered nation to serve as the nation's first president, including in a second term. Thereafter, the team of Washington and Hamilton was reunited in the first presidency, continuing a remarkable success story from beginning to end: one of the most important alliances and partnerships of not only the American Revolution and the early republic, but also in American history. Without the timely union of these two remarkable men and their close working relationship, the revolution might not have been won, and a long life for the American republic would not have been ensured after the war.

Clearly, Washington's heavy dependence on Hamilton as his capable chief of staff, close confidant, and adviser throughout the war years was a habit that the first president faithfully continued long after the American Revolution and fortunately for the fate of America. Hamilton wrote Washington's speeches, including his famous Farewell Address, as if the two men still wore blue Continental uniforms at headquarters, when it had seemed that the great dream of America was doomed to an early death. As during the war years at headquarters, Hamilton became the first president's chief political advisor, continuing to bestow sage advice and insight. All the while, Washington benefitted immensely from the contributions of his most brilliant adviser, who was truly King Solomon–like in wisdom, and the main driving force of his staff in war and peace.

As America's first Secretary of the Treasury, Hamilton served as the chief architect of the American banking system and stronger national government to lay the central foundation for today's United States of America. But of course, none of these successes were possible had not Washington and Hamilton first evolved into a highly successful team first in wartime during the lengthy struggle to ensure the Continental army's survival, but was the same as the republic's survival. Quite simply, the most effective high-level partnership and leadership team during the Revolutionary War became the key collaboration that led to the creation of the Constitution and a "more perfect Union" in the end: during both of these most crucial periods in the life of the United States, no one played a greater or more important role as Washington's vital supporter, advisor, confidant, and friend than Hamilton. Clearly, few individuals have made so many important contributions in the history of any nation.

One modern historian made the appropriate connection between Hamilton's key position in Washington's Administration, that was only a continuation of his all-important wartime role by Washington's side during the darkest days of the revolution, and his disproportionate contributions that played key roles in saving Washington, the army, and the infant republic from 1777 to 1781: "this supremely confidant and extraordinarily able young man threatened to dominate the executive and to emerge as a kind of Prime Minister, with Washington as a kind of limited constitutional" head.[18]

But while the native West Indian's accomplishments were forgotten in time by generations of Americans who were given the wrong view of Hamilton by educators, Hamilton's wife Betsey (Elizabeth Schuler Hamilton), who lost her husband and son to the madness of dueling for the sake of society's distorted views of the meaning of honor, perhaps said it best when she correctly informed one of his political opponents about one of her husband's most enduring legacies, not long after he died in New York City thirty-six hours after having been shot: "Never forget that my husband *made* your government" of the United States of America. Hamilton's final words to his wife were some of the most heartfelt that he had ever written, because he wished for "the sweet hope of meeting you in a better world. Adieu, best of wives and best of Women. Embrace all my darling Children for me."[19] For Hamilton, that better world existed at some place that he had never known in his eventful life.

In some strange, inexplicable cosmic equation that was a balancing of sorts, it was almost as if Hamilton's life had been ordained to meet a tragic end precisely because he was blessed with so many exceptional gifts possessed in total by so few others. As he sincerely lamented with some anguish as the years and the day's ever-changing values passed by him, Hamilton was indeed not made for this world. In the end, Hamilton's remarkable life was like a Greek Tragedy of the kind that he knew so well from his classical education, but also an American tragedy for America's most gifted and brilliant Founding Father.

But his legions of detractors could never take away Hamilton's lengthy list of achievements on and off the battlefield, and what he accomplished for America.

Emphasizing exactly why he had risked his life on so many fields of strife across America, Hamilton penned these late October 1787 words in imploring the American people to adopt the proposed United States Constitution because what was at stake was nothing less than "the fate of an empire in many respects, the most interesting in the world [and if not adopted then] deserve to be considered as the general misfortune of mankind."[20]

From early 1777 to early 1781, young Lieutenant Colonel Alexander Hamilton, only a few years removed from a miserable dead end in his native West Indies, was Washington's right hand man, closest confidant, and his irrepressible chief of staff, whose vital wartime roles on so many levels of supreme importance have been long unappreciated even today in the nation that he played such a large role in creating in war and peace.

And no list of Hamilton contributions were more important than when serving as Washington's chief of staff. It has been long thought that Napoleon had been the first commander to employ a chief of staff in the modern sense, but this was not the case. What young Hamilton accomplished from early 1777 to early 1781 was an achievement that was unprecedented in the annals of military history, because he served as the first chief of staff in the modern sense. Ironically, this remarkable achievement and crucial role—second only to General George Washington's role in terms of overall importance—has been the one most overlooked by historians to this day.

A key player in the success of Napoleon's campaigns across Europe, the brilliant Berthier became the most celebrated chief of staff in history, casting a giant shadow over Hamilton's earlier role that was equally, if not more, brilliant. As America's first chief of staff in the modern sense, Hamilton set a remarkable historical precedent and an incredibly high bar for military leaders far into the future and even to this day. In the end, Alexander Hamilton became the very embodiment of the American dream and much more, demonstrating that anything was possible by someone who refused to be limited by artificial boundaries of class, wealth, and society.

About the Author

Phillip Thomas Tucker received his PhD in American history from St. Louis University in 1990. Tucker has authored many books, especially about the Revolutionary War and the Civil War. He has written about some of the most iconic personae and moments in American history, including the Skyhorse books *George Washington's Surprise Attack: A New Look at the Battle That Decided the Fate of America*, *Pickett's Charge: A New Look at Gettysburg's Final Attack*, and *Death at the Little Bighorn: A New Look at Custer, His Tactics, and the Tragic Decisions Made at the Last Stand*. He lives near Washington, DC.

Notes

Chapter I

1. William F. Cissel, "Alexander Hamilton: The West Indian 'Founding Father'," July 2004, pp. 1–6, Christiansted National Historic Park, National Park Service, Christiansted, St. Croix; Ron Chernow, *Alexander Hamilton*, (New York: Penguin Books, 2004), pp. 8–28; John Ferling, *Jefferson and Hamilton, The Rivalry That Forged a Nation*, (New York: Bloomsbury Press, 2013), pp. 10–11; Lawrence S. Kaplan, *Alexander Hamilton, Ambivalent Anglophile*, (Wilmington, DE: Scholarly Resources, 2002), pp. 2–3; Jack Rakove, *Revolutionaries*, (New York: Mariner Books, 2010), pp. 401–402; Milton Lomask, *Odd Destiny, A Life of Alexander Hamilton*, (New York: Farrar, Straus and Giroux, 1969), pp. 3–4, 6, 7; John C. Miller, *Alexander Hamilton, Portrait in Paradox*, (New York: HarperCollins Publishers, 1959), pp. 3–4; John F. Roche, *Alexander Hamilton, Illustrious Americans*, (Morristown: Silver Burdett Company, 1967), pp. 9–10; Willard Sterne Randall, *Alexander Hamilton*, (New York: HarperCollins Publishers, Inc., 2003), pp. 17–18; Iain Zaczek, The Book of Scottish Clans, (London: Cico Books, 2001), p. 53; A. J. Langguth, *Patriots, The Men Who Started the American Revolution*, (New York: Simon and Schuster, 1988), p. 124.
2. Knott and Williams, *Washington and Hamilton*, p. 20; Chernow, *Alexander Hamilton*, pp. 17, 20–21; Ferling, *Jefferson and Hamilton*, pp. 10–11; Joyce Gordon, *Nevis, Queen of the Caribbean*, (New York: MacMillan Publishers, Ltd., 1990), pp. 12–15, 28–29, 43; Photograph, "Birthplace of Hamilton, Island of Nevis, B.W.I," Keystone View Company, Author's Collection; Lomask, *Odd Destiny*, pp. 3–4, 6; Miller, *Alexander Hamilton*, pp. 3–4.
3. Ferling, *Jefferson and Hamilton*, pp. 10–11; Kaplan, *Alexander Hamilton*, p. 3; Chernow, *Alexander Hamilton*, pp. 10–13, 16–17, 19, 139; Knott and Williams, *Washington and Hamilton*, p. 20; Langguth, *Patriots*, p. 124; Miller, *Alexander Hamilton*, p. 4; Rakove, *Revolutionaries*, pp. 401–402; Randall, *Alexander Hamilton*, p. 7; Lomask, *Odd Destiny*, pp. 4, 7.
4. Gordon, *Nevis*, pp. 1–43; Brian, *St. Kitts, Cradle of the Caribbean*, (New York: MacMillan Publishers, Ltd., 1989), pp. 1–13; Chernow, *Alexander Hamilton*, pp. 4, 7, 11–12, 16–17, 21; Ferling, *Jefferson and Hamilton*, pp. 10–11; Lomask, *Odd Destiny*, p. 4; Miller, *Alexander Hamilton*, p. 4; Rakove, *Revolutionaries*, p. 401.
5. Gordon, *Nevis*, pp. 4–5, 22–25; Chernow, *Alexander Hamilton*, pp. 4, 6, 8, 19, 23; Randall, *Alexander Hamilton*, p. 8; Lomask, *Odd Destiny*, pp. 5–6.

6.   Cissel, "Alexander Hamilton: The West Indian 'Founding Father'," p. 6, NPS; Chernow, *Alexander Hamilton*, pp. 7, 9–10, 16–17, 19, 22–24; Ferling, *Jefferson and Hamilton*, p. 14; Mary-Jo Kline, editor, *Alexander Hamilton, A Biography in His Own Words*, volume 1, (New York: Newsweek, 1973), p.15; Randall, *Alexander Hamilton*, p. 8; Miller, *Alexander Hamilton*, pp. 3–5; *Fodor's U.S. & British Virgin Islands*, (New York: Random House, 2010), pp. 135–139; Rakove, *Revolutionaries*, p. 401; Knott and Williams, Washington and Hamilton, pp. 20–21; Lomask, *Odd Destiny*, pp. 3–4, 7; Randall, *Alexander Hamilton*, p. 20; Langguth, *Patriots*, p. 124; Andrew Jackson O'Shaughnessy, *An Empire Divided, The American Revolution and the British Caribbean*, (Philadelphia: University of Pennsylvania Press, 2000), pp. 213–216.

7.   Chernow, *Alexander Hamilton*, pp. 24–26; Ferling, *Jefferson and Hamilton*, p. 15; Knott and Williams, *Washington and Hamilton*, pp. 21–22; National Park Service Brochure, Christiansted, Alexander Hamilton's Christiansted, Christiansted National Historic Site, National Park Service, United States Department of the Interior; Lomask, *Odd Destiny*, p. 7; Eric Burns, *Virtue, Valor, & Vanity, the Founding Fathers and the Pursuit of Fame*, (New York: Arcade Publishing, 2007), p. 46; Chernow, *Alexander Hamilton*, pp. 10–12, 16–22; Randall, *Alexander Hamilton*, pp. 7, 9.

8.   Lomask, *Odd Destiny*, p. 61; Chernow, *Alexander Hamilton*, pp. 29–31; Miller, *Alexander Hamilton*, p. 5.

9.   Chernow, *Alexander Hamilton*, p. 27; Miller, *Alexander Hamilton*, p. 4.

10.   Chernow, *Alexander Hamilton*, pp. 30–31, 33–38; Rakove, *Revolutionaries*, p. 402; Lomask, *Odd Destiny*, p. 7; Miller, *Alexander Hamilton*, pp. 3–5; Kline, ed., *Alexander Hamilton*, pp. 15, 17–23, 34–35; Randall, *Alexander Hamilton*, pp. 7, 20, 26–31, 33; Arthur Lefkowitz, *George Washington's Indispensable Men, The 32 Aides-de-Camp Who Helped Win American Independence*, (Mechanicsburg, PA: Stackpole Books, 2003), p. 109.

11.   Theodore Roosevelt, *New York*, (Delray Beach: Levenger Press, 2004), pp. 91–93; Ferling, *Jefferson and Washington*, pp. 10–11, 36; Francis Mulraney, "Hercules Mulligan—the Irish-born tailor and spy who saved Washington twice," IrishCentral, July 20, 2016; Rakove, *Revolutionaries*, pp. 401–402; Chernow, *Alexander Hamilton*, pp. 12–13, 34–51, 55–56; Ferling, *Jefferson and Hamilton*, pp. 15–16, 25–26; National Park Service Brochure, Christiansted: Alexander Hamilton's Christiansted, Christiansted National Historical Site, National Park Service, United States Department of the Interior; Miller, *Hamilton*, pp. 3, 5, 7–14; Kline, ed., *Alexander Hamilton*, p. 38; Mark Mayo Boatner, III, *Encyclopedia of the American Revolution*, (New York: David McKay Company, Inc., 1966), p. 477; Marcia L. Barnes, "The Son of Liberty from Islay," The Glasgow Islay Association, Glasgow, Scotland; Paul Martin, "He saved George Washington's Life . . . twice!," FoxNews.com, July 4, 2002; Randall, *Alexander Hamilton*, pp. 6–23, 34–37, 40–44, 46–47, 49–50, 65, 67, 77–79; Knott and Williams, *Washington and Hamilton*, pp. 24–31.

12.   Miller, *Alexander Hamilton*, pp. 93–94.

13.   Chernow, *Alexander Hamilton*, pp. 30–31; Kaplan, *Alexander Hamilton*, p. 23.

14.   Mary-Jo Kline, *Alexander Hamilton*, p. 15; Martin, "He saved George Washington's Life . . . twice!," FoxNews.com, July 4, 2002; Randall, *Alexander Hamilton*, p. 106.

15.   Chernow, *Alexander Hamilton*, pp. 49, 57–61, 63–64, 66–67, 70–72; Ferling, *Jefferson and Hamilton*, pp. 36–40; David Silbey, "Alexander Hamilton, Soldier," *Military History Quarterly*, (Spring 2017), p. 40; Justin Rohrlich, "Secrets of Alexander Hamilton's Powder

Horn Revealed," Minyanville Media, Inc., June 10, 2010; Phillip Thomas Tucker, *How the Irish Won the American Revolution, A New Look at the Forgotten Heroes of America's War of Independence*, (New York: Skyhorse Publishers, 2015), pp. 205–207; Knott and Williams, *Washington and Hamilton*, pp. 56–58; Rakove, *Revolutionaries*, p. 402; Shawn Marsh, "Powder horn that's believed to have been owned by Alexander Hamilton goes up for Auction," *Associated Press*, January 11, 2016; Randall, *Alexander Hamilton*, pp. 46–47, 79, 81, 87, 97–99; Alfred Hoyt Bill, *The Campaign of Princeton 1776–1777*, (Princeton: Princeton University Press, 1975), p. 50; Miller, *Alexander Hamilton*, p. 20; Martin, "He saved George Washington's Life . . . twice!," FoxNews.com, July 4, 2002; Kline, ed., *Alexander Hamilton*, pp. 24–30, 40–41, 69–70.

16. Knott and Williams, *Washington and Hamilton*, p. 71; Chernow, *Alexander Hamilton*, pp. 44–45, 58–61, 72; Ferling, *Jefferson and Hamilton*, pp. 38–40; Kaplan, *Alexander Hamilton*, pp. 21, 23–24; Silbey, "Alexander Hamilton, Soldier," *MHQ*, p. 40; David R. Petriello, *Bacteria and Bayonets, The Impact of Disease in American Military History*, (Philadelphia: Casemate, 2016), p. 98.

17. Burns, *Virtue, Valor, & Vanity*, p. 63; Randall, *Alexander Hamilton*, p. 99.

18. Chernow, *Alexander Hamilton*, pp. 63, 72; Knott and Williams, *Washington and Hamilton*, p. 71; Miller, *Alexander Hamilton*, p. 20; Randall, *Alexander Hamilton*, p. 99.

19. Knott and Williams, *Washington and Hamilton*, p. 58; Chernow, *Alexander Hamilton*, pp. 72–73; Miller, *Alexander Hamilton*, p. 20; Kaplan, *Alexander Hamilton*, p. 24; Randall, *Alexander Hamilton*, p. 95.

20. Chernow, *Alexander Hamilton*, p. 73; Randall, *Alexander Hamilton*, pp. 99, 108; Martin, "He saved George Washington's Life . . . . twice!," FoxNews.com, July 43, 2002; Michael C. Harris, *Brandywine, A Military History of the Battle that Lost Philadelphia but Saved America*, (El Dorado Hills, CA: Savas Beatie, 2016), p. 49; Miller, *Alexander Hamilton*, p. 20.

21. Miller, *Alexander Hamilton*, p. 20; Chernow, *Alexander Hamilton*, p. 73; Silbey, "Alexander Hamilton, Soldier," *MHQ*, p. 40; Kline, ed., *Alexander Hamilton*, p. 49; Randall, *Alexander Hamilton*, p. 99, 106.

22. Kline, ed., *Alexander Hamilton*, p. 49.

23. Chernow, *Alexander Hamilton*, p. 73; Ferling, *Jefferson and Hamilton*, pp. 37–38; Silbey, "Alexander Hamilton," *MHQ*, p. 40; Kline, ed, *Alexander Hamilton*, p. 43; Randall, *Alexander Hamilton*, p. 106

24. Chernow, Alexander Hamilton, pp. 73–74; Randall, *Alexander Hamilton*, pp. 108–109.

25. Knott and Williams, *Washington and Hamilton*, p. 71; Kline, ed., *Alexander Hamilton*, p. 49.

26. Nathaniel Philbrick, *Valiant Ambition, George Washington, Benedict Arnold, and the Fate of the American Revolution*, (New York: Viking, 2016), pp. 9–13, 19; Joseph J. Ellis, *Revolutionary Summer*, (New York: Alfred A. Knopf, 2013), pp. 78, 84, 114–118; Knott and Williams, *Washington and Hamilton*, p. 73; Ferling, *Jefferson and Hamilton*, p. 62; Thomas Fleming, *Liberty!, The American Revolution*, (New York: Viking, 1997), pp. 181–182, 186–189, 194; Chernow, *Alexander Hamilton*, pp. 74–80; Randall, *Alexander Hamilton*, pp. 108, 110.

27. Chernow, *Alexander Hamilton*, pp. 74–80; Philbrick, *Valiant Ambition*, pp. 25, 27, 29; Miller, *Alexander Hamilton*, pp. 557–576; Roosevelt, *New York*, pp. 108–109; Ellis, *Revolutionary Summer*, pp. 148–149; Fleming, *Liberty!*, pp. 198–202.

28. Roosevelt, *New York*, pp. 108–109.

29. Robert Leckie, *George Washington's War, The Saga of the American Revolution*, (New York: HarperCollins Publishers, 1992), pp. 285–286; Chernow, *Alexander Hamilton*, pp. 80–82; Knott and Williams, *Washington and Hamilton*, p. 75; Ferling, *Jefferson and Hamilton*, pp. 62–63; Ellis, *Revolutionary Summer*, p. 152; Charles Bracelen Flood, *Rise, And Fight Again, Perilous Times Along the Road to Independence*, (New York: Dodd, Mead and Company, 1976), pp. 86–90; Benson John Lossing, *Pictorial Field-book of the Revolution*, (New York: Harper Brothers, 1850) vol. 1, p. 616; Randall, *Alexander Hamilton*, pp. 111–112; Gregory T. Edgar, *Campaign of 1776, The Road to Trenton*, (Bowie, MD: Heritage Books, 2008), pp. 232–237; Fleming, *Liberty!*, pp. 202–209.

30. Fleming, *Liberty!*, pp. 209–210.

31. Knott and Williams, *Washington and Hamilton*, pp. 77–78; Chernow, *Alexander Hamilton*, pp. 83–84; Randall, *Alexander Hamilton*, pp. 113–114; John F. Roche, *Alexander Hamilton*, (Morristown, NJ: Silver Burdett Company, 1967), p. 130; Bill, *The Campaign of Princeton*, p. 50; Steven M. Richman, *The Bridges of New Jersey, Portraits of Garden State Crossings*, (New Brunswick, NJ: Rutgers University Press, 2005), p. 35.

32. Kline, ed., *Alexander Hamilton*, p. 104.

33. Randall, *Alexander Hamilton*, p. 115.

34. Lomask, *Alexander Hamilton*, p. 8; Chernow, *Alexander Hamilton*, pp. 61, 83; Ferling, *Jefferson and Hamilton*, pp. 37–38, 61.

35. Chernow, *Alexander Hamilton*, pp. 61, 83–84; Ferling, *Jefferson and Hamilton*, pp. 37–38, 63; Bruce Chadwick, *George Washington's War, The Forging of a Revolutionary Leader and the American Presidency*, (Naperville, IL: Sourcebooks, Inc., 2005), p. 10; Randall, *Alexander Hamilton*, pp. 113–115; Phillip Thomas Tucker, *George Washington's Surprise Attack, A New Look at the Battle that Decided the Fate of America*, (New York: Skyhorse Publishing, 2014), pp. 1–3; W. W. H. Davis, "Washington on the West Bank of the Delaware, 1776," *The Pennsylvania Magazine of History and Biography*, vol. 4, no. 2, (1880), p. 146.

36. Chernow, *Alexander Hamilton*, p. 84; Ferling, *Jefferson and Hamilton*, pp. 37–38; Miller, *Alexander Hamilton*, pp. 3–7, 21; Randall, *Alexander Hamilton*, pp. 27, 116; Tucker, *George Washington's Surprise Attack*, pp.1–56.

37. Randall, *Alexander Hamilton*, p. 114; Chadwick, *George Washington's War*, p. 17; Ferling, *Jefferson and Washington*, pp. 37–38.

38. Chadwick, *George Washington's War*, p. 18; Tucker, *George Washington's Surprise Attack*, pp. 56–311; Randall, *Alexander Hamilton*, p. 117.

39. Tucker, *George Washington's Surprise Attack*, pp. 352–500.

40. O'Shaughnessy, *An Empire Divided*, pp. 213–216; Chernow, *Alexander Hamilton*, p. 84.

41. Chernow, *Alexander Hamilton*, pp. 84–85; Benjamin Tallmadge and F. A. Tallmadge, *Memoir of Colonel Benjamin Tallmadge*, (New York: Thomas Holman Printer, 1858), p. 17; Bill, *The Campaign of Princeton*, pp. 112–113; Michael Williams Craig, *General Edward Hand, Winter's Doctor*, (Lancaster, PA: Rock Ford Foundation, 1984), pp. 50–52; Knott and Williams, *Washington and Hamilton*, pp. 80–81; Randall, *Alexander Hamilton*, p. 118; Chadwick, *George Washington's War*, p. 29; Edgar, *Campaign of 1776*, p. 392–393; Leckie, *George Washington's War*, p. 329.

42. Leckie, *George Washington's War*, p. 329; Bill, *The Campaign of Princeton*, p. 113; Randall, *Alexander Hamilton*, pp. 59–60, 118.

43. Chadwick, *George Washington's War*, p. 31; Knott and Williams, *Washington and Hamilton*, p. 81; Ferling, *Jefferson and Hamilton*, pp. 37–38, 63.

44. Alexander Hamilton to George Washington, February 13, 1783, Alexander Hamilton Papers, Manuscripts and Archives Division, New York Public Library, New York, New York; Ferling, *Jefferson and Washington*, pp. 67–68.

45. Ferling, *Jefferson and Hamilton*, pp. 64–68; Tallmadge and Tallmadge, *Memoir of Colonel Benjamin Tallmadge*, p. 18; Silbey, "Alexander Hamilton, Soldier," *MHQ*, p. 42; Randall, *Alexander Hamilton*, pp. 114, 120; Chernow, *Alexander Hamilton*, p. 85; Miller, *Alexander Hamilton*, pp. 3–5, 21; Burns, *Valor, Virtue, & Vanity*, p. 46; Kaplan, *Alexander Hamilton*, p. 26; Kline, ed., *Alexander Hamilton*, p. 96; Rakove, *Revolutionaries*, p. 402; Mark Puls, *Henry Knox, Visionary General of the American Revolution*, (New York: Palgrave MacMillan, 2008), pp. 1–97; Alexander Rose, *Washington's Spies, The Story of America's First Spy Ring*, (New York: Bantam Books, 2007), p. 33; Knott and Williams, *Washington and Hamilton*, p. 82; Lefkowitz, *George Washington's Indispensible Men*, p. 107.

46. Chernow, *Alexander Hamilton*, p. 87; Ferling, *Jefferson and Hamilton*, p. 68; Kline, ed., *Alexander Hamilton*, p. 96; Boatner, *The Encyclopedia of the American Revolution*, p. 478; Knott and Williams, *Washington and Hamilton*, pp. 80–82.

47. Rakove, *Revolutionaries*, p. 402.

48. Ferling, *Jefferson and Hamilton*, p. 68; Miller, *Alexander Hamilton*, p. 21; Lefkowitz, *George Washington's Indispensible Men*, pp. 15, 107; Randall, *Alexander Hamilton*, p. 121.

Chapter II

1. Philbrick, *Valiant Ambition*, p. 103; Burns, *Virtue, Valor, & Vanity*, p. 46; Kaplan, *Alexander Hamilton*, p. 26; Chadwick *George Washington's War*, pp. 73–74; Morristown, New Jersey, Wikipedia; Alfred Hoyt Bill, *Valley Forge, The Making of An Army*, (New York: Harper & Brothers, 1952), p. 17; George F. Scheer and Hugh F. Rankin, *Rebels and Redcoats*, (New York: Mentor Books, 1959), p. 255; Harry M. Ward, *Charles Scott and the 'Spirit of '76',"* (Charlottesville: University of Virginia Press, 1988), p. 28; Lefkowitz, *George Washington's Indispensible Men*, pp. 110–111.

2. Ferling, *Jefferson and Hamilton*, pp. 68–69; Chadwick, *George Washington's War*, pp. 74–78; Morristown, New Jersey, Wikipedia; Lomask, *Alexander Hamilton*, pp. 10–13; Chernow, *Alexander Hamilton*, p. 86.

3. Chernow, *Alexander Hamilton*, pp. 12–14, 17, 85; Kahn, *Alexander Hamilton*, p. 26; Ferling, *Jefferson and Hamilton*, pp. 68–69; Chadwick, *George Washington's War*, pp. 78, 132, 138–140; Lomask, *Odd Destiny*, p. 39; Lefkowitz, *George Washington's Indispensible Men*, pp. 108, 111; Randall, *Alexander Hamilton*, p. 119; Bill, *Valley Forge*, p. 17; Robert K. Wright, *The Continental Army*, (Washington, DC: U. S. Government Printing Office, 1983), p. 114.

4. Lomask, *Odd Destiny*, pp. 4, 7; *The Sacred Heart Review*, Boston, MA, vol. 41, no. 6, (January 30, 1909); Scheer and Rankin, *Rebels and Redcoats*, pp. 254–255.

5. *The Sacred Heart Review*, vol. 41, no. 6, (January 30,1909); Lefkowitz, *George Washington's Indispensable Men*, p. 111.

6. Scheer and Rankin, *Rebels and Redcoats*, p. 255; Lefkowitz, *George Washington's Indispensible Men*, pp. 103–104.

7. Scheer and Rankin, *Rebels and Redcoats*, p. 255.

8. "LTC John Fitzgerald (–1799)–Find a Grave Memorial," www.findagrave.com; Chadwick, *George Washington's War*, p. 132; Tucker, *George Washington's Surprise Attack*, pp. 469, 474; Lefkowitz, *George Washington's Indispensible Men*, pp. 15, 28, 34–35, 53, 62–64, 104–106; Massey, *John Laurens and the American Revolution*, p. 80; Ferling, *Jefferson and Hamilton*, p. 68; Scheer and Rankin, *Rebels and Redcoats*, p. 255; Randall, *Alexander Hamilton*, p. 123; Donald A. Moran, "George Washington's Military Family," Liberty Tree Newsletter, (December 1998); Samuel Blachley Webb Papers, Yale University Library, Yale University, New Haven, CT; David Hackett Fischer, *Washington's Crossing*, (New York: Oxford University Press, 2004), p. 385.

9. Michael Cecere, *An Officer of Very Extraordinary Merit, Charles Porterfield and the American War for Independence*, (Bowie, MD: Heritage Books, 2004), pp. 30–31; Flood, *Rise, and Fight Again*, p. 85; Randall, *Alexander Hamilton*, pp. 126–127; Edgar, *Campaign of 1776*, pp. 207–208.

10. Rakove, *Revolutionaries*, pp. 402–403; Lomask, *Alexander Hamilton*, p. 46; Ferling, *Jefferson and Hamilton*, p. 69; Randall, *Alexander Hamilton*, p. 119.

11. Harrison Clark, *All Cloudless Glory, The Life of George Washington, From Youth to Yorktown*, (Washington, DC: Regnery Publishing, Inc., 1995), p. 240; Ferling, *Jefferson and Hamilton*, pp. 68–69; Moran, "George Washington's Military Family," LTN; Chernow, *Alexander Hamilton*, p. 89.

12. Rakove, *Revolutionaries*, pp. 402–403; Ferling, *Jefferson and Hamilton*, pp. 68–69.

13. Rakove, *Revolutionaries*, pp. 402–403, p. 403; Gregory D. Massey, *John Laurens and the American Revolution*, (Columbia: University of South Carolina Press, 2000), p. 80; Lefkowitz, *George Washington's Indispensable Men*, p. 18.

14. Clark, *All Cloudless Glory*, p. 241; Ferling, *Jefferson and Hamilton*, pp. 68–69.

15. Edward G. Lengel, editor, *This Glorious Struggle, George Washington's Revolutionary War Letters*, (New York: HarperCollins Publishers, 2007), p. 35.

16. Chernow, *Alexander Hamilton*, pp. 88–91; Ferling, *Jefferson and Hamilton*, pp. 68–69; Miller, *Alexander Hamilton*, pp. 3–5, 22, 67; Rod Gragg, *By the Hand of Providence*, (New York: Howard Books, 2011), p. 17; Lefkowitz, *George Washington's Indispensible Men*, pp. 25, 109–111; Moran, "George Washington's Military Family," LTN.

17. George Washington's March 12, 1777 Smallpox Inoculation Orders, Morristown, New Jersey, George Washington's Mount Vernon, Mount Vernon, Virginia; Chadwick, *George Washington's War*, pp. 89–96, 132; Ellis, *Revolutionary Summer*, p. 85.

18. Clark, *All Cloudless Glory*, p. 528; Chadwick, *George Washington's War*, p. 94; Scheer and Rankin, *Rebels and Redcoats*, p. 255; Lefkowitz, *George Washington's Indispensable Men*, pp. 34–35.

19. Moran, "George Washington's Military Family," LTN; Chadwick, *George Washington's War*, p. 99.

20. Gragg, *By the Hand of Providence*, p. 17; Chernow, *Alexander Hamilton*, pp. 30–31; Chadwick, *George Washington's War*, pp. 132–135, 137–138; Philip J. Schwartz, editor, *Slavery at the Home of George Washington*, (Mount Vernon: Mount Vernon Ladies' Association, 2001), p. 1.

21. Kaplan, *Alexander Hamilton*, pp. 26, 50; Chernow, *Alexander Hamilton*, pp. 85–86; Chadwick, *George Washington's War*, pp. 132–134, 137–138; Kline, ed., *Alexander Hamilton*, p. 49.

22. Chadwick, *George Washington's War*, pp. 134–135, 137–138; Chernow, *Alexander Hamilton*, p. 86.

23. Petriello, *Bacteria and Bayonets*, p. 104; Chadwick, *George Washington's War*, pp. 135, 137; Kaplan, *Alexander Hamilton*, p. 26.

24. Gragg, *By the Hand of Providence*, p. 17.

25. Randall, *Alexander Hamilton*, pp. 149,162; Chadwick, *George Washington's War*, pp. 78–79, 134–135, 137–138, 143; Miller, *Alexander Hamilton*, pp. 32–35.

26. Chadwick, *George Washington's War*, pp. 137–139; Stephen F. Knott, *Alexander Hamilton and the Persistence of Myth*, (Lawrence: University Press of Kansas, 2002), p. 225; Chernow, *Alexander Hamilton*, pp. 86–89; Ferling, *Jefferson and Hamilton*, pp. 68–69; Kline, ed., *Alexander Hamilton*, p. 96; Chief of Staff, Wikipedia; Miller, *Alexander Hamilton*, pp. 21–67.

27. Chadwick *George Washington's War*, p. 138; Paul Cartledge, *Alexander the Great*, (New York: Vintage Books, 2004), pp. 167–168; Chernow, *Alexander Hamilton*, pp. 90–91; Thomas Fleming, *Beat the Last Drum, The Siege of Yorktown 1781*, (New York: St. Martin's Press, 1963), p. 68

28. Chadwick, *George Washington's War*, pp. 137–140; Chernow, *Alexander Hamilton*, p. 88.

29. Chernow, *Alexander Hamilton*, pp. 88–90; Chadwick, *George Washington's War*, p. 138.

30. Lomask, *Alexander Hamilton*, p. 46.

31. Chernow, *Alexander Hamilton*, p. 90; Massey, *John Laurens and the American Revolution*, p. 80.

32. Schachner, *Aaron Burr*, pp. 35, 39; Ferling, *Jefferson and Hamilton*, pp. 67–69; Chernow, *Alexander Hamilton*, pp. 88–90; Knott and Williams, *Washington and Hamilton*, pp. vii-257.

33. Chernow, *Alexander Hamilton*, pp. 51, 89–90; Schachner, *Aaron Burr*, pp. 44–45; Ferling, *Jefferson and Hamilton*, pp. 68–69; Miller, ed., *Alexander Hamilton*, p. 67.

34. Alexander Hamilton to John Laurance, March 1–April 10, 1777, Alexander Hamilton Papers, Digital Edition, Editor, Harold C. Syrett, Charlottesville: University of Virginia Press, Rotunda, 2011.

35. Scheer and Rankin, *Rebels and Redcoats*, pp. 255–256.

36. David A. Clary, *Adopted Son, Washington, Lafayette, and the Friendship That Saved the Revolution*, (New York: Bantam Books, 2008), pp. 3, 9, 106–107; Chadwick, *George Washington's War*, p. 138; Leckie, *George Washington's War*, p. 343.

37. Knott and Williams, *Washington and Hamilton*, pp. 104–105; Chernow, *Alexander Hamilton*, pp. 44, 61, 68–69. 73–74, 85–90; Kline, ed., *Alexander Hamilton*, pp. 45–47; Kaplan, *Alexander Hamilton*, pp. 40–41.

38. Ferling, *Jefferson and Hamilton*, pp. 37–38; Kline, ed., *Alexander Hamilton*, pp. 46–47.

39. Kline, ed., *Alexander Hamilton*, pp. 45–48.

40. Ibid., pp. 47–48.

41. Ibid.

42. Ibid., pp. 47–48.

43. Chernow, *Alexander Hamilton*, pp. 90–91; Kaplan, *Alexander Hamilton*, pp. 40–43.

44. Roche, *Alexander Hamilton*, p. 131; Chernow, *Alexander Hamilton*, pp. 90–91.

45. Moran, "George Washington's Military Family," LTN; Chadwick, *George Washington's War*, p. 138; Lt. Col. Richard Kidder Meade, Valley Forge National Historical Park, Pennsylvania, Online Biography.

46. Massey, *John Laurens and the American Revolution*, p. 80; Lt. Col. Richard Kidder Meade, VFNHP, Online Biography; Lefkowitz, *George Washington's Indispensable Men*, pp. 8–9.

47. Chernow, *Alexander Hamilton*, p. 92; Lt. Col. Richard Kidder Meade, VFNHP.

48. Tench Tilghman, *Memoir of Lieutenant Colonel Tench Tilghman, Secretary And Aid to Appendix, Containing Revolutionary Journals and Letters, Hitherto Unpublished* (1876), (Albany: J. Munsell, 1876), p. 114; Chernow, *Alexander Hamilton*, pp. 88–92; Ferling, *Jefferson and Hamilton*, pp. 68–69; Caroline Cox, *A Proper Sense of Honor, Service and Sacrifice in George Washington's Army*, (Chapel Hill: University of North Carolina Press, 2004), p. 56; Chadwick, *George Washington's War*, pp. 138–140; Ferling, *Jefferson and Hamilton*, pp. 68–69; Massey, *John Laurens and the American Revolution*, p. 80; Lefkowitz, *George Washington's Indispensable Men*, pp. 16, 95, 115.

49. Kline, ed., *Alexander Hamilton*, p. 73; Lefkowitz, *George Washington's Indispensable Men*, pp. 34, 114.

50. Kline, ed., *Alexander Hamilton*, pp. 71–72.

51. Ibid; Massey, *John Laurens and the American Revolution*, pp. 73, 80; Randall, *AlexanderHamilton*, pp. 15–23; Chernow, *Alexander Hamilton*, pp. 12, 26, 88–93.

52. Chernow, *Alexander Hamilton*, pp. 12–13, 88–91, 93; Ferling, *Jefferson and Hamilton*, pp. 67–68; Kline, ed., *Alexander Hamilton*, pp. 17–20, 38, 50, 77, 96; Lefkowitz, *George Washington's Indispensable Men*, pp. 110, 115; Lomask, *Odd Destiny*, p. 7; Miller, *Alexander Hamilton*, pp. 3–5, 21–22; Rakove, *Revolutionaries*, p. 403; Chadwick, *George Washington's War*, pp. 138–140;; Kaplan, *Alexander Hamilton*, p. 26; Randall, *Alexander Hamilton*, p. 123; Knott and Williams, *Washington and Hamilton*, p. 83

53. Kaplan, *Alexander Hamilton*, p. 27; Chernow, *Alexander Hamilton*, pp. 87–93; Miller, *Alexander Hamilton*, p. 21; Rakove, *Revolutionaries*, p. 403; Randall, *Alexander Hamilton*, p. 123; Chadwick, *George Washington's War*, pp. 138–140.

54. Chadwick, *George Washington's War*, pp. 138–140; Knott and Williams, *Washington and Hamilton*, p. 83; Chernow, *Alexander Hamilton*, p. 89.

55. Lefkowitz, *George Washington's Indispensible Men*, pp. xviii, 12; Randall, *Alexander Hamilton*, p. 119; Knott and Williams, *Washington and Hamilton*, pp. vii-257.

56. Chadwick, *George Washington's War*, p. 139; Kline, ed., *Alexander Hamilton*, pp. 45–48.

57. Massey, *John Laurens and the American Revolution*, p. 81; Chadwick, *George Washington's War*, p. 139.

58. Kaplan, *Alexander Hamilton*, p. 29.

59. Rakove, *Revolutionaries*, p. 404; Chadwick, *George Washington's War*, pp. 138–140; Miller, *Alexander Hamilton*, pp. 21–22; Cartledge, *Alexander the Great*, p. 137

60. Kaplan, *Alexander Hamilton*, p. 40; Lefkowitz, *George Washington's Indispensable Men*, p. 113; Chernow, *Alexander Hamilton*, p. 90; Kline, ed., *Alexander Hamilton*, p. 51; Randall, *Alexander Hamilton*, pp. 128–129; Rakove, *Revolutionaries*, pp. 404–405.

61. Randall, *Alexander Hamilton*, p. 129.

62. Roche, *Alexander Hamilton*, p. 130; Randall, *Alexander Hamilton*, p. 129.

63. Chernow, *Alexander Hamilton*, pp. 73–74; Clark, *All Cloudless Glory*, pp. 294–296; Chadwick, *George Washington's War*, pp. 138–139.

64. 63. Clark, *All Cloudless Glory*, pp. 294–297; Ellis, *Revolutionary Summer*, pp. 76–77; Miller, *Alexander Hamilton*, p. 67.

65. "LTC John Fitzgerald (–1799)-Find a Grave Memorial," www.findagrave.com; Chadwick, *George Washington's War*, pp. 78, 132.

66. Robert Hanson Harrison Biographical Sketch, Valley Forge, National Park Service, National Historic Park, Pennsylvania; "LTC John Fitzgerald (–1799)-Find A Grave Memorial," www.findagrave.com; Peter Kumpa, "Robert Hanson Harrison: Lost Hero of the Revolutionary Era," *Baltimore Sun*, December 31, 1990; Scheer and Rankin, *Rebels and Redcoats*, p. 255; Moran, "George Washington's Military Family," LTN; Lefkowitz, *George Washington's Indispensable Men*, p. 115.

67. Lefkowitz, *George Washington's Indispensable Men*, p. 111; Miller, *Alexander Hamilton*, p. 69.

68. Lomask, *Alexander Hamilton*, p. 48; Randall, *Alexander Hamilton*, p. 124.

69. Moran, "George Washington's Military Family," LTN; Ferling, *Jefferson and Hamilton*, pp. 69–70, 79–80; Bill, *Valley Forge*, p. 17; Lomask, *Alexander Hamilton*, p. 162; Chernow, *Alexander Hamilton*, pp. 92–93; David Hancock, *Oceans of Wine, Madiera and the Emergence of American Trade and Taste*, (New Haven: Yale University Press, 2009), pp. 289–290; Henry Wiencek, *Master of the Mountain, Thomas Jefferson and His Slaves*, (New York: Farrar, Straus and Giroux, 2012), p. 163.

70. Randall, *Alexander Hamilton*, p. 122.

71. Lomask, *Alexander Hamilton*, p. 162.

72. Ferling, *Jefferson and Hamilton*, p. 70; Kline, ed., *Alexander Hamilton*, p. 82.

73. Chernow, *Alexander Hamilton*, p. 112; Lomask, *Alexander Hamilton*, pp. 47, 162; Ferling, *Jefferson and Hamilton*, p. 70; Brendan Morrissey, *Yorktown 1781, The World Turned Upside Down*, (London: Osprey Books, 1997), pp. 52, 58.

74. Ferling, *Jefferson and Hamilton*, p. 70; Lomask, *Alexander Hamilton*, p. 48; John F. Roche, *Alexander Hamilton*, (Morristown: Silver Burdett Company, 1967), p. 145; Knott and Williams, *Washington and Hamilton*, p. 165.

75. Harrison Biographical Sketch, Valley Forge NPS; Marquis De Chastellux, *Travels in North-America in the Years 1780–81–82*, (New York 1828), p. 62.

76. Tilghman, *Memoir of Lieutenant Colonel Tench Tilghman*, pp. 8–9, 26, 28, 131–132; Randall, *Alexander Hamilton*, p. 123; Lefkowitz, *George Washington's Indispensable Men*, p. 111; Moran, "George Washington's Military Family," LTN.

77. Tilghman, *Memoir of Lieutenant Colonel Tench Tilghman*, pp. 8–9, 133.

78. Ibid., p. 28.
79. John Laurens, *The Army Correspondence of Colonel John Laurens in the Years 1777–8*, (New York: Nabu Press, 2001), pp.145–146; Lefkowitz, *George Washington's Indispensable Men*, pp. 8, 119–120; Chernow, *Alexander Hamilton*, pp. 94–95.
80. Laurens, *The Army Correspondence of Colonel John Laurens in the Years 1777–8*, p. 83.
81. Ibid., p. 69; Miller, *Alexander Hamilton*, p. 5.
82. Burns, *Virtue, Valor & Vanity*, pp. 46–47; Chernow, *Alexander Hamilton*, p. 91; Chadwick, *George Washington's War*, p. 78; Ferling, *Jefferson and Hamilton*, p. 69; Miller, *Alexander Hamilton*, p.67; Lefkowitz, *George Washington's Indispensable Men*, p. 10; Kaplan, *Alexander Hamilton*, p. 26.
83. Chernow, *Alexander Hamilton*, p. 90–91; Chadwick, *George Washington's War*, p. 138; Kline, ed., *Alexander Hamilton*, pp. 45–48.
84. Chernow, *Alexander Hamilton*, p. 37; Ferling, *Jefferson and Hamilton*, p.69; Kline, ed., *Alexander Hamilton*, pp. 15–25, 40–41; Randall, *Alexander Hamilton*, p. 85.
85. Kline, ed., *Alexander Hamilton*, p. 27.
86. Ibid., p. 28.
87. Ibid., p. 30.
88. Ibid., pp. 43–44
89. Ferling, *Jefferson and Hamilton*, p. 69; Chadwick, *George Washington's War*, p. 138.
90. Kaplan, *Alexander Hamilton*, pp. 40–41; Chernow, *Alexander Hamilton*, p. 91.
91. Knott and Williams, *Washington and Hamilton*, pp. vii-257; Ferling, *Jefferson and Hamilton*, pp. 68–69; Chernow, *Alexander Hamilton*, pp. 85–98; Miller, *Alexander Hamilton*, p. 22; Chadwick, *George Washington's War*, pp. 138–140, 380.
92. Chadwick, *George Washington's War*, p. 140.
93. Chernow, *Alexander Hamilton*, pp. 85–98; Ferling, *Jefferson and Hamilton*, pp. 37–38, 68–70; Randall, *Alexander Hamilton*, p. 127.
94. Lefkowitz, *George Washington's Indispensable Men*, p. 12; Chernow, *Alexander Hamilton*, pp. 85–98; Ferling, *Jefferson and Hamilton*, pp. 68–70; Miller, *Alexander Hamilton*, p. 22; Burns, *Virtue, Valor & Vanity*, p. 47; Chadwick, *George Washington's War*, pp. 138–140, 380.
95. Burns, *Virtue, Valor & Vanity*, p. 95; Chernow, *Alexander Hamilton*, pp. 85–98; Chadwick, *George Washington's War*, pp. 138–140, 362–363, 380; Ferling, *Jefferson and Hamilton*, pp. 68–70; Moran, "George Washington's Military Family," LTN.
96. Chastellux, *Travels in North-America in the Years 1780–81–82*, pp. 171–172, note; Miller, *Alexander Hamilton*, pp. 21–22, 67.
97. Hamilton, *The Life of Alexander Hamilton*, vol. 2, p. 69; Randall, *Alexander Hamilton*, pp. 66, 87; Lomask, *Alexander Hamilton*, p. 79.
98. Ferling, *Jefferson and Hamilton*, pp. 37–38; Burns, *Virtue, Valor & Vanity*, p. 47.
99. Laurens, *The Army Correspondence of Colonel John Laurens in the Years 1777–78*, p. 59.
100. Cox, *A Proper Sense of Honor*, pp. xv-xvi, 21–35; Massey, *John Laurens and the American Revolution*, p. 82.
101. Burns, *Virtue, Valor & Vanity*, p. 32.
102. Massey, *John Laurens and the American Revolution*, p. 83.

103. Kline, ed., *Alexander Hamilton*, pp. 45–46; Randall, *Alexander Hamilton*, p. 55.

104. James Thacher, *Military Journal, During the American Revolutionary War, form 1775 to 1783*, (Cranbury: The Scholar's Bookshelf, 2005), p. 60; Miller, *Alexander Hamilton*, p. xii.

105. Miller, *Alexander Hamilton*, p. xii; Kline, ed., *Alexander Hamilton*, p. 46.

106. Lomask, *Odd Destiny*, p. 39.

107. Chernow, *Alexander Hamilton*, pp. 85–97, 149; Ferling, *Jefferson and Hamilton*, pp. 68–70; Chadwick, *George Washington's War*, p. 143.

Chapter III

1. Chernow, *Alexander Hamilton*, pp. 85–97; Chadwick, *Washington's War*, 138–140, 380; Lefkowitz, *George Washington's Indispensable Men*, pp. 1, 25, 95, 101, 107–111, 114; Ferling, *Jefferson and Hamilton*, pp. 68–70; Fleming, *Beat the Last Drum*, p. 68; Knott and Williams, *Washington and Hamilton*, pp. vii–257; Knott and Williams, *Washington and Hamilton*, pp. vii–257.

2. Fleming, *Beat the Last Drum*, p. 68; Chernow, *Alexander Hamilton*, pp. 85–97; Ferling, *Jefferson and Hamilton*, pp. 69–71; Randall, *Alexander Hamilton*, pp. 120–124;; Miller, *Alexander Hamilton*, pp. 21–67; Chadwick *George Washington's War*, p. 138–140, 380; Knott and Williams, *Washington and Hamilton*, p. 227.

3. Chris McNabb, editor, *Armies of the Napoleonic Wars*, (Oxford: Osprey Publishing Ltd., 2009), pp. 38–42; Andrew Roberts, *Napoleon, A Life*, (New York: Penguin Books, 2014), p. 80; Scott Bowden and Bill Ward, *Last Chance for Victory, Robert E. Lee and the Gettysburg Campaign*, (New York: Da Capo Press, 2001), p. 24; Paul Strathern, *Napoleon in Egypt*, (New York: Bantam Books, 2007), p. 34.

4. Telford Taylor, *Sword and Swastika, Generals and Nazis in the Third Reich*, (Chicago: Quadrangle Paperbacks, 1969), pp. 35–36; Cartledge, *Alexander the Great*, pp. 167–168; Knott and Williams, *Washington and Hamilton*, p. 82.

5. Strathern, *Napoleon in Egypt*, p. 34; Chernow, *Alexander Hamilton*, p. 88; Chadwick, *George Washington's War*, pp. 138–140; Roberts, *Napoleon*, p. 80.

6. Chadwick, *George Washington's War*, pp. 138–140.

7. Miller, *Alexander Hamilton*, pp. 21–40.

8. Roberts, *Napoleon*, p. 80; Lomask, *Alexander Hamilton*, p. 46.

9. Chernow, *Alexander Hamilton*, pp. 85–93; Randall, *Alexander Hamilton*, pp. 29–33.

10. Ferling, *Jefferson and Hamilton*, pp. 37–38; Chernow, *Alexander Hamilton*, p. 61; Kline, ed., *Alexander Hamilton*, p. 51; Randall, *Alexander Hamilton*, pp. 77–79.

11. Kline, ed., *Alexander Hamilton*, pp. 52–53.

12. Alexander Hamilton to Major General Benjamin Lincoln, June 4, 1777, Alexander Hamilton Papers, Digital Edition, Editor, Harold C. Syrett, Charlottesville: University of Virginia Press, Rotunda, 2011.

13. Roche, *Alexander Hamilton*, p. 131.

14. Randall, *Alexander Hamilton*, p. 128.

15. Alexander Hamilton to Hugh Knox, The Papers of Alexander Hamilton, Digital Edition, Editor, Harold C. Syrett. Charlottesville: University of Virginia Press, Rotunda, 2011.

16. Ibid.

17. Ibid; Tallmadge and Tallmadge, *Memoir of Colonel Benjamin Tallmadge*, p. 18; Chernow, *Alexander Hamilton*, p. 61; Harris, *Brandywine*, p. 48.

18. Lefkowitz, *George Washington's Indispensable Men*, pp. 7, 116; Alexander Rose, *Washington's Spies, The Story of America's First Spy Ring*, (New York: Bantam Books, 2014), pp. 4–5, 33–34, 42–43, 67–280; "The Legacy of Hercules Mulligan," Central Intelligence Agency, www.cia.gov; Kline, ed., *Alexander Hamilton*, p. 51; Clark, *All Cloudless Glory*, pp. 395–396; Kaplan, *Alexander Hamilton*, p. 29; Rose, *Washington's Spies*, pp. 16–17, 41–42; Lomask, *Alexander* Hamilton, p. 49; Tallmadge and Tallmadge, *Memoir of Colonel Benjamin Tallmadge*, pp. 5–19; Fleming, *Beat the Last Drum*, p. 68; Edgar, *Campaign of 1776*, p. 207; Randall, *Alexander Hamilton*, pp. 121, 149; Brian Kilmeade and Don Yaeger, *George Washington's Secret Six, The Spy Ring That Saved the American Revolution*, (New York: Sentinel, 2014), pp. 26, 148.

19. Nathan Schachner, *Aaron Burr, A Biography*, (New York: A. S. Barnes and Company, Inc.,1961), pp. 52, 253–254; Chernow, *Alexander Hamilton*, pp. 43, 90; Lomask, *Odd Destiny*, pp. 46, 49.

20. Mulraney, "Hercules Mulligan," IrishCentral, July 20, 2016; Rose, *Washington's Spies*, pp. 224–226; Donald E. Markle, *The Fox and the Hound, The Birth of American Spying*, (New York: Fall River Press, 2014), p. 83.

21. Bill, *Valley Forge*, p. 17; Kline, *Alexander Hamilton*, pp. 23–24; Knott and Williams, *Washington and Hamilton*, p. 26; Chernow, *Alexander Hamilton*, p. 43; Chadwick, *George Washington's War*, pp. 146–147; Lomask, *Odd Destiny*, p. 20; Gragg, *By the Hand of Providence*, p. 186; Wright, *The Continental Army*, p. 114; Randall, *Alexander Hamilton*, pp. 50, 54.

22. Rose, *Washington's Spies*, p. 191; Kilmeade and Yaeger, *George Washington's Secret Six*, p. 124; Randall, *Alexander Hamilton*, p. 121.

23. Randall, *Alexander Hamilton*, pp. 129–130.

24. Chernow, *Alexander Hamilton*, pp. 20–26; Randall, *Alexander Hamilton*, p. 130.

25. Randall, *Alexander Hamilton*, pp. 123–124; Lefkowitz, *George Washington's Indispensable Men*, p. 115.

26. Kaplan, *Alexander Hamilton*, p. 28; Chernow, *Alexander Hamilton*, pp. 43–44, 93; Kline, ed., *Alexander Hamilton*, pp. 53–54; Randall, *Alexander Hamilton*, pp. 49–50, 55; Lomask, *Odd Destiny*, p. 63.

27. Chernow, *Alexander Hamilton*, pp. 93–94; Randall, *Alexander Hamilton*, pp. 189–190.

28. Roche, *Alexander Hamilton*, p. 131.

29. Gerald H. Clarfield, *Timothy Pickering and the American Republic*, (Pittsburgh: University of Pittsburgh Press, 1980), pp. 3–43.

30. Kline, ed., *Alexander Hamilton*, pp. 50–51, 55; Randall, Alexander Hamilton, p. 133; Lomask, *Odd Destiny*, p. 49; Lefkowitz, *George Washington's Indispensable Men*, p. 116.

31. Randall, *Alexander Hamilton*, p. 129.

32. Ibid., p. 133; Chernow, *Alexander Hamilton*, p. 61; Ferling, *Jefferson and Hamilton*, pp. 37–38.

33. Kline, ed., *Alexander Hamilton*, pp. 51–52; Kaplan, *Alexander Hamilton*, p. 40.

34. Kline, ed., *Alexander Hamilton*, p. 55.

35. Ibid., pp. 50–51, 55; Tallmadge and Tallmadge, *Memoir of Colonel Benjamin Tallmadge*, p. 18; Randall, *Alexander Hamilton*, p. 133.

36. Kline, ed., *Alexander Hamilton*, p. 55; Randall, *Alexander Hamilton*, p. 114.

37. Chernow, *Alexander Hamilton*, p. 61; Tallmadge and Tallmadge, *Memoir of Colonel Benjamin Tallmadge*, pp. 19–20; Randall, *Alexander Hamilton*, p. 114; Kline, ed., *Alexander Hamilton*, pp. 55–56.

38. Alexander Hamilton to Captain Francis Grice, May 30, 1777, Alexander Hamilton Papers, Digital Edition, Editor, Harold C. Syrett. Charlottesville: University of Virginia Press, Rotunda, 2011; Tallmadge and Tallmadge, *Memoir of Colonel Benjamin Tallmadge*, p. 18.

39. Alexander Hamilton to Hugh Knox, July 1, 1777, Alexander Hamilton Papers, Digital Edition, Editor, Harold C. Syrett, Charlottesville: University of Virginia Press, Rotunda, 2011.

40. Ibid; Philbrick, *Valiant Ambition*, p. 104; Chernow, *Alexander Hamilton*, pp. 86–92; Rose, *Washington's Spies*, pp. 191, 224–226; Mulraney, "Hercules Mulligan," IrishCentral, July 20, 2016; "The Legend of Hercules Mulligan," Central Intelligence Agency, June 30, 2016, internet.

41. Ibid; Brendan Morrissey, *Saratoga 1777, Turning point of a revolution*, (Oxford: Osprey Publishing, ltd., 2000), pp. 7, 11; Chernow, *Alexander Hamilton*, pp. 48, 61, 97; Tallmadge and Tallmadge, *Memoir of Colonel Benjamin Tallmadge*, pp. 18, 22; Kline, ed., *Alexander Hamilton*, pp. 56–57; Kaplan, *Alexander Hamilton*, p. 40; Arthur E. R. Boak and William G. Sinnigen, *A History of Rome to A.D. 565*, (New York: Macmillan Company, 1969), p. 117.

42. Jean Edward Smith, *John Marshall, Definer of a Nation*, (New York: Henry Holt and Company, Inc., 1996), p. 55.

43. Chernow, *Alexander Hamilton*, p. 98; Kline, ed., *Alexander Hamilton*, p. 57; Richard M. Ketchum, *Saratoga, Turning Point of America's Revolutionary War*, (New York: Henry Holt and Company, 1997), pp. 64–88.

44. Kline, ed., *Alexander Hamilton*, p. 57.

45. Chernow, *Alexander Hamilton*, p. 97; Kline, ed., *Alexander Hamilton*, p. 57.

46. Chernow, *Alexander Hamilton*, p. 98; Kline, ed., *Alexander Hamilton*, p. 58; Smith, *John Marshall*, pp. 55–56; Lomask, *Odd Destiny*, p. 49; Randall, *Alexander Hamilton*, pp. 128, 133.

47. Randall, *Alexander Hamilton*, p. 134; Kline, ed., *Alexander Hamilton*, p. 58.

48. Chernow, *Alexander Hamilton*, pp. 61, 98; Kaplan, *Alexander Hamilton*, p. 40; Lomask, *Odd Destiny*, pp. 45–49; Ferling, *Jefferson and Hamilton*, pp. 37–38; Randall, *Alexander Hamilton*, p. 133.

49. Walter A. McDougall, *Promised Land, Crusader State*, (New York: Houghton Mifflin Company, 1997), pp. 5, 10–20; Chernow, *Alexander Hamilton*, p. 17; Lomask, *Odd Destiny*, pp. 8, 10–12; Randall, *Alexander Hamilton*, pp. 34–35, 131–132,

50. Massey, *John Laurens and the American Revolution*, pp. 6, 8–40, 73; Biographical Information about John Laurens, John Laurens Papers, South Caroliniana Library, University of South Carolina, Columbia, South Carolina; Lefkowitz, *George Washington's Indispensable Men*, pp. 119, 123; Chernow, *Alexander Hamilton*, pp. 6, 8, 23, 94–95.

51. Massey, *John Laurens and the American Revolution*, p. 79; Chernow, *Alexander Hamilton*, pp. 94–95; Henry Savage, Jr., *River of the Carolinas: The Santee*, (Chapel Hill: University of North Carolina Press, 1968), pp. 100–106; Lefkowitz, *George Washington's Indispensable Men*, pp. 119, 121–123.

52. Chernow, *Alexander Hamilton*, p. 98; Smith, *John Marshall*, pp. 56–57.

53. Ibid., pp. 58–60; Philbrick, *Valiant Ambition*, pp. 136, 138–140; Massey, *John Laurens and the American Revolution*, p. 75; Fleming, *Liberty!*, pp. 263, 266; Randall, *Alexander Hamilton*, p. 134; Don Higginbotham and Kenneth Nebenzahl, *Atlas of the American Revolution*, (New York: Rand McNally and Company, 1974), pp. 113–114; Ferling, *Jefferson and Hamilton*, p. 71; Lefkowitz, *George Washington's Indispensable Men*, p. 125.

54. Chernow, *Alexander Hamilton*, p. 98; Emory M. Thomas, *Robert E. Lee, A Biography*, (New York: W. W. Norton and Company, 1995), pp. 30–31, 288–293; Puls, *Henry Knox*, p. 106; Randall, *Alexander Hamilton*, pp. 134–135; Miller, *Alexander Hamilton*, p. 22; Kline, ed., *Alexander Hamilton*, p. 58; Lomask, *Alexander Hamilton*, p. 50.

55. Chernow, *Alexander Hamilton*, p. 98; Puls, *Henry Knox*, p. 106; Kline, ed., *Alexander Hamilton*, pp. 58–59; Lomask, *Alexander Hamilton*, p. 50.

56. Kline, ed., *Alexander Hamilton*, pp. 58–59.

57. Ibid., p. 59; Chernow, *Alexander Hamilton*, p. 98; Ferling, *Jefferson and Hamilton*, p. 71; Randall, *Alexander Hamilton*, p. 135; Bill, *Valley Forge*, p. 96; Lomask, *Alexander Hamilton*, p. 50.

58. Chernow, *Alexander Hamilton*, pp. 98–99; Thomas Fleming, *Washington's Secret War, The Hidden History of Valley Forge*, (New York: HarperCollins, 2005), pp. 70–71; Lomask, *Alexander Hamilton*, p. 50; David Willis McCulloch, *Wars of the Irish Kings*, (New York: Crown Publishers, 2000), pp. 79–319.

59. Kline, ed., *Alexander Hamilton*, p. 59.

60. Ferling, *Jefferson and Hamilton*, p. 71; Fleming, *Washington's Secret War*, pp. 71–74; Chernow, *Alexander Hamilton*, p. 99; Randall, *Alexander Hamilton*, p. 135; Fleming, *Liberty!*, p. 266; Lomask, *Strange Destiny*, pp. 50–51.

61. Ferling, *Jefferson and Hamilton*, p. 72; Jim Piecuch, editor, *Cavalry of the American Revolution*, (Yardley: Westholme Publishing, 2012), pp. 109–111; Chernow, *Alexander Hamilton*, pp. 99–100; Fleming, *Washington's Secret War*, pp. 15–16, 74; Smith, *John Marshall*, p. 60; Randall, *Alexander Hamilton*, pp. 136, 140; Knott and Williams, *Washington and Hamilton*, pp. 85–86.

62. Philbrick, *Valiant Ambition*, pp. 157–158; Puls, *Henry Knox*, pp. 106–107; Fleming, *Washington's Secret War*, p. 74.

63. Puls, *Henry Knox*, pp. 107–108; Harris, *Brandywine*, p. 48; Smith, *John Marshall*, p. 60.

64. Tallmadge and Tallmadge, *Memoir of Colonel Benjamin Tallmadge*, pp. 22–23; Chernow, *Alexander Hamilton*, p. 100; Philbrick, *Valiant Ambition*, pp. 158, 160; Smith, John Marshall, pp. 60–62; Ferling, *Jefferson and Hamilton*, p. 72; Puls, *Henry Knox*, pp. 107–108; Massey, *John Laurens and the American Revolution*, pp. 76–77; Randall, *Alexander Hamilton*, pp. 136–137; Fleming, *Liberty!*, pp. 266–267; Lefkowitz, *George Washington's Indispensable Men*, pp. 126–127.

65. Tallmadge and Tallmadge, *Memoir of Colonel Benjamin Tallmadge*, pp. 22–23; Philbrick, *Valiant Ambition*, p. 160; Puls, *Henry Knox*, p. 108; Bill, *Valley Forge*, p. 126; Clarfield, *Timothy Pickering and the American Republic*, p. 45.

66. Tallmadge and Tallmadge, *Memoir of Colonel Benjamin Tallmadge*, pp. 22–23; Philbrick, *Valiant Ambition*, pp. 160–161; Tilghman, *Memoirs of Lieutenant Colonel Tench Tilghman*, pp. 127, 161; Smith, *John Marshall*, pp. 61–62.

67. Tallmadge and Tallmadge, *Memoir of Colonel Benjamin Tallmadge*, pp. 22–23; Lomask, *Alexander Hamilton*, p. 51; Philbrick, *Valiant Ambition*, pp. 160–161; Fleming, *Liberty!*, p. 266.

68. Chernow, *Alexander Hamilton*, pp. 99–100; Chadwick, *George Washington's War*, pp. 120–122; Lomask, *Alexander Hamilton*, pp. 69–70; Ferling, *Jefferson and Hamilton*, p. 72.

69. Chadwick, *George Washington's War*, p. 122.

70. Kaplan, *Alexander Hamilton*, pp. 27, 29; Lomask, *Alexander Hamilton*, p. 49.

71. Randall, *Alexander Hamilton*, pp. 130–131.

72. Ibid., p. 234.

73. Alexander Hamilton to John Jay, July 13, 1777, John Jay Papers, Columbia University Library, New York, New York; Chernow, *Alexander Hamilton*, p. 98.

74. Douglas Southall Freeman, *Washington*, (New York: Touchstone Books, 1995), p. 347; Chernow, *Alexander Hamilton*, p. 100.

75. Chernow, *Alexander Hamilton*, pp. 89–91, 97–98, 100; Fleming, *Liberty!*, pp. 237–262; Morrissey, *Saratoga 1777*, pp. 9–86.

76. Massey, *John Laurens and the American Revolution*, p. 79.

77. Lomask, *Alexander Hamilton*, p. 49.

78. Chernow, *Alexander Hamilton*, p. 100; Kline, ed., *Alexander Hamilton*, p. 59; Ferling, *Jefferson and Hamilton*, p. 72; Randall, *Alexander Hamilton*, p. 140; Lomask, *Odd Destiny*, pp. 52–53

79. Ferling, *Jefferson and Hamilton*, p. 72; Randall, *Alexander Hamilton*, p. 127; Chernow, *Alexander Hamilton*, p. 101; Lomask, *Old Destiny*, p. 52–53.

80. Ibid., p. 140; George Washington to Horatio Gates, October 30, 1777, Horatio Gates Papers, New York Historical Society, New York, New York; Lomask, Alexander Hamilton, pp. 52–53.

81. Rakove, *Revolutionaries*, p. 403; Ferling, *Jefferson and Hamilton*, pp. 72–73; Fleming, *Washington's Secret War*, p. 116; Chernow, *Alexander Hamilton*, p. 101; Chadwick, *George Washington's War*, pp. 208, 255; Bill, *Valley Forge*, p. 84; Noel F. Busch, *Winter Quarters, George Washington and the Continental Army at Valley Forge*, (New York: W. W. Norton and Company, 1975), p. 56; Randall, *Alexander Hamilton*, pp. 140–141; Lomask, *Alexander Hamilton*, p. 53; Knott and Williams, *Washington and Hamilton*, p. 85.

82. Busch, *Winter Quarters*, p. 56; Chernow, *Alexander Hamilton*, p. 101; Knott and Williams, *Washington and Hamilton*, p. 86.

83. Lomask, *Alexander Hamilton*, p. 53; Chernow, *Alexander Hamilton*, p. 101; Randall, *Alexander Hamilton*, p. 141.

84. Kline, ed., *Alexander Hamilton*, p. 59; Chernow, *Alexander Hamilton*, p. 102; Lomask, *Alexander Hamilton*, pp. 53–54; Randall, *Alexander Hamilton*, p. 144.

85. Randall, *Alexander Hamilton*, p. 144; Kline, ed., *Alexander Hamilton*, p. 60.

86. Ferling, *Jefferson and Hamilton*, pp. 72–73, 77; Chernow, *Alexander Hamilton*, pp. 100, 102; Kline, ed., *Alexander Hamilton*, pp. 60–61.

87. Chernow, *Alexander Hamilton*, p. 102; Randall, *Alexander Hamilton*, p. 144.

88. Chernow, *Alexander Hamilton*, pp. 101–102; Kline, ed., *Alexander Hamilton*, p. 88; Ferling, *Jefferson and Hamilton*, p. 77; Kaplan, *Alexander Hamilton*, pp. 29–30; Randall, *Alexander Hamilton*, p. 144; Lomask, *Odd Destiny*, p. 53; Miller, *Alexander Hamilton*, pp. 24–25.

89. Lomask, *Alexander Hamilton*, p. 54; Randall, *Alexander Hamilton*, pp. 144–145.

90. Massey, *John Laurens and the American Revolution*, pp. 89–91; Ferling, *Jefferson and Washington*, p. 77; Miller, *Alexander Hamilton*, pp. 26–28; Randall, *Alexander Hamilton*, pp. 148–149; Marcus Cunliffe, *George Washington, Man and Monument*, (New York: Mentor Book, 1958), p. 99.

91. Chernow, *Alexander Hamilton*, p. 103; Lomask, *Alexander Hamilton*, pp. 54–55; Randall, *Alexander Hamilton*, p. 145.

92. Randall, *Alexander Hamilton*, p. 145.

93. Chernow, *Alexander Hamilton*, pp. 102–103; Ferling *Jefferson and Hamilton*, p. 77; Randall, *Alexander Hamilton*, p. 145.

94. Chernow, *Alexander Hamilton*, pp. 102–103; Randall, *Alexander Hamilton*, pp. 145–146.

95. Laurens, *The Army Correspondence of Colonel John Laurens in the Years 1777–78*, pp. 92–93; Chernow, *Alexander Hamilton*, pp. 103–104; Ferling, *Jefferson and Hamilton*, p. 77; Miller, *Alexander Hamilton*, p. 26; Randall, *Alexander Hamilton*, p. 146.

96. Chadwick, *George Washington's War*, p. 208; Chernow, *Alexander Hamilton*, p. 104; Randall, *Alexander Hamilton*, p. 146; Lomask, *Odd Destiny*, p. 53

97. Chernow, *Alexander Hamilton*, pp. 101–104; Randall, *Alexander Hamilton*, p.147.

98. Randall, *Alexander Hamilton*, p. 147; Chernow, *Alexander Hamilton*, pp. 101–103.

99. Randall, *Alexander Hamilton*, p. 145.

100. Lomask, *Alexander Hamilton*, p. 55; Chernow, *Alexander Hamilton*, p. 103.

101. Chernow, *Alexander Hamilton*, pp. 102–103; Ferling, *Jefferson and Hamilton*, pp. 72–73, 77; Randall, *Alexander Hamilton*, p. 143.

102. Chernow, *Alexander Hamilton*, p. 104; Chadwick, *George Washington's War*, p. 208.

103. Chernow, *Alexander Hamilton*, pp. 104–107; Ferling, *Jefferson and Hamilton*, p. 77; Randall, *Alexander Hamilton*, pp. 139, 144–145, 148–149.

104. Burn, *Virtue, Valor & Vanity*, p. 47; Kline, ed., *Alexander Hamilton*, pp. 60–61; Chernow, Alexander Hamilton, pp. 101–103, 109; Ferling, *Jefferson and Hamilton*, p. 77; Chadwick, *George Washington's War*, pp. 138–140; 208; Randall, *Alexander Hamilton*, p. 149; Lomask, *Alexander Hamilton*, p. 49.

105. Nancy Isenberg, *Fallen Founder, The Life of Aaron Burr*, (New York: Viking, 2007), pp. 41–42; Randall, *Alexander Hamilton*, p. 147.

106. Isenberg, *Fallen Founder*, pp. 41–42; Schachner, *Aaron Burr*, p. 45.

107. Chernow, *Alexander Hamilton*, pp. 100–105; Ferling, *Jefferson and Hamilton*, p. 77; Miller, *Alexander Hamilton*, p. 37; Randall, *Alexander Hamilton*, p. 149; Lomask, *Alexander Hamilton*, p. 54.

108. Chernow, *Alexander Hamilton*, pp. 90–106; Randall, *Alexander Hamilton*, pp. 148–149.

109. Philbrick, *Valiant Ambition*, pp. 185–187; Chadwick, *George Washington's War*, pp. 255–257; Chernow, *Alexander Hamilton*, pp. 91, 100, 104–105, 107.

110. Erna Risch, *Quartermaster Support of the Army, A History of the Corps, 1775–1939*, (Washington, DC: Center of Military History, United States Army, 1989), pp. 29–33; Philbrick, *Valiant Ambition*, pp. 185–187, 191; Ferling, *Jefferson and Hamilton*, p. 72; Randall, *Alexander Hamilton*, p. 149; Chernow, *Alexander Hamilton*, pp. 104–105, 107–108; Fleming, *Washington's Secret War*, pp. 2, 11–12, 14–15; Smith, *John Marshall*, p. 64; "Isaac Potts," Historic Valley Forge, www.USHistory.com; Willard Sterne Randall, *Benedict*

Arnold, Patriot and Traitor, (New York: Quill/William Morrow, 1990), pp. 402–406; Clarfield, *Timothy Pickering and the American Republic*, p. 42.

111. Lefkowitz, *George Washington's Indispensable Men*, pp. 134, 136; Philbrick, *Valiant Ambition*, pp. 192–194; Randall, *Alexander Hamilton*, pp. 139, 144–145, 149; Fleming, *Washington's Secret War*, pp. 148–165; Chadwick, *George Washington's War*, pp. 253–257.

112. Philbrick, *Valiant Ambition*, pp. 191–192; Ferling, *Jefferson and Hamilton*, p. 74; Fleming, *Washington's Secret War*, p. 165; Lefkowitz, *George Washington's Indispensable Men*, p. 134.

113. Chernow, *Alexander Hamilton*, p. 109; Fleming, *Washington's Secret War*, pp. 175–178; Randall, *Alexander Hamilton*, pp. 150–151.

114. Fleming, *Washington's Secret War*, p. 178.

115. Randall, *Alexander Hamilton*, p.151.

116. Chernow, *Alexander Hamilton*, pp. 108–109; Chadwick, *George Washington's War*, p. 287; Randall, *Alexander Hamilton*, pp. 156–158; Ferling, *Jefferson and Hamilton*, p. 74.

117. Philbrick, *Valiant Ambition*, pp. 191–192; Kline, ed., *Alexander Hamilton*, p. 61; Randall, *Alexander Hamilton*, p. 157.

118. Randall, *Alexander Hamilton*, pp. 156–157; Miller, *Alexander Hamilton*, p. 36; Kline, ed., *Alexander Hamilton*, p. 61.

119. Philbrick, *Valiant Ambition*, pp. 192–193; Kline, ed. *Alexander Hamilton*, pp. 61–62; Miller, *Alexander Hamilton*, p. 36.

120. Kline, ed., *Alexander Hamilton*, pp. 61–62; Knott and Williams, *Washington and Hamilton*, pp. 106, 109.

121. Philbrick, *Valiant Ambition*, pp. 191–192; Bill, *Valley Forge*, pp. 144–145.

122. Busch, *Winter Quarters*, p. 145; Pierre-Étienne du Ponceau Biography Information, Pierre-Étienne du Ponceau Papers, 1781–1845, Special Collections, William and Mary College, Williamsburg, Virginia.

123. Busch, *Winter Quarters*. p. 146.

124. Ibid., pp. 146–147.

125. Robert Hanson Harrison Biographical Sketch, NPS, Valley Forge NHP.

126. Larrie D. Ferreiro, *Brothers at Arms, American Independence and the Men of France and Spain Who Saved It*, (New York: Alfred A.Knopf, 2016), pp.151-153; Fleming, *Washington's Secret War*, pp. 206–233; Bill, *Valley Forge*, p. 147; Busch, *Winter Quarters*, pp. 79, 83–84; Scheer and Rankin, *Rebels and Redcoats*, p. 353; Chernow, *Alexander Hamilton*, p. 109; Langguth, *Patriots*, p. 470; Randall, *Alexander Hamilton*, pp. 153–154; Taylor, *Sword and Swastika*, pp. 35–36.

127. Randall, *Alexander Hamilton*, p. 155; Bill, *Valley Forge*, p. 148; Busch, *Winter Quarters*, pp. 79, 83–84.

128. Leckie, *George Washington's War*, p. 440; Fleming, *Washington's Secret War*, pp. 212, 217–222, 230–233; Chernow, *Alexander Hamilton*, pp. 109–110; Busch, *Winters Quarters*, pp. 83–84; Smith, *John Marshall*, p. 65; Ferreiro, *Brothers at Arms*, p.153; Scheer and Rankin, *Rebels and Redcoats*, pp. 353–354; Randall, *Alexander Hamilton*, pp. 154–155; Langguth, *Patriots*, p. 470; Robert Middlekauff, *The Glorious Cause, The American Revolution, 1763–1789*, (New York: Oxford University Press, 2005), p. 424; Fleming, *George Washington's Secret War*, pp. 140–142, 285.

129. Charles Royster, *Light-Horse Harry Lee and the Legacy of the American Revolution*, (Cambridge: Cambridge University Press, 1986), pp. 24–25.

Chapter IV

1. Chadwick, *George Washington's War*, p. 342.
2. William C. Stinchcombe, *The American Revolution and the French Alliance*, (Syracuse: Syracuse University Press, 1969), pp. 1–11; Chernow, *Alexander Hamilton*, pp. 109, 112–113, 119–120; Lomask, *Odd Destiny*, pp. 7–9, 61; Miller, *Alexander Hamilton*, pp. 3; Clark, *All Cloudless Glory*, pp. 409, 505; Bill, *Valley Forge*, pp. 44, 145; Lomask, *Odd Destiny*, p. 8; Smith, *John Marshall*, p. 65; Randall, *Alexander Hamilton*, pp. 18, 154; Busch, *Winter Quarters*, p. 97.
3. Kaplan, *Alexander Hamilton*, p. 38.
4. Roche, *Alexander Hamilton*, p. 143.
5. Ferreiro, *Brothers at Arms*, pp. xv–xxv; Isenberg, *Fallen Founder*, p. 45; Stacy Schiff, *A Great Improvisation, Franklin, France, and the Birth of America*, (New York: Henry Holt and Company, 2005), pp. 164–167; Chernow, *Alexander Hamilton*, pp. 119–120; Bevin Alexander, *Sun Tzu at Gettysburg, Ancient Military Wisdom in the Modern World*, (New York: W. W. Norton and Company, 2011), pp. 16–19; Kaplan, *Alexander Hamilton*, pp. 29, 37–39; Stinchcombe, *The American Revolution and the French Alliance*, pp. 1–11.
6. Piers Mackesy, *The War for America 1775–1783*, (Lincoln: University of Nebraska Press, 1993), pp. 181–186; Alexander, *Sun Tzu at Gettysburg*, p. 18; Chernow, *Alexander Hamilton*, p. 119.
7. Tilghman, *Memoirs of Lieutenant Colonel Tench Tilghman*, p. 164.
8. Ibid., pp. 168–169.
9. Mackesy, *The War for America 1775–1783*, pp. 181–186.
10. Laurens, *The Army Correspondence of Colonel John Laurens in the Years 1777–8*, p. 177.
11. Tilghman, *Memoirs of Lieutenant Colonel Tench Tilghman*, pp. 168–169.
12. Philbrick, *Valiant Ambition*, p. 220; Fleming, *Washington's Secret War*, p. 307; Lefkowitz, *George Washington's Indispensable Men*, p. 145.
13. Alexander Hamilton to Marquis de Barbe-Marbois, February 7, 1781, Alexander Hamilton Papers, Manuscripts and Archives Division, New York Public Library, New York, New York; Lomask, *Odd Destiny*, p. 61.
14. Robert Hanson Harrison Biographical Sketch, NPS, Valley Forge, NHP; Chernow, Alexander Hamilton, pp. 107, 109; Kline, ed., *Alexander Hamilton*, p. 62; Cecere, *An Officer of Very Extraordinary Merit*, pp. 30–31; Randall, *Alexander Hamilton*, p. 127; Rose, *Washington's Spies*, p. 33; Piers Mackesy, *The War for America 1775–1783*, (Lincoln: University of Nebraska Press, 1993), p. 34; Randall, *Alexander Hamilton*, pp. 166–167; Moran, "George Washington's Military Family," LTN; Lefkowitz, *George Washington's Indispensable Men*, p. 156.
15. Lefkowitz, *George Washington's Indispensable Men*, p. 156; Chernow, *Alexander Hamilton*, pp. 98–99; Kline, ed., *Alexander Hamilton*, p. 62; Mackesy, *The War for America*, p. 34.
16. Kline, ed., *Alexander Hamilton*, pp. 62–63.
17. Ibid., p. 63.
18. Ibid; Smith, *John Marshall*, p. 65.
19. Chernow, *Alexander Hamilton*, p. 109; Randall, *Alexander Hamilton*, p. 161.
20. Randall, *Alexander Hamilton*, p. 168.

21. Ibid., p. 167

22. Ibid., p. 168.

23. Ibid., p. 169; Chernow, *Alexander Hamilton*, pp. 73–74.

24. Chernow, *Alexander Hamilton*, pp. 112–133; Fleming, *Washington's Secret War*, pp. 307–308.

25. Fleming, *Washington's Secret War*, pp. 308–309; Chernow, *Alexander Hamilton*, p. 98; Randall, *Alexander Hamilton*, p. 170; Bill, *Valley Forge*, p. 204; Lefkowitz, *George Washington's Indispensable Men*, p. 162.

26. Knott and Williams, *Washington and Hamilton*, p. 70; Clark, *All Cloudless Glory*, p. 398; Fleming, *Washington's Secret War*, p. 310; Lomask, *Alexander Hamilton*, p. 49; Randall, *Alexander Hamilton*, pp. 171–172.

27. Tilghman, *Memoir of Lieutenant Colonel Tench Tilghman*, p. 171; Langguth, *Patriots*, p. 478; Fleming, *Washington's Secret War*, pp. 312–313; Clark, *All Cloudless Glory*, p. 398; Chernow, *Alexander Hamilton*, p. 113; Kline, ed., *Alexander Hamilton*, p. 58; Randall, *Alexander Hamilton*, p. 172; Mackesy, *The War for America*, p. 215.

28. Clark, *All Cloudless Glory*, p. 401; Kline, ed., *Alexander Hamilton*, pp. 58, 65.

29. Kline, ed., *Alexander Hamilton*, p. 58.

30. Clark, *All Cloudless Glory*, p. 401; Bill, *Valley Forge*, p. 205.

31. Clark, *All Cloudless Glory*, pp. 312–313; Bill, *Valley Forge*, p. 205; Lefkowitz, *George Washington's Indispensable Men*, pp. 156–157.

32. Chernow, *Alexander Hamilton*, p. 113; Kline, ed., *Alexander Hamilton*, p. 66.

33. Clark, *All Cloudless Glory*, pp. 398, 402; Lomask, *Odd Destiny*, p. 8; Chernow, *Alexander Hamilton*, p. 112; Kline, ed., *Alexander Hamilton*, p. 64; Busch, *Winter Quarters*, p. 98; Lefkowitz, *George Washington's Indispensable Men*, p. 163.

34. Randall, *Alexander Hamilton*, pp. 171–172; Kline, ed., *Alexander Hamilton*, p. 64.

35. Kline, ed., *Alexander Hamilton*, p. 64

36. Ibid; Lefkowitz, *George Washington's Indispensable Men*, p. 164.

37. Mackesy, *The War for America*, p. 215; Lefkowitz, *George Washington's Indispensable Men*, p. 164; Chernow, *Alexander Hamilton*, p. 113; Miller, *Alexander Hamilton*, p. 29.

38. Chernow, *Alexander Hamilton*, p. 113; Randall, *Alexander Hamilton*, p. 173.

39. Lefkowitz, *George Washington's Indispensable Men*, p. 163; Chernow, *Alexander Hamilton*, p. 113; Kline, ed., *Alexander Hamilton*, p. 64; Randall, *Alexander Hamilton*, p. 173.

40. Kline, ed., *Alexander Hamilton*, p. 64; Lefkowitz, *George Washington's Indispensable Men*, p. 163; Fleming, *Washington's Secret War*, pp. 309–310

41. Chernow, *Alexander Hamilton*, p. 113; Randall, *Alexander Hamilton*, p. 172.

42. Bill, *Valley Forge*, p. 206; Chernow, *Alexander Hamilton*, p. 113; Randall, *Alexander Hamilton*, p. 173; Kline, ed., *Alexander Hamilton*, p. 64; Lomask, *Odd Destiny*, p. 59

43. Lefkowitz, *George Washington's Indispensable Men*, p. 162; Randall, *Alexander Hamilton*, p. 173.

44. Lefkowitz, *George Washington's Indispensable Men*, pp. 164, 168; Randall, *Alexander Hamilton*, p. 174.

45. Randall, *Alexander Hamilton*, p. 174; Lefkowitz, *George Washington's Indispensable Men*, p. 164.

46. Isenberg, *Fallen Founder*, pp. 3–4, 42, 45–46; Chernow, *Alexander Hamilton*, pp. 84, 111, 113; Bill, *Valley Forge*, p. 235; Schachner, *Aaron Burr*, pp. 32–68; Massey, *John Laurens and the American Revolution*, p. 81.

47. Clark, *All Cloudless Glory*, p. 402; Bill, *Valley Forge*, p. 208.

48. Kline, ed., *Alexander Hamilton*, p. 66.

49. Chernow, *Alexander Hamilton*, pp. 113–116; Randall, *Alexander Hamilton*, p. 174.

50. Chernow, *Alexander Hamilton*, pp. 113–114, 140; Ferling, *Jefferson and Hamilton*, p. 76; Clark, *All Cloudless Glory*, p. 403; Cecere, *An Officer of Very Extraordinary Merit*, pp. 101–102, 105; Lomask, *Alexander Hamilton*, p. 59; Bill, *Valley Forge*, pp. 212, 214–215, 217; Kline, ed., *Alexander Hamilton*, p. 66; Fleming, *Washington's Secret War*, pp. 314–317; Middlekauff, *The Glorious Cause*, pp. 430–433; Miller, *Alexander Hamilton*, pp. 30–31; Lefkowitz, *George Washington's Indispensable Men*, pp. 168, 171–172.

51. Bill, *Valley Forge*, p. 214; Kline, ed., *Alexander Hamilton*, p. 66; Chernow, *Alexander Hamilton*, p. 113; Randall, *Alexander Hamilton*, p. 174; Lefkowitz, *George Washington's Indispensable Men*, p. 162.

52. Leckie, *George Washington's War*, p. 484; Randall, *Alexander Hamilton*, p. 179; Lomask, *Alexander Hamilton*, p. 59.

53. Miller, *Alexander Hamilton*, p. 31.

54. Ibid., p. 31; Chernow, *Alexander Hamilton*, p. 114; Stephen F. Knott, *Alexander Hamilton and the Persistence of Myth*, (Lawrence: University Press of Kansas, 2002), pp. 1–2; Freeman, *Washington*, p. 399.

55. Chernow, *Alexander Hamilton*, pp. 114–115; Freeman, *Washington*, pp. 398–399; Lefkowitz, *George Washington's Indispensable Men*, p. 140; Fleming, *Washington's Secret War*, pp. 316–320; Kline, ed., *Alexander Hamilton*, p. 66; Clark, *All Cloudless Glory*, p. 403; Randall, *Alexander Hamilton*, p. 175; Middlekauff, *The Glorious Cause*, pp. 430, 432–434.

56. Kline, ed., *Alexander Hamilton*, p. 66.

57. Clark, *All Cloudless Glory*, p. 406.

58. Roche, *Alexander Hamilton*, p. 103.

59. Ibid; Chernow, *Alexander Hamilton*, p. 115; Ferling, *Jefferson and Hamilton*, pp. 76–77; Randall, *Alexander Hamilton*, p. 175; Miller, *Alexander Hamilton*, p. 31; Lomask, *Alexander Hamilton*, p. 59; Lefkowitz, *George Washington's Indispensable Men*, pp. 168, 171–172; Randall, *Alexander Hamilton*, pp. 175, 179.

60. Miller, *Alexander Hamilton*, p. 31; Chernow, *Alexander Hamilton*, pp. 80–85, 115; Puls, *Henry Knox*, p. 131; Randall, *Alexander Hamilton*, pp. 175, 179; Bill, *Valley Forge*, p. 219.

61. Kline, ed., *Alexander Hamilton*, p. 66.

62. Chernow, *Alexander Hamilton*, pp. 95, 115; "LTC John Fitzgerald (–1799)-Find A Grave Memorial," www.findagrave.com; Cecere, *An Officer of Very Extraordinary Merit*, p. 103; Kline, ed., *Alexander Hamilton*, p. 68; Massey, *John Laurens and the American Revolution*, pp. 80–81; Miller, *Alexander Hamilton*, p. 31; Randall, *Alexander Hamilton*, p. 175; Moran, "George Washington's Military Family," LTN.

63. Massey, *John Laurens and the American Revolution*, p. 110; Chernow, *Alexander Hamilton*, p. 95.

64. Kline, ed., *Alexander Hamilton*, p. 66; Randall, *Alexander Hamilton*, p. 175.

65. Chernow, *Alexander Hamilton*, pp. 109–110; Smith, *John Marshal*, p. 66.

66. Ferreiro, *Brothers at Arms*, p. 157; Randall, *Alexander Hamilton*, p. 176.

67. Ferling, *Jefferson and Hamilton*, p. 77; Miller, *Alexander Hamilton*, p. 32; Chernow, *Alexander Hamilton*, p. 115; Randall, *Alexander Hamilton*, p. 175.

68. Laurens, *The Army Correspondence of Colonel John Laurens in the Years 1777–8*, p. 202; Bill, *Valley Forge*, p. 215; Chernow, *Alexander Hamilton*, pp. 114–115; Lefkowitz, *George Washington's Indispensable Men*, p. 8.

69. Massey, *John Laurens and the American Revolution*, p. 110; Chernow, *Alexander Hamilton*, p. 115.

70. Lefkowitz, *George Washington's Indispensable Men*, p. 175; Randall, *Alexander Hamilton*, p. 177.

71. Ferling, *Jefferson and Hamilton*, p. 77; Randall, *Alexander Hamilton*, p. 176.

72. Miller, *Alexander Hamilton*, pp. 31–32.

73. Randall, *Alexander Hamilton*, p. 177.

74. Ferling, *Jefferson and Hamilton*, p. 77; Miller, *Alexander Hamilton*, p. 32.

75. Chernow, *Alexander Hamilton*, p. 115; Kline, ed., *Alexander Hamilton*, p. 65; Randall, *Alexander Hamilton*, p. 177; Lomask, *Alexander Hamilton*, p. 59.

76. Kline, ed., *Alexander Hamilton*, p. 65; Ferling, *Jefferson and Hamilton*, p. 77; Massey, *John Laurens and the American Revolution*, p. 110; Miller, *Alexander Hamilton*, p. 32.

77. Leckie, *George Washington's War*, p. 487; Chernow, *Alexander Hamilton*, p. 115; Ferling, *Jefferson and Hamilton*, p. 77; Miller, *Alexander Hamilton*, pp. 32, 35.

78. Massey, *John Laurens and the American Revolution*, pp. 110–111; Lefkowitz, *George Washington's Indispensable Men*, p. 177.

79. Ferling, *Jefferson and Hamilton*, pp. 77–78; Chernow, *Alexander Hamilton*, pp. 101–104; Miller, *Alexander Hamilton*, p. 33.

80. Chernow, *Alexander Hamilton*, p. 92; Randall, *Alexander Hamilton*, p. 146.

81. Massey, *John Laurens and the American Revolution*, pp. 112–113; Ferling, *Jefferson and Hamilton*, pp. 77–78; Miller, *Alexander Hamilton*, pp. 32–33; Chernow, *Alexander Hamilton*, pp. 102–104, 115–116; Randall, *Alexander Hamilton*, p. 176.

82. Chernow, *Alexander Hamilton*, pp. 84, 115–116; Ferling, *Jefferson and Hamilton*, pp. 77–79; Kaplan, *Alexander Hamilton*, p. 32.

83. James McHenry Biography Sketch, Center of Military History, United States Army, Washington, DC; Chernow, *Alexander Hamilton*, pp. 91–93, 113–114; Ferling, *Jefferson and Hamilton*, pp. 78–80; Clark, *All Cloudless Glory*, pp. 407–408; Chadwick, *George Washington's War*, p. 428; Scheer and Rankin, *Rebels and Redcoats*, p. 388; Lomask, *Alexander Hamilton*, p. 48; Randall, *Alexander Hamilton*, pp. 171,175–176, 179–180; Piers Mackesy, *The War for America, 1775–1783*, (Lincoln: University of Nebraska Press, 1993), p. 215; Brian Lalor, editor, *The Encyclopedia of Ireland*, (New Haven: Yale University Press, 2003), p. 66; John Beake, *Otho Holland Williams in the American Revolution*, (Mount Pleasant: The Nautical and Aviation Publishing Company, 2015), p. 23; Lefkowitz, *George Washington's Indispensable Men*, pp. 140–142.

84. Lomask, *Alexander Hamilton*, p. 48; Randall, *Alexander Hamilton*, pp. 171.

85. Roche, *Alexander Hamilton*, p. 102; Ferling, *Jefferson and Hamilton*, p. 74; Lomask, *Alexander Hamilton*, p. 48.

86. Lefkowitz, *George Washington's Indispensable Men*, p. 142; Lomask, *Alexander Hamilton*, p. 48; Chernow, *Alexander Hamilton*, pp. 92–93; Ferling, *Jefferson and Hamilton*, p.79; Hancock, *Oceans of Wine*, p. 326; Randall, *Alexander Randall*, p. 218.

87. Chernow, *Alexander Hamilton*, p. 90; Lomask, *Alexander Hamilton*, p. 162.

88. Chernow, *Alexander Hamilton*, p. 119; Philbrick, *Valiant Ambition*, pp. 217–218; Scheer and Rankin, *Rebels and Redcoats*, pp. 388–389; Massey, *John Laurens and the American Revolution*, pp. 113–115; Lomask, *Alexander Hamilton*, pp. 60–61; Freeman, *Washington*, p. 405.

89. Roche, *Alexander Hamilton*, p. 103; Chernow, *Alexander Hamilton*, p. 119; Lomask, *Odd Destiny*, p. 61.

90. Kline, ed., *Alexander Hamilton*, p. 68; Chernow, *Alexander Hamilton*, pp. 119–120; Leckie, *George Washington's War*, pp. 285, 358, 363–364; Lomask, *Odd Destiny*, p. 61; Mark Mayo Boatner III, *Encyclopedia of the American Revolution*, (New York: David McKay Company, Inc., 1966), p. 690; Freeman, *Washington*, p. 405.

91. Kline, ed., *Alexander Hamilton*, p. 68; Ferling, *Jefferson and Hamilton*, pp. 37–38; Miller, *Alexander Hamilton*, p. 46; Chernow, *Alexander Hamilton*, p. 98.

92. Chernow, *Alexander Hamilton*, pp. 117–118; Kline, ed., *Alexander Hamilton*, p. 68.

93. Alexander Hamilton to unidentified individual, September 12, 1778, Alexander Hamilton Papers, Manuscripts and Archives Division, New York Public Library, New York, New York; Ferreiro, *Brothers at Arms*, p. 171.

94. Massey, *John Laurens and the American Revolution*, p. 123.

95. Clark, *All Cloudless Glory*, p. 426; Beake, *Otho Holland Williams*, p. 53.

96. Lefkowitz, *George Washington's Indispensable Men*, p. 180; Ferling, *Jefferson and Hamilton*, pp. 77–78; Bill, *Valley Forge*, p. 235; Kline, ed., *Alexander Hamilton*, pp. 68–69; Massey, *John Laurens and the American Revolution*, pp. 112–113, 125–126; Chernow, *Alexander Hamilton*, pp. 116–117; Randall, *Alexander Hamilton*, pp. 176, 179–180; Miller, *Alexander Hamilton*, pp. 34–35.

97. Kline, ed., *Alexander Hamilton*, pp. 69–70; Massey, *John Laurens and the American Revolution*, p. 126; Chernow, *Alexander Hamilton*, pp. 116–117; Randall, *Alexander Hamilton*, p. 176.

98. Massey, *John Laurens and the American Revolution*, p. 126; Kline, ed., *Alexander Hamilton*, pp. 68–70.

99. Massey, *John Laurens and the American Revolution*, p. 127; Ferling, *Jefferson and Hamilton*, pp. 77–78.

100. Ibid; Chernow, *Alexander Hamilton*, pp. 105–106, 113–117; Ferling, *Jefferson and Hamilton*, pp. 77–78; Kaplan, *Alexander Hamilton*, p. 31.

101. Kaplan, *Alexander Hamilton*, p. 32; Chernow, *Alexander Hamilton*, pp. 88–91, 105–106, 113–117; Ferling, *Jefferson and Hamilton*, pp. 77–78.

102. Rakove, *Revolutionaries*, p. 405; Lefkowitz, *George Washington's Indispensable Men*, p. 187; Chernow, *Alexander Hamilton*, pp. 91, 108–109.

103. Ferling, *Jefferson and Hamilton*, p. 82; Clark, *All Cloudless Glory*, p. 426; Lefkowitz, *George Washington's Indispensable Men*, pp. 187–188; Miller, *Alexander Hamilton*, p. 40.

104. Clark, *All Cloudless Glory*, p. 428; Lefkowitz, *George Washington's Indispensable Men*, p. 188; Langguth, *Patriots*, p. 478.

105. Thacher, *Military Journal*, p. 160; Ferling, *Jefferson and Hamilton*, pp. 82–85.

106. Chernow, *Alexander Hamilton*, pp. 61, 98; Ferling, *Jefferson and Hamilton*, pp. 37–38, 79–85; Miller, *Alexander Hamilton*, p. 41.

107. Schiff, *A Great Improvisation*, pp. 13–62; Massey, *John Laurens and the American Revolution*, p. 116; Chernow, *Alexander Hamilton*, pp. 94–95, 113, 119–120; Ferling, *Jefferson and Hamilton*, pp. 84–85; Miller, *Alexander Hamilton*, p. 67; Roche, *Alexander Hamilton*, p. 103; Lomask, *Alexander Hamilton*, pp. 60–62.

108. Miller, *Alexander Hamilton*, pp. 3–5; Schiff, *A Great Improvisation*, pp. 166–167; Stinchcombe, *The American Revolution and the French Alliance*, pp. 1–12, 56; Hamilton, *The Life of Alexander Hamilton*, vol. 1, pp. 321–322; Chernow, *Alexander Hamilton*, pp. 29–30, 113, 119–120; Massey, *John Laurens and the American Revolution*, p. 121; Roche, *Alexander Hamilton*, p. 103; Lomask, *Alexander Hamilton*, pp. 60–61.

109. Clark, *All Cloudless Glory*, p. 44; Stinchcombe, *The American Revolution and the French Alliance*, p. 2.

110. Schiff, *A Great Improvisation*, pp. 166–167; Chernow, *Alexander Hamilton*, pp. 8, 12–13, 119–120; Ferling, *Jefferson and Hamilton*, p. 84; Miller, *Alexander Hamilton*, p. 3; Kaplan, *Alexander Hamilton*, p. 24; Stinchcombe, *The American Revolution and the French Alliance*, pp. 2, 56; Hamilton, *The Life of Alexander Hamilton*, vol. 1, pp. 321–322; Miller, *Alexander Hamilton*, p. 38; Milton Lomask, *John Carroll, Bishop and Patriot*, (New York: Farrar, Straus and Cudahy, 1956), p. 141.

111. Chadwick, *George Washington's War*, p. 380.

112. Philbrick, *Valiant Ambition*, pp. 218–219; Mackesy, *The War for America*, p. 192; Schiff, *A Great Improvisation*, pp. 167–168; Ferling, *Jefferson and Hamilton*, p. 85; John Shelby, *The Road to Yorktown*, (New York: St. Martin's Press, 1976), pp. 144–145; Stinchcombe, *The American Revolution and the French Alliance*, pp. 2, 12, 32, 48–56; Laurens, *The Army Correspondence of Colonel John Laurens in the Years 1777–8*, pp. 220–221; G. De Bertier de Sauvigny and David H. Pickney, *History of France*, (Wheeling: Forum Press, Inc., 1983), pp. 200–201; Massey, *John Laurens and the American Revolution*, pp. 121–122; Kaplan, *Alexander Hamilton*, pp. 37–39; Clark, *All Cloudless Glory*, pp. 408–409, 413; Ferreiro, *Brothers at Arms*, p. 171; Roche, *Alexander Hamilton*, p. 103.

113. Schiff, *A Great Improvisation*, pp. 167–170; Cox, *A Proper Sense of Honor*, pp. xv–xvi, 21–28; Chernow, *Alexander Hamilton*, pp. 95–97, 113; Lomask, *Alexander Hamilton*, p. 61; Roche, *Alexander Hamilton*, p. 103.

114. Stinchcombe, *The American Revolution and the French Alliance*, pp. 2, 51–52; Henry Steele Commager and Richard B. Morris, editors, *The Spirit of 'Seventy-Six, The Story of the American Revolution As Told By Participants*, (New York: Bonanza Books, 1983), p. 717; Chernow, *Alexander Hamilton*, pp. 29–30, 95–97; Ferling, *Jefferson and Hamilton*, pp. 84–85; Kaplan, *Alexander Hamilton*, pp. 37–39; Roche, *Alexander Hamilton*, p. 103.

115. Ferreiro, *Brothers at Arms*, p. 218; Stinchcombe, *The American Revolution and the French Alliance*, pp. 50–56; Lomask, *Odd Destiny*, pp. 60–61; Ferling, *Jefferson and Hamilton*, pp. 84–85.

116. Stinchcombe, *The American Revolution and the French Alliance*, p. 56.

117. Ferreiro, *Brothers at Arms*, p. 218; Kline, ed., *Alexander Hamilton*, p. 67; Ferling, *Jefferson and Hamilton*, pp. 84–85.

118. Ibid; Kaplan, *Alexander Hamilton*, pp. 37–39.

119. Massey, *John Laurens and the American Revolution*, p. 122.

120. Kaplan, *Alexander Hamilton*, pp. 37–39; Roche, *Alexander Hamilton*, p. 103; Chadwick, *George Washington's War*, p. 138.

121. Bill, *Valley Forge*, pp. 242–243; Lomask, *Odd Destiny*, pp. 60–61; Roche, *Alexander Hamilton*, p. 103.

Chapter V

1. Chernow, *Alexander Hamilton*, p. 121; Chadwick, *George Washington's War*, pp. 406-6–407, 412; Henry Wiencek, *Master of the Mountain, Thomas Jefferson and His Slaves* (New York: Farrar, Straus, and Giroux, 2012), p. 74; Ellis, *Revolutionary Summer*, p. 93; Randall, *Alexander Hamilton*, pp. 162–163, 291–292; The People's Bicentennial Commission, *Voices of the American Revolution*, (New York: Bantam Books, 1975), pp. 186–187.

2. Kline, ed., *Alexander Hamilton*, pp. 20, 35; Chernow, *Alexander Hamilton*, p. 32; Randall, *Alexander Hamilton*, pp. 6, 26; Chadwick, *George Washington's War*, p. 406

3. Ferling, *Jefferson and Hamilton*, p. 87; Chadwick, *George Washington's War*, pp. 78, 140, 342, 409–410; Randall, *Alexander Hamilton*, pp. 162–163, 291–292

4. Chadwick, *George Washington's War*, p. 410; Randall, *Alexander Hamilton*, pp. 162–163, 291–292; Knott and Williams, *Washington and Hamilton*, pp. 92–93.

5. Michael Lee Lanning, *Defenders of Liberty, African Americans in the Revolutionary War*, (New York: Kensington Publishing Corporation, 2000), pp. 66–68, 202–204; Massey, *John Laurens and the American Revolution*, pp. 92–97, 130–132; Chernow, *Alexander Hamilton*, p. 121; Ferling, *Jefferson and Hamilton*, p. 87; Randall, *Alexander Hamilton*, p. 163; Lomask, *Alexander Hamilton*, pp. 61–62.

6. Lanning, *Defenders of Liberty*, pp. 66–68, 202–204; Middlebrook encampment, Wikipedia; Kaplan, *Alexander Hamilton*, p. 24; Chernow, *Alexander Hamilton*, pp. 121–122; Schiff, *A Great Improvisation*, p. 166; Ferling, *Jefferson and Hamilton*, pp. 81–87; Miller, *Alexander Hamilton*, p. 3; Lomask, *Odd Destiny*, pp. 6, 61; Rakove, *Revolutionaries*, pp. 15–16; Wiencek, *Master of the Mountain*, p. 70; Randall, *Alexander Hamilton*, pp. 164–165; Massey, *John Laurens and the American Revolution*, p. 229.

7. Laurens, *The Army Correspondence of Colonel John Laurens in the Years 1777–78*, pp. 114–115.

8. Lomask, *Alexander Hamilton*, p. 61.

9. Lanning, *Defenders of Liberty*, p. 204.

10. Ibid., p. 203.

11. Ibid., pp. 66–67, 202.

12. Ibid., pp. 202–203; Ellis, *Revolutionary Summer*, p. 93.

13. Lanning, *Defenders of Liberty*; Wiencek, *Master of the Mountain*, pp. 51–52

14. Lanning, *Defenders of Liberty*, pp. 67–68, 203; Chernow, *Alexander Hamilton*, p. 122

15. Ferling, *Jefferson and Hamilton*, p. 87; Lanning, *Defenders of Liberty*, 203.

16. Lanning, *Defenders of Liberty*, p. 203; Ferling, *Jefferson and Hamilton*, p. 87; Michael P. Johnson and James L. Roark, *Black Masters, A Free Black Family in the Old South*, (New York: W. W. Norton and Company, 1984), p. 31.

17. Burns, *Virtue, Valor, & Vanity*, p. 95.

18. Ibid., *Defenders of Liberty*, p. 202.

19. Ferling, *Jefferson and Hamilton*, p. 87; Lanning, *Defenders of Liberty*, pp. 66–67, 202–204; Lomask, *Alexander Hamilton*, pp. 61–62; Randall, *Alexander Hamilton*, pp. 164–165.

20. Lanning, *Defenders of Liberty*, p. 67.

21. Laurens, *The Army Correspondence of Colonel John Laurens in the Years 1777–8*, p. 116.

22. Ibid., p. 115; Chernow, *Alexander Hamilton*, p. 122.

23. Ray Raphael, *Founders, The People Who Brought You A Nation*, (New York: MJF Books, 2009), p. 95.

24. Chernow, *Alexander Hamilton*, pp. 123–125; Ferling, *Jefferson and Hamilton*, p. 87; Kline, ed., *Alexander Hamilton*, pp. 88–89; Randall, *Alexander Hamilton*, p. 182.

25. Chernow, *Alexander Hamilton*, pp. 114–115; Roche, *Alexander Hamilton*, pp. 134–135; Randall, *Alexander Hamilton*, pp. 175–177; Beake, *Otho Holland Williams*, p. 23; Lefkowitz, *George Washington's Indispensable Men*, p. 193.

26. Chernow, *Alexander Hamilton*, pp. 114–115; Randall, *Alexander Hamilton*, p. 217.

27. Alexander Hamilton to James Duane, September 7, 1779, Lloyd W. Smith Collection, Morristown National Historical Park, Morristown, New Jersey; Alexander Hamilton to Major General Nathanael Greene, September 10, 1777, Alexander Hamilton Papers, Digital Edition, Editor, Harold C. Syrett, Charlottesville: University of Virginia Press, Rotunda, 2011.

28. Kline, ed., *Alexander Hamilton*, p. 75.

29. Ibid.

30. Ibid; Chernow, *Alexander Hamilton*, pp. 119–120.

31. Kline, ed., *Alexander Hamilton*, pp. 75–76.

32. Alexander Hamilton and Louis Du Portail to George Washington, November 8, 1779, Alexander Hamilton Papers, National Archives, Washington, DC.

33. Alexander Hamilton to Lieutenant Colonel John Taylor, October 29, 1779, Alexander Hamilton Papers, Digital Editor, Editor, Harold C. Syrett, Charlottesville: University of Virginia Press, Rotunda, 2011.

34. Kline, ed., *Alexander Hamilton*, pp. 75–76.

35. Ibid.

36. Ibid.

37. Randall, *Alexander Hamilton*, pp. 217–218.

38. Ibid., p.218; George Seldes, compiler, *The Great Thoughts*, (New York: Ballantine Books, 1985), p. 234.

39. Shelby, *The Road to Yorktown*, p. 149; Stinchcombe, *The American Revolution and the French Alliance*, pp. 133–134; Langguth, *Patriots*, p. 496.

40. Rakove, *Revolutionaries*, p. 403; Chernow, *Alexander Hamilton*, p. 123.

41. Puls, *Henry Knox*, p. 141; Chernow, *Alexander Hamilton*, p. 127; Chadwick, *George Washington's War*, pp. 361–362; Lomask, *Odd Destiny*, p. 4; Lefkowitz, *George Washington's Indispensable Men*, pp. 194–195.

42. Chernow, *Alexander Hamilton*, pp. 123–125; Kline, ed., *Alexander Hamilton*, pp. 77–78; Massey, *John Laurens and the American Revolution*, pp. 150–152, 170–172; Ferling, *Jefferson and Hamilton*, p. 79; Randall, *Alexander Hamilton*, pp. 182–185, 218; Lomask, *Alexander Hamilton*, pp. 67–68.

43. Massey, *John Laurens and the American Revolution*, pp. 150–152; Chernow, *Alexander Hamilton*, p. 124; Kline, ed., *Alexander Hamilton*, p. 77; Randall, *Alexander Hamilton*, p. 182.

44. Randall, *Alexander Hamilton*, p. 184.

45. Knott and Williams, *Washington and Hamilton*, p. 76; Chernow, *Alexander Hamilton*, p. 124; Ferling, *Jefferson and Hamilton*, p. 84; Randall, *Alexander Hamilton*, p. 182; Massey, *John Laurens and the American Revolution*, p. 152.

46. Kline, ed., *Alexander Hamilton*, p. 77; Ferling, *Jefferson and Hamilton*, p. 84.

47. Massey, *John Laurens and the American Revolution*, p. 152; Chernow, *Alexander Hamilton*, p. 125.

48. Leckie, *George Washington's War*, p. 505; Knott and Williams, *Washington and Hamilton*, pp. 104–113; Ferling, *Jefferson and Hamilton*, pp. 82–84.

49. Langguth, *Patriots*, pp. 497–498; Lomask, *Alexander Hamilton*, p. 63.

50. Randall, *Alexander Hamilton*, pp. 123–124.

51. Ibid., p. 187.

52. Ibid; Webb Papers, YUL.

53. Randall, *Alexander Hamilton*, p. 187; Chernow, *Alexander Hamilton*, pp. 126, 128.

54. Randall, *Alexander Hamilton*, p. 189.

55. Rakove, *Revolutionaries*, p. 141.

56. Ibid.

57. Chastellux, *Travels in North-America in the Years 1780–81–82*, pp. 67–68.

58. Ibid; Bill, *Valley Forge*, p. 145.

59. Chastellux, *Travels in North-America in the Years 1780–81–82*; Chadwick, *George Washington's War*, pp. 361–362; Chernow, *Alexander Hamilton*, p. 127; Lomask, *Alexander Hamilton*, pp. 62–63; Randall, *Alexander Hamilton*, pp. 187–188.

60. Ferling, *Jefferson and Hamilton*, pp. 80–85; Phillip Thomas Tucker, *How the Irish Won the American Revolution, A New Look at the Forgotten Heroes of America's War of Independence*, (New York: Skyhorse Publishing, 2015), pp. 241–242; Rakove, *Revolutionaries*, p. 404; Lefkowitz, *George Washington's Indispensable Men*, p. 198; Chernow, *Alexander Hamilton*, pp. 128–132; Randall, *Alexander Hamilton*, pp. 187–188, 190; Miller, *Alexander Hamilton*, p. 66; Chadwick, *George Washington's War*, pp. 362–364; Kline, ed., *Alexander Hamilton*, p. 78; Lomask, *Alexander Hamilton*, pp. 63–66.

61. Chernow, *Alexander Hamilton*, pp. 123, 128–132; Miller, *Alexander Hamilton*, p. 65; Randall, *Alexander Hamilton*, p. 190; Lomask, *Alexander Hamilton*, pp. 69–70.

62. Chernow, *Alexander Hamilton*, pp. 126, 128; Randall, *Alexander Hamilton*, p. 194.

63. Chadwick, *George Washington's War*, p. 380.

64. Ibid.

65. Ibid.

66. Ibid., p. 381; Randall, *Alexander Hamilton*, p. 190.

67. Kline, ed., *Alexander Hamilton*, p. 79; Randall, *Alexander Hamilton*, p. 191.

68. Roche, *Alexander Hamilton*, p. 138.

69. Ferling, *Jefferson and Hamilton*, p. 80; Randall, *Alexander Hamilton*, p. 192.

70. Kline, ed., *Alexander Hamilton*, p. 80; Chernow, *Alexander Hamilton*, pp. 132, 134–136, 147; Randall, *Alexander Hamilton*, pp. 193–194; Lomask, *Alexander Hamilton*, p. 66.

71. Chernow, *Alexander Hamilton*, p. 119; Chadwick, *George Washington's War*, pp. 381–382; Randall, *Alexander Hamilton*, p. 193.

72. Roche, *Alexander Hamilton*, p. 131.
73. Stinchcombe, *The American Revolution and the French Alliance*, pp. 134–135; Chernow, *Alexander Hamilton*, p. 139; G. De Bertier de Sauvigny and David H. Pinkney, *History of France*, pp. 200–201.
74. Roche, *Alexander Hamilton*, pp. 142–143.
75. Chernow, *Alexander Hamilton*, pp. 83–84, 112–113; Kline, ed., *Alexander Hamilton*, p. 80.
76. Kline, ed., *Alexander Hamilton*, p. 81; Lomask, *Alexander Hamilton*, p. 69.
77. Kline, ed., *Alexander Hamilton*, pp. 81–82.
78. Ibid., p. 82.
79. Randall, *Alexander Hamilton*, p. 195.
80. Ibid., pp. 197, 202; Kline, *ed., Alexander Hamilton*, p. 83; Alexander Hamilton to Henry Knox, July 9, 1780, The Papers of Alexander Hamilton, Digital Edition, Editor Harold C. Syrett. Charlottesville: University of Virginia Press, Rounda, 2011.
81. Kline, ed., *Alexander Hamilton*; Lomask, *Odd Destiny*, pp. 28–37.
82. Kline, ed., *Alexander Hamilton*, pp. 83–84.
83. Ibid., p. 88.
84. Randall, *Benedict Arnold*, p. 405; Chernow, *Alexander Hamilton*, p. 105; Randall, *Alexander Hamilton*, p. 145.
85. Kline, ed., *Alexander Hamilton*, p. 88.
86. Kline, ed., *Alexander Hamilton*, pp. 88–89.
87. Rakove, *Revolutionaries*, p. 405.
88. Chadwick, *George Washington's War*, p. 380; Chernow, *Alexander Hamilton*, p. 147.
89. Rakove, *Revolutionaries*, p. 405; Roche, *Alexander Hamilton*, p. 145; Lomask, *AlexanderHamilton*, pp. 68–69.
90. Chernow, *Alexander Hamilton*, pp. 137–139; Rakove, *Revolutionaries*, p. 405; Lomask, *Alexander Hamilton*, pp. 68–70; Ferling, *Jefferson and Hamilton*, pp. 82–84; Miller, *Alexander Hamilton*, p. 5.
91. Raphael, *Revolutionaries*, pp. 360–361; Chernow, *Alexander Hamilton*, pp. 138–139; Lomask, *Alexander Hamilton*, pp. 68–71; Randall, *Alexander Hamilton*, p. 218.
92. Rakove, *Revolutionaries*, p. 405; Lomask, *Alexander Hamilton*, pp. 68–71.
93. Miller, *Alexander Hamilton*, pp. 43–47; Chernow, *Alexander Hamilton*, pp. 138–139; Lomask, *Alexander Hamilton*, pp. 68–71.
94. Chernow, *Alexander Hamilton*, pp. 137–139; Miller, *Alexander Hamilton*, p. 51.
95. Miller, *Alexander Hamilton*, p. 58; Chernow, *Alexander Hamilton*, p. 139.
96. Roche, *Alexander Hamilton*, p. 148; Randall, *Alexander Hamilton*, p. 47.
97. Chernow, *Alexander Hamilton*, pp. 137–139; Randall, *Alexander Hamilton*, p. 216.
98. Chernow, *Alexander Hamilton*, pp. 139, 145; Kline, ed., *Alexander Hamilton*, p. 92.
99. Kline, ed., *Alexander Hamilton*, p. 92; Chernow, *Alexander Hamilton*, pp. 132, 150; Randall, *Alexander Hamilton*, pp. 216, 221.
100. Hamilton, *The Life of Alexander Hamilton*, vol. 1, pp. 308–310.

Chapter VI

1. Chernow, *Alexander Hamilton*, pp. 88–128; Chadwick, *George Washington's War*, pp. 138–140; Rakove, *Revolutionaries*, pp. 402–404; Randall, *Alexander Hamilton*, pp. 167, 216, 218.

2. Lefkowitz, *George Washington's Indispensable Men*, pp. 203–205; Ferling, *Jefferson and Hamilton*, pp. 77–78; Randall, *Alexander Hamilton*, p. 149.

3. Chadwick, *George Washington's War*, p. 426.

4. Leckie, *George Washington's War*, p. 450.

5. Burns, *Virtue, Valor, & Vanity*, p. 62; Chadwick, *George Washington's War*, pp. 138–140; 410; Miller, *Alexander Hamilton*, p. 22.

6. Chadwick, *George Washington's War*, pp. 426–427; Burns, *Virtue, Valor & Vanity*, pp. 63, 67.

7. Kline, ed., *Alexander Hamilton*, pp. 92–93; Randall, *Alexander Hamilton*, p. 217.

8. Kline, ed., *Alexander Hamilton*, pp. 92–93.

9. Ibid.

10. Burns, *Virtue, Valor, & Vanity*, p. 63.

11. Hamilton, *The Life of Alexander Hamilton*, vol. 1, p. 318.

12. Ibid., p. 319; Fort Bunker Hill, New York Military Museum and Veterans Research Center, Saratoga Springs, New York, internet; Randall, *Alexander Hamilton*, pp. 107–108.

13. Randall, *Alexander Hamilton*, p. 3.

14. Hamilton, *The Life of Alexander Hamilton*, vol. 1, p. 319; Chernow, *Alexander Hamilton*, pp. 137–139.

15. Hamilton, *The Life of Alexander Hamilton*, vol. 1, pp. 318–319.

16. Ibid., p. 319; Ferling, *Jefferson and Hamilton*, pp. 77–78.

17. Hamilton, *The Life of Alexander Hamilton*, vol. 1, p. 320.

18. Ibid; Chernow, *Alexander Hamilton*, p. 119; Randall, *Alexander Hamilton*, p. 216.

19. Hamilton, *The Life of Alexander Hamilton*, vol. 1, pp. 320–321.

20. Ibid., p. 321.

21. Ibid., pp. 321–322.

22. Ibid., p. 326; Stinchcombe, *The American Revolution and the French Alliance*, pp. 51–52, 54; Chernow, *Alexander Hamilton*, pp. 139, 150; Ferling, *Jefferson and Hamilton*, pp. 84–85; Randall, *Alexander Hamilton*, p. 218; Rakove, *Revolutionaries*, p. 403.

23. Hamilton, *The Life of Alexander Hamilton*, vol. 1, p. 327; Chernow, *Alexander Hamilton*, p. 150; Clark, *All Cloudless Glory*, p. 503.

24. Randall, *Alexander Hamilton*, p. 218; Chernow, *Alexander Hamilton*, pp. 138.

25. Hamilton, *The Life of Alexander Hamilton*, pp. 320–322; Kline, ed., *Alexander Hamilton*, p. 92; Miller, *Alexander Hamilton*, pp. 64–66; Chernow, *Alexander Hamilton*, pp. 132–137; Rakove, *Revolutionaries*, pp. 404–407; Lomax, *Alexander Hamilton*, pp. 64–65; Randall, *Alexander Hamilton*, p. 224.

26. Ferling, *Jefferson and Hamilton*, p. 79; Miller, *Alexander Hamilton*, pp. 21, 64–69; Chernow, *Alexander Hamilton*, pp. 124–125, 139.

27. Rakove, *Revolutionaries*, p. 405; Ferling, *Jefferson and Hamilton*, pp. 25–26, 79–81.

28. Isenberg, *Fallen Founder*, pp. 3–5, 15–16.

29. Ibid., pp. 19–34; Chernow, *Alexander Hamilton*, p.149; Miller, *Alexander Hamilton*, p. 22.

30. Isenberg, *Fallen Founder*, p. 37.

31. Chernow, *Alexander Hamilton*, p. 139; Kline, ed., *Alexander Hamilton*, p. 78.

32. Ibid; Massey, *John Laurens and the American Revolution*, pp. 42, 82, 110.

33. Rakove, *Revolutionaries*, pp. 404–405; Kaplan, *Alexander Hamilton*, p. 28.

34. Kaplan, *Alexander Hamilton*, p. 23; Ferling, *Jefferson and Hamilton*, p. 81; Randall, *Alexander Hamilton*, p. 189.

35. Chernow, *Alexander Hamilton*, pp. 128, 145; Kaplan, *Alexander Hamilton*, p. 23.

36. Tilghman, *Memoir of Lieutenant Colonel Tench Tilghman*, p. 90.

37. Ibid., p. 173; Chernow, *Alexander Hamilton*, pp. 139–140; Ferling, *Jefferson and Hamilton*, p. 81.

38. Charles Royster, *A Revolutionary People at War, The Continental Army and the American Character, 1775–1783*, (New York: W. W. Norton and Company, 1981), pp. 311–313; Chernow, *Alexander Hamilton*, pp. 137–140.

39. Randall, *Alexander Hamilton*, pp. 127–128.

40. Kilmeade and Yeager, *George Washington's Secret Six*, p. 165; Philbrick, *Valiant Ambition*, pp. 283–304; George C. Daughan, *Revolution on the Hudson, New York City and the Hudson River Valley in the American War of Independence*, (New York: W. W. Norton and Company, 2016), pp. 263–264; Ferreiro, *Brothers at Arms*, pp. 224–225; Puls, *Henry Knox*, p. 146; Schachner, *Aaron Burr*, p. 43; Chernow, *Alexander Hamilton*, pp. 119, 140–141; Ferling, *Jefferson and Hamilton*, pp. 72–73, 77–79; Randall, *Alexander Hamilton*, p. 202; Miller, *Alexander Hamilton*, p. 69; Freeman, *Washington*, p. 444; Randall, *Benedict Arnold*, p. 538; Knott and Williams, *Washington and Williams*, p. 94; Lefkowitz, *George Washington's Indispensable Men*, p. 209.

41. Freeman, *Washington*, p. 444; Knot and Williams, *Washington and Hamilton*, p. 95.

42. Kline, ed., *Alexander Hamilton*, p. 89; Freeman, *Washington*, p. 465.

43. Knott and Williams, *Washington and Hamilton*, p. 94; Clark, *All Cloudless Glory*, p. 485.

44. Philbrick, *Valiant Ambition*, p. 311; Randall, *Alexander Hamilton*, p. 207; Knott and Williams, *Washington and Hamilton*, p. 95.

45. Randall, *Alexander Hamilton*, p. 207.

46. Knott and Williams, *Washington and Hamilton*, p. 95; Chernow, *Alexander Hamilton*, pp. 140–141; Kline, ed., *Alexander Hamilton*, p. 90; Randall, *Alexander Hamilton*, pp. 206–208.

47. Kline, ed., *Alexander Hamilton*, pp. 90–91; Philbrick, *Valiant Ambition*, pp. 302, 304; Clark, *All Cloudless Glory*, pp. 484–486; Chernow, *Alexander Hamilton*, pp. 141–143; Randall, *Alexander Hamilton*, pp. 192, 216; Miller, *Alexander Hamilton*, p. 71.

48. Chernow, *Alexander Hamilton*, p. 143; Kline, ed., *Alexander Hamilton*, p. 91.

49. Kline, ed., *Alexander Hamilton*, p. 91; Chernow, *Alexander Hamilton*, p. 144; Randall, *Alexander Hamilton*, pp. 211, 213–214; Knott and Williams, *Washington and Hamilton*, p. 95

50. Kline, ed., *Alexander Hamilton*, pp. 91–92.

51. Alexander Hamilton to Lieutenant Colonel John Laurens, October 11, 1780, Founders Online, National Archives, Washington, DC; Chernow, *Alexander Hamilton*, p. 144; Randall, *Alexander Hamilton*, p. 213.

52. Philbrick, *Valiant Ambition*, p. 316; Randall, *Alexander Hamilton*, pp. 217–218; Chernow, *Alexander Hamilton*, p. 150; Clark, *All Cloudless Glory*, p. 503; Craig, *General Edward Hand*, p. 29, 86.

53. Chernow, *Alexander Hamilton*, pp. 143–147; Ferling, *Jefferson and Hamilton*, p. 81; Randall, *Alexander Hamilton*, p. 216.

54. Lomask, *Alexander Hamilton*, pp. 73–74; Ferling, *Jefferson and Hamilton*, p. 87; Langguth, *Patriots*, p. 517.

55. Chernow, *Alexander Hamilton*, pp. 147–148; Ferling, *Jefferson and Hamilton*, pp. 11, 81–82; Kline, ed., *Alexander Hamilton*, pp. 81, 93; Langguth, *Patriots*, p. 517; Randall, *Alexander Hamilton*, pp. 143, 218–219; Lefkowitz, *George Washington's Indispensable Men*, p. 216.

56. Randall, *Alexander Hamilton*, pp. 219–220.

57. Chastellux, *Travels in North-America in the Years 1780–81–82*, pp. 171–173; Randall, *Alexander Hamilton*, p. 220; Chernow, *Alexander Hamilton*, pp. 14–15, 145–149.

58. Hamilton, *The Life of Alexander Hamilton*, vol. 1, p. 324.

59. Chernow, *Alexander Hamilton*, pp. 130–131, 145, 150; Ferling, *Jefferson and Hamilton*, p. 81; Randall, *Alexander Hamilton*, pp. 212, 221; Kline, ed, *Alexander Hamilton*, p. 93; Donald T. Phillips, *On the Wing of Speed, George Washington and the Battle of Yorktown*, (New York: iUniverse Star, 2006), p. 3; Knott and Williams, *Washington and Hamilton*, p. 243.

60. Kline, ed., *Alexander Hamilton*, pp. 93–94.

61. Robert L. Tonsetic, *1781, The Decisive Year of the Revolutionary War*, (Philadelphia: Casemate Publishing, 2011), pp. viii, 12–13, 25; Ferling, *Jefferson and Hamilton*, pp. 86–87; Hamilton, *The Life of Alexander Hamilton*, pp. 323–324; Chernow, *Alexander Hamilton*, pp. 139, 150–151; Harvey, *"A Few Bloody Noses,"* pp. 394–395.

62. Hamilton, *The Life of Alexander Hamilton*, vol. 1, p. 325.

63. Ibid., pp. 325–326.

64. Knott and Williams, *Washington and Hamilton*, p. 71; Kline, ed., *Alexander Hamilton*, p. 77.

65. Ferling, *Jefferson and Hamilton*, p. 103; Randall, *Alexander Hamilton*, pp. 220–223; Kline, ed., *Alexander Hamilton*, pp. 92–93.

66. Miller, *Alexander Hamilton*, p. 61.

67. Ferling, *Jefferson and Hamilton*, p. 103; Randall, *Alexander Hamilton*, p. 218.

68. Massey, *John Laurens and the American Revolution*, pp. 173–175.

69. Ibid., pp. 176–177.

70. Alexander Hamilton to the Marquis de Barbe-Marbois, February 7, 1781, Alexander Hamilton Papers, Manuscripts and Archives Division, New York Public Library, New York, New York.

71. Alexander Hamilton to Colonel Timothy Pickering, February 9, 1781, Alexander Hamilton Papers, Digital Edition, Editor, Harold C. Syrett, Charlottesville: University of Virginia Press, Rotunda, 2011.

72. Ibid.

73. Alexander Hamilton to Timothy Pickering, February 15, 1871, Alexander Hamilton Papers, Manuscripts and Archives Division, New York Public Library, New York, New York.

74. Freeman, *Washington*, p. 451; Craig, *General Edward Hand*, pp. 1–7, 23, 85.

75. Kline, ed., *Alexander Hamilton*, p. 94.

76. Ibid., pp. 15, 76–77, 94–97; Rakove, *Revolutionaries*, pp. 402–406; Ferling, *Jefferson and Hamilton*, pp. 102–104; Miller, *Alexander Hamilton*, pp. 67, 69, 71; Freeman, *Washington*, p. 451; Chernow, *Alexander Hamilton*, pp. 85–151; Chadwick, *George Washington's War*, pp. 426–427; Schachner, *Aaron Burr*, pp. 44–45; Knott and Williams, *Washington and Hamilton*, pp. vii-x, 22; Royster, *Light-Horse Harry Lee*, pp. 24–25; Lomask, *Alexander Hamilton*, pp. 73–75; Chief of Staff, Wikipedia; Randall, *Alexander Hamilton*, pp. 217–218, 225; David G. Chandler, *The Campaigns of Napoleon, The Mind and Method of History's Greatest Soldier*, (New York: Scribner, 1966), pp. 1108, 1102.

77. Lomask, *Alexander Hamilton*, p. 73; Randall, *Alexander Hamilton*, p. 220.

78. Miller, *Alexander Hamilton*, p. 5; Rakove, *Revolutionaries*, p. 401; Randall, *Alexander Hamilton*, pp. 26–28

79. Rakove, *Revolutionaries*, p. 402.

80. Tonsetic, *1781*, p. x; Langguth, *Patriots*, p. 517; Kline, ed., *Alexander Hamilton*, pp. 91–92; Chernow, *Alexander Hamilton*, p. 150; Miller, *Alexander Hamilton*, p. 71; Lefkowitz, *George Washington's Indispensable Men*, p. 227.

81. Burns, *Virtue, Valor, & Vanity*, p. 63; Knott and Williams, *Washington and Hamilton*, pp. ix-x; Clark, *All Cloudless Glory*, p. 503; Chernow, *Alexander Hamilton*, pp. 149–151; Rakove, *Revolutionaries*, pp. 402–406; Busch, *Winter Quarters*, pp. 97–98; Chadwick, *George Washington's War*, pp. 426–427; Kline, ed., *Alexander Hamilton*, pp. 94–96; Lomask, *Alexander Hamilton*, pp. 73–74.

82. Lanning, *Defenders of Liberty*, pp. 66–67, 202–204; Chadwick, *George Washington's War*, pp. 406–410; Henry Wiencek, *Master of the Mountain, Thomas Jefferson and His Slaves*, (New York: Farrar, Straus and Giroux, 2012), p. 74–75; Knott and Williams, *Washington and Hamilton*, p. 92.

83. Lomask, *Alexander Hamilton*, p. 75; Chadwick, *George Washington's War*, pp. 406–407.

84. Chernow, *Alexander Hamilton*, p. 149; Randall, *Alexander Hamilton*, p. 225.

85. Miller, *Alexander Hamilton*, pp. 21–22; Chernow, *Alexander Hamilton*, pp. 88, 107, 149; Kaplan, *Alexander Hamilton*, pp. 26–27; Chadwick, *George Washington's War*, p. 79; Lomask, *Alexander Hamilton*, pp. 74–75; Massey, *John Laurens and the American Revolution*, p. 197.

86. Chernow, *Alexander Hamilton*, pp. 88, 107, 149; Chadwick, *George Washington's War*, p. 428; Randall, *Alexander Hamilton*, pp. 220–222.

87. Randall, *Alexander Hamilton*, pp. 122, 225.

88. Kaplan, *Alexander Hamilton*, p. 32; Miller, *Alexander Hamilton*, p. 71; Clarfield, *Timothy Pickering and the American Republic*, pp. 44–46.

89. Kaplan, *Alexander Hamilton*, p. 32.

90. Harvey, *"A Few Bloody Noses,"* pp. 394–396; Randall, *Alexander Hamilton*, pp. 221, 224; Freeman, *Washington*, p. 460; Phillips, *On the Wing of Speed*, pp. 3, 24.

91. Randall, *Alexander Hamilton*, p. 224.

92. Kaplan, *Alexander Hamilton*, pp. 23–24; Chernow, *Alexander Hamilton*, p. 151; Miller, *Alexander Hamilton*, p. 71; Langguth, *Patriots*, p. 517; Randall, *Alexander Hamilton*, p. 221.

93. Kline, ed., *Alexander Hamilton*, p. 96.

94. Langguth, *Patriots*, p. 517; Chernow, *Alexander Hamilton*, pp. 149–151; Randall, *Alexander Hamilton*, pp. 220–222.

95. Thacher, *Military Journal*, p. 160; Chernow, *Alexander Hamilton*, pp. 149–151; Chadwick, *George Washington's War*, p. 406; Lomask, *Alexander Hamilton*, pp. 74–75; Randall, *Alexander Hamilton*, pp. 220–222.

96. Kline, ed., *Alexander Hamilton*, p. 96.

97. Chernow, *Alexander Hamilton*, pp. 88, 107, 149; Lomask, *Alexander Hamilton*, p. 75; Randall, *Alexander Hamilton*, p. 221.

98. Kaplan, *Alexander Hamilton*, p. 34; Chernow, *Alexander Hamilton*, pp. 88, 107, 149; Lomask, *Alexander Hamilton*, pp. 74–75.

99. Chernow, *Alexander Hamilton*, p. 151; Chadwick, *George Washington's War*, pp. 426–427; Rakove, *Revolutionaries*, p. 406; Kline, ed., *Alexander Hamilton*, pp. 94–96; Langguth, *Patriots*, p. 517; Kaplan, *Alexander Hamilton*, pp. 34–35; Randall, *Alexander Hamilton*, pp. 145, 147, 221, 223; Freeman, *Washington*, pp. 451, 460.

100. Kline, ed., *Alexander Hamilton*, p. 95.

101. Ibid; Langguth, *Patriots*, p. 518; Chernow, *Alexander Hamilton*, pp. 88, 107, 149; Randall, *Alexander Hamilton*, p. 223; Miller, *Alexander Hamilton*, p. 72; Lomask, *Alexander Hamilton*, pp. 74–75.

102. Kaplan, *Alexander Hamilton*, p. 35; Chernow, *Alexander Hamilton*, pp. 88, 107, 149, 152; Kline, ed., *Alexander Hamilton*, p. 95; Langguth, *Patriots*, p. 518; Miller, *Alexander Hamilton*, pp. 72–75; Knott and Williams, *Washington and Hamilton*, p. 96.

103. Kaplan, *Alexander Hamilton*, p. 35.

104. Kline, ed., *Alexander Hamilton*, p. 95; Randall, *Alexander Hamilton*, pp. 225–226.

105. Kline, ed., *Alexander Hamilton*, pp. 95–96.

106. Lomask, *Alexander Hamilton*, p. 76.

107. Rakove, *Revolutionaries*, p. 406.

108. Kline, ed., *Alexander Hamilton*, p. 96.

109. Miller, *Alexander Hamilton*, p. 35.

110. Ibid., pp. 74–75.

111. Randall, *Alexander Hamilton*, pp. 182–185, 220.

112. Randall, *Alexander Hamilton*, pp. 223–224.

113. Ibid., p. 224.

114. Knott and Williams, *Washington and Hamilton*, p. 98; Kline, ed., *Alexander Hamilton*, p. 96; Chernow, *Alexander Hamilton*, pp. 88, 107, 149, 153; Miller, *Alexander Hamilton*, p. 35.

115. Chernow, *Alexander Hamilton*, p. 153; Kline, ed., *Alexander Hamilton*, pp. 88–89.

116. Randall, *Alexander Hamilton*, p. 224.

117. Philbrick, *Valiant Ambition*, p. 101; Clark, *All Cloudless Glory*, pp. 294–297; Knott and Williams, *Washington and Hamilton*, pp. vii–257; Chernow, *Alexander Hamilton*, pp. 21, 147–148, 153.

118. Chernow, *Alexander Hamilton*, pp. 147–148; Randall, *Alexander Hamilton*, p. 195.

119. Kline, ed., *Alexander Hamilton*, p. 94; Langguth, *Patriots*, p. 518; Chernow, *Alexander Hamilton*, pp. 119–120, 153; Miller, *Alexander Hamilton*, p. 75; Tonsetic, *1781*, pp. 72–73; Knott and Williams, *Washington and Hamilton*, pp. 98, 113.

120. Lomask, *Alexander Hamilton*, p. 75.

121. Langguth, *Patriots*, p. 518; Knott and Williams, *Washington and Hamilton*, pp. 105–113; John Ferling, *The Ascent of George Washington, The Hidden Political Genius of an American Icon*, (New York: Bloomsbury Press, 2009), p. 225.

Conclusion

1. Knott, *Alexander Hamilton and the Persistence of Myth*, p. 221.

2. Chadwick, *George Washington's War*, pp. 138–140; Tonsetic, *1781*, p. 157.

3. Knott, *Alexander Hamilton and the Persistence of Myth*, pp. 2–232; Lefkowitz, *George Washington's Indispensable Men*, pp. 108–109; Fleming, *Washington's Secret War*, pp.

164–165, 175–179; Knott and Williams, *Washington and Hamilton*, pp. vii-257; Chadwick, *George Washington's War*, pp. 138–140; Randall, *Alexander Hamilton*, pp. 145–149.

4. Knott, *Alexander Hamilton and the Persistence of Myth*, pp. vii-257; Burns, *Virtue, Valor, & Vanity*, p. 49; Kaplan, *Alexander Hamilton*, p. 167; Knott and Williams, *Washington and Hamilton*, pp. vii-257; Edward J. Larson, *The Return of George Washington, 1783–1789*, (New York: HarperCollins Publishers, 2014), pp. 3-303

5. Kline, ed., *Alexander Hamilton*, p. 78.

6. Ibid., p. 88.

7. Ibid., p. 89.

8. Alexander Hamilton to George Washington, February 13, 1783, Alexander Hamilton Papers, Manuscripts and Archives Division, New York Public Library, New York, New York.

9. Kline, ed., *Alexander Hamilton*, pp. 99–101; Miller, *Alexander Hamilton*, pp. 548–549, 572; Randall, *Alexander Hamilton*, pp. 412–424; Knott and Williams, *Washington and Hamilton*, pp. 236–237.

10. Kline, ed., *Alexander Hamilton*, pp. 80–101; Randall, *Alexander Hamilton*, pp. 422–424

11. Alexander Hamilton to James Hamilton, June 1785, Alexander Hamilton Papers, Manuscripts and Archives Division, New York Public Library, New York, New York.

12. Fleming, *Beat the Last Drum*, pp. 281–286; Davis, *The Campaign That Won America*, pp. 198–220; Morrissey, *Yorktown 1781*, pp. 66–77; Joanne B. Freeman, *Affairs of Honor*, (New Haven: Yale University Press, 2001), pp. 281–282; Chadwick, *George Washington's War*, pp. 138–140, 426; Schachner, *Aaron Burr*, pp. 44–45, 252–253; Miller, *Alexander Hamilton*, pp. 36–37; Randall, *Alexander Hamilton*, pp. 176, 184–185, 247–248, 412–424; Knott and Williams, *Washington and Hamilton*, pp. vii-257; Kline, ed., *Alexander Hamilton*, pp. 49–102; Lomask, *Alexander Hamilton*, pp. 162–166.

13. Knott, *Alexander Hamilton and the Persistence of Myth*, pp. 2–232; Raphael, *Founders*, pp. 436; Chadwick, *George Washington's War*, pp. 138–140, 426; Miller, *Alexander Hamilton*, pp. 21–67; Clark, *All Cloudless Glory*, pp. 247, 251–252; Randall, *Alexander Hamilton*, p. 234; Fleming, *Beat the Drum*, p. 75; David T. Zabecki, editor, *Chief of Staff, The Principal Officers Behind History's Great Commanders, Napoleonic Wars to World War I*, (2 vols., Annapolis: Naval Institute Press, 2008), vol. 1, pp. 29–39; Chandler, *The Campaigns of Napoleon*, pp. 1021, 1057.

14. Francis Rufus Bellamy, *The Private Life of George Washington*, (New York: Thomas Y. Crowell Company, 1951), p. 318.

15. Randall, *Alexander Hamilton*, p. 149.

16. Randall, *Alexander Hamilton*, p. 121.

17. Kline, ed., *Alexander Hamilton*, p. 102.

18. Marcus Cunliffe, *George Washington, Man and Monument*, (New York: Mentor Books, 1958), p. 137; Miller, *Alexander Hamilton*, p. 67; Randall, *Alexander Hamilton*, pp. 119–421; Knott and Williams, *Washington and Hamilton*, pp. vii-257.

19. Lomask, *Alexander Hamilton*, pp. 171–172; Knott and Williams, *Washington and Hamilton*, pp. 239–242.

20. Robert C. Baron, editor, *Soul of America, Documenting Our Past, 1492–1974*, (Golden: Fulcrum, Inc., 1989), p. 102.

INDEX